Dispossession and Displacement
Forced Migration in the Middle East and North

British Academy Occasional Paper · 14

Dispossession and Displacement
Forced Migration in the Middle East and North Africa

Edited by
Dawn Chatty and Bill Finlayson

Published for THE BRITISH ACADEMY
by OXFORD UNIVERSITY PRESS

Oxford University Press, Great Clarendon Street, Oxford OX2 6DP

Oxford New York

Auckland Cape Town Dar es Salaam Hong Kong Karachi
Kuala Lumpur Madrid Melbourne Mexico City Nairobi
New Delhi Shanghai Taipei Toronto

With offices in

Argentina Austria Brazil Chile Czech Republic France Greece
Guatemala Hungary Italy Japan Poland Portugal Singapore
South Korea Switzerland Thailand Turkey Ukraine Vietnam

Published in the United States
by Oxford University Press Inc., New York

© The British Academy, 2010

Database right The British Academy (maker)

First published 2010

British Library Cataloguing in Publication Data
Data available

Library of Congress Cataloging in Publication Data
Data available

Typeset by
New Leaf Design, Scarborough, North Yorkshire
Printed in Great Britain
on acid-free paper by
CPI Antony Rowe,
Chippenham, Wiltshire

ISBN 978-0-19-726459-1

Contents

List of Illustrations   vii

Notes on Contributors   ix

Introduction   1
     Dawn Chatty and Bill Finlayson

Part I
Displacement

1. What Visibility Conceals: Re-embedding Refugee Migration
    from Iraq   17
     Géraldine Chatelard

2. The Transnational Turn in Migration Studies and the
    Afghan Social Networks   45
     Alessandro Monsutti

3. Internal Displacement in the Occupied Palestinian Territories:
    Politics and the Loss of Livelihood   69
     Maher Anawati Bitar

4. Displacement by Repatriation: The Future of Turkish Settlers
    in Northern Cyprus   97
     Yaël Ronen

Part II
Repatriation

5. From *Mohajer* to *Hamwatan*: The Reintegration Experiences of
    Second-generation Afghans Returning from Pakistan and Iran   123
     Mamiko Saito and Paula Kantor

6. Repatriation and Reconstruction: Afghan Youth as a 'Burnt
    Generation' in Post-conflict Return   147
     Sarah Kamal

Contents

Part III
Identity in Exile

7. When the Self Becomes Other: Representations of Gender,
    Islam, and the Politics of Survival in the Sahrawi Refugee
    Camps   171
    Elena Fiddian-Qasmiyeh

8. 'Hey, Afghani!' Identity Contentions among Iranians and
    Afghan Refugees   197
    Zuzanna Olszewska

9. Narrative as Identity: Perspectives from an Iraqi Women
    Refugees' Oral History Project   215
    Laura Hamblin and Hala Al-Sarraf

Part IV
Policy

10. The Refugee Factor in Two Protracted Conflicts: Cyprus and
    Palestine Compared   227
    Peter Loizos and Tobias Kelly

11. There Go the Neighbourhoods: Policy Effects vis-à-vis Iraqi
    Forced Migration   249
    Nabil Al-Tikriti

Epilogue
    Dispossession and Forced Migration in the Twenty-first-
    century Middle East and North Africa: The Way Forward   273
    Dawn Chatty

Abstracts   281
Index   289

Illustrations

3.1	The occupied Palestinian territories	71
4.1	Map of Cyprus	98
5.1	Flow of Afghan returnees, 2002–4	126
7.1	Map of Western Sahara	174
8.1	Map of Afghanistan and Iran	199
10.1	Map of the West Bank and Gaza Strip, 2000	229
12.1	Palestinians fleeing in 1948	274

Notes on Contributors

Maher Anawati Bitar is a doctoral candidate in International Relations at Oxford University and is concurrently pursuing a law degree at the Georgetown University Law Center in Washington, DC. He received an MSc in Forced Migration from the Refugee Studies Centre at Oxford while on a Marshall Scholarship. He has worked with the United Nations Relief and Works Agency (UNRWA) and the United Nations High Commissioner for Refugees (UNHCR).

Géraldine Chatelard is a Research Fellow with the French Institute for the Near East (IFPO) in Amman. She holds a PhD in History from the Ecoles des hautes études en sciences sociales (EHESS) in Paris, and was a post-doctoral Marie Curie Fellow at the European University Institute (2001–4). She has published works on Jordan and on migration and refugee trends from Iraq, including 'Iraqi Asylum Migrants in Jordan: Conditions, Religious Networks and the Smuggling Process', in G. Borjas and J. Crisp (eds), *Poverty, International Migration and Asylum* (2005) and 'Migration from Iraq between the Gulf and the Iraq Wars (1990–2003): Historical and Sociospacial Dimensions', COMPAS Working Paper (2009).

Dawn Chatty is University Reader in Anthropology and Forced Migration and deputy director of the Refugee Studies Centre at the Department for International Development, University of Oxford, UK. Her research interests include the coping strategies and resilience of refugee youth, nomadic pastoralism and conservation, gender and development, health, illness, and culture. Her most recent books include *Conservation and Mobile Peoples: Displacement, Forced Settlement and Sustainable Development* (ed. with Marcus Colchester, 2002), *Children of Palestine: Experiencing Forced Migration in the Middle East* (ed. with Gillian Lewando-Hundt, 2005), and *Handbook on Nomads in the Middle East and North Africa* (2006). Her edited volume, *Deterritorialized Youth: Sahrawi and Afghan Refugees at the Margins of the Middle East*, will be published in 2010.

Elena Fiddian-Qasmiyeh is a Senior Teaching Fellow in Development Studies at the School of Oriental and African Studies, University of

London. Before completing her doctoral research at Oxford University's Department of International Development, she worked as a legal adviser for refugees in Cairo (with AMERA-Egypt), and was a legal clerk at the International Criminal Court, conducting research on crimes committed in Darfur, Sudan. She has conducted research with sub-Saharan African asylum-seekers and refugees in Cairo; Palestinian, Kurdish and Afghan refugees living in the UK; Palestinian, Syrian, Yemeni, and Sahrawi university students based in Havana, Cuba; and Sahrawi refugees in Cuba, Syria, Spain, and their Algerian-based refugee camps. Her work has appeared in various journals and in edited volumes, including *Living through Intended and Unintended Suffering: War, Medicine and Gender* (ed. Hannah Bradby and Gillian Lewando-Hundt, 2009) and *Deterritorialized Youth: Sahrawi and Afghan Refugees at the Margins of the Middle East* (ed. Dawn Chatty, 2010).

Bill Finlayson ran the University of Edinburgh's Centre for Field Archaeology before moving to Amman in 1999 to become the director of the Council for British Research in the Levant and is a Visiting Professor at the University of Reading. The main focus of his research is hunter-gatherers in prehistory. Recent publications include *The Early Prehistory of Wadi Faynan, Southern Jordan: Archaeological Survey of Wadis Faynan, Ghuwayr and al-Bustan and Evaluation of the Pre-Pottery Neolithic A Site of WF16* (with Steven Mithen, 2007) and numerous journal articles. He has also been working on the nature of the ideas of 'East' and 'West' considered from a long-time perspective, and will publish this research with Jordanian colleagues in the *Bulletin of the Royal Institute for Interfaith Studies*.

Laura Hamblin is a Full Professor at Utah Valley University where she has received awards including the first UVU Faculty Ethics Fellowship, Service Fellow Award, School of HASS Dean's Faculty Creative Award, UVU Board of Trustees' Award of Excellence, Faculty Excellence Award, and Outstanding Service-learning Award. She has also taught at the University of Nevada, Las Vegas. During 2007–8 she lived in Amman, Jordan, where she and Hala Al-Sarraf gathered oral histories of Iraqi women refugees. She teaches women's literature, the history and theory of the genre of poetry, ethics and values, and has published a book of poetry, *The Eyes of a Flounder* (2005). Hamblin is part of the faculty which established Utah Valley University's Peace and Justice Studies Program.

Sarah Kamal worked on social development practice, policy, and research in Canada, Nicaragua, Uganda, India, and Iran. Her interests turned towards media systems after a visit to Taliban-controlled Afghanistan in 2001. She helped launch a women's radio station in western Afghanistan, coordinated participatory team research on Afghan refugee youth in Iran for the Oxford Refugee Studies Centre, promoted gender equality in Afghan media for UNIFEM, and set up an aid project on Afghan family law reform for Rights and Democracy. She was editor of the National Action Plan for the Women of Afghanistan, a ten-year policy platform for the Afghan Ministry of Women's Affairs to improve the status of Afghan women. Sarah holds an MSc in Comparative Media Studies from MIT, and has written for Oxford Analytica, the *UN Chronicle*, and Oxfam's *Gender and Development* journal. She is currently a Trudeau Scholar, engaged in doctoral studies in Media and Communications at the London School of Economics, UK.

Paula Kantor has a PhD in City and Regional Planning from the University of North Carolina at Chapel Hill. She is director of the Afghanistan Research and Evaluation Unit (AREU). During 2005–7 she managed AREU's livelihoods and gender research portfolio, including studies on the role of informal and micro credit in rural livelihoods; the refugee, return, and reintegration experiences of second-generation Afghans; household decision-making processes around the use of child labour; and family dynamics and violence. Prior to her work with AREU she taught at the School of Development Studies at the University of East Anglia, UK, and at the University of Wisconsin-Madison, USA.

Tobias Kelly is Senior Lecturer in Social Anthropology at the University of Edinburgh. His research interests include human rights, legal anthropology, law and development, and the Israeli/Palestinian conflict. He has also carried out long-term fieldwork among West Bank Palestinians, concentrating on issues of citizenship and everyday experiences of violence. More recently he has been carrying out research on the documentation of torture. He received a PhD in Anthropology from the London School of Economics in 2003, and has worked at the Institute of Law of Birzeit University, the Crisis States Programme at the LSE, and the Centre for Socio-Legal Studies at Oxford University.

Peter Loizos taught Anthropology at the London School of Economics from 1969 to 2002, and retired as Professor Emeritus. He has written three monographs about the people of Argaki village in West Cyprus, the most recent being *Iron in the Soul: Displacement, Livelihood and Health in Cyprus* (2008). A collection of his Cyprus essays was published in 2001 as *Unofficial Views: Cyprus: Society and Politics.* He also made two documentary films about the people of the village: one before their displacement, the other after it.

Alessandro Monsutti has carried out fieldwork in Afghanistan, Pakistan, and Iran since 1993, and more recently in Western countries among Afghan refugees and migrants. His research and teaching interests focus on the Middle East (in particular Afghanistan and its neighbouring countries), migration and refugees, transnational networks, kinship and ethnicity, qualitative methods in social sciences, development, and humanitarian assistance. He taught at the Graduate Institute of International and Development Studies, Geneva, until 2008 and is currently based at Yale University. His publications include *War and Migration: Social Networks and Economic Strategies of the Hazaras of Afghanistan* (2005), *Entre ordre et subversion: logiques plurielles, alternatives, écarts, paradoxes* (ed. with Suzanne Chappaz-Wirthner and Olivier Schinz, 2007), *The Other Shiites: From the Mediterranean to Central Asia* (ed. with Silvia Naef and Farian Sabahi, 2007), *Le monde turco-iranien en question* (ed. with Mohammad-Reza Djalili and Anna Neubauer, 2008), and *Migration et développement, un mariage arrangé* (ed. with Denise Efionayi-Mäder, Gérard Perroulaz, and Catherine Schümperli, 2008).

Zuzanna Olszewska is a Junior Research Fellow in Oriental Studies at St John's College, Oxford. She recently completed her doctorate, 'Poetry and Its Social Contexts among Afghan Refugees in Iran', at the Institute of Social and Cultural Anthropology, University of Oxford, and holds a master's degree from Oxford's Refugee Studies Centre. She has published articles on Afghan refugees in Iran for *Iranian Studies* journal and *Encyclopedia Iranica*, and on Afghan women's poetry for *Women of Afghanistan in the Post-9/11 Era: Paths to Empowerment* (ed. Jennifer Heath and Ashraf Zahedi, forthcoming).

Yaël Ronen teaches public international law. She is currently a faculty member at Sha'arei Mishpat Law College, Israel. Previously she held a post-doctoral fellowship at the Minerva Centre for Human Rights in the Hebrew University in Jerusalem. Prior to embarking on an academic career, she served as a lawyer and diplomat in the Israeli foreign service. Her areas of expertise within international law include statehood and territorial status, human rights, and international humanitarian law. Her doctoral dissertation, on transition from illegal regimes under international law, will be published in 2010.

Mamiko Saito was the senior research officer on migration at the Afghanistan Research and Evaluation Unit (AREU) in Kabul. Having started work in Afghanistan and Pakistan in 2003 with a particular focus on refugees, she currently works at the South Asia Division, Japan International Cooperation Agency (JICA). She holds a master's degree in Education and Development Studies from the University of East Anglia.

Hala Al-Sarraf received her masters in Public Health from Columbia University where she was a Fullbright Scholar. Her areas of expertise include civil society, conflict resolution, education, health, psycho-social health, and refugees. She is the CEO and director of the Iraq Health Aid Organization (IHAO) which is involved in health education, providing health-care access, training health-care workers, and establishing health-care policy. During 2007–8 she collaborated with Laura Hamblin, gathering oral histories of Iraqi women refugees living in Amman, Jordan. Currently she is researching the impact of conflict on health, including the psychological impact, and the issue of the 'brain drain' in Iraq, and its impact on health.

Nabil Al-Tikriti was a member of the team that operated the Catholic Relief Services humanitarian assistance project in Iraq in 1991–2, and later served with Medécins Sans Frontières as a relief worker in Somalia, Iran, Albania, Turkey, and Jordan. After serving as a field administrator and election monitor in various programme assignments, he joined the Department of History at the University of Mary Washington in Fredericksburg, Virginia, in 2004. He has been awarded a US Institute of Peace Senior Fellowship, two Fulbright grants, and research support from both the University of Chicago and the University of Mary Washington.

Introduction

Dawn Chatty and Bill Finlayson

Dispossession and forced migration have been an indelible part of life in the modern history of the Middle East and North Africa. At the end of the nineteenth century waves of Circassian Muslim and Jewish groups were dispossessed of their homes and lands in Eurasia and the Caucuses and forced into the region. This was closely followed by the displacement, death marches, and massacres of Armenians and other Christian groups such as the Nestorian Chaldeans and Assyrians in Anatolia at the end of the First World War. Between the two world wars the Kurds emerged as the next victims of dispossession. They were followed by the Palestinians—Christian and Muslim—who fled their homes in the struggle for control over the formerly British-mandated Palestine shortly after the end of the Second World War. In recent years, nearly 4 million Iraqis have fled their country or have been internally displaced. Two million of these fled into Syria and Jordan between 2006 and 2007. In the summer of 2006, around 1 million Lebanese took refuge in Syria. During this same period, Sudanese and Somali refugees continued to flood into Egypt and Yemen seeking peace, security, and sustainable livelihoods. These events have resulted in penetrating media coverage as well as serious research interest. Submissions for research and travel grants to study the growing phenomenon of forced migration in the region have been increasing. As a result, the Council for British Research in the Levant took the lead in looking more carefully at the subject as whole and, whenever possible, encouraging comparative studies.

As an outcome of a preliminary meeting on the subject held at the Refugee Studies Centre, University of Oxford, in January 2007, representatives from the Council for British Research in the Levant, the British Institute in East Africa, the British Institute at Ankara, the British Institute of Persian Studies, the British Institute for the Study of Iraq, and the British Society for Middle Eastern Studies agreed that the time had come to hold a conference on dispossession and displacement in the Middle East aimed at identifying areas of research which need to be further

1

explored. Although there were some sensitivities regarding the term 'Middle East', it was decided to accept the broadest definition of the area as extending from Mauretania and Morocco in the west to Afghanistan in the east. The lives of refugees and other forced migrants were recognized as a growing, highly pertinent area of contemporary research. Although the majority of people falling into the category of refugees and forced migrants arose from generally well known complex humanitarian emergencies or natural disasters, the topic encompassed many others, including those who have been resettled due to development programmes and government policies to reduce nomadic mobility, as well as biodiversity conservation programmes. It was generally agreed that the nature of displacement, forced or otherwise, as well as processes of repatriation needed further study. The complexity of identity in exile, particularly with reference to gender roles and generation, as well as policy implications of such dispossession and migration were also considered to be important areas for further research.

The British Academy sponsored a conference in London on 28–9 February 2008, which brought together a wide range of scholars and development/aid professionals working on the theme of forced migration in the region. The conference explored the extent to which forced migration has come to be a defining feature of life in the Middle East and North Africa. It presented research on refugees, internally displaced peoples (IDPs) and those who remain behind from Afghanistan in the east, to Morocco in the west, and to Sudan in the south. The papers were grouped around four related themes: displacement, repatriation, identity in exile, and refugee policy. The eleven essays in this collection originated as papers at the conference. They cover themes as disparate as the future of the Turkish immigrant settlers in northern Cyprus; the continuing internal displacement among Kurds in Iraq and Palestinians in the West Bank and East Jerusalem; the Afghan Hazara migratory networks between Afghanistan, Pakistan, Iran, and the Western countries; Afghan refugee youth as a 'burnt generation' in post-conflict return; Sahrawi identity in refugee camps; and expression of the 'self' in poetry among refugees in Iran and oral history among Iraqi refugees in Jordan. The essays in this volume give both precise examination of some specific refugee situations as well as impressionistic and richly ethnographic accounts of life of the dispossessed and exiled.

DISPLACEMENT

Chapter 1 by Géraldine Chatelard, 'What Visibility Conceals: Re-embedding Refugee Migration from Iraq', considers the historical and political context of Iraqi displacement to the northern regions of Iraq as well as to Syria and Jordan. Chatelard examines what the international human-itarian aid regime's designation of 'unprecedented refugee crisis' for the approximately 2 million Iraqi refugees has meant to both forced migrants and political actors in the region. She contends that by making Iraqi refugees visible, and at the same time promoting a state-centred approach to dealing with their relief, other invisibilities were created. Her essay explores these 'invisibilities' including previous forced migrations from Iraq as well as the cross-border ties which have existed for decades and are part of the history of the region with pre-existing exile communities playing an important role in migratory projects. The global social organization of Iraqi migration, Chatelard maintains, has been shaped as much by the nature of successive coercive Iraqi regimes, which have fragmented the population along religious, ethnic, and ideological orientations, as by the nature of the polities within which the majority of forced migrants from Iraq had sought security.

Chatelard's analysis makes clear that the 'Iraqi refugee agenda' is in essence a particular angle of vision which prevents analysts from distin-guishing between those who are forced out by violence or fear and do not have the necessary social capital to 'buy protection' in Iraq or a neigh-bouring country, and those who have been able through their own access to financial and social assets to adopt a form of trans-local mobility. This narrow 'refugee lens' obscures the complexities of migratory strategies from and to Iraq. It precludes an understanding of the articulations between previous and current movements and the links maintained over time and across space by Iraqis at home and in migration. These percep-tions can also be applied to other situations of armed conflict, human insecurity, and prolonged forced, in particular in the essays by Bitar and Monsutti that follow.

The theme of displacement is particularly relevant to the remaining essays in Part I. In Chapter 2, 'The Transnational Turn in Migration Studies and the Afghan Social Networks', Alessandro Monsutti examines the change in understanding migration as a time-bound process. Basing his work theoretically on that of James Clifford and Arjun Appaduria, he sees the normal in the diasporic; where the world is deterritorialized; where travel becomes more significant than being rooted in a nation state; and where social relations are more important than locations. Since the 1980s the idea that migration should end in either return or the integration of the migrant within their host society has given way to a more complex understanding of the trajectories of migration and multiple ties and links established across boundaries. Socio-cultural groups are no longer understood as territorially defined. By concentrating on mobility it is possible to develop a global ethnography which understands the transnational strategies adopted. These approaches, initially developed to study voluntary migration, are now being used in forced migration studies, partly to recognize the agency of forced migrants, and also because of the difficulty in differentiating between different types of migrant. Monsutti considers the Hazaras of Afghanistan, often believed to have been part of the population displacement starting with the late 1970s Soviet intervention in Afghanistan, but who have a long tradition of movement, and for whom mobility may be a planned strategy. Here, movement is not followed by integration or definitive return, the society is truly transnational. Travel is a normal part of life cycles. The flow of migration is not uni-directional. Hazaras have long-established networks in Pakistan and Iran: each network is operated differently to make use of differing local opportunities, but the Hazaras have generally not sought refugee status. Hazaras have more recently started to migrate to Australia (illegally) and North America (legally), expanding their migratory networks.

The theme of displacement in a confined place is the focus of Maher Bitar in Chapter 3, 'Internal Displacement in the Occupied Palestinian Territories: Politics and the Loss of Livelihood'. The problem of 'internally stuck persons' no longer able to flee to safer ground is the current description of Palestinians who are increasingly at risk of internal displacement within circumscribed territorial boundaries. Internally displaced persons (IDPs) in Palestine receive much less assistance and protection than refugees. IDPs in the West Bank comprise internally displaced people and refugees who have been moved a second time. Sometimes the cause of the second displacement is 'indirect' and thus attracts less attention, but still contributes to a worsening humanitarian situation. Bitar's essay carefully identifies Israeli policies of land expropriation and confiscation in the West Bank and East Jerusalem that directly cause displacement, especially following the Oslo Accords, and illustrates how these have divided Palestinian population centres from one another. While home demolitions—sometimes combined with forced expulsions, military incursions, and clearing operations, such as in areas adjacent to the 'Wall'—are the most direct form of displacement, the building of Israeli settlements (and associated infrastructure and security zones) in the Occupied Territories is, according to Bitar, probably the main cause of displacement. Violence and intimidation from settlers have been a contributing factor. Revocation of residency rights, mainly of Jerusalem residents, also forces Palestinians out of Jerusalem.

Bitar is also concerned with the indirect causes of displacement which create untenable living conditions. Building restrictions, checkpoints, segregated roads, walls—all contribute, indirectly, to the displacement of Palestinians. The Wall, itself, falls into both categories as it complements many of the direct and indirect causes mentioned. Controls, closed areas, new permits, and new closed access roads all further limit Palestinian movement. Areas taken in by the Wall include prime agricultural and water-rich land. Bitar concludes that the Wall, when combined with settlements and other measures, is bringing 45.5 per cent of the West Bank, including East Jerusalem, within consolidated Israeli hold. The Wall is causing significant numbers of West Bank and East Jerusalem residents to become 'internally stuck', as are residents of Gaza. Bitar argues that this ongoing displacement of Palestinians is a direct consequence of deliberate Israeli policy.

Yaël Ronen moves the analysis of displacement west to Cyprus in Chapter 4, 'Displacement by Repatriation: The Future of Turkish Settlers in Northern Cyprus'. Large numbers of poor mainland Turks were settled in Cyprus in the 1970s, which, Ronen maintains, was an attempt to effect demographic change. She argues that these settlers had little in common with Turkish Cypriots and still less with Greek Cypriots. Their numbers possibly exceeded those of the Turkish Cypriots, but accurate figures were hard to come by as many have been granted citizenship in the Turkish Republic of Northern Cyprus. Settlement of the Cyprus problem, she finds, includes calls for the removal of these settlers. But there are two conflicting pulls: the illegal act of settlement and granting of citizenship opposed to the reality of settlement and the human rights of the settlers. Whatever Cyprus finally agrees in relation to these settlers, Ronen argues, will be closely watched by other countries which have either forcibly displaced populations or have accepted forced migrants. Ronen examines the Annan Plan and finds that it essentially denies the settlers any status in post-conflict Cyprus, although it would give each side the ability to grant citizenship to a substantial number of people. Under this plan, the number of settlers who might be forced to leave is possibly not as high as might be predicted, but the basic principle of the plan is that settlers should leave unless exempted. Tempering the Annan Plan is the right to private life protected by the European Convention on Human Rights and Fundamental Freedoms. This Convention provides some protection to settlers against expulsion, depending upon the extent of their integration in the state of residence, and how long a person has been residing there. Among the Turkish settlers, there are those who may never have been to Turkey, their state of nationality. However, the Convention does provide some reasons to justify expulsion, and the government of Cyprus objects to their presence on a number of grounds. Ronen queries these and finds that the 'illegality of their presence' is a weak justification compared to the hardship expulsion would cause. Furthermore, Ronen finds that demanding expulsion of all settlers because of their previous military training appears out of proportion.

Ronen closes her essay with the important consideration that the 'Cyprus problem' has been dealt with by legal means from the outset, unlike other national occupations. This strategy, Ronen suggests, means that as the Greek Cypriot minority is determined to protect its cultural character, expulsion of Turkish settlers is more likely to occur than in other similar crises.

REPATRIATION

The theme of repatriation is explored in the second part of this volume. In Chapter 5, 'From *Mohajer* to *Hamwatan*: The Reintegration Experiences of Second-generation Afghans Returning from Pakistan and Iran', Mamiko Saito and Paula Kantor use an anthropological perspective to consider social and emotional trajectories experienced by young Afghan refugees returning to their 'homeland'. Ninety-six per cent of displaced Afghans live in Pakistan and Iran: half were born in these countries in second or third generations, over 70 per cent being under 29. There is a gap in research on these young Afghans. However, the authors remind us that this group cannot be treated as a single unit: there are significant differences depending on place of residence, gender, language, religiosity, education, and many other factors. Attitudes to return and reintegration differ markedly.

Saito and Kantor base their essay on a sample of 199 Afghan refugees. The young refugees expressed conflicting and multiple identities. Making the decision to return is not easy, as many have developed links to where they grew up, hold mixed perceptions of Afghanistan, and have immediate concerns, such as potential disruption to education if they return. Growing up in a country not their own exacerbates development of identity and normal adolescent challenges. Afghan national consciousness barely existed before the Soviet invasion. Invasions by foreigners and exile among others has helped develop this so that while Afghan sub-group identities appear to be more of an issue for first-generation refugees, second generations are less interested in an idealized past than in gaining access to property and citizenship.

Saito and Kantor also explore the situation of those who return to Afghanistan. Although often better educated and possibly wealthier, they continue to suffer from a mix of stresses. For some the experience of being a non-citizen continues. Social rejection of returnees is problematic, especially as the desire to return is often the result of experiences of not belonging abroad. Rejection as returnees is compounded by discrimination based on background, such as ethnicity, religion, gender—distinctions that had been overshadowed when abroad. Regardless of background or experience on return, nearly all returnees expressed negative stereotypical views of Afghans at home, although many try to fit in. Women have particular problems, with poor access to health facilities, more domestic work, poor security, reduced mobility, and shame attached to working. The authors conclude that no simple generalizations can be made about the ongoing process of reintegration because it requires renegotiating core values, developing resilience, and external economic facilitation.

Sarah Kamal's Chapter 6, 'Repatriation and Reconstruction: Afghan Youth as a "Burnt Generation" in Post-conflict Return', addresses some of the coercive repatriation programmes to Afghanistan which have often created circumstances where families return under less than optimal conditions to the land they had fled. The long-term fortunes of young refugees who return to unstable post-conflict societies are difficult to determine. Kamal follows the movements and perspectives of four long-term Afghan refugee youths across a five-year period. She draws from in-depth interviews and participant observation in 2003, 2006, and 2007 to contrast the youths' pre-repatriation perspectives in Iran against their post-repatriation experiences in Afghanistan. She demonstrates that while their parents often characterized themselves as the 'burnt generation' of the exile period, the youths feel that they themselves are bereft of opportunity post-'return'. Such perspectives are tempered and change with time as they work through ambivalence over their relationship with

Iran and changing circumstances in Afghanistan. The challenge for refugee youth is multifaceted. They must position themselves psychologically relative to their childhood and adulthood as well as national affiliation in order to make sense of their past, present, and future aspirations. Repatriation can engender a highly conflicted outlook on life leaving many refugee youths, especially in return situations after prolonged exile, with suboptimal solutions.

IDENTITY IN EXILE

The third part of this volume focuses on identity in exile. Elena Fiddian-Qasmiyeh's Chapter 7, 'When the Self Becomes Other: Representation of Gender, Islam, and the Politics of Survival in the Sahrawi Refugee Camps', examines the Sahrawi refugee case, where the Polisario, the Sahrawi 'government-in exile', markets itself in such a way as to fulfil what it perceives to be the conditions and values of sponsors in the international aid regime. The essay focuses on the solidarity network in Spain for the Sahrawi refugees. The movement, which includes many Spanish institutions such as municipal councils, lobbies the Spanish government. It also coordinates a programme of support by Spanish families for refugees, providing material, financial, and social assistance that is highly appreciated by the Sahrawis, marginalizing official but less visible humanitarian projects. Fiddian-Qasmiyeh maintains that the Polisario Front cultivates this sympathy by projecting an image of the refugees that focuses on Sahrawi women and their liberated and empowered status. Visitors to camps are taken on organized tours to see the successes of the refugees. Sahrawi women are contrasted to the 'rest' of the Arab and Muslim world. The essay is not concerned with whether this empowered status is real, but assesses why the Polisario Front has concentrated so much on this aspect of camp life. It suggests that the language of women's rights is seen by the Polisario as important to capture the attention of external observers, in particular the solidarity network. The refugee camps are seen as locations of democracy and gender equality. In contrast, there have been high-profile cases of girls fostered in Spain being allegedly forced to return to the camps, and the imagery used in campaigns surrounding these events has centred on orientalist visions of the oppression of women. While many solidarity groups denounced this use of stereotypes, others threatened to disengage from the Sahrawi cause, revealing the leverage their support gives. In the end, Fiddian-Qasmiyeh has been able to show that the Polisario Front has succumbed to such pressure, despite trying to argue that such cases should be treated as private matters between families. The Polisario Front has to reproduce the camps within the image it has created in order to maintain the support of Spanish solidarity groups.

Chapter 8 by Zuzanna Olszewska, '"Hey, Afghani!" Identity Contentions among Iranians and Afghan Refugees', addresses issues of identity as expressed through poetry. Olszewska's focus is the second generation of Afghan refugees in Iran who are often portrayed as a confused generation experiencing an 'identity crisis'. She argues that this generation often has few memories of Afghanistan and little desire to return; they do not have the opportunity of naturalizing as Iranian citizens and exist, for the most part, on the margins of society. To Iranians, Afghans are seen as a problem and should be pressured to leave the country: almost 1 million documented refugees are perceived as a burden on the social welfare infrastructure of the state. However, at a cultural level, as Iranians wrestle with their own multi-stranded identity as 'Islamic', 'modern', and 'Iranian', or a combination of these, Afghans also represent a mute interlocutor for these concerns: a stereotypical, backward Other against whom the Self may be defined.

This essay, based on ethnographic fieldwork in Afghan communities in Iran, explores the representations of Afghans in Iran and examines the ways in which Iran-educated Shi'a Afghans respond to and defy the marginalizing positions through their own discourse and poetry. Through the careful examination of a number of highly evocative poems Olszewska helps us to understand both social transformations taking place in this group of refugees, and the broader tensions inherent in Iranian society. The poems clearly illustrate the distressing ambivalence experienced by second-generation Afghan refugees in Iran. This ambivalence can also be extrapolated to other groups in situations of long-term displacement. The essay brings to light the rich and sophisticated ferment in ideas, aesthetics, and identities that take place in this and other refugee populations.

Chapter 9, 'Narrative as Identity: Perspectives from an Iraqi Women Refugees' Oral History Project' by Laura Hamblin and Hala Al-Sarraf, is based on the collected oral histories of Iraqi women refugees in Jordan. Whereas the old Iraqi Ba'ath rule emphasized Arab identity, the new regime stresses Iraqi identity within the concepts of ethnic and sectarian power sharing. Sectarian identities did not appear to divide the Iraqi exile community to a great extent and Iraqi women refugees interviewed by the authors still see themselves as Arabs, and do not accept the new sectarian criteria. Their identity is thus being challenged by contemporary realities. Hamblin and Sarraf found that although about half of the women interviewed were employed, only one worked in her professional discipline. Many of these women's children also worked to support the group. Even where fathers were present it was often easier for women to work than men. This has fostered problems with gender roles, with women being responsible for income and acting as head of the family. This refugee reality has led to family problems with domestic violence emerging as a worrying concern. The authors also note that traditional marriage patterns have being disrupted as girls are starting to work when young. Educating the next generation has become problematic. Although the Jordanian host government has revised its initial exclusionary position regarding education, the largely illegal Iraqi refugee residents are not registering their children for schooling; many are missing necessary papers, and others are still afraid of being identified as Iraqis. Their identity as illegal residents blights their perception of future opportunities and darkens their daily life. Hamblin and Sarraf found that few of these Iraqi refugee women see themselves returning to Iraq, and for the present it would appear that for most of them the current state of limbo will continue.

POLICY

The final part of this volume considers policy. In Chapter 10, 'The Refugee Factor in Two Protracted Conflicts: Cyprus and Palestine Compared', Peter Loizos and Tobias Kelly examine the ways in which Greek-Cypriot and Palestinian refugees played a part in the collapse of the respective peace processes. The essay provides an historical overview of the development of both these refugee populations, differentiating the Palestinian conflict between indigenous nationalists against colonial settlers, and the Cypriot conflict between two indigenous movements. In both countries large numbers of people were displaced, but the Greek-Cypriots gained a state with rare continuing violence, while the Palestinians did not, and violence has remained common. The dispossessed Palestinians, whether or not they had crossed an international border, were given refugee status, which has been inherited by their children. This has resulted in their having limited legal rights—many of them remaining as stateless persons—and poor economic circumstances. Even where they have full citizenship rights in Jordan, in reality they face socio-economic prejudices. The Greek-Cypriots, on the other hand, continued to have a state and were seen as internally displaced persons. Unlike the Palestinian refugees, the Cypriot refugees were given enhanced social, economic, and citizenship rights. Greek-Cypriot refugees have always been directly involved in the political process, having kept the right to vote in Greek Cyprus; Palestinian refugees have been marginalized in peace discussions.

Loizos and Kelly draw four significant conclusions from their comparative study. The most important is that refugees need to become a national issue, so their desires become hard to distinguish from those of non-refugees, and agreements have to be worked with reference to the whole population. Second, refugees are an issue of morality and memory, not just rights. Third, access to political and economic resources is important, and in this comparative study emerged as a key difference between the two refugee populations. Finally, the different way each case study's peace negotiations collapsed suggests that the 'refugee issue' is not enough, on its own, to lead to violence. In Cyprus political and economic circumstances gave the Greek-Cypriots many more options, whereas for Palestinians Israeli military violence and a disjointed Palestinian leadership have meant that the 'refugee issue' and armed struggle remain the fundamental option for the Palestinians.

In Chapter 11, 'There Go the Neighbourhoods: Policy Effects vis-à-vis Iraqi Forced Migration', Nabil Al-Tikriti examines the emergence of sectarianism in Iraq. Sectarian identities have long existed in the country, although they tend to erupt in violence only as a result of highly specific causes. Some observers have regarded Iraq as falling into three ethno-sectarian divisions, approximating to the 1991 no-fly zone borders. Since 2003 these have been consolidated into real divisions. Yet Tikriti shows that, in reality, there were more ethno-sectarian identities present in Iraq predating Ottoman rule but they were consolidated in the reformed *millet* system of the second half of the nineteenth century. With the end of the Ottoman Empire in the early 1920s more secular, nationalistic movements emerged. Intermarriage and mixed neighbourhoods became more common and were reasonably stable until the end of the twentieth century.

Tikriti places forced migration in its proper context and reminds us that it is not new to modern Iraq. Massacres in the 1930s led to Chaldo-Assyrian Christians moving out of the area, some to Syria and others to Europe and the USA. In the 1950s, Iraqi Jews left in great numbers in a process largely organized by joint Israeli/Iraqi government policies. By the late 1950s with the overthrow of the king, many royalists fled the country; though few in number they were wealthy and represented prominent families. Saddam Hussein then expelled 'Persian' Iraqis. Further large movements occurred after 1991, during which period many Sunnis were settled around Baghdad.

The past few decades saw a secular state suppressing communitarian and ethnic groups, instead dividing people into Ba'ath party members and the others. Communal violence since 2003 has reshaped the country and forced migration has made the tripartite division established by the Coalition authorities more real. Tikriti maintains that in fact Coalition authorities intentionally encouraged the breaking down of institutions supportive of national identity, which thus allowed sectarian actors to step into the breech. Apparent use of assassination to gain political control resulted in the flight of middle-class professionals by 2005. De-Ba'athification and the dismantling of the former economic state system then led to the dissolution of the secular system and the strengthening of sectarian organizations. The interim governing council was also founded on sectarian lines while increasing sectarian violence led to a growing reliance on sectarian protection. Tikriti shows that the 'surge' strategy of the Coalition continued to force population displacement and formally institutionalize the new segregated communities and sectarian interests.

CONCLUSION

The essays in this volume cover a wide range of case studies including Sahrawi refugees in Algeria and Spain, Palestinian refugees in the West Bank and Gaza, Turkish settlers and Greek-Cypriot refugees, Iraqi refugees in Jordan as well as internally displaced Iraqis in northern Iraq, and Afghan refugees in Iran and in diaspora. The authors construct their analyses from a range of disciplines including anthropology, sociology, political science, and literature. The notion of unidirectional migration is challenged, as is the humanitarian aid regime's response of 're-rooting' the dispossessed where forced migrants are regarded as either candidates for resettlement or repatriation. The contributing authors contest such ideas and instead refer to global movements and networks, circulatory migration, and historical contexts.

Not surprisingly a particular interest in gender and generation runs through the essays, with the impact the upheaval of forced migration has on relations between men and women as well as between generations coming under significant scrutiny. Whether regarded as 'burnt-out' by elders or generally traumatized and alienated, many refugee youth, particularly in urban contexts, find their identity shaped by social narratives not of their own making. Their sense of discrimination and lack of opportunity emerges as an important theme. The plight of Iraqi refugees in the region and the very limited humanitarian assistance they receive is also closely considered. Very few Iraqis, we are told, apply for third-country resettlement. Most, it seems, prefer to wait in a bordering country—even with little or no international aid—in order to take the first safe opportunity to return to their homeland. Yet, these Iraqis are running out of funds to keep their families together, while at the same time little is being done internationally or at the state level to extend humanitarian aid, or legal protection to this largely self-settled refugee group. The need for protection and human security continues to increase as these dispossessed Iraqis—both refugees and internally displaced people— struggle to shield their families and keep their society from fragmenting any further.

Human security, legal protection, coping, resilience, and resistance are all issues of crucial importance in understanding the social upheaval and the loss of citizenship and in some cases political identity when people are forced to leave their homes, give up their livelihoods, and find new ways to survive. The essays in this collection make a significant contribution not only to understanding the plight of refugees and displaced people but also in comprehending the larger political and economic universe in which they must operate. Refugees, whether internally displaced or pushed across international borders, are categories of people, not objects. They are individuals who have lost the political protection of their country and who find themselves outside or at the margins of the global nation-state system. Their struggle to survive and to thrive depends upon turning their exile or forced migration around; to regain the protection of a government and to become 'citizens' once again either in the original homeland or a new nation. It is a quest we can all sympathize with and support. This volume is a step in the direction of making the refugee story more transparent. With that knowledge, we can hope that the future of the Middle East and North Africa will contain a lessening of dispossession and forced migration.

REFERENCES

Appadurai, Arjun (1991), 'Notes and Queries for Transnational Anthropology', in Richard Fox (ed.), *Recapturing Anthropology: Working in the Present* (Santa Fe, NM, School of American Research Press), p. 191.

—— (1999), 'Disjuncture and Difference in the Global Cultural Economy', in Simon During (ed.), *The Cultural Studies Reader* (London and New York, Routledge), pp. 220–30.

Clifford, James and Marcus, George E. (eds) (1986), *Writing Culture: The Poetics and Politics of Ethnography* (Berkeley, LA, and London, University of California Press).

Part I
Displacement

1.
What Visibility Conceals: Re-embedding Refugee Migration from Iraq

Géraldine Chatelard

INTRODUCTION

Iraq has undergone profound changes since the Anglo-American invasion and the fall of the Ba'athist regime in April–May 2003. New and heightened levels of human insecurity have led to large refugee flows towards neighbouring Arab countries—mostly Syria and, to a lesser extent, Jordan—and to internal displacement, in particular to the Kurdish autonomous region in the north of Iraq. Refugee migration started in anticipation of the 2003 American invasion with Iraqis looking for security in those neighbouring countries that allowed them entry. The number of refugees increased in subsequent years and reached a peak between early 2006 and early 2008 in response to the widespread development of communal and criminal violence in the country, but also following sweeping policies of economic liberalization and the dismantling of the army and public sector that resulted in increasingly high levels of unemployment (Marfleet 2007). Those who left during that two-year period looked for refuge mostly in Syria, after Jordan restricted entries of Iraqis following bombing attacks on hotels in Amman carried out by Iraqi nationals in November 2005. While new regulations on exit from Iraq were imposed in late 2005/early 2006 (conditional granting of a new type of passport, in particular), both Syria and Jordan introduced formal advanced visa procedures for Iraqis—the former in September 2007, the latter in January 2008—further reducing the number of those able to exit Iraq in their quest for security.

Towards the end of 2006, and after a process of policy agenda-setting in which international refugee and human rights advocates and humanitarian organizations, many of them US-based, played major roles in bringing Iraqi refugees from invisibility to visibility, the post-Saddam Hussein mass displacement from Iraq was designated for the first time as an unprecedented refugee crisis of huge proportions with figures as high as 2.2 million refugees gaining currency.[1] A complex set-up was deployed to protect and assist the refugees in neighbouring countries and further afield, supported by international funding and refugee resettlement schemes to Western states (Sassoon 2008). These humanitarian operations and the politically laden aspects of the Iraq refugee crisis, in which the responsibility of the US government for failing to restore governance and maintain order and security in Iraq was pointed out, have led humanitarian practitioners, refugee advocacy groups, the media, and most scholars to focus their interventions and/or analyses on post-Saddam Hussein refugee movements.

The assumption upon which this essay is based is that the magnifying effect of the 'unprecedented refugee crisis' designation together with the state-centred bias of the international refugee regime and, to some extent, of the academic field of refugee studies (Malkki 1995) have created other invisibilities by obscuring the question of the embeddedness of the recent forced migration in the longer-term political history of Iraq and in regional dynamics that span Iraq and the neighbouring countries that have played host to the majority of refugees from Iraq before and after

---

[1] In September 2007 public estimates by the UNHCR, based on figures provided by host governments, put the number of Iraqi refugees at 2.2 million, concentrated mostly in Syria and Jordan, with another 2.2 million displaced inside Iraq. Although the UNHCR mentioned that 1 million were displaced before the 2003 war, it was not clear from its published documents how many of those were displaced inside Iraq and how many had sought refuge across borders (UNHCR 2007). At the time of writing (February 2009) recent interviews in Jordan and Syria with the UNHCR, NGOs, funding agencies, and researchers engaged in field-work with Iraqi refugees revealed that figures published by host governments were the subject of debate among humanitarian and refugee practitioners and that credible numbers were thought to be between half a million and 1 million refugees having left Iraq since April/May 2003. For Jordan, the figures published by the government and the UNHCR have ranged between 450,000 and 750,000. By contrast, a demographic survey conducted by the Norwegian research institute FAFO in early 2007 estimated the total stock of Iraqis as 161,000 (FAFO 2007: 7). However, the Jordanian authorities contested these figures as being too low, basing their argument on the number of Iraqis subscribing to telephone lines and on statistics on arrivals and departures at borders. This led FAFO, in its final report, to use a revised number of between 450,000 and 500,000 Iraqis in the country, while advising that mobile phone lines are used by a large number of temporary visitors and that Jordanian statistics on departure underestimate more than those on arrival (FAFO 2007: 7–8). On the last point, see also Arouri (2008: 12). For the politics of counting refugees, see Bakewell (1999) and Crisp (1999).

2003. Additionally, the short-term, operationally bounded, humanitarian perspective has disregarded the articulations between several types and scales of migratory movements from Iraq. In both Syria and Jordan current refugee migration is a continuation, and only partial amplification, of previous trends, and takes place alongside a variety of other mobilities and circulations from and to Iraq (Chatelard and Dorai 2009). Refugee movements are not necessarily unidirectional and can include return visits to Iraq and subsequent migration to other Arab countries or to asylum states in the West. Large numbers of Iraqi migrants and refugees maintain ties across borders with those who have remained in Iraq and those who have settled in migration or asylum countries in the West in previous decades. The result is that pre-existing exile communities play an important role in the migratory projects of those who have left more recently. Finally many Iraqis who had left their country before 2003 and settled in the West are also now engaged in circulations between their current country of residence and the main regional Arab states that have been hosting the latest wave of refugees from Iraq.

As is often the case with major refugee crises in the contemporary world, the recent mass displacement from Iraq is overlaid on a continuum of previous displacements. Modern Iraq is in fact a classic case of twentieth-century post-imperial nation-state formation of the type Aristide Zolberg analysed in his seminal 1983 article, 'The Formation of New States as a Refugee-generating Process'. Successive Iraqi regimes have exerted control over population movements both by limiting the mobility of certain categories of the population inside the national territory and across borders, and by forcibly displacing other categories internally or outside the national space. In Iraq the phenomenon of forced migration has proved particularly durable and variegated, almost exhausting the typology of reactive migration proposed by Anthony Richmond (1993). Inscribed in the *longue durée* of state–population relations, forced-migration movements from Iraq have long taken a broad regional and worldwide scope (Chatelard 2009). The global social organization of Iraqi migration has been shaped as much by the nature of the coercion subsequent Iraqi regimes have exerted upon the society—by fragmenting the population along corporate lines based on kinship, religion, ethnicity, ideological orientations, and class, and by exerting control upon the mobilities of individuals (Dawod and Bozarslan 2003)—as by the nature of the polities within which the vast majority of migrants and refugees from Iraq have sought security.

Between the late 1970s and early 2003, Iran received the largest number of forced migrants from Iraq within a refugee regime (Alborzi

2006; Al-Meehy 2004), whereas in Arab states and Turkey the majority of Iraqis compelled to leave their country have been received as irregular migrants (Mannaert 2003; Zaiotti 2006). Despite these notable differences, all regional hosts exhibit a set of common characteristics.

The political orientations of host states vis-à-vis Iraq and the various components of its polity and population, together with references to meta-regional ideologies (pan-Islamism, pan-Shi'ism, pan-Arabism, pan-Turkism, or Europeanism, etc.) have created differentials in the context of opportunities of migrants from Iraq once again along ethnic, religious, political, and class lines that have determined the unequal allocation of economic and social resources and of individual and group security. Most of the social fragmentations existing in Iraq have also been maintained among those who have settled in liberal countries in the West where multiple communities of migrants originating in Iraq have been forming since the 1940s in Great Britain, Australia, the USA, Germany, Sweden, and several other countries. It is within socially fragmented transnational spaces that Iraqis from subsequent waves of emigration have maintained ties that span borders between Iraq, neighbouring states, and more distant emigration and asylum countries. The result is that an understanding of migratory trends and the circumstances of migrants from Iraq in any given temporal or spatial context needs to be based on an examination of the dynamics of such social units as the family, the socio-religious, or ethnic group. These, together with migrants' social or professional class, appear to be as relevant as policies vis-à-vis migrants or refugees and normative/legal categories in countries of transit or settlement.

Furthermore, the highly political nature of the causes that have led to reactive migration from Iraq, even when proximate causes appear to be economic (such as was the case under the embargo between 1990 and 2003, and continues to be the case under a neo-liberal system imposed by occupying powers), renders the distinction between refugees or political exiles on the one hand and economic migrants or expatriates on the other hand particularly difficult. Another difficulty in upholding these categories stems from the context of opportunities offered to qualified professionals and holders of capital from Iraq in a number of other Arab countries that have long practised selective migration policies (De Bel Air 2006, 2007). Large numbers of those who have been compelled to leave Iraq since 1990 in response to a combination of economic and political threats to their security and that of their families have found employment as qualified migrant workers in several Arab countries where others have invested capital in properties and businesses and obtained residence rights. A further issue is that of what Jordanian anthropologist Seteney Shami (1996) has deemed 'the forces of regionalism' in shaping migratory trends and experiences in the Middle East. Senses of alienation or, conversely, proximity between migrants from Iraq and host societies in the region are largely shaped by social and cultural determinants such as language, religion, and pre-existing family or other ties.

If the general categories of refugee or forced migrant are used in this essay to encompass all those Iraqis who left their country under duress, it remains nevertheless that many of them have not framed their experiences in such terms. Migrants' self-perceptions of the experiences that prompted their departure from Iraq and their self-definition along migration categories and other collective identities are important elements to consider to account for their migratory trajectories and experiences in time and space and are dealt with in this essay, premised on the necessity to explore what lies beyond academic, normative, and policy-relevant categories when looking at the sociological dynamics of refugees and forced migration (Bakewell 2008; Polzer 2008).

For all the above reasons it seems heuristic to look not only beyond the spaces, time-frames, and social/legal categories that international humanitarian and advocacy actors define as those of their engagement but equally beyond the recent disruptions in Iraqi political history and, hence, following on Elizabeth Colson (2007), to adopt a multidisciplinary linkage methodology. Whereas a systematic history of forced-migration movements from Iraq remains to be written, this essay aims to reconnect the mass refugee migration from Iraq that has followed the fall of the regime of Saddam Hussein with previous and concomitant social and spatial migratory trends through a combination of disciplinary approaches from the fields of the sociology of migration and social anthropology. Due to the limitations imposed by the format of this essay, the focus is on the movements of Iraqis between Iraq and Jordan, covering a period that extends from 1990 to 2008, set within broader migratory trends and trajectories. The argument developed, based on original research conducted since 1998 among Iraqi migrants and exiles and relevant institutional actors, is that the recent visibility of the former, a factor of the international engagement with the post-2003 Iraq refugee crisis, conceals previous dynamics of forced migration from Iraq, the embededdness of current refugee migration in other migration movements of Iraqis, and the variegated experiences and self-perceptions of refugees from Iraq.

21

BETWEEN THE GULF WAR AND THE IRAQ WAR: INVISIBLE IRAQIS IN JORDAN

The context of refugee migration from Iraq

According to accounts from humanitarian and refugee organizations during the 1990–1 Gulf War, 1 million Iraqis and foreigners working in Iraq crossed into Jordan over a period of two months. In the following years, while some refugees returned to Iraq, successive groups of individuals kept arriving in Jordan, the only country neighbouring Iraq whose border remained open between 1990 and 2003. Iraqis were fleeing the deteriorating economic situation ensuing from the UN-imposed embargo on Iraq, various types of violence exerted by the regime on active or perceived opponents (especially the Shi'ite Islamist Da'wa party), and, for some groups, such as Christians and Sabeans[2] from rural areas, vexations that were unhindered by the security forces. Most Iraqis identified themselves as members of the educated middle class, with a large proportion of them professionals, both men and women, and former civil servants. Because the regime imposed strict control on the exit of its nationals, leaving Iraq was a long, costly, and arduous undertaking, especially for holders of university degrees who faced financial disincentives imposed by the authorities, and those who were targeted by the Iraqi repressive apparatus. Most migrants had to prepare their departure secretly over several months, or even years, and many had to bribe their way out and/or pay for forged travel documents. The cost of emigration (compulsory bank guarantee, exit tax, etc.) had a selective effect on migrants, allowing out only those who could mobilize enough financial capital and/or social relations; hence migrants who arrived in Jordan belonged in their majority to the educated middle class (Chatelard 2009, 2005).

The number of Iraqis in Jordan in the year 2002 was estimated by the UNHCR at 300,000 in a country of 5 million people (UNHCR 2003). Iraqis were mostly concentrated in Amman, a city of 1.5 million inhabitants. Large flows had also transited Jordan in the previous twelve years, mostly on their way to western Europe where over 200,000 Iraqi nationals claimed asylum during that period. The Jordanian authorities, however,

---

[2] Sabeans (also called Mandeans) are a demographically small religious community specific to the Shatt el-Arab, a region spanning south-east Iraq and south-west Iran. They are attached neither to Islam nor Christianity.

barely acknowledged the presence and transit of this vast number of migrants, and Iraqis remained in many ways invisible to the eyes of the Jordanian public or national and foreign relief agencies. At the request of the Jordanian government, the latter concentrated their operations on the poorer sectors of the Jordanian population, including the most vulnerable of the Palestinian refugees displaced from the 1948 and 1967 wars with Israel, and, until the mid-1990s, on the 300,000 Jordanian nationals (the majority of Palestinian origin) who had been expelled from Kuwait in 1990–1 and had to be integrated in Jordan (Van Hear 1995).

Jordan did not have, even in 2009, a domestic asylum regime, nor is the country a signatory of international refugee conventions (Zaiotti 2006).[3] In 2002 only 5 per cent of the total estimate of Iraqis in the country were registered with the local office of the UNHCR that had started operating in Jordan during the 1990–1 Gulf War to conduct status determination and resettlement of refugees to third countries. The refugee recognition rate for Iraqis was notoriously low and registration as an asylum seeker did not guarantee any form of social benefit nor did it protect against *refoulement* to Iraq by the Jordanian authorities that was said to happen albeit in very limited numbers. This last fact acted as a particularly strong deterrent on those who might have considered approaching the UNHCR since the Iraqi government had de facto created the categories of 'illegal emigrant' and 'illegal asylum seeker'. Members of the latter category were those who had formally launched an asylum claim with the UNHCR in an Arab country or Turkey, or with national asylum agencies in a Western country, or who had been received as prima facie refugees in Iran. They were liable to the death penalty in case of return to Iraq, while their family members left in Iraq could incur serious threats from the authorities. The Iraqi secret services were also said to carry out assassinations of refugees with a high political profile in Jordan and in countries of asylum further afield, including in Europe.

Illegality of status was making the situation of Iraqi residents precarious: most had overstayed the visit permit on which they had entered Jordan. Access of the majority of Iraqis to the employment market was confined to the informal sector where they were unprotected by labour laws. They were denied welfare benefits and free access to health. On the

---

[3] Palestinian refugees in Jordan, the majority of whom are also Jordanian citizens, benefit from a particular status under the assistance mandate of the UN Works and Relief Agency (UNRWA) created in 1949–50 (Al-Husseini 2007). On the Jordanian legislation on refugees and other forced migrants, see Olwan (2007).

other hand, very few availed themselves of the possibility of registering their children in the public school system although it was by royal decree available to Iraqi children even when parents did not have a residence. In the vast majority of cases, Iraqis experienced a painful social degradation in Jordan. Informality and irregularity compelled them to keep a low profile and to establish residency in several poor or lower middle-class neighbourhoods of Amman with clusterings particularly around the existing churches that served Jordanian Christians. Whatever their socio-economic background and geographical origin, the majority were cut off from possible sources of income or remittances from inside Iraq at a time when the blockade precipitated a dramatic economic crisis and the deval-uation of the Iraqi currency. Those who managed employment in the formal or informal sectors in Jordan sent income back to dependants through informal systems of money transfer (*hawala*). Other forms of communication with Iraq were very limited: telephones were tapped by the Iraqi security services, the Iraqi postal service read letters, and the internet was unavailable to the public in Iraq (Chatelard 2005).

Social fragmentation and solidarity networks

There was an older group of Iraqi migrants to Jordan dating back from 1958 when the Iraqi monarchy was toppled and members of the former ruling elite were welcomed by King Hussein of Jordan, a close relative of the assassinated Iraqi monarch. This group, and successive ones who came before the large influx of the 1990s, was composed of members of the political, intellectual, and business elites who were either incorporated into the equivalent social class in Jordan or later migrated to third countries, mostly in Europe and America (Fattah 2007).

Relations maintained between the 'old' and 'new' generations of Iraqi migrants to Jordan and between Iraqis and Jordanians were primarily a factor of class and professional identity. Artists and intellectuals, academics, and members of the professions and the business elite repre-sented throughout the various periods of Iraqi migration to Jordan formed solidarity networks encompassing Jordanians and Iraqis who had arrived at different periods, therefore playing an efficient role in anchoring the newcomers socially and professionally. A few thousand Iraqi professionals and academics who arrived in the 1990s received status as foreign residents with a work contract. Many of them were still professionally active in Jordan in the early twenty-first century.

Other Iraqis, who had less social or professional capital to negotiate in Jordan with members of the previous generation of exiles, did not form a cohesive group. Interactions were limited by the absence of financial means, feelings of insecurity and mistrust, and several layers of social barriers that resulted in socializations and solidarities taking place along religious lines. Whereas Iraqi Christians could associate with Jordanian Christians of the same social class, Sabean families remained socially isolated although they received help from several Christian congregations. The religiously oriented Shi'ites were the most marginalized in a staunchly Sunni country that denied them the right to communal organization and political activism (Chatelard 2005).

A quest for security

As I was gathering the testimonies of Iraqis staying in Amman without a legal status and trying to understand their coping strategies and which factors, apart from institutional ones, explained their invisibility, three recurrent themes kept surfacing in informal face-to-face interviews or collective discussions. These were the situations that they had fled in Iraq, their anger and anxiety in the face of their new conditions in Jordan, and their projects of further migration.

Those who had fled to escape direct coercion exerted by the agents of the regime, and who were mainly active members or sympathizers of political Shi'ite currents (in particular the Da'wa party), described Iraq as hell, the locus of terror and of unlimited and inescapable tyranny exerted by Saddam Hussein and his security forces, and the site of torture, death, social dislocation, and the unbearable division of family and friendship groups. Their widespread sentiment was that their physical integrity and that of their close associates was never guaranteed. They considered the economic deprivation that had affected many of them under the embargo, or as a result of discriminatory policies (many had been dismissed from their jobs as civil servants), within the context of regime coercion. Religiously oriented refugees were likely to interpret their experience within a metaphor of divinely imposed suffering and redemption that fitted well within both Christian and Shi'ite world-views, and entertained the hope of punishment for the tyrant although this was not projected within human but eschatological times.[4] These individual experiences

---

[4] On Iraqi Shi'ites living in 'religious time and space' in Dearborn (USA), see Shoeb et al. (2007).

and collective representations were incommunicable to most Jordanians. The Jordanians' general feeling was of support for and admiration for Saddam Hussein, perceived as the champion of Arabs vis-à-vis Western imperialism and whose attributes of masculinity, authority, strong leadership, unchecked power, and military force were precisely the ones that had been used so brutally on the minds and bodies of refugees.

For those who had suffered at the hands of the regime and those who had left Iraq to escape deteriorating economic circumstances, Jordan was rarely mentally constructed as a place of permanent abode. It was spoken of as a locus of economic and social insecurity where one could be nothing but uncertain about the future. Iraqis were sharing a diffuse sentiment of anxiety in part lingering from past trauma, in part fuelled by rumours of deportation carried out by the Jordanian authorities or of assassinations conducted inside Jordan by agents of Saddam's regime, or by the widespread belief that one such agent had infiltrated the local office of the UNHCR. Unlike Iraq, Jordan was not a site of terror, but it was still a site of fear because it was not perceived as an entity totally separated from Iraq where individual security could be guaranteed. Hence, many migrants adopted strategies of physical and identity concealment that resulted in their social invisibility. As a whole, and excluding those who had secured a legal status via professional, class, or family connections or investment capacities, most Iraqis interacted with Jordanians only when it was necessary to ensure their basic living requirements. Mistrust was the norm, accompanied by a feeling of bitterness that what they had expected from Arab brothers in Jordan, a country that had championed Arabness, was unmet. The corollary was withdrawal into the close circle of family members, friends, and co-religionists with whom to share trust, mutual assistance, and the feeling of a common experience in Iraq and in Jordan.

As their stay endured, so grew their desire to travel further afield and reconstruct livelihoods in what many interviewees termed as 'safe' (*amin*) countries. By this they always meant western Europe, North America, or Australia. A large part of the every-day discussions of the Iraqis I met dealt with the feeling that they were at one stage of an unfinished journey, with imaginations of the destination as a place where they would escape physical threats and economic insecurity, with the project of raising a family, but also narratives of the uncertainties faced by relatives and friends who had taken the underground routes to such destinations, and finally discussions and exchange of information about the means to that end.

It is almost exclusively in this type of narrative that references to actors in the international refugee regime such as the UNHCR or national asylum agencies in prospective host countries were made. Often, they were simply juxtaposed with mentions of other facilitating institutions or individuals, such as churches that sponsored refugee arrivals through national schemes in Australia or Canada, embassies of various 'safe' countries in Amman, migrant smugglers who operated travel services in the city, religious leaders—Christian or Shi'ite—who were in Amman or had made it to a safe country, or the International Committee of the Red Cross which offered an international family identification service that some migrants used to locate relatives in the diaspora, reconnect with them to gather information on destination countries, and sometimes request financial assistance. The only hierarchy of preference was that of all other means over smugglers. The UNHCR was neither trusted nor favoured for the reasons mentioned above, but also because the UN system in general was perceived to be responsible for imposing the economic blockade over Iraq, and because many migrants feared being resettled in a country that they had not chosen. Most Iraqis knew rather precisely where they wanted to go: places where they had friends or relatives (who were not necessarily under a refugee status and with whom the UNHCR-sponsored family reunification schemes could not be activated), or destinations about which they had formed an idea and which they thought would meet their moral, social, or economic expectations.

For that group of Iraqis who had constructed a vision of Iraq as intrinsically unsafe, return was never on the agenda. They had no hope that tyranny in Iraq was about to come to an end in the near future. The only ones who attempted to go back did so with the aim of rescuing close family members, a spouse, children, sometimes a father or mother left behind, and bringing them to Jordan, or to sell a property in order to sustain themselves in exile or pay for a journey to safety. Others, whose motives for living in exile were based on strict economic considerations, also refrained from going back to Iraq on a regular basis. Their movements were impeded by the limitations the regime placed on the exit of its nationals, and those who re-entered Iraq were rarely confident that they would to be able to leave again.

Mobilities, circulations, and the redistribution of migrants

In the pre-2003 period the composition of the newly arrived Iraqi population in Amman changed quickly over just more than a decade: many of the original working-age males were joined by their spouses and children, and families experienced natural growth through births. The Iraqi migrant population in Jordan was in permanent recomposition as many of its members were in transit for variable time-lengths, sometimes as long as several years, and a large number of Iraqis were circulating between Iraq and Jordan: cross-border traders living off the embargo; business people and other members of the Iraqi elite whose movements out of Iraq and residence in Jordan were facilitated; bus, taxi, and truck drivers who connected Iraq to Jordan. As new migrants seeking economic or physical security arrived from Iraq, other ones left Jordan. Many sought employment in Libya, Yemen, and Arab Gulf states that recruited trained professionals. But the largest number travelled to countries where they applied for asylum and subsequently appeared in the statistics of national refugee agencies in Western states.

In this instance again, secondary migration often took place in stages, one family member—not systematically a male head of household—leaving ahead of their spouse and children who were reunited with them either after a long institutional process within the framework of asylum, more rarely migration regimes, or who embarked on a clandestine journey across continents (Chatelard 2005). In contrast to previous generations of Iraqi exiles who had been able to enter and settle in Europe or the USA through labour or student migration regimes, the post-1990 migrants were faced with the non-entry policies that most wealthy states had started to adopt in the 1980s and had little choice but to acquire legal status through asylum regimes. At that point, they started talking about themselves as asylum-seekers (*talbin luju'*) or as refugees (*laji'in*) to denote the legal category the UNHCR or asylum states had placed them in. However, they did not use these terms to qualify Iraqi migrants collectively, but spoke of themselves using various Arabic terms, such as *muhajirin* (emigrants), *manfiyin*, or *mughtaribin*, the latter two carrying the same sense of alienation as the English 'exiles'.

Over that period, Jordan played the role of a sieve and filter, or frontier zone, between Iraq and the rest of the world. The control and coercion mechanisms put in place by the Iraqi regime exerted a selection on would-be migrants, allowing out only specific categories who could mobilize financial and relational capital. In Jordan other mechanisms were at play that redistributed Iraqi migrants and refugees regionally and globally. Amman was a meeting point for Iraqis from previous decades who had accessed the nationality of their country of settlement in the West and those who had left Iraq more recently, allowing for marriages and other family or communal-based strategies of secondary migration. The country's integration in international communication and transport networks, the presence of several foreign embassies, and the availability of technologies for forging sophisticated identity and other documents allowed the development of a trade in services for irregular migration to Europe or, for a smaller number, to Australia or North America. Air transport to other Arab countries offering employment opportunities was available. UNHCR-operated resettlement and family-reunification programmes, together with the refugee-sponsorship schemes of Australia and Canada accessible from these countries' embassies in Amman, further distributed a few thousand refugees to Western countries. Class, political and professional identities, and previous migration histories of members of the family or the religious or ethnic group were all factors liable to direct the migratory strategies and trajectories of those who used Jordan as a stepping stone for further migration.

It is the interplay between the policy choices of Western countries on selective migration, asylum, refugee resettlement, and family-reunification on the one hand and the dynamics of migrants' social networks on the other hand that shaped the global distribution of Iraqi migration along a pattern of geographical convergence and social fragmentation. Pre-existing migratory poles specific to certain categories of Iraqis were further reinforced (Australia and California for Christians; the UK for the secular middle class; Germany for the Kurds who had left Iraq across Turkey), while new ones emerged (Canada for Christians; Sweden for Christians and Kurds; the suburbs of Detroit and London for religious Shi'ites). In each of these migratory poles, several discrete communities of migrants/refugees from Iraq maintained limited interactions.

In the Arab region the distribution of those who could or would not migrate further also happened along class and socio-religious or socio-political lines, once again as a combined factor of the policy choices of Arab states and of the social networks migrants could access. Within Arab migration regimes, those well integrated into Jordan through class or professional networks remained in the long term or maintained facilitated circulations between Iraq and Jordan whereas multi-directional migration of professionals took place between Jordan, Libya, and Yemen according to opportunities for labour and social connections. By contrast, supporters of the Da'wa party who had fled to Jordan later left for Syria where the authorities allowed the religious activities of Iraqi and other Shi'ites based both on the legal recognition of a Shi'ite community in the country and on regional politics such as Syria's ties with Iran and Hezbollah in Lebanon.

A CONCEALING VISIBILITY

The post-2003 Iraq crisis has not only brought Iraqi refugees in Jordan—and in other regional host states, particularly Syria—attention at the international level, it has also made them much more visible in the social landscape of Jordan and the objects of a discourse from the part of the Jordanian authorities, media, and public. However, by framing population movements from Iraq exclusively in refugee terms and by isolating post-2003 trends from previous ones, such as that of the late 1990s, this visibility conceals more than it reveals.

The new context of refugee migration to Jordan

Immediately after the collapse of the regime of Saddam Hussein in April 2003, the new context in Iraq prompted new refugees to come to Jordan: initially those who were closely associated with the former regime and feared arrest and/or retribution, then many others who had been unable to realize their migratory projects during previous years and who took the opportunity of the lifting of restrictions on exit from Iraq, and, finally, from early 2006, those who experienced or feared sectarian, political, and criminal violence, including retribution for having worked with the occupying forces or foreign companies. Members of the second category soon became 'displaced by absence' (Kunz 1973, quoted by Richmond 1993: 8) after insecurity in Iraq prevented them from returning.

The flow of Iraqis to Jordan, unhindered before attacks were carried out on hotels in Amman by Iraqi nationals in November 2005, was thereafter curbed at entry points (with adult males and those carrying identifiable Shi'ite names liable to be refused entry) and a formal visa procedure was introduced in early 2008 favouring holders of capital and those who had an institutional guarantor in Jordan or in Iraq. The result is that a very large part of those who fled generalized violence as of 2006, particularly those who expected to be refused entry into Jordan, had no choice but to flee to Syria.

Although motives for flight have been different from those of refugees of the previous period, Iraqis who have made it to Jordan still belong to the same social category: the educated urban middle and upper middle class, originating mostly from Baghdad. The major change in the sociological profile of the refugees before and after the fall of Saddam Hussein concerns religiously oriented Shi'ites who, having been made more welcome in Syria, have redirected their migration there. Among the current wave of Iraqis in Jordan a majority define themselves as secular, thus categories of Sunni or Shi'ite sectarian affiliation appear of little relevance. Yet those who seek assistance or protection from the UNHCR or non-government organizations (NGOs) are systematically required to identify along these categories. Forcing such statistical categories upon people has the effect of making communal identities performative in the context of humanitarian intervention. On the other hand, religious minorities such as Christians and Sabeans, who face higher levels of insecurity in today's Iraq, continue to be well represented among the refugees. Demographically, and according to a survey conducted by FAFO (2007), there is also now a higher proportion of women to men, with numbers of women on their own, and, most probably, a higher proportion of children, although this is difficult to verify in the absence of systematic statistics covering this population before and after 2003. In terms of spacial distribution, the newcomers to Jordan have settled mostly in Amman and in lower numbers in other cities in the north of the country, with those with less financial capacity finding rented accommodation in middle- and lower-middle-class neighbourhoods, and others, who could pay higher rents or buy properties, in more affluent areas of the capital. Distribution has therefore happened on a class and income basis, with a few clusterings along the lines of those Iraqis who arrived between 1990 and 2002, in particular for poorer Christians and Sabeans in the vicinity of existing churches that offered them social services.

In Jordan, Iraqis, especially since the bombing attacks of 2005, have become highly visible in the public discourse of the government and the local media, the latter generally reproducing uncritically the rhetoric of the former in a country where the Arabic press has limited scope for diverging from the official line. The Jordanian public have composed a shared imagining of the Iraqi presence in Jordan assembled out of the representations offered by the local media and government officials in which the sectarian conflict in Iraq and the fear of a Shi'ite expansion figure prominently, and of their own individual and collective concerns for political, societal, and economic security in Jordan. This imagining of the presence of Iraqis combines two main elements. On the one hand, a vision of their role as predators on the scarce natural and economic resources of Jordan and a primary force in driving up prices of goods and properties legitimizes claims to international assistance to 'relieve the burden' on Jordan. On the other hand, Iraqis are perceived as a risk to the religious and national identity of Jordan that needs to be contained by the security apparatus of the host state. Other perceptions of the Iraqi presence in Jordan that are not grounded in the predation and security discursive orders are not uncommon among Jordanian intellectuals, academics, professionals, artists, and Jordanian employees of relief organizations who are those most likely to maintain regular exchanges with Iraqis in the work place—as colleagues or as beneficiaries of assistance—or in social circles. However, these perceptions do not inform the content of the government-controlled information that flows in the direction of the general public, while there is no public sphere where diverging voices, including that of the Iraqis themselves, could debate the realities and implications of the Iraqi presence in the country. Therefore the prominence of the issue in public and popular discourses renders Iraqis in Jordan both highly conspicuous and equally misrepresented by a hegemonizing state-driven rhetoric.

Circulations, mobilities, and immobility

As was the case in the pre-2003 period, transit refugees and migrants from Iraq have also been using Jordan as a stepping stone towards Yemen, the Arab Gulf, or more distant destinations. Via Jordan, Egypt has replaced Libya as an Arab destination, offering markedly different opportunities, with irregularity and absence of employment being the norm (Fargues et al. 2008). Conversely, those Iraqis who had left Iraq in previous decades and settled in a Western country within a migration or refugee regime, and who have accessed the nationality of their country of residence, have been using Amman as a safe base from which to explore possibilities of visiting Iraq or establishing business links. Amman has reinforced its previous role as a meeting point between members of the distant diasporas who come to visit those relatives and friends who remained secluded in Iraq under the Ba'athist regime. Iraqi marriages held in the Jordanian capital are occasions for family reunions, bringing together people still living in Iraq, others who have taken residence in Jordan, and those who come from abroad. Frequent unions also take place between those from abroad and those from Iraq, or those newly arrived in Jordan as refugees, with a view to transferring residency rights and/or citizenship of a Western country to the Iraqi spouse.

Amman is perceived by Iraqis as Iraq's second economic capital. Jordan plays a broader social, political, and cultural role as a safe frontier to which to withdraw temporarily and conduct a number of activities in the context of the fragmentation of the Iraqi territory where entire areas, between 2006 and 2008, had fallen outside the control of a central government, thus restricting and making unsafe the movements of people. This is why a considerable circular flow of migrants has also kept shuttling between Baghdad and Amman in what can be conceptualized as a translocal space: Iraqi business people use Amman as a regional centre in which some have made investments and in which Iraqi business associations are active; members of the Iraqi government and public institutions hold meetings with international organizations that operate their activities in Iraq from Amman; Iraqi employees of foreign NGOs and international organizations come to meet their foreign colleagues whose trips to Iraq are restricted; new recruits from the Iraqi police forces and employees from an array of institutions and NGOs have received training in Jordan; patients flown in from Iraq are treated in Jordanian hospitals; students complete their education in Jordanian private universities before returning to Iraq, etc. Among the Iraqi governmental and business elite and also less prominent socio-economic categories such as civil society activists, a possible way of capitalizing on the safety and stability offered by Amman while maintaining professional, business, or political opportunities in Iraq has been to buy a property in Amman and secure a Jordanian residence permit either as an Iraqi or as a national of a Western country. While spouses and children live in Jordan, the head of the household, or both parents in some cases, travel frequently between Baghdad and Amman.

Business people are the only category of Iraqi residents to have been allowed to form associations whereas membership of Jordanian civil society organizations or the establishment of NGOs by non-nationals is prevented under Jordanian law. In February 2009, Jordan further reinforced its inclination towards Iraqi holders-of-capital over other migrants by facilitating visa and residence procedures for investors and business people from Iraq. Françoise De Bel-Air has qualified this policy as one of 'segmented assimilation (assimilation of the migrant to a sub-group within the host population)' where 'rich migrants from Palestine, Iraq and elsewhere continue to be welcome, thus composing a transversal, globalised elite, involved in consumption and select leisure infrastructure' (De Bel-Air 2007).

Strategies of mobility across the Iraqi–Jordanian border (or air space) are conditional upon a number of economic, social, administrative, or legal pre-requisites: either enough financial capital to make productive or consumptive investments that entitle Iraqis to residence rights in Jordan, or the backing of institutions or prominent individuals in Iraq or in Jordan that act as guarantors vis-à-vis the visa-granting Jordanian authorities, or the possession of a passport from a Western country that facilitates entry and an up-to-six-month stay in Jordan. At the other end, in Iraq, the main pre-requisite is the availability of a system of social or armed protection that allows circulation and the conduct of activities, or the restriction of these activities within secured spaces, like the Green Zone in Baghdad, or some 'pacified' neighbourhoods. Those most mobile across the border generally accumulate several of these assets. Their circulation between Jordan and Iraq does not preclude many of them being registered with the UNHCR in Amman or having applied to various humanitarian schemes for resettlement operated by such countries as Australia and Canada.

Mobility is not available to all Iraqis who have come to Jordan and many are immobilized either for lack of the financial assets or social connections that would allow them residency in Jordan. This group includes those who entered before restrictions were placed on entries or, in later years, migrants with a visa that they have overstayed. Applying a discretionary toleration regime grounded in commitments, somehow eroded, to pan-Arabism, the Jordanian authorities define those Iraqis who lack a legal residence as 'temporary guests' who can stay in Jordan pending return or secondary migration, but who then need to apply for a visa for re-entry into Jordan. The guest status is not legally binding for Jordan and can be revoked at any time (Olwan 2007). It maintains Iraqi 'guests' in a situation of legal and social insecurity, with limited opportunities for engaging in professional pursuits or collective social or advocacy activities.

Since late 2008, with the improved security situation in Iraq, many of those immobilized would like to undertake a visit back home to see relatives or friends, check on businesses, or evaluate the conditions of their properties or the situation in their neighbourhoods, often with a view to plan for return in stages or to engage in cross-border livelihood strategies. However, these projects have been impeded by the fact that they have no guarantee of being allowed back into Jordan and that they are liable to be asked to pay upon exit a substantial financial penalty for overstaying their visit permits.

Others who have the administrative and/or financial possibility to travel back to Iraq opt not to. They are prevented by concerns for their physical security as former prominent Ba'athists or for having worked for companies or armies of occupying countries; or, following traumatic experiences as objects or witnesses of violence, by their lack of trust in the fragile stability to which Baghdad and other areas of Iraq have been restored; or by their absence of interest in maintaining ties with Iraq, a feeling prevalent among Christians and others whose entire family groups have left Iraq before or after 2003. Most of these are engaged in projects of secondary migration to a Western country (in particular through registration with the UNHCR with a view to resettlement, by the activation of ties within transnational family and communal networks, and by the facilitating services of migrant smugglers), although the time factor and changes in the situation inside Iraq play a role in shifting migratory strategies, directions, and priorities for those who still have stakes, assets, and family or social connections inside Iraq.

Many of those immobilized, whether they are registered with the UNHCR or not, maintain connections with Iraq through other types of circulation and exchange. Information technologies and a free-market economy, both introduced in Iraq under its new governance regime, have considerably reshaped the relations between the Iraqi community in Amman and Iraq. Remittances changed direction after 2003 and now flow from Iraq to Jordan, either because families have split with breadwinners staying in Iraq, or because business-owners have settled in Jordan and have left their establishments under the care of employees. Those who were not high-ranking Ba'thists and have retired from the Iraqi public sector or the army can also collect pensions at the Amman branches of the Rafidain Bank, a nationalized Iraqi financial institution. Mobile phones and internet connections that were unavailable to the public under Saddam Hussein are now widespread. Information flows freely between Jordan and Iraq, with a host of internet sites and discussion forums in which Iraqis from 'inside' and 'outside' participate, and Iraqi journalists and academics-turned-experts based in Jordan receive payments for reports written on the situation in Iraq in collaboration with colleagues who have remained there.

The space of humanitarian intervention

Compared to the pre-2003 period, another important novelty in the opportunity context of Iraqis in Jordan has been the high-level involvement of institutional humanitarian actors and refugee organizations. On the occasion of a UN conference on displaced Iraqis held in Geneva in April 2007, the Jordanian government publicly acknowledged the presence of large numbers of Iraqis on its soil, calling for international support and expressing willingness to allow the operations of international relief and assistance NGOs. However, the conditions posed by the Jordanian authorities have been that Western countries, and especially the USA, commit to resettle those whose refugee status is recognized by the

UNHCR in Amman and that bilateral or multilateral aid be allocated to Jordan within a development framework to benefit all sectors affected by the presence of Iraqis. No parallel system of refugee assistance has been put in place. Within this context, the UNHCR in Amman resumed its registration operations that had been put to a near halt after the American invasion of Iraq under the assumption that refugees from the previous period were going to return to Iraq. As of early 2009, some 55,000 Iraqis in Jordan had registered as asylum seekers, the majority with a view to being resettled. In 2007 and 2008 a few thousand had been accepted as refugees in the USA, Australia, Canada, Sweden, and some other European countries. Many more are likely if one considers the 240,000 Iraqis registered with the UNHCR in Syria in early 2009. However, registration figures are not precise indications of the number of those who will be proposed for resettlement because they also include those who will eventually be denied refugee status by the UNHCR.

Although aid to Jordan in the framework of the country's assistance to Iraqis has been largely used to develop public institutions (in particular the educational and medical sectors) it has benefited Iraqis only marginally (Chatelard 2008). Donors (the USA, the EU, the UN, etc.) have also allocated budgets to more than twenty international and local NGOs that started operating programmes for Iraqi refugees in most large cities of Jordan, with beneficiaries selected on the basis of vulnerabilities (legal, social, economic, or psychological), rather than registration with the UNHCR. Between 40,000 and 60,000 Iraqis benefit from one or several of these programmes. These initiatives are particularly important for those who lack other forms of social protection, have limited or no access to incomes from employment or remittances from relatives, or who have been deeply affected by the violence they have experienced in Iraq: women on their own, many whose husbands have been killed in Iraq, and other isolated individuals; households where breadwinners are unable to work; children who find difficulties joining Jordanian schools; former victims of torture, etc. NGOs, together with some churches, provide social support and financial help to several families, paying schooling or medical fees, or delivering food and cash assistance to those most in need. Several community centres in various neighbourhoods in Amman and secondary cities welcome those Iraqis who lack other spaces to socialize or exchange their experiences of violence in Iraq and exile in Jordan.

It remains that such initiatives as income-generating projects or professional or vocational training for Iraqis are not permitted by the Jordanian authorities who want to prevent competition with their own nationals on an already congested work market and who strive to maintain the temporary nature of the stay of poorer Iraqis on their soil. Nevertheless, foreign NGOs play an economic role vis-à-vis this population by providing employment opportunities for many qualified Iraqis: administrative or medical personnel or social workers, some with a work contract and an attached residence permit, but an even larger number as paid volunteers without legal protection. The space of humanitarian action is therefore mostly limited to relief and assistance, catering for the immediate needs of those most socially or economically marginalized and physically or psychologically affected refugees, but with little scope for supporting either long-term stay in Jordan or even for preparing families for repatriation to Iraq.

What the UNHCR terms 'the urban context' of refugee protection and assistance in Jordan, in contrast with situations where refugees are regrouped in camps or other specific areas, has been viewed as a challenge by all institutional actors involved with Iraqi refugees. Such challenges have been identifying and reaching out to beneficiaries scattered in several neighbourhoods of Amman and in other cities; providing services that meet the needs of Iraqis while, upon the request of the Jordanian authorities, serving a broader population of vulnerable Jordanians; and tailoring programmes for individuals whose needs, expectations, and context of vulnerabilities and opportunities in Jordan are different from those of refugees in other relief operations that NGOs are familiar with. International institutional actors have been slowly coming to terms with the reality that vulnerable Iraqis in Jordan exhibit characteristics both of irregular migrants, due to their legal and social context of reception in Jordan, and of refugees socially, psychologically, and/or physically affected by violence in Iraq. Humanitarian actors have also started to admit that those in need of international assistance and protection might be much less numerous than was initially expected based on the very high figures publicized by Jordan in its funding appeals.

Locating 'refugeeness'

More Iraqis than in the previous period readily define their experiences in refugee terms, a label which has gained currency among those submitted to successive interviews with the UNHCR and various NGOs, and those offered a range of opportunities (assistance, employment, paid expertise, resettlement, etc.) within a refugee framework. The international political, humanitarian, and media discourse on the Iraq refugee crisis has undeniably come to provide an interpretative framework, largely unavailable in the previous period, within which those who find themselves displaced in Jordan and other Arab countries can recast their individual and collective experiences as refugees from conflict and violence. Many Iraqis in Jordan, however, remain uncomfortable with the term: some outwardly refuse the label, others shift, in their discourses, from one terminology to other ones to describe their migratory experiences and statuses, with some qualifying themselves as refugees exclusively when they evoke their dealings with specialized agencies. It remains that whatever the level of appropriation of and identification with the refugee category, Iraqis do not locate their 'refugeeness' inside the political, social, cultural, or physical spaces of Jordan, nor do they expect or claim 'refugeeness' within these spaces. The subjectivities of Iraqis in Jordan are as much a factor of the externalization of the framework of intervention in favour of Iraqi refugees—manifested in the involvement of international institutions within Jordan and mechanisms of resettlement outside the Middle East that are the ones shaping the experiences of Iraqis as *refugees*—as of the internalization of 'the forces of regionalism' (Shami 1996: 3) in shaping forced-migration dynamics and the identities of refugees in the Middle East.

In the Arab world regional linkages, Seteney Shami recalls, 'are salient in shaping identity, allocating mutual responsibility and hence informing the geographical trajectories and consequences of migration' (Shami 1996: 4). Beyond consideration of the political economy of hosting Iraqis (De Bel-Air 2007), the perspective of Jordan on the presence of Iraqis in its territory, and the expectations of Iraqis vis-à-vis their Jordanian hosts—be they the state or the society—is inseparable from Arab nationalism, or pan-Arabism, as a political ideology or Arabness as a sense of common identity, but also from the Sunni religious identity of the Hashemite monarchy, the country, and the people.

It is within that context that one must read the resistance of the Jordanian authorities and public to the labelling of Iraqis as refugees and their preferred use of the terms migrants (*muhajirin*) or guests (*dhuyuf*). So far the legitimacy of this resistance has largely remained uncontested within the Arab region. In Jordan, as in other Arab countries, the notions of refugee and refugeeness have come to be inseparable from the Palestinian experience with the result that, between Arabs, refugeeness can signify only the experience of individuals who have been denied national existence. Other Arab forced migrants are conceived of (and usually conceive of themselves) as migrants or simply as nationals of another Arab country by which they express a link to an existing Arab state that allows them to make claims to specific entitlements vis-à-vis their Arab hosts. It is the nature, quality, durability, and guarantee of these entitlements as Arab migrants or guests and the differentials that exist between Arab countries over time that may constitute an object of dissatisfaction on the part of Iraqis who have taken refuge in Jordan and in other Arab countries.

Islam as an historical and cultural framework or reference, including in its capacity to accommodate non-Muslim communities such as the Christians, together with the geopolitics of Sunnism and Shi'ism, represents other major regional forces that account, on the one hand, for the various inclinations of regional countries towards hosting specific groups of forced migrants, but also for the inclinations of these migrants to seek security in one or another country of the region. Religiously oriented Shi'ites from Iraq feel more exiled in Sunni Jordan than in Syria whose religious fabric is more pluralistic. In the 1980s and 1990s, many Iraqi Shi'ites who bene-fited from a generous refugee status in Iran later established themselves in Syria where they felt less culturally exiled as Arabs although they were received within a migration regime.

Iraqi refugees and other exiles in Jordan express their claims, identi-ties, experiences, and expectations along a variety of *relational* categories of self-definition, and rarely along mutually exclusive normative ones. Therefore one can think of oneself as a refugee to make claims to an inter-national (perceived as Western) refugee order that grants entitlements, security, and futures, while at the same time thinking of oneself as an Iraqi, an Arab, or a Muslim to make claims to a Jordanian or Syrian migra-tion order that grants others types of entitlements such as temporary safety, and continue to make claims to an Iraqi national order from which one does not want to be detached even as a migrant or refugee. Based on these relational identities, individual migratory strategies can be single or multiple, concomitant or subsequent with choices and configurations that vary over time based on a multiplicity of variables that pertain to the national and international contexts of migratory opportunities and to the experiences, assets, and projects of individuals, families, and broader collectives. It is within this relational field and within changing contexts of opportunities and constraints that the location of refugeeness for Iraqis needs to be re-embedded.

CONCLUSION: REVEALING AND CONCEALING

Iraqis refugees in Jordan and other Arab host countries have become highly visible at the international level: as refugees in the humanitarian and human-rights discourses and spaces of intervention; as objects of contested representations (as voluntary or involuntary migrants, as guests or refugees) by various political actors (the Iraqi government, the authorities of Arab host states, those of donor governments and agencies and resettlement countries in the West, and so on); and as objects of debate between these various actors as regards their future generally envisioned as either resettlement, return, or local integration. This visibility has revealed extreme levels of human suffering and created scope for international humanitarian operations in countries that were previously disinclined to such interventions. It has also compelled governments of countries that have played a direct role in precipitating a new order of insecurity in Iraq to engage with the issue of displacement in and from Iraq. Nevertheless, this recent visibility has arguably merely redressed the imbalance of the previous oblivion within which forced migrants from Iraq had fallen under the last period of the regime of Saddam Hussein. For over a decade Iran bore the burden of hosting hundreds of thousands of Iraqis in addition to 2 million Afghans with minimal international support (Alborzi 2006). No international pressure was exerted in the face of Jordan's denial of the situation of a majority of Iraqis on its soil, and advocacy campaigns did not identify Iraqi refugees as the responsibility of the UN, the USA, and some of the latter's allies that had created a context of economic and political insecurity in Iraq that led to the durable outmigration of at least 1 million Iraqis.

From a social sciences perspective, the new 'Iraq refugees agenda' conceals the multi-layered embeddedness of migratory movements from Iraq and the socially and spatially stratified patterns of security and protection available to current migrants and refugees. This angle of vision prevents analysts distinguishing between those Iraqis who have been forced out by violence or fear and do not have the necessary social or financial capital to 'buy protection' in Iraq or in a country of the region, and between those who have been able, through their access to financial and relation assets, to adopt a form of translocal mobility as a response to the uneven distribution of security and opportunities between Iraq and neighbouring countries. The narrow 'refugee lens' obscures the complexities of migratory strategies from and to Iraq and the nature of the challenges those who need to be mobile across borders are facing ensuing

from shifts in systems and mechanisms of control over population movements in Iraq and neighbouring countries. Furthermore, it precludes an
understanding of the articulations between previous movements and
current ones, of the links maintained across time and space by Iraqis at
home and in migration, and of the dynamics of current migratory trajectories that are based on the policies of states as much as on transnational
ties with previous generations of migrants in various locations across the
globe. It obviates the need to situate the identities, expectations, and
coping strategies of refugees in a multi-relational field. Finally, it obliter-
ates the fact that the aspirations of those Iraqis who cannot or will not
return to Iraq are rooted as much in their experiences of the Iraq of today
as in the memories of the Iraq of yesterday.

A final note on the comparability of the current refugee migration from
Iraq and the Palestinian exodus of 1948. Equating both phenomena has
become a *topos* of reports by refugee advocacy organizations and the media.
Parallels exist between the two displacement crises: prominent Palestinian
refugee scholar Julie Peteet has pointed out a communal sorting-out, territorial fragmentation, the absence of a framework for the protection of
refugees in neighbouring countries, and the creation of spaces of refugee
containment as common policy contexts facing Palestinians in 1948 and
Iraqis after 2003 (Peteet 2007). The two displacement phenomena, however,
are not analogous. Historical and political circumstances are markedly
different not least because, unlike Palestinians, Iraqis have a state. The
legacy of the Palestinian refugee issue, on the other hand, has shaped
Arab perceptions of and policies towards subsequent waves of refugees.
Socio-economic characteristics and the social capital of refugees in migration are also not equitable: whereas the vast majority of the Palestinian
refugees of 1948 were of rural background, the Iraqi refugees of post-2003
belong to the urban middle and upper middle classes with a high level of
education. But perhaps the most significant difference is that the recent
forced migration from Iraq is engrafted in long histories and broad geogra-
phies of migration under constraint with the result that, unlike Palestinians
in 1948, and in an era of widely available information and communication
technologies, recent refugees from Iraq have to be considered in relation to
vast pre-existing Iraqi disporas.

If a comparison is to be attempted between these two very large
refugee populations at regional and global scales, a more relevant
endeavour would be to question the politics and sociological dynamics of
identity and diaspora formation among Iraqi refugees since the 1970s
(after the Ba'ath party took power in Iraq and began to repress entities

with competing nationalist claims, such as the Kurds, and leftist oppositions parties, leading to recurrent large-scale forced migration) and Palestinian refugees after 1967 (when one generation had lived in exile, Palestinians were becoming the population with the highest rate of education in the Arab world, and the PLO was starting to formulate political claims).

REFERENCES

Alborzi, M. R. (2006), *Evaluating the Effectiveness of International Refugee Law: The Protection of Iraqi Refugees* (Leiden, Martinus Nijhoff Publishers).

Arouri, F. (2008), 'Irregular Migration in Jordan 1995–2007', CARIM Analytic and Synthetic Note 2008/71, European University Institute, Robert Schuman Center for Advanced Studies, http://cadmus.eui.eu/dspace/bitstream/1814/10116/1/CARIM_AS%26N _2008_ 71.pdf.

Bakewell, O. (1999), 'Can We Ever Rely On Refugee Statistics?', *Radical Statistics*, 72, www.radstats.org.uk/no072/article1.htm.

—— (2008), 'Research Beyond the Categories: The Importance of Policy Irrelevant Research into Forced Migration', *Journal of Refugee Studies*, 21, 4: 433–53.

Chatelard, G. (2005), 'Iraqi Asylum Migrants in Jordan: Conditions, Religious Networks and the Smuggling Process', in G. Borjas and J. Crisp (eds), *Poverty, International Migration and Asylum* (Basingstoke, Palgrave Macmillan), pp. 341–70, http://hal.archives-ouvertes.fr/docs/00/33/84/56/PDF/Asylum_migration.pdf.

—— (2008), 'Jordan's Transient Iraqi Guests: Transnational Dynamics and National Agenda', in *Viewpoints*, Special Edition on Iraq's Refugee and IDP Crisis, Middle East Institute, Washington, DC: 20–2, www.mideasti.org/publications/iraqs-refugee-idp-crisis/uprooted-populations-and-their-reluctant-hosts.

—— (2009), 'Migration from Iraq between the Gulf and the Iraq Wars (1990–2003): Historical and Sociospacial Dimensions', ESRC Centre on Migration, Policy and Society (COMPAS), University of Oxford, Working Paper, www.compas.ox.ac.uk/publications/working-papers/wp-09-68/#c221.

—— and Dorai, K. (2009), 'La présence irakienne en Syrie et en Jordanie: dynamiques sociales et spatiales, et modes de gestion par les pays d'accueil', *Maghreb-Machrek*, Paris, http://hal.archives-ouvertes.fr/hal-00338403/fr.

Colson, E. (2007), 'Linkages Methodology: No Man is an Island', *Journal of Refugee Studies*, 20, 2: 320–32.

Crisp, J. (1999), '"Who has Counted the Refugees?" UNHCR and the Politics of Numbers', *New Issues in Refugee Research*, Working Paper 12, Geneva, Policy Research Unit, UNHCR, www.unhcr.org/3ae6a0c22.html.

Dawod, H. and Bozarslan, H. (eds) (2003), *La société irakienne: communautés, pouvoirs et violences* (Paris, Karthala).

De Bel-Air, F. (2006), 'Intoduction. Migrations et politique au Moyen-Orient: populations, territoires, citoyennetes a l'aube du XXIe siecle', in F. De Bel Air (ed.), *Migrations et politique au Moyen-Orient* (Beirut and Amman, Institut Francais du Proche-Orient), pp. 7–36.

—— (2007), 'State Policies on Migration and Refugees in Jordan', Paper Prepared for the Meeting on Migration and Refugee Movements in the Middle East and North Africa, The American University in Cairo, Forced Migration and Refugee Studies Program, 23–5 October, www.aucegypt.edu/Researchat AUC/rc/cmrs/ reports/ Documents/ Francoise%20de%20Belair.pdf .

FAFO (2007), *Iraqis in Jordan: Their Number and Characteristics*, www.fafo.no/ais/ middeast/jordan/IJ.pdf.

Fargues, P., El-Masry, S., Sadek, S., and Shaban, A. (2008), 'Iraqis in Egypt: A Statistical Survey in 2008', The American University in Cairo, Center for Migration and Refugee Studies, www.aucegypt.edu/ResearchatAUC/rc/ cmrs/Documents/Iraqis%20in %20 Egypt %20Provisional%20Copy.pdf.

Fattah, H. (2007), 'Les autres Irakiens: émigrés et exilés d'avant 2003 en Jordanie et leurs récits d'appartenance', *Revue des mondes musulmans et de la Méditerranée*, 117–18: 127–36.

Al-Husseini, J. (2007), 'The Arab States and the Refugee Issue: A Retrospective View', in E. Benvenisti, C. Gans, and S. Hanafi (eds), *Israel and the Palestinian refugees* (Berlin, Springer), pp. 435–64, http://halshs.archives-ouvertes.fr/ docs/00/34/38/93/ PDF/The_Arab_States_and_the_Refugee_Issue.pdf.

Kunz, E. (1973), 'The Refugee in Flight: Kinetic Models and Forms of Displacement', *International Migration Review*, 7, 2: 125–46.

Malkki, L. (1995), 'Refugees and Exile: From "Refugee Studies" to the National Order of Things', *Annual Review of Anthropology*, 24: 495–523.

Mannaert, C. (2003), 'Irregular Migration and Asylum in Turkey', *New Issues in Refugee Research*, Working Paper 89, Geneva, Policy Research Unit, UNHCR, www.unhcr.org/3ebf5c054.html.

Marfleet, P. (2007), 'Iraq's Refugees: "Exit" from the State', *International Journal of Contemporary Iraqi Studies*, 1, 3: 397–419.

Al-Meehy, A. (2004), 'Regional Dynamic of Refugee Flows: The Case of Iran', in B. F. Salloukh and R. Brynen (eds) *Persistent Permeability? Regionalism, Localism, and Globalization in the Middle East* (Aldershot, Ashgate), pp. 105–24.

Olwan, M. (2007), 'The Legal Framework of Forced Migration and Refugee Movements in Jordan', Paper Prepared for the Meeting on Migration and Refugee Movements in the Middle East and North Africa, The American University in Cairo, Forced Migration and Refugee Studies Program, 23–5 October, www.aucegypt.edu/ResearchatAUC/rc/cmrs/Documents/Mohamed Olwan.pdf.

Peteet, J. (2007), 'Unsettling the Categories of Displacement', *MERIP Middle East Report* (244), www.merip.org/mer/mer244/peteet.html.

Polzer, T. (2008), 'Invisible Integration: How Bureaucratic, Academic and Social Categories Obscure Integrated Refugees', *Journal of Refugee Studies*, 21, 4: 477–97.

Richmond, A. H. (1993), 'Reactive Migration: Sociological Perspectives on Refugee Movements', *Journal of Refugee Studies*, 6, 1: 7–24.

Sassoon, J. (2008), *The Iraqi Refugees: The New Crisis in the Middle East* (London, I. B. Tauris).

Shami, S. (1996), 'Transnationalism and Refugee Studies: Rethinking Forced Migration and Identity in the Middle East', *Journal of Refugee Studies*, 9, 1: 3–26.

Shoeb, M., Weinstein, H., and Halpern, J. (2007), 'Living in Religious Time and Space: Iraqi Refugees in Dearborn, Michigan', *Journal of Refugee Studies*, 20, 3: 441–60.

UNHCR (2003), *Iraqi Refugees and Asylum-seekers Statistics* (Geneva, UNHCR).

—— (2007), *Statistics on Displaced Iraqis around the World: Global Overview, September 2007* (Geneva, UNHCR).

Van Hear, N. (1995), 'The Impact of Involuntary Mass "Return" to Jordan in the Wake of the Gulf Crisis', *International Migration Review*, 29, 2: 352–74.

Zaiotti, R. (2006), 'Dealing with non-Palestinian Refugees in the Middle East: Policies and Practices in an Uncertain Environment', *International Journal of Refugee Law*, 18: 333–53.

Zolberg, A. (1983), 'The Formation of New States as a Refugee-generating Process', *Annals of the American Academy of Social and Political Science*, 467: 24–38.

2.
The Transnational Turn in Migration Studies and the Afghan Social Networks

Alessandro Monsutti

TRANSNATIONALISM IN ANTHROPOLOGY: FROM THEORY TO THE FIELD

Migration studies have undergone considerable development since the 1980s, particularly in social anthropology, despite the fact that the subject has long been included in the field of social sciences.[1] This expansion has taken place alongside new thinking on the very subject and methods of the discipline which was proposed by the authors of *Writing Culture* (Clifford and Marcus 1986) in North America, among others. Many researchers have addressed the issue of the links between sociocultural groups and territory. According to them, anthropologists had, over many decades, defined their object of research as socially and linguistically homogenous territorial entities. By travelling from one location to another and from one culture to another, migrants challenged this vision of a world composed of a mosaic of discrete sociocultural groups. Therefore migration was understood as a time-bound process which terminated in the more or less successful integration of the migrant in his/her host society or returning to his/her society of origin. By contrast, an increasing number of recent studies no longer focus on the cultural and identity changes brought about by spatial movement, but rather on the complex trajectories of people who cross political and cultural borders including the multiplicity of links which they establish during their travels. The term 'transnationalism' has now become dominant to describe this

---

[1] See, for example, the seminal texts by Ravenstein (1885, 1889) as well as that by Fairchild (1925).

approach. Here we use the definition given by Steven Vertovec, who summarizes the debate as follows:

> most social scientists working in the field may agree that 'transnationalism' broadly refers to multiple ties and interactions linking people or institutions across the borders of nation-states (Vertovec 1999: 447).

It has thus now been established that sociocultural groups can no longer be understood as discrete territorially defined entities. Increasingly, migration is no longer seen as mere passage from one location to another, but instead as a complex phenomenon characterized by recurrent and multidirectional movements during which a variety of links are woven. For example, the dispersal of family groups can be the result of a strategy aimed at diversifying resources and minimizing risks: it does not always lead to a weakening of social ties. By concentrating on the mobility of people between a number of nation states, the exchange of material and symbolic goods, the circulation of information, or even political, economic, or social investment by migrants across international borders, it is possible to construct an ethnography which is both global and detailed.[2]

A number of researchers have used the concept of a transnational network to study forced migrations (Marx 1990; Shami 1996; Al-Ali et al. 2001; Chatelard 2002). Without denying the specificity of refugees with respect to legal status or the risks which they face, these researchers have been inspired by theoretical and methodological approaches which had originally been developed to discuss voluntary migrations. This is justified by a number of observations. First, people who are recognized as refugees are not mere victims of a fate beyond their control; they are actors who attempt to respond to difficult conditions by relying on the social and cultural resources which remain under their control. Next, the strategies they develop are often similar to those used by people consid-

---

[2] Issues around migration in a globalized context are also of concern to international organizations and to state authorities which increasingly concentrate on them, as is suggested by the establishment in 2003 in Geneva of the Global Commission on International Migration (2005). Its mandate was to propose a framework to provide a global and coherent response to migration problems. Its final report points out that there are structural reasons which explain that the number of migrants will continue to increase in coming years (demographic gaps, economic and political disparities, etc.). In the autumn of 2006, the sixty-first session of the United Nations opened with the first high-level dialogue on international migration and development. It demonstrates the importance given in the agenda of the international community to the need to understand and manage migrations globally, even if this community continues to be made up of sovereign states who supposedly maintain legitimate and exclusive control over disjointed territories.

ered to be migrant labourers. Finally, the borders between the different types of status (internally displaced people, refugees, migrant workers) are not airtight: by adapting to a constantly changing context and by manipulating labels, the same people may belong to different categories simultaneously or sequentially.

This essay is thus intended to illustrate the broad potential of the transnational approach by analysing one particular group, Afghan refugees and migrants, particularly the Hazaras who originate in the mountainous centre of Afghanistan. The conflict which Afghanistan has suffered after the communist coup in 1978 and the Soviet intervention of 1979 led to one of the largest population movements of the end of the twentieth century. At the beginning of the 1980s, the United Nations High Commissioner for Refugees (UNHCR) counted over 6 million Afghan refugees, mostly distributed between Pakistan and Iran.[3] They then formed the largest displaced population on the earth and nearly half the people under the responsibility and mandate of the UN agency.

However, this exodus has not always had the traumatic dimension which humanitarian agencies and the media tend to attribute to it. A long-term historical perspective leads us to relativize its exceptional character (Hanifi 2000). Nomads who travel seasonally with their herds in search of better pasture but who use their movements to trade with settled people, mountain populations who travel to cities or to the lowlands to find seasonal work, pilgrims, escapees, or conquerors—Afghans have a long experience of mobility in all its forms. The migration of Afghans to Pakistan, Iran, and the countries of the Persian Gulf, as well as to Europe, North America, and Australia is not merely a response to insecurity and poverty. The war has been an opportunity for a deep redefinition of social organization rather than the cause of a massive but reversible exile. Groups are not structured by reference to a place of common residence but by links of solidarity and mutual assistance which cross international borders. Geographical dispersal and economic diversification are a con-sequence of these kinship links and allow people to spread risks: thus mobility is often a planned strategy. Afghans have established a 'circula-tory territory', to adopt the expression of Alain Tarrius (1995). On the one hand, there are very few Afghan refugees who have never returned home after their initial departure; on the other, almost all family groups have at least one of their members abroad. Migration and exile are not followed

---

[3] Approximately a further 1,500,000 people were internally displaced (Colville 1998).

by a process of integration in the host country or a definitive return to the country of origin: movement is continuous and a truly transnational community is ultimately created. In the light of the transnational networks established by the Afghans, two theses are suggested here. First, mobility is a structural feature of their way of life, it is not mere coercion or imposed by external circumstances. Second, the strategies they have developed blur the distinction between forced and voluntary migration.

NORTH AMERICAN CRITICAL ANTHROPOLOGY: DIASPORAS, ETHNOSCAPES, AND TRANSMIGRANTS

The debate around migration studies and transnationalism has been particularly lively in North America as illustrated by the controversy surrounding the word 'diaspora', which was initiated by the creation of a journal in its name in 1991. The word's origin is the Greek word meaning 'dispersion' and it has historically been used to describe the dispersal of Jews within the Roman Empire.[4] In a programmatic text published in the first issue of this journal, William Safran describes the concept as follows:

> expatriate communities whose members share several of the following character-
> istics: 1) they, or their ancestors, have been dispersed from a specific original
> 'center' to two or more 'peripheral', or foreign, regions; 2) they retain a collec-
> tive memory, vision, or myth about their original homeland—its physical location,
> history, and achievements; 3) they believe that they are not—and perhaps
> cannot be—fully accepted by their host society and therefore feel partly alien-
> ated and insulated from it; 4) they regard their ancestral homeland as their true,
> ideal home and as the place to which they or their descendants would (or should)
> eventually return—when conditions are appropriate; 5) they believe that they
> should, collectively, be committed to the maintenance or restoration of their orig-
> inal homeland and to its safety and prosperity; and 6) they continue to relate,
> personally or vicariously, to that homeland in one way or another, and their ethno-
> communal consciousness and solidarity are importantly defined by the existence
> of such relationship (Safran 1991: 83–4).

Although this definition retains some traces of the Jewish origin of the concept and its extension to certain specific communities (Armenians and Greeks), the word has been used to describe numerous migrant popula-tions, ranging from the Turks in Germany to Indians and Pakistanis in

---

[4] The complex history of the word 'diaspora' from its origins to date is recorded by Tölölyan (1996).

Great Britain, Chinese in south-east Asia, and Palestinians (for example, Bruneau 1994; Van Hear 1998; Centlivres 2000; Schnapper 2001).

According to James Clifford (1994), however, Safran's definition remains too formal and narrow to reflect the changing global conditions of the current period. He estimates that it is sterile to ossify the meaning of a word such as diaspora by referring to an 'ideal type' and then describing different groups as being more or less diasporic according to the number of characteristics of this ideal type which they manifest. He argues in favour of an anthropology which allows for an open rather than normative analysis of decolonization, migrations, global communications, transport, and all other phenomena connected with multi-locality and mobility. At the end of the twentieth and the beginning of the twenty-first centuries, in a rapidly changing world, diffused social links and transnational relations including the place of origin as one anchor among many are becoming more common. The existence of diasporic communities, like the Jewish one, reveals how misleading it is to conceive cultures as self-sufficient, internally focused, and rooted in a single location. Far from representing an epiphenomenon of the nation state or global capitalism, they are a basic characteristic component of the contemporary world.

Clifford's thoughts about diasporas are part of his efforts to redefine the conceptual tools and methods of anthropology (see also Clifford 1986, 1988, 1992, 1997). He recognizes that there have always been tendencies to challenge but, reflecting on Malinowski's heritage, he emphasizes the fact that fieldwork was conceived as a form of co-residence rather than a trip or a visit. This method found its source in a particular understanding of culture: an integrated and homogeneous[5] unit defined in space. Clifford offers a different vision: culture as a journey—journey being understood not only in its literal sense but implying all kinds of more or less allegorical or imagined movements. Thus, the field is not defined here as the study of remote populations, of the essence of the Other, but as a decentring experience which is no longer conceptualized primarily in spatial terms. Besides, Clifford considers that anthropologists should seek inspiration in some travel-writing techniques to allow more room for personal perspective and feelings.

In a text originally published in 1990, Arjun Appadurai (1999) also wonders how anthropology can grasp the contemporary world. He seeks to go beyond a vision of words in dichotomous opposition: global/local,

---

[5] For a critique which leads in the same direction, see Gupta and Ferguson (1992, 1997).

North/South, etc. He suggests five conceptual categories to organize the anthropology of culture and of global economies: *ethnoscapes* produced by movements of people (refugees and migrants of course, but also seasonal labourers and tourists); *technoscapes* created by the circulation of technologies; *financescapes* linked to capital flows and stock exchanges; *mediascapes* made by the circulation of information and images produced by television, radio, newspapers, cinema, and other media; and, finally, *ideoscapes* resulting from political ideologies whether state or otherwise (liberty, public goods, rights, sovereignty, etc.). Far from homogenizing the world culturally, these five types of flow produce new differences and feelings of belonging. Appadurai reviews these distinctions in a text which was published shortly after the first one:

> As groups migrate, regroup in new locations, reconstruct their histories, and reconfigure their ethnic 'project', the ethno in ethnography takes on a slippery, nonlocalized quality . . . groups are no longer tightly territorialized, spatially bounded, historically unselfconscious, or culturally homogenous (Appadurai 1991: 191).

The fact that societies, cultures, and nations appear to be distinct entities arises from a specific understanding of space, whereas people's mobility is, according to Appadurai, a basic characteristic of the contemporary world. He argues for a 'cosmopolitan ethnography' based on new research strategies allowing one to understand the deterritorialized world in which we live. This new ethnography must not limit itself to studying real movements but must also address imagination and representations.

Theories of transnationalism are an extension of these general theoretical efforts to the field of migration studies. Indeed, their promoters do not consider their subject of study to be closed units of analysis or localized communities: they show how migrants and refugees question the connection between culture and territory. Nina Glick Schiller, Linda Basch, and Cristina Szanton Blanc (1992, 1995) have specialized in transnationalism which they define as a social process through which migrants establish relations which cross geographic, political, and cultural borders and link their country of origin with their country of settlement. They call 'transmigrants' those who develop and maintain multiple types of relations—be they family, economic, social, religious, or political—which cross state, cultural, and geographic borders. In other words, they are people whose identity and practices are linked to networks extending simultaneously across a number of nation states. According to Glick Schiller and her colleagues, globalization is characterized at the world level by an intensification of relations between distant locations, in such a way that a local situation is influenced by events which take place very far away. Rather than study isolated phenomena, anthropologists should focus on flows of people, commodities, capital, images, and information. The subject of anthropology shifts from communities which are—or are supposed to be—territorialized within a nation state to a series of separate locations where nations are a mere component and no longer the frame of reference.

The work of Liisa Malkki (1992, 1995, 1997) focuses more specifically on refugees, but it is part of the same project to rethink the general framework of the migration problematic. She addresses the rooting metaphor which has metaphysical connotations as it naturalizes links between people and territory. According to Malkki, the notion of point of origin becomes difficult to use because more and more people identify with deterritorialized categories. The study of people in motion demands a new theoretical sensitivity which gives priority to borders and their crossing. This change of paradigm allows us to examine critically the impact which the national reference framework can have on researching refugees and other displaced people.

Migrations are seen as an anomaly not only by certain social scientists for whom societies and cultures are rooted in a territory—which implies that numerous studies address the issues through a medical and psychologizing perspective—but this approach is also a consequence of the political organization of the world, since it is divided into nation states (Zolberg 1981: 6). The usual understanding of the concept of culture tends 'towards rooting rather than travel', writes Malkki (1992: 33), referring to Clifford. Alongside Glick Schiller and her colleagues as well as many others, she deplores the fact that preconceptions of sedentarity are echoed in xenophobia and anti-immigrant discourses. The 'order of things' to which she refers is that of the natural division of the world into a number of sovereign states.

Malkki summarizes her argument in four points: 1) the world of nations tends to be conceptualized as an enclosed space of separate territories; 2) the relationship of people with space tends to be naturalized through botanical metaphors; 3) the concept of culture has many common characteristics with that of nation as both imply the idea of rooting in specific locations, thus revealing a 'metaphysical sedentarism' or a 'metaphysics of sedentarity'; 4) the naturalization of links between populations and locations implies that movement is an anomaly, an idea expressed through the metaphor of 'uprootedness'.

This rapid survey[6] allows us to see that transnational studies are characterized by at least three features: the phenomena concerned cross the borders of autonomous political entities; links are established over significant distances; a variety of cultural indicators and forms are implied. To go beyond the vision of a world made up of a mosaic of disjointed sociocultural units and to underline that these social relations are more decisive than the locations, Hannerz thus proposes the expression 'global Ecumene'[7] and underlines the contribution of anthropology to the study of the contemporary transnational processes in a variety of research fields: 'translocalities', 'border studies', 'migration', 'diasporas', 'transnational corporations and occupations', 'tourism', 'cyberspace', 'media', and 'commodities' (Hannerz 1998: 237).

A MULTI-SITED ETHNOGRAPHY

In order to study the multiplicity of links that connect people living in locations distant from one another, the transnational approach requires a renewed field methodology, which takes its inspiration from the 'multi-sited ethnography' proposed by George Marcus (1995). He suggests different strategies to implement his programme: these include following and reconstructing the circulation of people, things, metaphors (particularly in the media), stories and allegories (as in the structural analysis of myths undertaken by Levi-Strauss), life stories, and conflicts. Ethnographic inquiry carried out in a single location does not allow mapping of the circulation of goods and the life itineraries of mobile people; it is instead necessary to place the research theme in a world system. This delocalization of ethnographic practice is not an academic trick, but corresponds to the conditions of the daily life of an increasing

---

[6] Among the vast body of literature on transnationalism, see also Portes et al. (1999), Olwig (2003), Levitt et al. (2003), Levitt and Nyberg-Sørensen (2004), Levitt and Jaworsky (2007), and Brettell (2008). My aim here is to illustrate the potential of this approach through the study of Afghan migratory networks. Elsewhere I have commented on the excesses of this literature which tends to exaggerate the novelty of human mobility and to oversimplify the theoretical and methodological sensitivies of earlier anthropologists (Monsutti 2005). More generally, for a critique of postmodernist North American anthropology, see Brightman (1995), Darnell (1995), Lindholm (1997), Sahlins (1999), Amselle (2000), and Friedman (2000).

[7] 'Ecumene', transcription of a word used by the Ancient Greeks to describe the totality of the inhabited world (Hannerz 1992: 37).

number of people. Within this framework, the contrast between local and global is weakened and concern is with relations between different places.

This approach to understanding migratory movements partially rehabilitates, both as a framework for observation and as a subject of study, a methodological tool which was considered outdated: social networks. Network analysis developed from the 1950s onwards but mainly flourished during the following two decades before running progressively out of steam. The principal reasons for the bad reputation it developed at that time are an undifferentiated understanding of social relations (to understand the behaviour of people, research focused on the structure of social networks and the frequency of interaction rather than the contents of exchanges and of individual relations), formalism, the difficulties involved in gathering empirical data which could be integrated in the theoretical framework, and relatively marginal themes. However, networks remain a useful methodological tool to understand the situations of mobility which characterize contemporary societies. In the old but still famous study of a Norwegian parish, John A. Barnes provides a definition of the concept of 'network'. It remains useful to this day, due to its very simplicity:

> The image I have is of a set of points some of which are joined by lines. The points of the image are people, or sometimes groups, and the lines indicate which people interact with each other. We can of course think of the whole of social life as generating a network of this kind (Barnes 1954: 43).

In other words, starting from a person or a group of people, social relations are to be reconstructed. Society is no longer understood within the functionalist paradigm as a series of integrated and distinct communities but as a set of social relations ramifying from each individual. They are not linked to a specific territory and have neither spatial nor social specific borders. Links between two distant people can be intense, while those between certain neighbours can be very loose. Networks can be understood as the web of effective or potential social relations which are mobilized in specific situations.

Used with care and cleansed of certain formalist and individualist extremes characteristic of the network analysis of the 1960s and 1970s, the concept of social networks can be very useful. The work of Hannerz (1967, 1986, 1992, 1996) is indicative of this evolution. In his most recent writings, he reduces the egocentric dimension of networks and gives them a broader scope, thus enabling the concept to include not only individual strategies but also those of broader groups, such as households, lineages, neighbouring groups, even tribal segments. By its flexibility, the method-ological tool of networks allows us to study the cultural complexity of the contemporary world which can be seen as a 'network of networks', also allowing us to understand how the local level is articulated within the global system and to put into perspective the links people settled in places distant from one another maintain with each other.

This research programme can be implemented by avoiding focus on clearly defined village communities. On the contrary, the researcher is guided by the relations which have emerged over time, in order to extract from them the strategies of what starts off as a small group of interlocu-tors and, from this, to gradually reconstitute their networks and build a living and precise image of the links which unite the dispersed members of social groups whose limits are not determined in advance. How do people move? What are the stages of their migratory journeys? Where do they live? Who do they contact when seeking employment, residence permits, visas, identity cards, or passports? How do they send money and goods from one country to another? How do they retain contact with each other despite the weak technical means at their disposal? What solidarity links can they rely on? In addressing these questions, we can illustrate the sociocultural resources which, for example, Afghan migrants mobilize and the strategies which they use to react to the destruction brought about by war and exile, and not just the motives which push them to migrate or the causes of their exile.

Travelling between Afghanistan, Pakistan, and Iran and then Europe, North America, Australia, and New Zealand to follow the migratory network of what was initially a very small group of people creates a serious risk of dispersal of work and loss of ethnographic depth. However, the population or the phenomenon which are the subject of the research can retain a smaller scale. Rather than narrow data collection to a single location, the aim is to reconstitute the links woven by a migrant popula-tion between the different settlement locations which form a coherent social field despite their spatial dispersal. Fieldwork has not been multi-sited merely in the sense of having different locations of inquiry but also, and even more so, through the will to understand the structural links which connect these different locations.

By following this approach, are we missing important issues? Edwards (1994) expressed the concerns of an anthropologist working in Afghanistan who had to give up his original project of working within a defined community, be it a mountain village or a nomadic tribal group.

Forced by circumstances, he had to carry out his fieldwork in a variety of locations—in Peshawar, in refugee camps, by travelling inside Afghanistan but also working with Afghans in Washington and carrying out a survey of internet users. Beyond his worries, Edwards demonstrated a new way of carrying out fieldwork, simultaneously multi-locally (from Peshawar to Washington) and delocalized (internet). My experience among the Hazaras is comparable. The explosion of locations where members of the group under study live has led to a diversification of locations of study. A population living in a multiplicity of locations means that the study also has to be multi-local.

THE AFGHAN TRANSNATIONAL SYSTEM

Afghanistan

Modern Afghanistan emerged in the middle of the eighteenth century through military action by Pashtun tribes at a time when the large regional empires—Safavid in Iran, Moghul in India, Shaibani in central Asia—were in decline. During the last two and half centuries, the country has known hardly any periods of peace. The conflict which emerged after the Communist coup in April 1978 did, however, result in an unprecedented level of violence. Using ancient migratory routes, millions of Afghans sought refuge in neighbouring countries. After the withdrawal of the Red Army in 1989 and the fall of the pro-Soviet regime in 1992, the country sank into an endless internal war between the different factions of the earlier resistance. The US intervention which followed the 11 September 2001 attacks on New York and Washington brought about the defeat of the Taliban and the installation in Kabul of a government supported by the international community and legitimized by a democratic process. But any hopes of achieving normality rapidly vanished. Rampant corruption at all levels of the administration has reduced the state's credibility, while the Taliban have reorganized in their southern bastions by capitalizing on the discontent of large segments of the population. International and non-governmental institutions appear to be incapable of taking effective measures and contribute to the confusion which currently prevails in Afghanistan.

However, insecurity and the lack of the rule of law are not the only factors which explain ongoing Afghan migration—despite a massive wave of returns.[8] According to the United Nations Fund for Population Activities (UNFPA) the population of Afghanistan will treble by 2050, increasing from 32.3 million to 97.3 million. With an average population increase of 3.5 per cent per annum between 2005 and 2010, the country has one of the highest levels of demographic growth in the world.[9] Demographic pressure is thus enormous and will continue to increase in the coming years and decades. According to a UN report, the population density of the Behsud area, in the Hazarajat (a region which covers the mountainous centre of the country), is sixty-one inhabitants per square km. However, once recalculated on the basis of cultivable land, it is 1,210 inhabitants per square km, higher than that of Bangladesh (Johnson 2000: 46). It is thus not surprising that the low-rainfall highland and plateau regions are unable to feed their populations.

Hazarajat society is composed mainly of sedentary smallholder farmers. The local economy is essentially based on modest agriculture and supplementary livestock herding. It is strongly dependent on the financial contribution of migrants who travel and seek opportunities in urban centres or abroad. In such a context, migration is not merely a response to violence and poverty. It is normal for young men to travel for the first time before their marriage. This is to enable them to acquire some experience by living apart from their families, and thus demonstrate their capacity to survive as well as to save the capital needed to get married and start a family. These trips abroad are thus an integral part of their life cycle.[10]

The geographical dispersal of the members of a household or an extended kin group as well as the resulting economic diversification enables such groups to spread risks and this dispersion is often a planned strategy. Thus, it is really a principle of life which translates itself in the transnational networks which Hazaras, as well as other Afghans, have established on a global scale.

---

[8] The UNHCR considers that over 4 million Afghans have returned home with its support between 2002 and 2007; to this must be added 1.2 million who returned spontaneously (UNHCR 2007: iv). In fact, the number of returnees dropped after 2005. Moreover, very early on, these figures were challenged due to the probably high proportion of people 'recycling' their movements, returning to Pakistan or Iran after having received the assistance available to returnees (Turton and Marsden 2002: 1, 20–1).

[9] See www.unfpa.org/emergencies/afghanistan/factsheet.htm.

[10] In this respect, migration is a rite of passage to adulthood during which young men assert their masculinity through the toughness of the trials they have to endure (Monsutti 2007).

Pakistan and Iran

The first Hazaras went to the Indian subcontinent to seek work during the time of the British Raj or to escape from Amir Abdur Rahman's subjugation of Hazarajat between 1891 and 1893. From 1879 onwards, some of them participated in the construction of the Bolan Pass railway, which links the plains of Sind to the highlands of Baluchistan and beyond that to the Afghan border. Others joined the British Army, specifically the 106th Hazara Pioneers. This military unit, which existed from 1904 to 1933 and which participated in the battle of Ypres during the First World War, gave Hazaras who left Afghanistan a number of opportunities for self-improvement beyond those which they could hope for in their country of origin: a career, social recognition, and economic success.

Their migration was effectively continuous after that period and Hazaras now form one of the main communities in Quetta, the capital of Pakistani Baluchistan (Collective for Social Science Research 2006). Indeed, the dreadful famine which struck many parts of Afghanistan in the early 1970s, the communist coup of 1978, then the Soviet intervention of the following year increased migratory movements. But this flow is not unidirectional. Despite variations in intensity, there is a migratory continuum between Hazarajat and Quetta. Few Hazaras have settled in refugee camps in Pakistan. They immediately preferred to take their chances in an urban environment where they could rely on a host community and in fact have hardly ever needed to rely on humanitarian aid aimed at refugees. Many farmers from southern Hazarajat migrate seasonally; each winter they go to work in the coal mines of the Quetta region, before returning to Afghanistan in early spring to carry on their agricultural activities. Thanks to the relationships they have established in local society, migrants coming from Afghanistan can obtain a Pakistani identity card, even a passport. The city acts as a migration and trade hub as well as a refuge. In case of expulsion from Iran or conflict in Afghanistan, people can always rely on being received in Quetta by a relative or a friend. However, the capital of Pakistani Baluchistan offers few economic opportunities other than coal mining and trade for those who have some start-up capital.

Hazaras fleeing the conquest of Abdur Rahman also went to Iran during the Qajar period. Concentrated around Mashhad where they are known as Berberi, descendants of these migrants have maintained very few relationships with their region of origin. By comparison with Pakistan, Iran thus presents a clear contrast. In Iran, Afghans have faced a xenophobic atmosphere and are restricted to manual labour (Adelkhah and Olszewska 2007). Even the Shia Hazaras do not really have access to a host group. However, families always seem to have one of their members there to ensure a financial income. The determining factor in this context is the hiring networks. Workers group around certain entrepreneurial and competent individuals to form temporary work teams. They move from one building site to the next according to the availability of work; information on their location is passed on by word of mouth. Hazaras who travel to the Islamic Republic are thus fairly likely to find work through the intermediary of a relative or neighbour. They stay there for long periods, rarely less than a year, often far longer. Older men who have family responsibilities are reluctant to leave for such long periods and prefer to stay closer to their wives and children in the village of origin and therefore they go to Quetta which offers the possibility of temporary migration, while also providing a more favourable hosting environment.

Since the 1970s oil boom started, many young Hazaras have sought employment in Iran and often stay there for many years. There, although it is easy to find fairly well paid employment by activating family and tribal networks, many activities are prohibited to Afghans. They are mainly employed in Iranian enterprises as bricklayers, agricultural labourers, or guards. There is a constant risk of expulsion, and police harassment and violence are regular features of their life. Afghans have a very precarious status and it is difficult for them to settle in a stable manner, whether with or without their families.

Australia

The first Afghans arrived on the Australian continent during the last decades of the nineteenth century as camel drivers.[11] More recently, in the 1980s but mainly in the first half of the 1990s, middle- and upper-class urban Afghans arrived in Australia—often after having resided in India—and have settled mostly in Sydney and Melbourne. A third migratory wave was composed of people escaping from the Taliban regime between 1998 and 2001. They were mostly Hazaras. Many of them travelled on—sometimes forged—Pakistani passports acquired in Quetta and giving them the right to travel to Malaysia or Indonesia without a visa. They then continued their journey to Australian territories nearest to

[11] Their caravans supplied the workers who laboured in the isolated mines and quarries of the desert as well as those who participated in the construction of railways (Stevens 1989).

the great archipelago (Christmas Island and Ashmore Reef, in particular) on precarious Indonesian boats. About 9,000 boat people arrived in Australia during this period[12] (in addition to Afghans there were also many Iraqis).

Australia's receiving policy in response to this flow of migrants landing illegally became increasingly restrictive and the government proposed the Pacific Solution, a set of strict measures aimed at preventing the illegal arrival of people by sea.[13] This involved first the exclusion from the Australian migratory zone of the places most easily accessible from Indonesia, thus making it impossible to put a request for asylum for those who reached these places. As a parallel measure the Navy strengthened its efforts to intercept and send back Indonesian boats transporting migrants before they were able to reach Australian territory. Finally, the Canberra government gave itself the means to deport many hundreds of asylum seekers to certain small islands in the Pacific, Manus in particular, north of Papua New Guinea, and Nauru. This policy was complementary to the use of different detention camps.[14]

Such drastic measures effectively closed this migration route. Many migrants who arrived between 1998 and 2001 were interned, sometimes for two or three years. With the support of some human-rights associations, most of them finally managed to obtain residence permits, often after having brought their cases to the Refugee Review Tribunal (RRT) which in many cases took decisions contradicting the—initially negative—ones of the Department of Immigration and Citizenship. After having been freed from detention centres at Curtin (former Australian air force base, near Derby in the north of Western Australia) or Port Hedland (a former mining centre, also in the north of Western Australia), for example, many Hazaras then moved to the Perth region in south-west Australia. Some of them found work in industrial abattoirs or vineyards (in Mount Barker, Albany, Bunbury, and Margaret River). Elsewhere they became labourers on building sites. In many cities which faced economic difficulties, groups mobilized to support Afghan requests to the authorities

---

[12] The 2001 census counts 12,410 people born in Afghanistan. See www.censusdata.abs. gov.au.

[13] Set up by the Conservative government of John Howard in late 2001, it was abandoned after the electoral victory of the Labour party in November 2007.

[14] For example, Woomera (in the southern Australian desert). Administered by a private American company specializing in prison management, it is said to have received up to 1,500 asylum seekers. It is infamous for the many cases of abuse committed there between its opening in 1999 and its closure in 2003.

for regularization of their status, in particular Albany (WA), Murray Bridge (SA), or Young (NSW). Having sorted out their legal status, many Hazaras then sought opportunities in Melbourne, Sydney, or even Adelaide. There they developed their own mutual assistance networks and contributed to the expansion of the vast Afghan diaspora in the world.

North America

The Afghan community consists of many thousands in North America. Mostly members of the urban middle and upper classes (Oeppen forthcoming), Afghans are well represented in the San Francisco Bay area (Fremont in particular) as well as in Washington DC (and the neighbouring states of Virginia and Maryland), but also in Toronto, Montreal, and Vancouver.

As in Australia, rural Hazaras arrived only recently as a result of the territorial expansion of the community's migratory networks beyond the Middle East. However, given the geographical position of the North American continent, it is almost impossible to arrive there illegally. In Canada, for example, migrants must be sponsored[15] publicly (by the federal state or a province) or privately (generally through a charitable or community association). As for the USA, one of the immigration mechanisms used is the visa lottery organized by the authorities which issues annually about 50,000 green cards for permanent residence. This procedure is open to nationals of a list of countries which changes each year and which is intended to maintain a degree of diversity within the immigrant population. After five years of residence, people having a green card are able to request naturalization.

A few Hazaras have successfully arrived through this route in the second half of the 1990s, most often with Pakistani papers. They formed the initial nucleus of a small community established in New York which today numbers between 150 and 200 people. It has gradually grown through family reunion or through marriage, as first arrivals brought wives from Afghanistan or Pakistan. These transnational marriages often allow successful migrants to upgrade their social status: many beneficiaries of a green card and others with US passports have managed to marry women from families of higher social status than themselves, who

---

[15] Supported by their community associations many Hazaras who successfully travel to Canada are Ismailis (Guilbert 1999; Monsutti 2006).

would probably have been inaccessible in their home country. Very soon after their arrival, a few Hazaras with connections to other Middle Eastern migrants who had been settled in the megalopolis for longer managed to achieve professional status in the catering business. They acquired pushcarts for the sale of coffee and pastries. This socio-economic niche is difficult to penetrate. The problem is not getting a permit from the municipality (which costs a few hundred dollars per year), but rather negotiating with a largely self-managed group to acquire the right of usage of a pitch. The most desirable spots (on the corners of certain street in Manhattan, near underground stations, etc.) can cost many thousands of dollars which must be paid to the previous user.

This is both a social and an economic investment. People who achieve success gradually get closer to the most central locations while reselling at a profit their previous pitch to a younger member of the community. They introduce these newcomers into the profession by acting as mentor and thus strengthen their own social capital. Migration here seems to open new possibilities and to contribute to a redefinition of hierarchies and social status.

A TRANSNATIONAL PERSPECTIVE ON AFGHAN MIGRATORY NETWORKS

It is clear, from the description of the means used to establish themselves in each of the locations which form part of their vast circulatory territory, that the Hazaras are not mere victims of forces beyond their control. They are actors who adapt to the world system by relying on the cultural and social resources at their disposal. They have created migratory networks which form a truly transnational system. Scattered between the Middle East, Western Europe,[16] North America, Australia, and New Zealand, the Hazaras, like other Afghans, have retained and even developed their mechanisms of solidarity and mutual support.

Escape from violence is not necessarily incompatible with a real migratory strategy. The geographical dispersion and the resulting economic diversification can become an asset. Afghan refugees and migrants have known how to adapt to each context. People with similar identity and sociological profile have defined themselves differently according to

---

[16] With respect to Europe, see Centlivres and Centlivres-Demont (2000) and Tarrius (2007).

their migratory trajectory and their final destination. We have focused our attention on rural Hazaras. In Pakistan, they have relied on a host community which was created by population movements caused by earlier conflicts, and they have not sought official recognition as refugees or taken advantage of the presence of the numerous humanitarian organizations aiding Afghans. In Iran they have forged a place for themselves in the national labour market by ensuring that local employers appreciate their work without hoping for long-term integration in the society of the host country. A small kernel of entrepreneurial individuals arrived officially in the USA with Pakistani papers after having obtained a residence permit through the lottery. Their *alter ego*, however, travelled illegally to Australia where they benefited from the active support of numerous human-rights groups which fought the government's hard line.

The ethnographic description of the strategies used by Afghans throughout their movements thus blurs the distinction between voluntary and forced migration. Depending on the context and the choices made, the same individuals can be labelled as refugees or as economic migrants. In fact, refugees and other types of migrants share numerous social characteristics, and whether a person belongs to this category or that is rarely straightforward.

While the international regime for the management of refugees is based on the assumption that movement must end, mobility as well as dispersion can sometimes be considered social, economic, and political capital (Monsutti 2008). In the course of their global travels, Hazaras have not merely adapted to context. They retain links with their land of origin, links which are concretized through the transfer of important amounts of money, through political activities focused on Afghanistan, or even investment in reconstruction projects and the rehabilitation of a family home in Kabul or elsewhere. In addition they have created transversal links between the different places where they settle, materialized through internet fora, numerous trips between Sweden and the UK, between Germany and the USA, as well as through the circulation of male and female marriage partners.[17] By being sensitive to the fact that migration is not a unilinear process, a transnational perspective implemented through a mobile ethnography leads to a better understanding of these many

---

[17] 'Afghans use transnational networks to find women of marriageable age—identifying women in Afghanistan as brides for Afghan men living in Iran, and identifying Afghan women living in Iran as brides for Afghan men living in Europe, the United States, Canada and Australia' (Abbasi-Shavazi and Glazebrook 2006: 5).

practices and links beyond the opposition between refugees and labour migrants.

Note. This text has been translated from the French by Helen Lackner. It is based on data collected during different field visits from 1993 onwards to Afghanistan, Pakistan, and Iran and, more recently, in Europe, North America, Australia, and New Zealand, in particular within the framework of a research project entitled 'Beyond the Boundaries: Hazara Migratory Networks from Afghanistan, Pakistan and Iran toward Western Countries' financed by the MacArthur Foundation (Chicago) between 2004 and 2006.

REFERENCES

Abbasi-Shavazi, M. J. and Glazebrook, D. (2006), *Continued Protection, Sustainable Reintegration: Afghan Refugees and Migrants in Iran* (Kabul, Afghanistan Research and Evaluation Unit).

Adelkhah, F. and Olszewska, Z. (2007), 'The Iranian Afghans', *Iranian Studies*, 40, 2: 137–65.

Al-Ali, N., Black, R., and Koser, K. (2001), 'Refugees and Transnationalism: The Experience of Bosnians and Eritreans in Europe', *Journal of Ethnic and Migration Studies*, 27, 4: 615–34.

Amselle, J.-L. (2000), 'La globalisation: 'Grand partage' ou mauvais cadrage?', *L'Homme*, 156: 207–26.

Appadurai, A. (1991), 'Global Ethnoscapes: Notes and Queries for Transnational Anthropology', in R. Fox (ed.), *Recapturing Anthropology: Working in the Present* (Santa Fe, NM, School of American Research Press), pp. 191–210.

—— (1999), 'Disjuncture and Difference in the Global Cultural Economy', in S. During (ed.), *The Cultural Studies Reader* (London and New York, Routledge), pp. 220–30.

Barnes, J. A. (1954), 'Class and Committee in a Norwegian Island Parish', *Human Relations*, 7: 39–58.

Brettell, C. B. (2008), 'Theorizing Migration in Anthropology: The Social Construction of Networks, Identities, Communities, and Globalscapes', in C. B. Brettell and J. F. Hollfield (eds), *Migration Theory: Talking across Disciplines*, 2nd edn (New York and London, Routledge), pp. 113–59.

Brightman, R. (1995), 'Forget Culture: Replacement, Transcendence, Relexification', *Cultural Anthropology*, 10, 4: 509–46.

Bruneau, M. (1994), 'Espaces et territoires de diasporas', *L'Espace géographique*, 1: 5–18.

Centlivres, P. (2000), 'Introduction: portée et limites de la notion de diaspora', *Cahiers d'études sur la Méditerranée orientale et le monde turco-iranien*, 30: 5–12.

—— and Centlivres-Demont, M. (2000), 'Exil et diaspora afghane en Suisse et en Europe', *Cahiers d'études sur la Méditerranée orientale et le monde turco-iranien*, 30: 151–71.

Chatelard, G. (2002), *Iraqi Forced Migrants in Jordan: Conditions, Religious Networks, and the Smuggling Process*, Working Paper 49 (Florence, Robert Schuman Center for Advanced Studies, European University Institute).

Clifford, J. (1986), 'Introduction: Partial Truths', in J. Clifford and G. E. Marcus (eds), *Writing Culture: The Poetics and Politics of Ethnography* (Berkeley and London, University of California Press), pp. 1–26.

—— (1988), *The Predicament of Culture: Twentieth-century Ethnography, Literature, and Art* (Cambridge, MA, Harvard University Press).

—— (1992), 'Travelling Cultures', in L. Grossberg, C. Nelson, and P. Treichler (eds), *Cultural Studies* (New York, Routledge), pp. 96–116.

—— (1994), 'Diasporas', *Cultural Anthropology*, 9, 3: 302–38.

—— (1997), 'Spatial Practices: Fieldwork, Travel, and the Disciplining of Anthropology', in A. Gupta and J. Ferguson (eds), *Anthropological Locations: Boundaries and Grounds of a Field Science* (Berkeley, University of California Press), pp. 185–222.

—— and Marcus, G. E. (eds) (1986), *Writing Culture: The Poetics and Politics of Ethnography* (Berkeley and London, University of California Press).

Collective for Social Science Research (2006), *Afghans in Quetta: Settlements, Livelihoods, Support Networks and Cross-border Linkages* (Kabul, Afghanistan Research and Evaluation Unit).

Colville, R. (1998), 'Afghan Refugees: Is International Support Draining Away After Two Decades in Exile?', *Refuge*, 17, 4: 6–11.

Darnell, R. (1995), 'Deux ou trois choses que je sais du postmodernisme: le "moment expérimental" dans l'anthropologie nord-américaine', *Gradhiva*, 17: 3–15.

Edwards, D. B. (1994), 'Afghanistan, Ethnography, and the New World Order', *Cultural Anthropology*, 9: 345–60.

Fairchild, H. P. (1925), *Immigration: A World Movement and Its American Significance* (New York, Macmillan).

Friedman, J. (2000), 'Des racines et (dé)routes: tropes pour trekkers', *L'Homme*, 156: 187–206.

Glick Schiller, N., Basch, L., and Szanton Blanc, C. (eds) (1992), *Towards a Transnational Perspective on Migration: Race, Class, Ethnicity, and Nationalism Reconsidered* (New York, New York Academy of Sciences).

——, ——, and —— (1995), 'From Immigrant to Transmigrant: Theorizing Transnational Migration', *Anthropological Quarterly*, 68, 1: 48–63.

Global Commission on International Migration (2005), *Migration in an Interconnected World: New Directions for Action* (Geneva, Global Commission on International Migration).

Guilbert, L. (1999), *Les réfugiés publics afghans ismaïlis dans la région de Québec: médiation citoyenne interculturelle* (Quebec, Université Laval).

Gupta, A. and Ferguson, J. (1992), 'Beyond "Culture": Space, Identity, and the Politics of Difference', *Cultural Anthropology*, 7, 1: 6–23.

—— and —— (1997), 'Discipline and Practice: "The Field" as Site, Method, and Location in Anthropology', in A. Gupta and J. Ferguson (eds), *Anthropological Locations: Boundaries and Grounds of a Field Science* (Berkeley, University of California Press), pp. 1–46.

Hanifi, M. J. (2000), 'Anthropology and the Representations of Recent Migrations from Afghanistan', in E. M. Gozdziak and D. J. Shandy (eds), *Rethinking Refuge and Displacement: Selected Papers on Refugees and Immigrants*, Vol. 8 (Arlington, VA, American Anthropological Association), pp. 291–321.

Hannerz, U. (1967), 'Gossip, Networks, and Culture in a Black American Ghetto', *Ethnos*, 32: 35–60.

—— (1986), 'Theory in Anthropology: Small is Beautiful? The Problem of Complex Cultures', *Comparative Studies in Sociology and History*, 28: 362–7.

—— (1992), 'The Global Ecumene as a Network of Networks', in A. Kuper (ed.), *Conceptualizing Society* (London, Routledge), pp. 34–56.

—— (1996), *Transnational Connections: Culture, People, Places* (London, Routledge).

—— (1998), 'Transnational Research', in H. R. Bernard (ed.), *Handbook of Methods in Cultural Anthropology* (Walnut Creek, CA, London, and New Delhi, AltaMira Press), pp. 235–56.

Johnson, C. (2000), *Hazarajat Baseline Study: Interim Report* (Islamabad, UN Co-ordinator's Office).

Levitt, P., Dewind, J., and Vertovec, S. (2003), 'International Perspective on Transnational Migration: An Introduction', *International Migration Review*, 37, 3: 565–75.

—— and Jaworsky, B. N. (2007), 'Transnational Migration Studies: Past Developments and Future Trends', *Annual Review of Sociology*, 33: 129–56.

—— and Nyberg-Sørensen, N. (2004), *The Transnational Turn in Migration Studies* (Geneva, Global Commission on International Migration).

Lindholm, C. (1997), 'Logical and Moral Dilemmas of Postmodernism', *Journal of the Royal Anthropological Institute*, 3, 4: 747–60.

Malkki, L. H. (1992), 'National Geographic: The Rooting of Peoples and the Territorialization of National Identity Among Scholars and Refugees', *Cultural Anthropology*, 7, 1: 24–44.

—— (1995), 'Refugees and Exile: From "Refugees Studies" to the National Order of Things', *Annual Review of Anthropology*, 24: 495–523.

—— (1997), 'News and Culture: Transitory Phenomena and the Fieldwork Tradition', in A. Gupta and J. Ferguson (eds), *Anthropological Locations: Boundaries and Grounds of a Field Science* (Berkeley, University of California Press), pp. 86–101.

Marcus, G. E. (1995), 'Ethnography in/of the World System: The Emergence of Multi-sited Ethnography', *Annual Review of Anthropology*, 24: 105–10.

Marx, E. (1990), 'The Social World of Refugees: A Conceptual Framework', *Journal of Refugee Studies*, 3, 3: 189–203.

Monsutti, A. (2005), *War and Migration: Social Networks and Economic Strategies of the Hazaras of Afghanistan* (New York and London, Routledge).

—— (2006), 'La diaspora ismaélienne: des hautes vallées du Hadjigak aux faubourgs du Québec', *Afghanistan Info*, 59: 15–17.

—— (2007), 'Migration as a Rite of Passage: Young Afghans Building Masculinity and Adulthood in Iran', *Iranian Studies*, 40, 2: 167–85.

—— (2008), 'Afghan Migratory Strategies and the Three Solutions to the Refugee Problem', *Refugee Survey Quarterly*, 27, 1: 58–73.

Oeppen, C. (forthcoming), 'The Afghan Diaspora and Its Involvement in the Reconstruction of Afghanistan', in A. Schlenkhoff and C. Oeppen (eds), *Understanding Afghanistan: A Multidisciplinary Approach* (Oxford and New York, Hurst).

Olwig, K. F. (2003), '"Transnational" Socio-cultural Systems and Ethnographic Research: Views from Extended Field Site', *International Migration Review*, 37, 3: 787–811.

Portes, A., Guarnizo, L. E., and Landolt, P. (1999), 'The Study of Transnationalism: Pitfalls and Promise of an Emergent Research Field', *Ethnic and Racial Studies*, 22, 2: 217–37.

Ravenstein, E. G. (1885 and 1889), 'The Laws of Migration', *Journal of the Royal Statistical Society*, 48, 2: 167–235 and 52, 2: 241–305, reprint (New York, Arno Press, 1976), pp. 165–305.

Safran, W. (1991), 'Diasporas in Modern Society: Myths of Homeland and Return', *Diaspora*, 1, 1: 83–4.

Sahlins, M. (1999), 'Two or Three Things That I Know About Culture', *Journal of the Royal Anthropological Institute*, 5, 3: 399–421.

Schnapper, D. (2001), 'De l'Etat-nation au monde transnational: du sens et de l'utilité du concept de diaspora', *Revue européenne des migrations internationales*, 17, 2: 9–39.

Shami, S. (1996), 'Transnationalism and Refugee Studies: Rethinking Forced Migration and Identity in the Middle East', *Journal of Refugee Studies*, 9, 1: 3–26.

Stevens, C. (1989), *Tin Mosques and Ghantowns: A History of Afghan Cameldrivers in Australia* (Melbourne, Oxford University Press).

Tarrius, A. (1995), 'Territoires circulatoires des entrepreneurs commerciaux maghrébins de Marseille: du commerce communautaire aux réseaux de l'économie souterraine mondiale', *Journal des anthropologues*, 59: 15–35.

—— (2007), *La remontée des Sud: Afghans et Marocains en Europe méridionale* (La Tour d'Aigues, Editions de l'Aube).

Tölölyan, K. (1996), 'Rethinking *Diaspora(s)*: Stateless Power in the Transnational Moment', *Diaspora*, 5, 1: 3–36.

Turton, D. and Marsden, P. (2002), *Taking Refugees for a Ride? The Politics of Refugee Return to Afghanistan* (Kabul, Afghanistan Research and Evaluation Unit).

United Nations High Commissioner for Refugees (UNHCR) (2007), *Operational Information: Monthly Summary Report—October 07* (Kabul, UNHCR), p. iv.

Van Hear, N. (1998), *New Diasporas: The Mass Exodus, Dispersal and Regrouping of Migrant Communities* (Seattle, University of Washington Press).

Vertovec, S. (1999), 'Conceiving and Researching Transnationalism', *Ethnic and Racial Studies*, 22, 2: 447–62.

Zolberg, A. R. (1981), 'International Migrations in Political Perspective', in M. M. Kritz, C. B. Keely, and S. M. Tomasi (eds), *Global Trends in Migration: Theory and Research on International Population Movements* (Staten Island, NY, Center for Migration Studies), pp. 3–27.

3.
Internal Displacement in the Occupied Palestinian Territories: Politics and the Loss of Livelihood
Maher Anawati Bitar

INTRODUCTION

Between 27 December 2008 and 17 January 2009, 1,314 Palestinians were killed, over 5,300 severely injured, and over 50,000 were forced to find shelter with the United Nations. As of 21 January 2009, 'the total number of people displaced by the military operation remain[ed] unknown' (UN OCHA 2009: 1). The Israeli military assault on the Gaza Strip compounded an already alarming and deteriorating humanitarian crisis and accentuated a new reality in the long history of Palestinian forced displacement: the inability to flee conflict for safer ground. In Gaza, the concept of 'internally stuck persons' (ISPs)—a recent term in the field of forced migration—has taken on an even more consequential meaning. The Gaza Strip has become a physical prison, with every conventional entry and exit route—by ground, air, or sea—controlled by an outside power (Khalidi 2009). And in such an open-air prison, most displaced persons become, by definition, 'internally displaced persons' (IDPs), because the large majority are compelled to remain within these circum-scribed boundaries. Yet, such IDPs are precluded from the established legal and physical protection guarantees afforded to refugees—those with the ability to cross an international border. Gaza, it seems, high-lights—in stark terms—a humanitarian and human rights paradox: populations unable to flee are also the least protected.

In certain respects, the situation in the Gaza Strip can no longer be compared to the West Bank. Yet, for all the differences—in domestic political governance, the scale of the humanitarian crisis, and the nature of Israel's military occupation—the ramifications and patterns of displacement in both locations reflect a converging reality: Gaza presents a prospective—and unsettling—model for forecasting the possible consequences that the Government of Israel's (GoI) military and infra-structural grip may have on populations at risk of displacement in the West Bank and East Jerusalem. The GoI's military occupation, with its associated policies and infrastructure, is accelerating and, in certain cases, redefining the nature of forced displacement among Palestinians in the occupied Palestinian territories (oPt). Historically, Palestinians have been vulnerable to waves of displacement across international borders. However, Palestinians in the oPt are increasingly at risk of internal displacement within the circumscribed territorial boundaries determined by the GoI's military occupation.

In light of these rapid developments, this essay examines the scope, extent, and repercussions of involuntary migratory movements within the oPt of the West Bank and East Jerusalem, with a particular emphasis on the physical barrier (hereinafter the Wall) that the GoI is building within the oPt (see Figure 3.1). Although displacement in Gaza, the West Bank, and East Jerusalem is often triggered by similar direct and indirect factors, the latter two areas face a particular set of triggers that are alto-gether distinct. This essay argues that displacement cannot be viewed simply as a humanitarian crisis, or as an inadvertent consequence of conflict or Israel's security needs. A review of preliminary displacement patterns,[1] coupled with an analysis of current and projected territorial and demographic changes, strongly suggests that forced displacement is both a result of and a means by which the GoI has expanded its hold of East Jerusalem and key areas in the West Bank.

Although the United Nations and a number of Palestinian, Israeli, and international non-governmental organizations have conducted field research to highlight the problem of internal displacement, the phe-nomenon remains crucially under-researched (UN OCHA 2008a; CARE International et al. 2008). Moreover, local authorities and the international community have not adequately responded to the protection and assis-tance needs of IDPs. According to the International Displacement Monitoring Centre (IDMC), a leading research centre on internal displace-ment, 'the international community has largely failed to address the situ-ation of forced displacement in the oPt in a systematic and comprehensive

---

[1] The figures presented in this essay are based primarily on studies conducted by the United Nations Office for the Coordination of Humanitarian Affairs and, to a lesser extent, non-governmental agencies operating in the oPt. Due to the volatile and ongoing nature of developments on the ground, the data presented in this essay are subject to constant change.

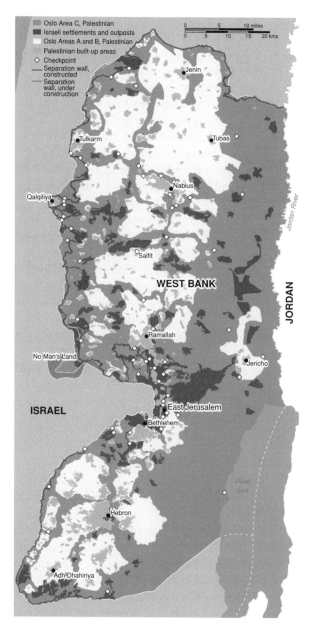

Figure 3.1.   The occupied Palestinian territories.
Source: Rajaie Batniji et al. (2009), 'Health as Human Security in the Occupied Palestinian Territory', *The Lancet*, 373 (© Elsevier, reproduced with permission from Elsevier).

manner' (IDMC 2008: 20). This essay, therefore, seeks to spur a larger interdisciplinary assessment of the causes and consequences of internal displacement in the oPt, which, in turn, may serve to inform local and international protection and assistance responses.

The first section provides a brief historical analysis of internal displacement in the oPt, and identifies various triggers of displacement affecting Palestinians in East Jerusalem and the West Bank.

The second section examines these displacement triggers in more depth. It differentiates between two categories of displacement—direct and indirect. This analysis highlights the fact that most displacement is caused by multiple displacement triggers, often a combination of direct and indirect factors.

The essay then focuses in on the territorial, political, and displacement impact of the Wall and its associated regime of restrictive policies and regulations. This section attempts to show that repercussions of the Wall are blurring the distinction between direct and indirect displacement. The Wall and its associated regime present the most recent and visible manifestation of an integrated set of policies and physical barriers that continue to allow the GoI to secure territorial gains in East Jerusalem and the West Bank, while simultaneously reducing the number of Palestinians in these same areas.

The essay concludes with a brief look at the political and humanitarian consequences of the Wall and its associated regime. In light of the growing displacement crisis in the oPt, it emphasizes the need for more robust and comprehensive data collection, so as to ensure that responsive and preventive assistance and protection programmes meet the needs of IDPs and at-risk communities.

IDENTIFYING AND DEFINING INTERNAL DISPLACEMENT

Forced displacement is an ongoing and recurring phenomenon in modern Palestinian history. Although this essay focuses primarily on Palestinians displaced or at risk of displacement in the West Bank and East Jerusalem, it is imperative to situate internal displacement within the larger political and displacement history of Palestinians.

Palestinian refugees represent the largest and oldest refugee population in the world (Shiblak 2006: 8). Over three-quarters of Gaza's estimated 1.4 million residents are registered refugees with the United Nations Relief and Works Agency (UNRWA), the UN agency mandated to provide assistance to Palestinian refugees. Over 750,000 of 2.4 million residents of the West Bank are UNRWA-registered refugees (UNRWA 2006). Moreover, internal displacement in the oPt is not a recent occurrence. Many Palestinians have been displaced—both internally and externally—multiple times during and following pivotal periods of conflict, such as in 1948 and 1967. Since Israel began its military occupation of East Jerusalem and the West Bank in 1967, an estimated 110,000 Palestinians have suffered displacement to areas within the West Bank as well as across international borders (IDMC 2008: 14). As the subsequent analysis of displacement triggers shows, displacement has and continues to affect all sectors of Palestinian society and must be understood as a dynamic, ongoing, and long-running process.

In this context, applying the designation of IDP can be misleading, because a displaced person in the West Bank may very likely already be a refugee. The IDMC therefore adopts two separate designations: (1) *displaced persons* for 'Palestinians who are forcibly displaced from their homes in the oPt but have not left the Territory', and (2) *secondary displaced Palestinians* for 'Palestinian *refugees* who are forcibly displaced from their homes in the oPt, but have not left the Territory' (IDMC 2008: 28; emphasis added). For the IDMC, incorporating secondary displaced persons into all assessments of internal displacement is crucial for three distinct reasons:

1   UNRWA does not have an express protection mandate, and therefore refugees who are also subject to internal displacement continue to suffer from an acute protection gap.
2   First-time and secondary displaced persons 'show similar protection and humanitarian needs'.
3   'Excluding secondary displaced refugees would fail to take note of the nature, scope and severity of displacement taking place' (IDMC 2008: 28).

Although cognizant of the distinct challenges facing secondary displaced persons, this essay merges these two groups—first-time and secondary displaced persons—under the umbrella term of IDP.

Because of the oPt's troubled history of displacement, defining what constitutes forced internal displacement and, in extension, who may be considered an IDP often remains complex and case-specific. The United Nations Guiding Principles on Internal Displacement—although not internationally binding—are helpful in distinguishing between various causes of displacement:

> Internally displaced persons are persons or groups of persons who have been forced or obliged to leave their homes or places of habitual residence, in particular as a result of or in order to avoid the effects of armed conflict, situations of generalized violence, violations of human rights or natural or human-made disasters, and who have not crossed an internationally recognized State border (UNHCHR 1998).

To be considered an IDP for the purposes of this study, a resident of East Jerusalem or the West Bank must have been forced or obliged to leave his or her home or place of habitual residence, while remaining within the internationally recognized borders of the oPt.[2] Such displacement can occur as a result of or in order to avoid the following four categories of displacement triggers, which cover a wide range of direct and indirect displacement-inducing activities identified by existing field research in the oPt:

1. armed conflict, including, but not limited to, military incursions, clearing operations, and directed violence and intimidation by Israeli soldiers as well as settlers;
2. situations of generalized violence, which also arise from military operations and settler violence;
3. violations of human rights, which occur as a result of the violence described above as well as because of home demolitions, forcible expulsion, land confiscation, and restrictions on freedom of movement, all in large part a consequence of settlement building and the imposition of the Wall and its associated regime; and
4. human-made disasters, which, in the case of the oPt, include a host of targeted economic, movement, building, and environmental restrictions that have combined to economically de-develop large swaths of the oPt, create untenable living conditions, and induce increased forced migration from specific areas of the West Bank and East Jerusalem.

Combined with the consolidation of the Wall and its associated regime, these various policies and practices have and will continue to directly and indirectly produce displacement. As the following section details, although direct displacement may attract the most attention because of its

---

[2] In accordance with the Oslo Accords of 1993, 'Gaza and the West Bank are considered a single territorial unit, so forced displacement between the two areas does not create refugee status' (IDMC 2008: 9).

visibility, the indirect causes of displacement, including those that fall within the broad umbrella of 'human-made disasters' above, should be of particular concern to researchers and human-rights practitioners. A worsening humanitarian situation threatens the livelihood of large segments of Palestinian society and continues to heighten the risk of displacement for vulnerable groups in the oPt, in particular for Bedouin communities, UNRWA-registered refugees, children, people with disabilities, and female-headed households (CARE International et al. 2008).

DIRECT AND INDIRECT CAUSES OF DISPLACEMENT

This section examines the various triggers of displacement in more depth. It distinguishes between two separate—although deeply interconnected —forms of displacement: direct and indirect displacement. Direct displacement encompasses all policies, activities, and human-rights violations that directly lead to the expulsion or coerced dislocation of individuals, families, or even entire communities. In contrast, indirect displacement occurs as a consequence of a combination of policies, activities, and human-rights violations that compel individuals to relocate because of untenable living conditions. Unlike direct displacement, indirect displacement is more difficult to track and quantify.

Distinguishing neatly between direct and indirect causes of displacement can be difficult and impractical, if not impossible, given the messy reality on the ground. As is often the case, ostensibly indirect causes of displacement manifest themselves in decidedly direct ways. The multifaceted impact of the Wall—discussed in the next section—is a case in point. To the researcher, therefore, distinguishing between direct and indirect causes of displacement often turns on a rather abstract determination of degree. The challenge ahead for displacement research in the oPt, as in other contexts of displacement across the world, is to create effective research strategies that will be able to account for the complex set of variables—both direct and indirect—causing displacement. Such research would not only identify and quantify past and present cases of displacement more accurately, it would also allow for the identification of communities at risk of displacement and the development of preventive and forward-looking protection measures. The following analysis is but an initial foray into developing such a systematic research framework.

Administrative cantonization: land expropriation and confiscation in the oPt

To comprehend the scale of and territorial basis for displacement, it is imperative to flesh out the GoI's land policies and activities in the oPt since 1967, and particularly following the Oslo Accords of the early 1990s. Although settlement activity and land confiscation in East Jerusalem and the wider West Bank began shortly after the military occupation of the oPt, the formal contours of Israel's hold of significant areas of the West Bank emerged with the Oslo Accords. Under the Accords, the oPt 'was divided into three zones: Area A under full Palestinian control; Area B under Israeli security control; and Area C, compromising 60 percent of the West Bank, under full Israeli control' (IDMC 2008: 7–8). Area A, and to a lesser extent Area B, encompasses the largest Palestinian population centres. Area C, in contrast, is the focal point of Israel's construction and expansion of settlements and associated transportation and military infrastructure. According to a study conducted by the United Nations Office for the Coordination of Humanitarian Affairs (UN OCHA):

> more than 38 percent of the West Bank consists of Israeli settlements, outposts, military bases, closed military areas and Israeli-designated nature reserves. These areas are tightly controlled or off-limits to Palestinians and virtually all of them are located in Area C (UN OCHA 2008a: 11).

The territorial, demographic, political, and displacement consequences of the GoI's land policies cannot be overstated. By consolidating its hold of Area C and East Jerusalem, the GoI has effectively severed multiple Palestinian population centres from each other. Area C, encompassing most of the West Bank, is pivotal to Palestinian economic and political development. 'Over 400 Palestinian villages and towns (excluding East Jerusalem) have at least part of their built-up area in Area C', with a population estimated at over 228,000. Of these, 'about 44,000 reside in 130 communities, whose built-up area lies entirely in Area C' (UN OCHA 2008a: 1). Moreover, as UN OCHA documents, 'Area C holds the land reserves necessary for the expansion of Palestinian population centres, the development of national infrastructure and the agricultural and private sector' (UN OCHA 2008a: 11). To be effective, 'any infrastructure connecting Palestinian communities (roads, water and electricity networks, etc.) needs to cross Area C' (UN OCHA 2008a: 11). As is argued in the next section, this process of cantonization and colonization has been buttressed by the construction of the Wall and its associated regime. Together, these policies continue to severely damage the economic, political, and social viability of Palestinian society in the oPt and, in extension, contribute to the current displacement crisis.

It is crucial to keep this larger context in mind as we turn to look at the various triggers of displacement individually. As noted above, each of the variables—be they direct or indirect—do not, by any means, act in isolation to spur displacement. Rather, cases of displacement can involve numerous, interdependent triggers, which can often combine to impose unprecedented hardship and pressures on individuals, families, and entire communities.

Direct displacement triggers

Settlement building and expansion

Illegal under international law,[3] settlements are arguably the principal driving force spurring displacement in the West Bank and East Jerusalem. According to UN OCHA:

> over the course of its prolonged military occupation, Israel has facilitated and encouraged the settling of nearly 470,000 Israelis into the occupied Palestinian territory, resulting in the takeover of Palestinian land, natural resources and transportation routes (UN OCHA 2008b: 2).

The construction, expansion, servicing, and protection of settlements significantly influence many of the GoI's policies in East Jerusalem and the West Bank, and can therefore be considered a crucial catalyst for displacement. The settlements provide a powerful political, military, and economic rationale and incentive for Israel's strengthened grip of key areas in the oPt, the strategic routing of the Wall, and the extensive network of 'Israeli-used roads built to connect the settlements to one another and to Israel' (UN OCHA 2008a: 11). According to the IDMC, the humanitarian and human-rights consequences of the settlements and their associated restriction regime on Palestinians are multifaceted. The establishment of settlements 'has entailed the expropriation of private Palestinian land, undermined the safety of Palestinian civilians, and entailed policies discriminatory against Palestinians' (IDMC 2008: 71).

Many of the policies and actions described below are thus intimately tied to and carried out to shore up the settlement enterprise. These include policies that result in the direct expulsion and evacuation of

---

[3] In a 2004 Advisory Opinion, the International Court of Justice 'concluded that Israeli settlements in the oPt are in breach of international law' (UN OCHA 2008b: 2).

Palestinians from key locations in East Jerusalem and the West Bank, the confiscation and clearing of land for settlement use, and the military protection of the settlements and settler population (IDMC 2008: 75).

Home demolitions

Home demolitions are the most direct and quantifiable form of displacement in the oPt. Since the beginning of the military occupation in 1967, Israel has demolished more than 18,000 homes under the auspices of 'clearing operations based on security concerns, punitive demolitions, and administrative demolitions for lack of building permits' (IDMC 2008: 10). The United Nations Committee Against Torture has expressed 'concern about . . . Israeli policies of house demolitions, which may, in certain instances, amount to cruel, inhuman or degrading treatment or punishment (Article 16 of the Convention Against Torture)' (UN CAT 2001).

Punitive demolitions, in particular, have a long history in the oPt. From 1987 to 2005, '1,115 houses were completely demolished' as a means of punishing the relatives of individuals deemed militants by the GoI (IDMC 2008: 54). Between October 2001 and January 2005 alone, 667 Palestinian homes were demolished for punitive reasons, 'which left more than 4,200 persons homeless' (IDMC 2008: 55).

The greatest risk of displacement, however, arises from administrative demolitions carried out because of a lack of building permits issued by the GoI, particularly in East Jerusalem and in Area C of the West Bank. Due specifically to a lack of building permits, more than 2,200 homes have been destroyed and 13,000 Palestinians have become homeless since 1998 (IDMC 2008: 10). In both East Jerusalem and Area C, Palestinians must request and receive a specific building permit from the GoI to build or expand on any property. In carrying out this policy, Israel has effectively frozen legal construction in many of these locations by overwhelmingly denying the vast majority of permit applications. According to a study conducted by UN OCHA, 'more than 94 percent of applicants for such permits submitted by Palestinians between 2000 and 2007 were denied' (UN OCHA 2008c: 3). If the GoI rejects the application, or if no application is submitted, 'a demolition order is issued [and] no further steps are required before a demolition order is executed' (UN OCHA 2008c: 3). In East Jerusalem, such administrative demolitions, combined with punitive demolitions, have resulted in the demolition of approximately 800 houses from 1991 to 2007. From 2003 to 2007 alone, 993 individuals were displaced as a result of these home demolitions (IDMC 2008: 10).

Area C has been similarly targeted. Between January and November 2008, 586 people were displaced due to home demolitions (UN OCHA 2008f: 3). Between 2000 and 2007, '5,000 demolition orders were issued, and over 1,600 Palestinian buildings were demolished' (UN OCHA 2008a: 1). Currently, 'more than 3,000 Palestinian-owned structures in Area C of the West Bank have pending demolition orders that can be executed at any moment' (UN OCHA 2008e: 3). Moreover, 'since obtaining a building permit for construction in Area C is virtually impossible, Palestinians are forced to build without permits, in spite of the threat of demolition' (UN OCHA 2008e: 5). This creates a vicious cycle, where the threat of direct displacement by demolition causes untenable living conditions in East Jerusalem and Area C. The GoI does not permit families and communities to build new or expand existing homes to accommodate natural growth. To build illegally, as many inevitably do, triggers a demolition order and looming forced displacement. The economic consequences, in short, have and will continue to be drastic. According to the World Bank:

> these restrictions have created an artificial land shortage, resulting in a distortion of land markets; as Area C became largely inaccessible or not desirable for investment, land prices in Areas A and B have increased and, in certain towns, are cost-prohibitive, thus severely inhibiting urban and industrial development (UN OCHA 2008e: 5).

Although the political and demographic ramifications of such land policies are discussed in more depth in the next section, it is important to note the strong correlation between demolition and displacement patterns in East Jerusalem and Area C and the strategic territorial significance of both these areas to the GoI's land and settlement policies.

Forced expulsion

Forced expulsion—the uprooting and dispersion of entire communities in order to take over specific tracts of land—also has a long, indelible history in Palestine. This essay treats it as a distinct category of displacement, even though it is often carried out using home demolitions. Forced expulsion differs from home demolition in its scope and impact. It is primarily used against Palestinian collectivities, rather than particular homes, and most often involves the large-scale demolition of community structures with the intent of relocating entire populations away from newly cleared sites.

Unlike its large-scale use in 1948 and 1967, forced expulsion in the West Bank and East Jerusalem has been more targeted since 1967, but with equally devastating effects. Its use has been concentrated primarily in rural Palestinian areas within Area C, most often to clear areas adjacent to settlements or military bases of remaining Palestinian communities. As of May 2008, 'at least ten small communities throughout the West Bank are at risk of being almost entirely displaced due to the large number of pending demolition orders' (UN OCHA 2008a: 1). One community, Khirbet Qassa, was forcibly relocated beyond the Wall on 29 October 2007, when:

> the IDF removed all of the community members while hired workers were used to collect all of the belongings of the residents, as well as their sheep, and removed them beyond the Tarqumiya Terminal which became operational on 28 October 2007. In total, . . . 180 people were displaced (UN OCHA 2007a).

A year later, on 30 October 2008, the Bedouin community of Mughayir Al Dir suffered a similar fate: thirty-six structures, including twenty-three residential buildings which constituted the seasonal dwelling of ninety-seven people (fifty-one of them children), were destroyed after the Israel Defense Forces (IDF) declared the area a 'closed military zone' because of its proximity to an Israeli settlement outpost (UN OCHA 2008d: 4).

As with many of the home demolitions, forced expulsion cases cannot and should not be viewed in isolation from the political and territorial transformations on the ground, particularly in Area C and East Jerusalem. As the examples above indicate, forced expulsion and home demolition cases are integrally tied to the expansion of the GoI settlement and military infrastructure in strategic areas of the oPt.

Military incursions and clearing operations

Military incursions and clearing operations can also lead to large-scale displacement. The scale of displacement in the oPt often depends on the military strategies executed by the Israeli military. These can include the aerial bombardment of urban areas, ground military operations that result in the extensive destruction of homes, apartment buildings, and schools, and the creation of buffer zones, or 'security corridors', such as in areas adjacent to the Wall and settlements. In Gaza, a buffer zone along the border with Israel 'extends from 500 meters to a kilometre inside the Gaza Strip. Communities living in or in close proximity to this buffer zone remain at risk of displacement' (IDMC 2008: 11). Moreover, following military operations, Palestinians 'displaced or at risk of displacement in areas in proximity to Israeli installations or security zones established by the IDF remain vulnerable to arrest, or physical harm' (IDMC 2008: 119).

Revocation of residency rights

The GoI has maintained a long-standing policy of confiscating or revoking identification documents, primarily of Jerusalem residents, in order to compel their relocation to the West Bank or abroad. The Israeli human-rights group B'Tselem estimates that, between 1967 and 2007, 8,269 Jerusalem ID cards were confiscated, effectively disenfranchising and forcing these ID card holders out of Jerusalem (B'Tselem 2008). From 1996 to 1999, for instance, the Interior Ministry of Israel 'implemented a policy of "quiet deportation"' in which the Ministry permanently revoked the residency rights of hundreds of Palestinians on the grounds that they lived for a prolonged period outside of Israel, including the oPt (B'Tselem and HaMoked 2004). Official statistics, however, do 'not include persons under the age of 16 years, which means that thousands more were affected by the revocation of Jerusalem IDs' (Badil 2007). As is discussed in the next section, the policy of revoking identification cards has been reinforced by the consolidation of the Wall and its associated regime. Although less visible than other forms of direct displacement, available evidence suggests this policy has and continues to be used as a tool to alter the demographic landscape of East Jerusalem.

Directed violence and intimidation

Internal displacement has also been a direct consequence of systematic violence and intimidation at the hands of Israeli settlers (IDMC 2008: 16). As with home demolitions, forced expulsions, and the revocation of residency rights, settler violence has been concentrated in key areas in Jerusalem and in the vicinity of Israeli settlements in Area C. According to a study conducted by UN OCHA:

> in some cases, settler attacks have been so systematic—and the response of the relevant Israeli authorities so absent—as to directly contribute to the displacement of Palestinian residents from targeted areas. . . . Examples include the H2 area of Hebron, Palestinian hamlets in Massafer Yatta, and the village of Yanoun, in the northern West Bank (whose residents subsequently returned) (UN OCHA 2008b: 2, 6).

Settler violence has long been tacitly accepted, or at least tolerated, by the Israeli authorities in the oPt:

> The absence of action points to a lack of will, a point underscored by [Israeli advocate] Talia Sasson, who noted that it was unrealistic to expect the Israeli state and its organs to enforce law upon the settlers, when those very entities are responsible for unlawful settlement activity on a daily basis (UN OCHA 2008b: 15).

Residents of the city of Hebron have suffered acutely from such violence. By late 2006, more than 40 per cent of residences in downtown Hebron had been vacated and 'over 75 percent of Palestinian businesses had closed due to difficult living conditions caused by settler harassment and restrictive IDF policies' (UN OCHA 2008b: 6). In the old city of Hebron, where between 400 and 800 settlers live under the protection of the Israeli military, 'a combination of stringent security restrictions in movement and settler intimidation and violence has led over 1,800 businesses to shut down and over 1,000 Palestinian homes to be vacated, the majority since 2000' (IDMC 2008: 16).

Indirect displacement triggers

Indirect displacement triggers encompass a diverse set of policies and restrictions that induce displacement through the creation of untenable living conditions. As discussed with respect to home demolitions, a central, albeit indirect, factor in inducing displacement is the imposition of building restrictions in strategic areas, primarily Area C and East Jerusalem (see above).

Israel's 'closure regime'—consisting of checkpoints, roadblocks, terminals, segregated roads, and walls—is another indirect factor contributing to internal displacement. The closure regime, when 'combined with Israeli infrastructure and discriminatory policies, serves to limit Palestinian access to, and claims to, land and compel Palestinians to leave their homes' (IDMC 2008: 15). 2008 saw an in increase in the overall number of obstacles and a further entrenchment of 'the complex system of restrictions . . ., leading to further social and economic fragmentation of Palestinian areas' (UN OCHA 2008g: 10). For instance, as of September 2008, UN OCHA 'observed 630 obstacles blocking Palestinian movement, including 93 staffed checkpoints and 537 unstaffed obstacles (earthmounds, roadblocks, barriers, etc)' (UN OCHA 2008h). Moreover, contrary to popular perception, many policies promoted as facilitating Palestinian movement in the West Bank have instead served to further institutionalize the closure regime:

> Some of the steps taken by the Government of Israel to ease Palestinian movement in the West Bank and ensure transportation contiguity between physically disconnected communities, including through the construction of 'fabric of life' roads and the expansion of staffed IDF checkpoints on main terminal routes, came at the price of further entrenching the system of movement restrictions (UN OCHA 2008g: 16).

Even as the closure regime becomes firmly institutionalized, its effects on displacement remain a challenge to monitor. There is a serious lack of accurate data, because 'figures of displacement linked to the closures remain difficult to identify for lack of systematic study and for the fact that such restrictions have usually combined with, or preceded, other factors to cause of displacement' (IDMC 2008: 114). Indeed, as the following section shows, direct and indirect displacement triggers most often act in tandem and reinforce each other to create unsafe and untenable living conditions and place communities at great risk of displacement.

CREATING DISPLACEMENT: THE WALL AND ITS ASSOCIATED REGIME

The Wall is the most recent factor creating internal displacement in the oPt. To date, however, 'there have been no comprehensive assessments of actual or potential displacement' caused by the Wall and its associated regime (IDMC 2008: 12). Preliminary research and data, nonetheless, provide substantial evidence that displacement is linked to the construction of the Wall and the consolidation of its associated regime. Even so, the Wall defies simple categorization because of the multiple ways in which it complements and entrenches many of the direct and indirect displacement triggers discussed above. On the one hand, its construction has entailed large-scale direct displacement of Palestinians from key areas in East Jerusalem and Area C in the West Bank. At the same time, its consolidation has served to further exacerbate deteriorating living conditions in these same strategic areas, thereby becoming a major indirect cause of displacement.

The territorial and demographic politics of the Wall

In 2002, after a series of attacks on civilians inside Israel, the GoI presented the Wall as a pragmatic security response. Since then, however, the planning and construction of the Wall's route have instead demonstrated the primacy of significant Israeli political, demographic, and territorial interests in the oPt.

The Wall is projected to be more than 709 km long (over double the length of the 1949 Armistice Line) and consists of a concrete wall in urban areas as well as electronic fencing (IDMC 2008: 11). The latter is particularly damaging. The fencing, which is 60–100 m wide, 'includes buffer zones with trenches and barbed wire, trace paths to register footprints, an electric fence with sensors to warn of any intrusion, a two-lane patrol road and fortified watchtowers at regular intervals' (IDMC and NRC 2006: 10). Recent figures indicate that 57 per cent of the structure has been completed, with a further 9 per cent under construction (UN OCHA 2008d: 6). Approximately 87 per cent of the Wall will be located within the West Bank, some of it as deep as around the large settlement blocks of Ma'ale Adumim, Gush Etzion, Ariel, and Qedumim (UN OCHA 2008d: 6). UN OCHA estimates that more than 500,000 Palestinians will live within a one-kilometre strip of the Wall, on both its eastern and western sides (UN OCHA 2006: 1).

The structure of the Wall is buttressed by an extensive 'associated regime', which is a 'set of administrative decisions composed of military orders (land, property confiscation), closed areas, a new permit system, and new regulations at checkpoints (or terminals) and gates' (Badil et al. 2006: 14). In addition, a network of 1,661 kilometres of roads and highways exclusively for the use of Israeli citizens 'connects settlements, outposts, military bases, national parks and closed military areas' (IDMC 2008: 15). The roads act as de facto barriers because Palestinians are prohibited from using them or crossing over them, which serves to further prohibit movement and fragment the West Bank.

The Wall and its associated regime also consolidate the GoI's hold of a number of existing closed areas—areas in the West Bank where Palestinian presence and movement are generally restricted by permit or expressly forbidden. These include the 'seam zones', the term used by the GoI to describe areas between the Wall and the Green Line.[4] They are projected to encompass an estimated 9.5 per cent of the occupied West Bank, including most of East Jerusalem, much of it prime agricultural land and water-rich areas (UN OCHA 2008d: 6; PLO NAD 2007a).

The Wall and its associated regime, moreover, cannot be examined in isolation from other policies and practices carried out by the GoI in the oPt. They reinforce a number of long-standing practices: 'The wall marks

[4] The term 'Green Line' refers to the Armistice line that delineates the pre-1967 borders of the West Bank, East Jerusalem, and Gaza Strip. Although this essay uses the term 'seam zone' to denote the areas between the Wall and the Green Line, the use of this term should not obfuscate the legal and humanitarian reality that a 'seam zone' is a form of closed area, as it imposes similar restrictions on access and movement for Palestinians and international agencies as other areas in the West Bank that enclose or are closed to Palestinians.

the summation of Israel's policies in Jerusalem since 1967, literally setting in concrete the fruits of decades of annexation and settlement building' (Dolphin 2006: 124). Three main functions of the Wall stand out. First, the Wall is being utilized as an instrument to expropriate and annex land. In conjunction with other closure measures and policies, particularly in the Jordan Valley, the GoI is gradually consolidating its long-term hold of a projected 45.5 per cent of the occupied West Bank, including East Jerusalem and much of Area C (PLO NAD 2007b). In particular, the Wall incorporates most Israeli settlements into Israel proper. The 2004 International Court of Justice Advisory Opinion (ICJ AO) affirms the find-ings of numerous UN reports, which show that the actual 'sinuous' route of the Wall 'has been traced in such a way to include in that area the great majority of the Israeli settlements in the occupied Palestinian Territory (including East Jerusalem)' (ICJ AO 2004: para. 119). In its completed form, it will incorporate an estimated 83 per cent of the West Bank settler population and over 360,000 settlers, of which almost 190,000 are settled in East Jerusalem (IDMC 2008: 11). Crucially, the route of the Wall leaves ample room for these settlements to continue expanding. The Wall and its associated regime are thus symbiotically tied to the Israeli settlements in the oPt: 'They are integrated legally, spatially, culturally and materially into Israel through laws, services, infrastructure and a road network that reaches all the way from Tel Aviv to the Jordan River' (Usher 2006: 7–8).

The GoI's systematic appropriation of Palestinian land has been facil-itated by the mutually reinforcing manner in which the Wall's strategic route has combined with the permit regime's limitations on Palestinian residence and movement. Together, they enable the GoI to expropriate land by activating many of the complex Israeli land and property laws that legitimize state confiscation, including the 1950 Absentees' Property Law (5710–1950) as well as subsequent laws and amendments.[5] In light of this evidence, Special Rapporteur of the Human Rights Council, John Dugard, explains that 'what we are presently witnessing in the West Bank is a visible and clear act of territorial annexation under the guise of secu-rity' (UNHCHR 2003: para. 6). Israeli Prime Minister Ehud Olmert has publicly affirmed such parallel interests, stating that 'the course of the fence—which until now has been a security fence—will be in line with the new course of the permanent border' (Myre 2006).

---

[5] For a more detailed examination of Israel's land and property laws, see Akram (2000).

Second, the Wall is an instrument for restricting freedom of movement—not only to Israel proper, but also to and between areas within the oPt. It severs cities and towns from each other, thus shattering their crucial economic, political, social, and religious interdependence. Moreover, it has served to buttress and enhance existing closure and restriction practices through the extension of a permit regime to newly enclosed areas in the seam zones. Even as such restrictions on access disproportionately affect Palestinians, they have compounded a worsening humanitarian situation because the operational capabilities of humanitarian agencies and non-governmental organizations have also been curtailed to varying degrees (UN OCHA 2007e: 14). Upon the basis of relevant instruments and provisions of international refugee law, international human-rights law, as well as international humanitarian law,[6] the rights violations resulting from the Wall are staggering. The ICJ AO thus concludes that the construction of the Wall and its associated regime impede the liberty of movement of the inhabitants of the oPt (with the exception of Israeli citizens and those assimilated thereto) as guaranteed under Article 12, paragraph 1, of the International Convention on Civil and Political Rights. They also impede the right to work, to health, to education, and to an adequate standard of living as proclaimed in the International Convention on Economic, Social and Cultural Rights and in the United Nations Convention on the Rights of the Child (ICJ AO 2004: para. 134).[7]

Third, the Wall and its associated regime are directly and indirectly inducing forced displacement. At the same time, the territorial expansion of the GoI inside the West Bank—through its dense network of settlements, roads, military bases, and the Wall—and the concomitant shrinking of areas permitted to Palestinians act to limit the refuge options

[6] The ICJ AO has affirmed the full applicability of international human rights and humanitarian law in the oPt, including East Jerusalem (see ICJ AO 2004: paras 81–113). In relation to international humanitarian law, it affirms the applicability of the provisions of the Hague Regulations (due to their elevation to customary international law), as well as those of the Fourth Geneva Convention, the latter to which Israel is a party. In terms of human-rights law, the Court affirmed the applicability of the International Convention on Civil and Political Rights, the International Convention on Economic, Social and Cultural Rights, and the United Nations Convention on the Rights of the Child, all three of which the GoI has ratified.

[7] The Court is also of the opinion that the Wall contravenes relevant provisions in the Fourth Geneva Convention and pertinent Security Council resolutions due to its role in illegally annexing land and contributing to the demographic alteration of the occupied territory.

available to IDPs. Many IDPs 'are forced to relocate away from Israeli settlements and related infrastructure, military zones and security strips, and areas under construction of the Wall and its associated regime' (IDMC 2008: 16). In other words, the present reality in Gaza—displacement within circumscribed boundaries—is becoming more apparent in the West Bank. The following case studies of Jerusalem and the seam zones offer a snapshot view of how the Wall, displacement, and territorial control go hand in hand.

Jerusalem: the largest seam zone

In Jerusalem specifically, the Wall has emerged as a significant tool in artificially upholding the Israeli government's long-standing demographic policies aimed at keeping Palestinian residents to 30 per cent or less of the city's population (IDMC 2008: 13).

In January 2009, the Wall was nearing completion around Jerusalem,[8] which is effectively the largest seam zone. At over 168 km in length, the Wall's route envelopes occupied East Jerusalem as well as its outlying environs, thus seamlessly integrating them into the larger Jerusalem municipality and Israel proper. Its current route has resulted in almost a quarter of the more than 250,000 Palestinians living in East Jerusalem— but outside the Wall—being sealed off from the city (IDMC 2008: 61). These Jerusalemites as well as most West Bank residents are thus cut off from their natural access to workplaces, health and education facilities, and places of worship.

Tracking displacement in and around Jerusalem remains difficult, because of the complex interaction of direct and indirect factors causing displacement. According to the United Nations Commission on Human Rights (UNCHR), the Palestinian population of East Jerusalem is being actively reduced 'by a number of stratagems', which include house demolitions, 'routing the wall to the west of neighbourhoods previously part of East Jerusalem, [and] transferring neighbourhoods previously integrated

---

[8] As the ICJ AO has stressed, any demographic or structural changes that seek to alter the occupied status of East Jerusalem are illegal under international law. The Court stated that all territories within the 1949 Armistice Line, including East Jerusalem, 'remain occupied territories and Israel has continued to have the status of occupying Power'. As such, and in accordance with UN Security Council resolutions, all 'legislative and administrative actions taken by Israel to change the status of the City of Jerusalem, including expropriation of land and properties, transfer of populations and legislation aimed at the incorporation of the occupied section, are totally invalid and cannot change that status' (ICJ AO 2004: para. 78).

into East Jerusalem by means of the Wall', among a host of interconnected policies. The Commission concludes, in a clear condemnation: 'We judge that this is a deliberate Israeli policy—the completion of the annexation of East Jerusalem' (UNCHR 2006).

Preliminary research shows a Palestinian population under increasing stress. A 2006 survey found that, based on the overall Jerusalem district population of '407,090 in mid-2006, 23,170 persons have thus already been displaced as a result of the Wall' (Badil et al. 2006: 27). The IDMC has found that the Wall is 'already responsible for the economic and social decline of entire communities as they are in practice cut off from Jerusalem and essential services they previously had access to' (IDMC and NRC 2006: 14).

East Jerusalem also presents a unique case because Israel's permit policies are leading to an unforeseen boomerang effect. In 1995, the GoI instituted a 'centre of life' policy for Palestinian residents of East Jerusalem, which allows Israel to revoke residency and social benefits for Palestinians who cannot prove that their 'centre of life' is in Jerusalem. In 2006 alone, 'over 1360 Palestinians had their ID card revoked [,] five times more than in 2005, and more than in any previous year since 1967' (UN OCHA 2007b: 11). The Wall and its associated regime—in particular the tracking systems built into the terminals—facilitate the implementation of the centre of life policy. Jerusalem ID card holders living outside the city's designated municipal boundaries must now cross through the terminals and their movements can be tracked in order to ascertain whether they are fulfilling the stringent requirements necessary to keep their Jerusalem residency. As a result, there has been an upsurge in the number of Jerusalemite Palestinians moving back into the municipal boundaries to retain Jerusalem residence status, even as the Wall's route has effectively cut off significant numbers of Palestinians, including many Jerusalem ID holders, from the city (IDMC 2008: 100).

The Wall and its associated regime also reinforce a family reunification and child registration ban, which was estimated to affect 16,000–24,000 families in 2004. The ban 'discriminately denies spouses from the oPt who are married to Israeli citizens or Palestinian permanent residents the opportunity to acquire Israeli citizenship or residency rights' (IDMC 2008: 14). As such, a Jerusalem resident must choose between continuing to live in Jerusalem apart from his or her partner, or move to the West Bank or abroad and therefore forfeit his or her residency rights as a consequence of the centre of life policy. In the words of the UN Special Rapporteur of the Commission on Human Rights, 'Israel hopes to further reduce the

Palestinian population of East Jerusalem by compelling spouses to move to the West Bank side of the Wall' (UNCHR 2006).

Seam zones and internally stuck persons

Just as with Jerusalem and its environs, seam zone and Wall-affected communities, particularly in the northern West Bank, are vulnerable to displacement. UN OCHA estimates that approximately 35,000 individuals will be living in a precarious limbo between the Wall and the 1949 Armistice Line. This figure reaches almost 300,000 individuals when affected Palestinian residents of East Jerusalem are included. Moreover, 'another 151,000 Palestinians will be surrounded on three or four sides by the Barrier' (UN OCHA 2008d: 6). Without including Jerusalem, this number reaches '125,000 Palestinians in 28 communities who live or will soon live in enclaves surrounded on three sides by the wall . . . An additional 26,000 Palestinians will be surrounded on four sides with a tunnel or road connecting them to the rest of the West Bank' (UNRWA and UN OCHA 2008).

Preliminary empirical evidence indicates that displacement patterns are becoming more pronounced in these areas. An early study conducted by Refugees International in 2003 found that the Wall, still in its early stage, threatened to displace an estimated 90,000 persons once completed (Refugees International 2003). Already in May 2005, the Palestinian Central Bureau of Statistics found that 14,364 persons (2,448 households) had been displaced from 145 localities near the route of the Wall (IDMC and NRC 2006: 7). According to the IDMC, minimum estimates point to between 24,500 and 57,000 persons being subjected to internal displacement (IDMC 2007: 6). In 2006, a Palestinian-led study found powerful empirical evidence that the Wall and its associated regime 'represent a measure which both has and is likely to continue to induce forced displacement among Palestinians' (Badil et al. 2006: 38).

Palestinians directly in the seam zones—between the Wall and the Green Line—are isolated from the rest of the West Bank and subject to a special permit regime. This permit regime is especially threatening the livelihoods of local farmers, as its increasingly restrictive application is limiting who may have access to the land. Permits 'are now mostly denied because the owner or user of the land has not been able to prove ownership sufficiently (although land titles are alien to many Palestinian communities) or direct relationships to the land' (IDMC and NRC 2006: 13). Dolphin argues that 'the constraints resulting from the gate and permit regime are not just inevitable bureaucratic "snafus" but a deliberate policy, the objective being to cause despair among the landowners in the hope they will cease working their land in the seam area' (2006: 99).

Seam zone communities in the northern West Bank are particularly at risk.[9] Approximately 10,000 Palestinians live in completely enclosed enclaves in the northern West Bank and need 'long-term' or 'permanent resident' permits to continue residing in their homes and on their lands (UN OCHA 2008d: 6). Those unable—due to financial or health reasons—or unwilling to move are increasingly finding themselves in economic, social, legal, and political limbo. The informal designation of internally stuck person—noted in the introduction with regard to Gaza—has been adopted by a number of NGOs, including Save the Children (United Kingdom) and the Badil Resource Centre (Badil 2005: 22). The notion of individuals unable or unwilling to move from areas of risk is of particular resonance with regard to the seam zone areas. These seam zone communities are especially vulnerable due to their isolation from both the West Bank and from Israel across the 1949 Armistice Line. Many are cut off from regular access to health, education, and social services, as well as regular economic, communal, and family ties within the West Bank. Due to the route of the Wall, most 'services are generally located on the east side of the Wall, so children, patients, and workers have to pass through Wall gates to reach schools, health services and workplaces' (UN OCHA 2007c). For example, approximately 79 per cent of families in the seam zones are 'separated from health centres and hospitals' (IDMC 2008: 145). An initial survey conducted by UN OCHA and UNRWA in 2007 has found that 1,200 households have left areas between the Wall and the Green Line, more than 3 per cent of the population surveyed. Moreover, by November 2007, '36 of the 67 communities identified in the seam zones' have reported that 'heads of households have left to find work elsewhere, representing about 1,100 additional individuals' (UN OCHA 2007d).

---

[9] Particular urban centres close to the Wall are also significantly impacted. The city of Qalqiliya, for instance, has been hard hit by out-migration due to the impact of the Wall. As early as 2003, an estimated 6,000–8,000 residents were found to have left the northern West Bank city since it was enclosed by concrete wall on three sides (IDMC 2008: 13). Qalqiliya's environs have also suffered. By early 2005, only 30 per cent of applicants were allocated agricultural permits, 'leading to a decline in agricultural productivity and food production as land, crops and orchards in the closed areas went neglected and untended' (Dolphin 2006: 76).

THE WALL AND THE FUTURE OF PALESTINE

This essay has assessed the growing crisis of internal displacement in the oPt. In doing so, it has taken a critical look at various direct and indirect displacement triggers: settlement construction and expansion, home demolitions, forced expulsion, military incursions, the revocation of residency rights, directed violence by Israeli settlers, and the Wall and its associated permit and closure regime.

The essay has thus argued that an analysis of existing data and the geographic distribution of displacement provide strong evidence to suggest that economic de-development and displacement of Palestinians have been and continue to be spatially concentrated and highly targeted, in a manner that significantly correlates with the larger political, territorial, and demographic aims of the GoI in East Jerusalem and the West Bank. Current evidence points to a process of gradual depopulation, especially in seam zone areas, in rural communities close to the Wall, as well as in locations in and around Jerusalem, including in 'enclave' areas completely surrounded by the Wall. IDPs are increasingly compelled to seek employment and residence in existing Palestinian urban centres in the West Bank, away from Jerusalem and the seam zones. Permit and building restrictions in Zones B and C prevent other migratory movements, such as rural-to-rural migration. Thus, through a form of accelerated urbanization, the Wall and its associated regime have the potential to radically alter the demographic distribution of Palestinians within the occupied West Bank, including East Jerusalem. Placing this scenario within an analysis of the possible strategic aims of the GoI in the oPt, it becomes clear that the Wall and its associated regime are facilitating the creation of not only a territorial but also a political fait accompli.

Rather than the Wall being a unilateral imposition of future international borders, as noted earlier, it may be more prudent for scholars and practitioners to view developments on the ground as consolidating a two-tiered reality. On the one hand, the Wall may very likely present a fixed boundary demarcation for Palestinians and non-Israeli individuals and entities, including international organizations, residing and operating in areas that will remain designated as 'West Bank'. OCHA explains that 'in conjunction with the complex system of permits, checkpoints and gates, the Wall has become a *de facto* border' (UN OCHA 2007b: 14). On the other hand, the Wall and its associated regime currently do not and, very possibly, will not act as a border for persons in Israel: 'Israeli citizens, Israeli permanent residents and those eligible to immigrate to Israel in accordance with the [Israeli] Law of Return may remain in, or move freely to, from and within' areas of the oPt under full Israeli control (ICJ AO 2004: para. 85; UN OCHA 2007b: 14). Already, the vast transportation network linking the settlements to Jerusalem and Israel provides contiguity between Israel, occupied East Jerusalem, and Israeli-controlled areas of the occupied West Bank (Zones B and C). As such, the Wall will present a significant obstacle for humanitarian agencies operating among Palestinian residents of the West Bank, including the 'seam zones'. They will face increasing access restrictions into areas gradually incorporated into Israeli jurisdiction, as is presently the case in Jerusalem and, more recently, in the northern 'seam zones'.

According to virtually all available accounts, this reality is producing a steadily enlarging humanitarian ripple effect. It affects the livelihoods and increases the vulnerability of those in the direct vicinity of the Wall as well as those in urban centres—internally displaced and internally stuck persons alike. The Wall has negatively impacted economic activity and development, agricultural output, education, social and health services, family and community relations, and religious worship, in addition to a host of other indicators. If current trends continue, the humanitarian impact of the Wall is likely to have an enduring effect on internal displace-ment in the oPt. The full scale of displacement, however, remains unknown due to the scarcity of comprehensive and actionable data. As this essay has repeatedly emphasized, further research is needed to ascertain the extent of the present predicament of internal displacement, to deter-mine the location and needs of IDPs, and to identify communities and individuals at risk of displacement. Without such information, interna-tional agencies and non-governmental organizations will be hard pressed to respond in a proactive manner to current cases of displacement and to develop preventive programmes specifically aimed at protecting commu-nities at serious risk of displacement. In this context, where the humani-tarian situation in the West Bank is rapidly deteriorating and Palestinian territory is gradually shrinking because of the Wall, the closure regime, and the settlements, reactionary humanitarian programmes are simply not sufficient.

REFERENCES

Akram, S. (2000), 'Palestinian Refugee Rights: Part Two—Israel's Legal Manoeuvres', *Information Briefs*, Washington, DC, Center for Policy Analysis on Palestine, www.thejerusalemfund.org/ht/a/GeneratePdfAction/url/ h~ttp, !!www*thejerusalemfund*org!h~t!display!ContentDetails!i!2143/filename/ %27Palestinian%20Refugee%20Rights:.pdf.

Badil (2005), 'Follow-up Information Submitted to the Committee for the Elimination of Discrimination Against Women, for the Convening of the Committee on Its 33rd Session of 5–22 July 2005 Regarding Israel's Serious Breaches of Its Obligations under the International Convention for the Elimination of Discrimination Against Women (CEDAW)', Bethlehem, Badil Resource Centre for Palestinian Residency and Refugee Rights, www.badil. org/Publications/Legal_Papers/BADIL-report-for-CEDAW.pdf.

—— (2007), 'Survey of Palestinian Refugees and Internally Displaced Persons 2006–2007', Bethlehem, Badil Resource Centre for Palestinian Residency and Refugee Rights, www.badil.org/Publications/Books/Survey2006–2007–Ch1. pdf.

—— et al. (2006), 'Displaced by the Wall: Pilot Study on Forced Displacement Caused by the Construction of the West Bank Wall and its Associated Regime in the Occupied Palestinian territories', Bethlehem and Geneva, Badil Resource Centre for Palestinian Residency Refugee Rights, Norwegian Refugee Council and the Internal Displacement Monitoring Centre, www.badil.org/ Publications/Books/Wall-Report.pdf.

Batniji, R., Rabaia, Y., Nguyen-Gilham, V., Giacaman, R., Sarraj, E., Punamaki, R., Saab, H., and Boyce, W. (2009), 'Health as Human Security in the Occupied Palestinian Territory', *The Lancet*, 373: 1133–43.

B'Tselem (2008), 'Revocation of Residency in East Jerusalem', www.btselem.org/ English/Jerusalem/Revocation_of_Residency.asp.

—— and HaMoked (2004), 'Forbidden Families: Family Unification and Child Registration in East Jerusalem', www.btselem.org/English/Publications/ Summaries/200401_Forbidden_Families.asp.

CARE International et al. (2008), 'Joint Submission to Human Rights Council on Human Rights Situation in Palestine and other Arab Occupied Territories', A/HRC/7/NGO/71, CARE International, Norwegian Refugee Council, DIAKONIA, Doctors without Borders, Premiere Urgence, The Israeli Committee Against House Demolitions (ICAHD), MA'AN Development Centre, and the Comitato Internationale per lo Suiluppo dei Popoli (CISP), http://unispal.un.org/UNISPAL.NSF/0080ef30efce525585256c38006eacae/ 067fe905b6c8d57885257408006604f2?OpenDocument.

Dolphin, R. (2006), *The West Bank Wall: Unmaking Palestine* (London, Pluto Press).

International Court of Justice Advisory Opinion (ICJ AO) (2004), 'The Legal Consequences of the Construction of a Wall in the Occupied Palestinian Territories', The Hague, www.icj-cij.org/docket/index.php?p1=3&p2=4& code=mwp&case=131&k=5a.

International Displacement Monitoring Centre (IDMC) (2007), 'Internal Displacement: Global Overview of Trends and Developments in 2006', Geneva, IDMC, www.internal-displacement.org/8025708F004BE3B1/(http

Info Files)/9251510E3E5B6FC3C12572BF0029C267/$file/Global_Overview_
2006.pdf.

—— (2008), 'Occupied Palestinian Territory: Forced Displacement Continues',
Geneva, IDMC, www.internal-displacement.org/countries/opt.

—— and Norwegian Refugee Council (NRC) (2006), 'Occupied Palestinian
Territories: West Bank Wall Main Cause of New Displacement Amid Worsening
Humanitarian Situation', Geneva, Internal Displacement Monitoring Centre
and Norwegian Refugee Council, www.reliefweb.int/rw/rwb.nsf/db900SID/
ACIO-6QYGXA?OpenDocument&RSS20=18–P.

Khalidi, R. (2009), 'What You Don't Know about Gaza', *New York Times*, 7 January,
www.nytimes.com/2009/01/08/opinion/08khalidi.html.

Myre, G. (2006), 'Olmert Wants to Set Border by 2010', *International Herald Tribune*,
10 March, www.iht.com/articles/2006/03/09/news/mideast.php.

Palestine Liberation Organization Negotiations Affairs Department (PLO NAD)
(2007a), 'Barrier to Peace: Assessment of Israel's Revised Wall Route',
Ramallah, PLO NAD, www.nad-plo.org/facts/wall/FS%20–%20Barrier%20
to%20Peace.pdf.

—— (2007b), 'Israel's Wall and Settlements (Colonies)', Ramallah, PLO NAD,
www.nad-plo.org/facts/wall/FS%20–%20Barrier%20to%20Peace.pdf.

Refugees International (2003), 'More than Just a Wall', Refugees International,
www.reliefweb.int/rw/rwb.nsf/db900sid/ACOS-64DD87?OpenDocument.

Shiblak, A. (2006), 'Stateless Palestinians', *Forced Migration Review*, 26: 8–9.

United Nations Commission on Human Rights (UNCHR) (2006), 'Report of the
Special Rapporteur of the Commission on Human Rights, John Dugard, on the
Situation of Human Rights in the Palestinian Territories Occupied by Israel
since 1967', UNCHR, E/CN.4/2006/29.

United Nations Committee Against Torture (UN CAT) (2001), 'Conclusions and
Recommendations of the Committee Against Torture: Israel', CAT/C/XXVII/
Concl.5, UN CAT, 23 November, www.unhchr.ch/tbs/doc.nsf/0/60df85db
0169438ac1256b110052aac5.

United Nations Office of the High Commissioner on Human Rights (UNHCHR),
(1998), *Guiding Principles on Internal Displacement*, UN Doc. E/CN.4/1998/
53/Add.2, UNHCHR, www.reliefweb.int/ocha_ol/pub/idp_gp/idp.html.

—— (2003), 'Question of the Violation of Human Rights in the Occupied Arab
Territories, including Palestine: Report of the Special Rapporteur of the
Commission on Human Rights, John Dugard, on the Situation of Human
Rights in the Palestinian Territories Occupied by Israel since 1967, to the
Sixtieth Session of the Commission on Human Rights', UNHCHR,
www.unhchr.ch/Huridocda/Huridoca.nsf/(Symbol)/E.CN.4.RES.2003.6.En?
Opendocument.

United Nations Office for the Coordination of Humanitarian Affairs (UN OCHA)
(2006), 'Preliminary Analysis of the Humanitarian Implications of the April
2006 Wall Projections', Jerusalem, UN OCHA, www.ochaopt.org/documents/
OCHABarrierProj_6jul06_web.pdf.

—— (2007a), 'Qassa Eviction Impact', Jerusalem, UN OCHA.

—— (2007b), 'The Humanitarian Impact of the West Bank Barrier on Palestinian Communities: East Jerusalem', Jerusalem, UN OCHA, www.ochaopt.org/documents/Jerusalem-30July2007.pdf.

—— (2007c), 'Three Years Later: The Humanitarian Impact of the Wall since the International Court of Justice Opinion', Jerusalem, UN OCHA, www.ochaopt.org/documents/ICJ3_Special_Focus_July2007.pdf.

—— (2007d), 'Special Focus: The Barrier Gate and Permit Regime Four Years On: Humanitarian Impact in the Northern West Bank', Jerusalem, UN OCHA, www.ochaopt.org/documents/OCHA_SpecialFocus_BarrierGates_2007_11.pdf.

—— (2007e), 'Occupied Palestinian Territory: 2007 Consolidated Appeal Mid-Year Review', Jerusalem, UN OCHA, www.ochaopt.org/documents/MYR_2007_oPt.doc.

—— (2008a), 'Special Focus: Lack of Permit Demolitions and Resultant Displacement in Area C', Jerusalem, UN OCHA, www.ochaopt.org/documents/Demolitions_in_Area_C_May_2008_English.pdf.

—— (2008b), 'Special Focus: Unprotected: Israeli Settler Violence against Palestinian Civilians and their Property', Jerusalem, UN OCHA, www.ochaopt.org/documents/ocha_opt_settler_vilonce_special_focus_2008_12_18.pdf.

—— (2008c), 'The Humanitarian Monitor: Number 26', Jerusalem, UN OCHA, www.ochaopt.org/documents/HM_June_2008.pdf.

—— (2008d), 'The Humanitarian Monitor: Number 27', Jerusalem, UN OCHA, www.ochaopt.org/documents/ocha_opt_humanitarian_monitor_table_2008_07_english.pdf.

—— (2008e), 'The Humanitarian Monitor: Number 30', Jerusalem, UN OCHA, www.ochaopt.org/documents/ocha_opt_humanitarian_monitor_oct_2008_10_english.pdf.

—— (2008f), 'The Humanitarian Monitor: Number 31', Jerusalem, UN OCHA, http://unispal.un.org/unispal.nsf/3822b5e39951876a85256b6e0058a478/655e09e48f408d64852575220054f7c6?OpenDocument.

—— (2008g), 'Occupied Palestinian Territory: 2009 Consolidated Appeal', Jerusalem, UN OCHA, http://ocha.unog.ch/fts/reports/daily/ocha_R32_A834.PDF.

—— (2008h), 'Closure Update: Main Findings and Analysis (30 April–11 September 2008)', Jerusalem, UN OCHA, www.reliefweb.int/rw/rwb.nsf/db900sid/EDIS-7JMMZU?OpenDocument&rc=3&emid=ACOS-635PFR.

—— (2009), 'Field Update on Gaza from the Humanitarian Coordinator: 20–21 January 2009, 1700 hours', Jerusalem, UN OCHA, www.ochaopt.org/gazacrisis/admin/output/files/ocha_opt_gaza_humanitarian_situation_report_2009_01_21_english.pdf.

United Nations Relief and Works Agency (UNRWA) (2006), 'Gaza Refugee Camp Profiles', United Nations Relief and Works Agency for Palestine Refugees in the Near East, www.un.org/unrwa/refugees/gaza.html.

—— and UN OCHA (2008), 'Four Years Later: The Humanitarian Impact of the Barrier: Four Years After the Advisory Opinion of the ICJ on the Barrier', Jerusalem, United Nations Relief and Works Agency for Palestine Refugees in the Near East and UN OCHA, www.un.org/unrwa/access/BarrierReport_July2008.pdf.

Usher, G. (2006), 'Introduction', in R. Dolphin, *The West Bank Wall: Unmaking Palestine* (London, Pluto Press).

4.
Displacement by Repatriation: The Future of Turkish Settlers in Northern Cyprus
Yaël Ronen

INTRODUCTION

This essay concerns the future of Turkish settlers in Northern Cyprus. It examines the prospect of their repatriation to Turkey in the framework of a peaceful settlement of the Cyprus conflict. While ordinarily the term 'repatriation' has a positive connotation, of returning home, the case of the Turkish settlers in Northern Cyprus demonstrates that what is homecoming for one may be displacement for another.

The essay gives a brief description of the history of the settlers issue in Northern Cyprus and its evolution. It then considers the dilemma facing the architects of the future unified Cyprus with respect to Turkish settlers. The next section describes the modalities currently being negotiated for addressing this issue. Since these modalities have been formulated very much in the shadow of international human rights law, the implications of certain human rights standards for the conflict are examined. Finally, the proposed modalities are evaluated by comparison with alternative solutions for the settler problem, adopted in the Baltic states in the early 1990s.

CYPRUS BACKGROUND

Brief history of the conflict

The population of the island of Cyprus, about 1 million in 2009,[1] comprises approximately 80 per cent Greek Cypriots of Christian faith

---

[1] The government of Cyprus estimates the population of government-controlled areas at 867,600. See Government of Cyprus Statistical Service Demographic Report 2006, p. 11. The TRNC estimates its population at about 260,000.

and 20 per cent Turkish Cypriots of Muslim faith. In 1960, Cyprus gained independence from British rule. Division between the two populations and civil disturbances erupted almost immediately.[2] They peaked in July 1974, following a coup d'état by Greek Cypriots favouring a union of Cyprus with Greece. In response to the coup, Turkish forces landed in Cyprus, with Turkey claiming that it was exercising its rights under the 1960 Treaty of Guarantee to protect the Turkish-Cypriot population. During the military conflict which ensued between Turkish and Cypriot forces until early 1975, practically all Greek Cypriots fled their homes in the northern part of the island and moved to the south, while most Turkish Cypriots fled from their homes in the southern part of the island to the north. The Turkish-held territory set up its own administration under the name Turkish Federated State of Cyprus (TFSC). In November 1983 the Turkish-Cypriot community declared the independence of the Turkish Republic of Northern Cyprus (TRNC) (Dugard 1987).[3] See Figure 4.1.

The TRNC was immediately recognized as an independent state by Turkey. The Security Council declared the declaration of independence legally invalid and called upon all states not to recognize any Cypriot

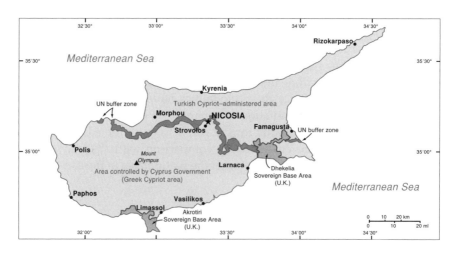

Figure 4.1.   Map of Cyprus.
Source: CIA *World Factbook* (reproduced with permission of CIA).

---

[2] UN Doc. S/RES/186 (4 March 1964).
[3] Declaration of Independence by Turkish Cypriot Parliament on 15 November 1983, UN Doc. A/38/586–S/16148 (16 November 1983).

state other than the Republic of Cyprus.[4] The refusal to recognize the TRNC is based on the violation by Turkey in 1974 of the prohibition on the use of force and of the right of Cyprus to self-determination.[5] The Security Council's call has been adhered to by all states[6] except Turkey.

At the same time, attempts to resolve the Cyprus conflict took place in various forms (Richmond 1998; Necatigil 1993; Palley 2005).[7] They climaxed in April 2004, when the UN Secretary-General presented the populations of both parts of the island with a draft Comprehensive Settlement of the Cyprus Problem (the 'Annan Plan'), proposing a federated United Cyprus Republic (UCR), composed of two constituent states, one Greek-Cypriot and one Turkish-Cypriot.[8] In simultaneously held referenda on 24 April 2004, a majority of TRNC voters approved the Plan, while in the south, the majority of voters rejected it. Without acceptance on both sides, the Plan did not materialize, nor is it binding on either party or on the UN. Nonetheless, it remains valuable as an indication of what the international community, acting through the UN Secretary-General, considers an acceptable compromise.[9] Moreover, at the time of writing

---

[4] UN Doc. S/RES/541 (18 November 1983), UN Doc. S/RES/550 (11 May 1984).

[5] For example, Council of Europe Parliamentary Assembly Recommendation 974 (1983) on the Situation in Cyprus (23 November 1983), 12(c). This aspect of the affair is entirely absent from the opinion of Sir (then Mr) Eli Lauterpacht CBE QC, 'Turkish Republic of Northern Cyprus, the Status of the Two Communities in Cyprus', UN Doc. A/44/968–S/21463, Letter from the Permanent Representative of Turkey to the United Nations Addressed to the Secretary-General (9 August 1990). The TRNC argues that Turkey's recourse to force was within its rights—and obligation—under the 1960 Treaty of Guarantee, to protect the Turkish-Cypriot population (Necatigil 1993). Yet even if the Treaty of Guarantee permits the use of force, it could not override the customary prohibition on the use of force embodied in the UN Charter (Dodd 1998; Nedjatigil 1982). Security Council Resolutions give the impression that the unlawfulness with which the Security Council was concerned was the violation of the 1960 Treaties—a point disputed by the TRNC (e.g. Necatigil 1993), and possibly the secession. It is submitted that the violation of the 1960 Treaties is not opposable to states not parties to the Treaties, while secession is not an unlawful act (Crawford 1998).

[6] European Community (EC) Bulletin 11–1983 point 2.4.1 (16 November 1983); Press communiqué of the Commonwealth Heads of Government (29 November 1983), cited in ECtHR *Loizidou v. Turkey (Merits)*, Judgment of 18 December 1996, Reports of Judgments & Decisions 1996–VI 2216, 23.

[7] For example, UN Doc. S/24472, Report of the Secretary-General on his Mission of Good Offices in Cyprus, containing Proximity Talks Leading to Set of Ideas on an Overall Framework Agreement on Cyprus (21 August 1992).

[8] The discussion in this essay is based on the final version of the Comprehensive Settlement of the Cyprus Problem as finalized on 31 March 2004, www.hri.org/docs/annan (hereafter 'Annan Plan').

[9] European Parliament Resolution, 'Prospects for the Unification of Cyprus' (21 April 2004); Matthew Bryza, Deputy Assistant Secretary for European and Eurasian Affairs, Roundtable

negotiations are underway between the Greek and Turkish communities on the island. Insofar as the future of settlers is concerned, these negotiations have the Annan Plan as their unspoken point of departure.[10] Accordingly, the Annan Plan serves as the basis for the current analysis, with certain modifications.

Settlers in the TRNC

In 1974, Turkish Cypriots numbered about 118,000 (Cuco 1992). Since then the composition of this population, residing mostly in the territory now under TRNC rule, has changed dramatically. In addition to the flight of over 40,000 Greek Cypriots from the north (Laakso 2003), the arrival of displaced Turkish Cypriots from the south,[11] and massive emigration of Turkish Cypriots in later years,[12] the most significant demographic change in the TRNC, and on which this essay focuses, is the settlement of mainland Turks, with the encouragement of both Turkey and the TRNC. Two large waves of settlers arrived in 1975 and 1977. These were estimated to add more than 10 per cent to the Turkish-Cypriot population of the territory at the time (Cuco 1992). Another wave of mainland Turks arrived in the early 2000s as construction workers, following a building boom in the TRNC.

Turkish settlers fall into two main categories. The vast majority are peasants and shepherds who arrived between 1975 and 1977 from poor regions in Turkey, i.e. Trabzon (East Black Sea), Antalya, Mersin, Adana (southern Turkey), Çaramba, Samsun (West Black Sea), Konya (central Anatolia), and south-eastern Turkey. These farmers were invited by radio and by announcements by *muhtars* (village headmen) made in Turkish village coffee shops. A small but politically significant minority comprises professionals, business people, retired military officers, and former students (Cuco 1992). They live mainly in mixed urban neighbourhoods

---

with Turkish Journalists, Washington, DC (1 February, 2007), http://turkey.usembassy.gov/statement_020107.html.

[10] Interview with Dr Kudret Özersay, Eastern Mediterranean University, Nicosia (27 November 2008). See also UK House of Commons Foreign Affairs Committee, 'Visit to Turkey and Cyprus', Fifth Report of Session 2006–7, Doc. No. HC 473 (9 May 2007) (hereafter 'HC 5th report 2007').

[11] The TRNC reports 65,000 displaced Turkish Cypriots.

[12] UK House of Commons Foreign Affairs Committee, 'Cyprus', Second Report of Session 2004–5, Doc. No. 113–I (22 February 2005), para. 201 (hereafter 'HC 2nd report 2005'), based on Laakso 2003.

and are often married to Turkish Cypriots.[13] The rural Turks have low professional skills and their customs and traditions differ in a significant way from those prevalent in Cyprus (Hatay 2005). The government of Cyprus claims (with the endorsement of the Council of Europe) that these differences are the main reason for the tensions and dissatisfaction of the indigenous Turkish-Cypriot population who tend to view the settlers as a foreign element (Doob 1986; Laakso 2003).[14] The UK House of Commons mission to Cyprus reported that the settlers, unlike Turkish Cypriots, feel they have nothing in common with Greek Cypriots.[15] Although their immigration to the TRNC was politically motivated and facilitated by the Turkish and TRNC governments, the settlers themselves were not politically motivated. It is quite plausible that a substantial number of them had little or no clear idea of where Cyprus was located before their arrival. They do not form a monolithic group and they do not all support a nationalist agenda (Hatay 2005; Anastasakis et al. 2004). Nonetheless, because of their number, Turkish settlers have a growing impact on the political climate in the TRNC.

The demographic composition of the TRNC is difficult to establish (Hatay 2007). Censuses carried out by the TRNC are rejected by the government of Cyprus as unreliable and intentionally misleading about the number of Turkish settlers. The population categories used by the opposing sides are defined differently, frustrating any attempt at comparing data.[16] The Council of Europe has initiated a number of studies on the population of the TRNC (Cuco 1992; Laakso 2003).[17] Palley argues that the TRNC government objected to these initiatives because it was reluctant to expose the large number of Turkish settlers (Palley 2005). Data on the number of settlers vary enormously: a 2003–4 Turkish government estimate gives a figure of 31,000; a 2003 estimate, endorsed by the Parliamentary Assembly of the Council of Europe, of 115,000 settlers, concludes that by 2000, at the latest, mainland Turkish settlers outnumbered indigenous Turkish

---

[13] HC 2nd report 2005. In 1992, the Cuco Report quoted the figure of 1,500 intermarriages notified between 1974 and 1990 to the Turkish Consulate in the TRNC, para. 82. Hatay (2005) quotes the number of Peace Force veterans married to Turkish Cypriots at around 800.

[14] PACE Recommendation 1197 (1992) on the demographic structure of the Cypriot communities.

[15] HC 5th report 2007.

[16] 'How Many Turkish Cypriots Remain in Cyprus', Written evidence before the select committee of the House of Commons, www.publications.parliament.uk/pa/cm200405/cmselect/cmfaff/113/113we33.htm.

[17] HC 2nd report 2005.

Cypriots (Laakso 2003); a 2006 TRNC census quotes the total number of immigrants from Turkey since the 1970s at close to 95,000, and of immigrants from other origins at over 7,500;[18] and a government of Cyprus estimate based on the same census arrives at 150,000–160,000.[19]

Until 2004, TRNC legislation was very permissive with regard to acquisition of TRNC citizenship. Law 3/1975 of the TFSC made it discretionary upon request and, in particular, available to members of the Turkish armed forces who had served in Cyprus and their families (Hatay 2005). In 1981 complementary provisions were established according to which Turkish-Cypriot nationality could be granted to persons permanently resident in the territory for at least one year, those who made or could make an important contribution to the economy, or social and cultural life, and those who have rendered services to the security forces (Laakso 2003). The 1983 constitution of the TRNC provides that original citizens of the TRNC include original citizens of the Republic of Cyprus ordinarily resident in the TRNC when it declared independence, and citizens of the TFSC.[20] A 1993 TRNC law confers original TRNC citizenship on persons born to a TRNC parent, and TRNC citizenship is also available to spouses of TRNC citizens.[21] In addition, the law provides for discretionary naturalization for various categories of aliens. Ordinarily, naturalization is contingent upon a five-year residence in the TRNC.[22] However, certain categories of individuals are exempt from this requirement. These include veterans of the 1974 peace operation and their families,[23] and persons 'who have rendered services after 1 August 1958 in the cadres of the Turkish Resistance Organization in the TRNC'[24] and their families.[25]

According to the government of Cyprus, on 12 October 2004 a protocol was signed between Turkey and the TRNC to regularize the presence of

---

[18] The Final Results of TRNC General Population and Housing Unit Census, Additional Tables, http://nufussayimi.devplan.org/Kesin-sonuc-index_en.html.

[19] Analysis of the '2006 Population Census' in the Occupied Area of Cyprus and Aide Memoire, produced by the government of Cyprus PIO, on file with the author.

[20] TRNC Constitution, Art. 67

[21] Law 52/1993 of 27 May 1993, Art. 4(1), 7.

[22] Art. 8(B).

[23] Art. 9(1)(D).

[24] Art. 9(1)(E). The Turkish Resistance Organization (TMT) was a locally established paramilitary force, engaged according to the Turkish-Cypriot narrative in protection of Turkish Cypriots against Greek-Cypriot violence, and in terrorism, according to the Greek-Cypriot narrative.

[25] Art. 9(2).

the construction workers arriving in the 2000s, adding some 40,000 new residents—and potential citizens—to the TRNC.[26]

Since 2004, granting TRNC citizenship has become a more selective process,[27] and mass grants, which were apparently a common occurrence, subsided. In 2007 a draft law was tabled, under which naturalization would be contingent upon five years' work followed by five years' residence in the TRNC.[28]

Turkish nationals may retain their nationality even when acquiring a new one.[29] Their children are Turkish nationals from birth.[30] At the same time, under Cypriot law, pre-1974 Cypriot nationals and their descendants are eligible for Cypriot citizenship.[31] Accordingly, children of mixed marriages between settlers and local Turkish Cypriots are also nationals of the Republic of Cyprus, although the Republic does not routinely acknowledge their status.[32]

THE DILEMMA AT REUNIFICATION

Ordinarily, when speaking about dispossessed and displaced persons in the context of the Cyprus conflict, what comes to mind is the plight of the Greek Cypriots, who have been denied access to their homes and property

---

[26] The Protocol authorized the residence of Turkish nationals present in the TRNC and employed there at the time of the Protocol's entry into force, namely 1 January 2005. This means that Turkish nationals who on 12 October 2004 were residing in Turkey had a three-month window wherein to transfer to the TRNC so as to take advantage of the Protocol. Observations made by the Ministry of Foreign Affairs of Cyprus, annexed to European Commission against Racism and Intolerance (ECRI), Third Report on Cyprus (adopted 16 December 2005) (hereafter 'ECRI 2005'). The mass arrival of construction workers was partly linked to the release of bonds related to Greek-Cypriot abandoned property that until then prevented building improvements.

[27] HC 5th report 2007.

[28] There are indications that the toughening of requirements is causing tension in TRNC–Turkish relations. For example, 'Fifty Thousand Persons Will Reportedly Be Gradually Made "Citizens" of the "TRNC"', Turkish Mass Media Bulletin (18 December 2007), Republic of Cyprus Press and Information Office, www.pio.gov.cy/moi/pio/pio.nsf/All/93E64B0FF93CE004C22573B5003F5F17?OpenDocument.

[29] The Turkish Nationality Law as amended in 1981 permits the acquisition of another nationality (TRNC nationality being recognized by Turkey) without renunciation of Turkish nationality. The only condition for dual nationality is to obtain permission of the Ministry of Interior. Dual nationality has been encouraged since the 1980s (Tiryakioğlu 2006).

[30] Turkish Nationality Law, Art. 1 as amended in 2004.

[31] The Republic of Cyprus Citizenship Law, No. 43 of 1967, Art. 4.

[32] US Human Rights Country Practice 2006 Report on Cyprus; HC 5th report 2007.

for over thirty years. The Turkish settlement in the TRNC is considered the cause for dispossession and displacement. Yet this population may itself become subject to forced displacement as part of the conflict resolution.

In the late 1970s the TRNC openly pursued a policy of encouraging Turkish immigration in order to effect a demographic change in Northern Cyprus. Such a policy is common among regimes which suffer from international illegitimacy, and is a means of entrenching their presence in the territory despite international censure. Thus, previous illegal regimes have attempted to change the demographic composition of the territory under dispute through the transfer of their own populations or populations loyal to them into the territory, and subsequently granting these populations residence or nationality in the territory.[33]

At the time of transition to the post-conflict regime, it is not surprising that there are calls at various levels, either for the physical removal of settlers from the country or at least for their exclusion from the body politic. These calls represent a variety of interests and sentiments. Common to most situations is resentment towards the settlers as representatives of the exploiting regime and a common thirst for retribution. This sentiment hardly singles out situations where an illegal regime ends; rather, it is common to many post-colonial regimes. Another motive for expulsion is concern of the post-conflict regime that despite its formal withdrawal, the previous regime will continue to exert political, economic, or military pressure on the territory under the new regime. The existence of a diaspora population of the previous regime in the territory exacerbates this concern, as that diaspora may be used as an excuse for intervention at various levels. A further reason for the indigenous population to call for the removal of settlers is where local resources are limited. The architects of the post-conflict regime must therefore decide the future of persons who had settled in the territory during the existence of the illegal regime and under its instruction or with its blessing. The legal power of the post-conflict regime to reverse the acts of its predecessor by removal of settlers may be limited in various ways. There may be an obligation to give effect to whatever status the previous regime conferred upon the settlers; expulsion may also be limited by the operation of human rights law and standards applicable to long-term

---

[33] For example, the implantation of Russophone settlers in the Baltic states by the Soviet Union (discussed below); settlement of Indonesians in East Timor; Moroccan settlement in Western Sahara.

residents, regardless of the original impermissibility of their arrival in the territory.[34]

Two opposite principles operate here. The first one is that *ex injuria jus non oritur*, namely an illegal act cannot produce legal consequences. Instead, the situation should revert to *status quo ante*. Indeed, the government of Cyprus originally demanded that all Turkish settlers return to Turkey. In contrast, facts do generate legal consequences—*ex factis jus oritur*. New factual situations come to exist which may have legal consequences because of their effectiveness, despite their illegal origins. They cannot simply be undone on the basis of their original illegality. The question is how to balance the two legal pulls.

THE ANNAN PLAN

The Annan Plan does not take a position on the status of the TRNC. This is an obvious consequence of the attempt to satisfy both Greek and Turkish Cypriots. Main Article 12 of the Foundation Agreement, entitled 'Past Acts', provides for legal continuity between the TRNC and the united Cyrus, the UCR. However, an observation appended to Main Article 12 excludes citizenship and immigration from this arrangement, and states:

> Matters of citizenship, immigration, and properties affected by events since 1963 are dealt with in a comprehensive way by this Agreement; any validity of acts prior to entry into force of this Agreement regarding these matters shall thus end unless they are in conformity with the relevant provisions of this Agreement.

On the basis of the return to 1963, the Annan Plan provides that original citizens of the UCR would include primarily persons who had Cypriot citizenship in 1963 and their descendants. It also makes limited provisions for residents and their subsequent naturalization.[35] But

---

[34] There are other limitations. The Special ILC Rapporteur on the expulsion of aliens also catalogues limits inherent in the international legal order and limits relating to the procedure of expulsion: UN Doc. A/CN.4/581, para. 27. The latter category is generally unaffected by the identity of potential expellees or the circumstances of expulsion, except with respect to national security grounds for expulsion, e.g. ICCPR Art. 13, ECHR Protocol 7 Art. 1(2). Therefore it is of limited interest in the current context. Moreover, procedural guarantees, around which a large part of jurisprudence revolves, usually become operative with respect to actual acts of expulsion. Accordingly, procedural guarantees will be considered only when they affect policy or are affected by it.

[35] Draft Federal Law on Citizenship of the United Cyprus Republic, Annex III, Attachment IV, Art. 5; Article 3 of the Foundation Agreement, echoed in Art. 3 of the Draft Act of

generally speaking, since most Turkish settlers arrived in North Cyprus in the late 1970s and in the early 2000s, the outcome of the Plan is that they would be denied any status in the UCR. As non-nationals and even non-residents, the UCR would be free to remove them from its territory.

The Plan does provide that in addition to the pre-1963 citizens, each side would be entitled to grant UCR citizenship to up to 45,000 persons. Priority for inclusion on the list is given on the basis of length of resi-dence, with top priority to adults who had lived in Cyprus from child-hood and their children.[36] This would include Turkish settlers. Following the resumption of negotiations between the two sides in 2008, Cypriot President Chrisafios has agreed to allow 50,000 settlers to naturalize immediately upon reunification.[37]

The implications of the Plan remain controversial. This is partly because of different readings of the Plan. The UN team made different representations to each of the parties. For example, the Turkish-Cypriot side was told that spouses of Turkish Cypriots would be entitled to citizenship outside the 45,000 quota,[38] while the Greek-Cypriot side was given to understand differently. Different expectations also exist with regard to thousands of students and academic staff. In addition, there are the vastly disparate estimates of the number of settlers, as noted above. The ambiguity of the situation is apparent in the difference between the July 2003 statement of the Secretary-General's special adviser's own legal adviser, that 'the Plan does not foresee that anybody will be forced to leave';[39] and the Secretary-General's 2004

Adaptation of the Terms of Accession of the United Cyprus Republic to the European Union.

[36] Draft Federal Law on Citizenship of the United Cyprus Republic, Annex III, Attachment IV, Art. 3. Part F of the Annan Plan (see note 8), entitled 'Measures to be taken during April 2004', includes the following item: 'Hand over by 10 April 2004 to the Secretary-General the list numbering no more than 45,000 persons as specified in the proposed Federal Law on Citizenship of the United Cyprus Republic (failing which the Citizenship Board shall, after entry into force of the Foundation Agreement, prepare the list in accordance with that law).'

[37] 'Christafios Firm on Settlers', www.cyprusemb.se/Dbase/cypemb/ref1162.asp.

[38] Draft Federal Law on Citizenship of the United Cyprus Republic, Annex III, Attachment IV, Art. 6. See also Statement by the Secretary-General's Special Adviser on Cyprus, Alvaro de Soto, at the Joint Meeting of the Foreign Affairs Committee and the Delegation of the European Parliamentary Committee with the Republic of Cyprus, Brussels (14 April 2004).

[39] Didier Pfirter, Statement at conference, 'The Annan Plan: Myths and Realities', Boğaziçi University, Istanbul (17 July 2003), quoted in 'Comments by the Government of Cyprus on the Report of the Secretary General on his Mission of Good Offices in Cyprus', UN Doc. S/2004/437 (28 May 2004), para. 41; HC 2nd report 2005.

statement that 'about half' of the settlers would have to leave the island.[40]

These ambiguities suggest that the removal of Turkish settlers might not be as dramatic as the Annan Plan appears to suggest. Indeed, it is reported that the Turkish-Cypriot side prepared a list of candidates for immediate naturalization, which contained no more than 41,000 names. But it is beyond doubt that the basic principle of the Plan is that settlers must leave, unless they qualify for a specific category which permits them to remain.[41]

HUMAN RIGHTS CONSTRAINTS ON REPATRIATION

Introduction

New factual situations come to exist which may have legal consequences because of their effectiveness. Accordingly, the presence of settlers may generate legal consequences embodied in international human rights law, that limit the post-transition regime's discretion in expelling them despite the original illegality of the transfer of settlers to the territory.

Various international human rights may be implicated in measures of expulsion. These include the right to a hearing, the prohibition on racial and other discrimination, the right to property (for example, when the freedom of ownership is conditional upon status, or when expulsion is carried out in a manner that prevents individuals from benefiting from their property), the prohibition against inhuman treatment, and more. Particularly pertinent to expulsion of long-term settlers from Cyprus is the right to private life, which is protected under the European Convention of Human Rights and Fundamental Freedoms (ECHR),[42] to which Cyprus and Turkey adhere, and which under the modified Annan Plan would also be binding upon the UCR.[43]

[40] 'Report of the Secretary-General on his Mission of Good Offices in Cyprus', UN Doc. S/2004/437, para. 60.

[41] The Cypriot Ministry of Foreign Affairs claimed that under the 2004 version of the Plan, 111,000 Turkish settlers are either entitled to UCR citizenship or to residence. The UK House of Commons concludes that thousands of the Turkish settlers would have to leave the territory: HC 2nd report 2005. The UK Foreign Affairs Committee pointed out that about 42,000 Turkish settlers who are not married to Turkish Cypriots would have to leave: HC 5th report 2007.

[42] 213 UNTS 222.

[43] Annan Plan (see note 8), Foundation Agreement, Annex V, Item 204 in the multilateral treaty list binding upon the UCR.

The right to private life

ECHR Article 8 stipulates:

1   Everyone has the right to respect for his private and family life, his home and his correspondence.

2   There shall be no interference by a public authority with the exercise of this right except such as is in accordance with the law and is necessary in a democratic society in the interests of national security, public safety or the economic well-being of the country, for the prevention of disorder or crime, for the protection of health or morals, or for the protection of the rights and freedoms of others.

Under ECHR jurisprudence, the totality of social ties between individuals and the community in which they are living constitutes part of the concept of 'private life' within the meaning of Article 8.[44] The right to private life protects 'the right to establish and develop relationships with other human beings and the outside world' and 'can sometimes embrace aspects of an individual's social identity'.[45] The expulsion of an integrated immigrant therefore constitutes an interference with his or her right to respect for private life. The criteria for assessing a person's integration within the state were developed mostly with respect to expulsion of criminal convicts, but are applicable *mutatis mutandis* to expulsion on other grounds, including settlement under an illegal regime. The extent of integration is measured through the solidity of social, cultural, and family ties with the state of residence and with the state of destination (usually the state of nationality).[46] These depend on the length of the person's stay in the country from which he or she is to be expelled; the nationalities of

[44] *Üner v. The Netherlands* (GC), Application No. 46410/99, Judgment of 18 October 2006, para. 59.

[45] Both quotes from *Pretty v. The United Kingdom*, Application No. 2346/02, ECHR 2002–III, para. 61: cf. ACHR Art. 11(2). According to the jurisprudence of the Inter-American Commission on Human Rights, private life: 'The requirements of Art. 11 encompass a range of factors pertaining to the dignity of the individual, including, for example, the ability to pursue the development of one's personality and aspirations, determine one's identity, and define one's personal relationships.' Report No. 4/01, Case 11.625, María Eugenia Morales de Sierra, Guatemala (19 January 2001), para. 46.

[46] *Üner v. Netherlands* (see note 44), para. 58. The ECtHR uses (para. 59) the term 'settled' in the sense of 'integrated', which is more common with Council of Europe documents and ECtHR judgments.

other persons affected; the person's family situation; and the seriousness of the difficulties which family members are likely to encounter in the country of origin of the expellee. The European Court of Human Rights (ECtHR) has emphasized that the longer a person has been residing in a particular state, the stronger his or her ties with that country will be, and the weaker the ties with the state of nationality. Therefore the Court has regard to the special situation of foreigners who have spent most, if not all, their childhood in the state of residence, who were brought up there and received their education there.[47] When the illegal regime lasts over two decades, as has happened in Northern Cyprus, there are likely to be many members of the settler community who consider the territory their home both geographically and socially, having lived there a large part of their life or even all of it. They may never have been to their state of origin (possibly their state of nationality but not necessarily).

However, the fact that an act of expulsion interferes with a person's family or private life does not mean that it is impermissible. ECHR Article 8 provides an exhaustive list of grounds that would justify interference with one's private life: 'national security, public safety or economic well-being of the country, for the prevention of disorder or crime, for the protection of health or morals, or for the protection of rights and freedoms of others'.[48] Expulsion would be justified if it is a proportionate response to one of these interests. The government of Cyprus objects to the presence of the Turkish settlers for a variety of reasons. The following sections examine these objections in light of the limitation clause of Article 8.

---

[47] In *Cyprus v. Turkey*, Application No. 8007/77 decided by the European Commission on Human Rights, Judge Schermers in a separate opinion on rights in residential property in the TRNC wrote: 'As Article 8 guarantees the right to respect for his home to everyone, the rights of the new occupant should be taken into account, even if the occupation was originally established on an invalid title. After a long period of time restoration of the *status quo ante* will become a violation of Article 8 with respect to the new occupant. It is difficult to establish how long this period is to be, because in fact it is a gradual process. . . . children will be born in the house who have no other place which they could consider as their home . . . I cannot accept as the only possible remedy that Turkey should be obliged to break up the homes of all present occupants in order to allow the original occupants to return.' This reasoning is all the more applicable to issues of personal status, where validation of the settler's status given his or her association with the territory does not come at the expense of an identifiable dispossessed other.

[48] The American Convention on Human Rights, Art. 30 allows a wider scope of restriction, requiring that restrictions be placed only in accordance with law, for reasons of general interest and in accordance with the purpose for which such restrictions have been established.

Permissible limitations on the right to private life

Law and order: illegality of the settlers' presence

Since the transfer of settlers is prohibited both under international law and under the domestic law of the ousted regime, the expulsion of settlers may formally fall within the category of 'prevention of disorder and crime' for the purpose of the ECHR, which includes enforcement of immigration law. This ground invokes the right of a state to control the entry and residence of non-nationals within its territory through immigration legislation.[49] This raises the question as to the 'order' that the post-conflict regime wishes to maintain.

The ECtHR clearly had domestic law in mind when it confirmed that the prevention of disorder entitles the state to take dissuasive measures such as expulsion against persons who have broken the domestic law on immigration. On the one hand, persons who voluntarily settle in territory which is under dispute bear the risk that in due course it will transpire that their settlement was illegal. On the other hand, the expulsion of persons who had not exercised any choice in relocating to the territory carries little weight in the way of ensuring domestic order and preventing crime.[50] Dissuasive measures such as expulsion are valuable against people who act in bad faith with knowledge of the domestic law they are violating. This is not clearly the case of settlers. Not only does their knowledge of the actual situation differ from one individual to another, but the legal status of the territory was sufficiently indeterminate that it would be excessive to hold them in full knowledge of the implications of their conduct. Indeed, it is questionable whether the domestic law of the pre-conflict, ousted regime, which was purportedly violated, was even applicable at the time that the settlers arrived.

Yet the weighty violation of law through the transfer of settlers is not that of domestic law but of international law. The 'order' which their expulsion may maintain is the international one. The link between the individual and the disruption of international order is so distant that it seems inappropriate to rely on it under the 'prevention of disorder and crime' ground. Furthermore, the responsibility for disruption of order does not attach to the settlers themselves but to the illegal regime. In

---

[49] *Shevanova v. Latvia*, Application No. 58822/00, Judgment of 15 June 2006, para. 74; *Kaftailova v. Lithuania*, Application No. 59643/00, Judgment of 22 June 2006, para. 66.
[50] The weight of the person's bad faith is evident when comparing *Shevanova v. Latvia* and *Kaftailova v. Lithuania* (see note 49).

addition to the issues of faith and knowledge of the law, it can be queried whether individuals should be held responsible, even under administrative measures, for the illegal regime's action.

To conclude, technically it may be possible to justify the expulsion of settlers on the basis of their illegal presence. However, because of its weakness this ground is likely to be outbalanced by the hardship it causes when the proportionality test is applied to individual cases. International jurisprudence indicates that even where individuals knowingly and consciously violate immigration law, law enforcement may give way to individual circumstances.[51] Such an outcome is all the more expected when individual conduct is in good faith.

National security: fifth column

A state may legitimately regard the presence of foreign military forces on its territory as a national security threat.[52] Many Turkish settlers—the majority, according to Greek Cypriots (Palley 2005)—are military reservists, who have immigrated after completing compulsory military service.[53] Greek Cypriots are concerned that even if the UCR is demilitarized, Turkey would have a ready army waiting, merely requiring air drops of equipment and some target practice.[54] The question is, however, how far beyond active military personnel this ground for expulsion can expand without constituting excessive interference with private life. Ordinarily, previous military training does not justify a presumption of danger emanating from a person, and demanding the departure of all settlers appears in excess of the requirement of a pressing social need and the test of proportionality.[55]

National security: the settler minority would serve as an excuse for political intervention by Turkey

The link between the settlers and their state of origin raises another problem, particularly when that link is formalized through international

---

[51] *Shevanova v. Latvia* (see note 49), *Winata v. Australia*, Communication No. 930/2000, views of 26 July 2001, CCPR/C/72/D/930/2000.

[52] *Slivenko v. Latvia*, Application No. 48321/99, Judgment of 9 October 2003; Letter of the HCNM to the Minister of Foreign Affairs of Estonia, No. 206/93/L (6 April 1993); CSCE Secretariat, CSCE Communication No. 124 (23 April 1993); Letter of the HCNM to the Minister of Foreign Affairs of Latvia, No. 238/93/L (6 April 1993).

[53] Professional Turkish military personnel had for the most part left the TRNC in the 1980s.

[54] Observations made by the Ministry of Foreign Affairs of Cyprus, annexed to ECRI 2005.

[55] Compare *Slivenko v. Latvia* (see note 52).

instruments as is the link between Turkey and the Turkish-Cypriot community.[56] This is the concern that the presence of the settler community in its territory would serve as an excuse for the withdrawn, illegal regime to intervene in the post-transition regime. Such intervention may go so far as to involve military force. In fact, this was the scenario that led to the Turkish military intervention in Cyprus in 1974. Yet the danger perceived by post-transition regimes is much wider and more subtle. Non-military pressure can be even more pervasive than a military one, because it is less overt and there are fewer constraints on resorting to it.

This apprehension exceeds the sociological or internal political impact of a large population perceived as foreign. For example, the presence of the Turkish settlers is regarded as a means by which Turkey will have direct influence over the whole of the UCR. The 1992 Cuco Report noted that most of the settlers were transferred to Cyprus as the result of a decision of the Turkish authorities: they feel indebted to Turkey for the resulting improvement in their standard of life. For this reason they are particularly sensitive to signals from the Turkish authorities, especially at election time. The elite of the settlers are also said to be highly susceptible to Turkish influence (Cuco 1992). This concern was reinforced by Turkey's characterization of the settlers as 'security' for Turkey, giving rise to the fear that in case of intercommunal clashes, Turkey would jump at the opportunity to intervene in the UCR (Palley 2005).

As real as the danger may be that Turkey would use the presence of its kin population as a pretext to intervene in the island, it is paradoxically weak as a justification for the expulsion of the Turkish settlers. Even if all mainland Turks leave the island, there is still a substantial population—indigenous Turkish Cypriots—that Turkey regards as its kin and claims to protect. Moreover, Turkey's interests in Cyprus have been acknowledged and accepted as legitimate with limits, both historically and under the Annan Plan. Expulsion of the settlers will not eliminate these interests. In fact, Greek Cypriots objected to the Annan Plan's perpetuation of Turkish involvement and influence. In their view, Turkish influence should have been limited, *inter alia* by removal of the settlers, rather than expanded as it was by the inclusion of the security and constitutional order of the constituent states under the amended Treaty of Guarantee.[57]

---

[56] Annan Plan (see note 8), Part C, Treaty on Matters Related to the New State of Affairs in Cyprus, Annex III: Additional Protocol to the Treaty of Guarantee.
[57] Ibid., Article 2.

The settler community would undermine the national character of the UCR

Turkish settlers are regarded as culturally different from Turkish Cypriots; it is feared that they will change the character of Cyprus, and turn the northern part in effect into another province of Turkey (Doob 1986; Loucaides 1995; Palley 2005). This concern is heightened by the fact that Turkish settlers are already a majority on the electoral rolls of the TRNC, which under the Annan Plan is the future Turkish-Cypriot constituent state of the UCR. They would therefore control its government and consequently share in the federal system, as representatives of the Turkish Constituent State.[58]

Rights of others: property

The presence of settlers may have immediate repercussions for the local population. One particular problem is that of immovable property. One of the main grounds for the rejection of the Annan Plan by Greek Cypriots was the concern that if mainland Turks remain, Greek Cypriots whose property the settlers occupy would never be able to recover their property (Palley 2005). Turkish settlers were given, under a variety of legislative and other arrangements, rights in property previously owned by Greek Cypriots. The Annan Plan regulates these property issues. Formally this regulation is unrelated to the residence issue; in practice the two issues are related. While removal of settlers would not necessarily deprive them of rights to property, clearly their remaining in the territory exacerbates potential conflicts between original owners and current occupants. Thus, the presence of Turkish settlers is perceived as rendering remote the prospect of reinstatement of Greek Cypriots in their home and properties.

ASSESSMENT

In order to obtain some perspective on the international approach towards the demand for expulsion of Turkish settlers, it is useful to compare the Annan Plan with another case of transition from illegal regime, namely that of the Baltic states. In the early 1990s, when the Soviet Union disintegrated, the Baltic states of Estonia, Lithuania, and Latvia became independent after fifty years of occupation. Difficult questions arose then with respect to Soviet-era settlers who were not of Baltic origin,

---

[58] Observations made by the Ministry of Foreign Affairs of Cyprus, annexed to ECRI 2005.

but were brought in by the Soviets (Ziemele 2005; Mälksoo 2003). Expulsion of the settlers was soon taken off the agenda. It was made clear that settlers would remain in the territory and eventually become nationals. The pressure exerted on the post-transition regimes concerned the regulation of nationality, not of residence. With respect to Cyprus, the internationally sponsored agreement provided for large-scale removal of settlers, even if not large enough for the liking of Greek Cypriots. The legal principles underlying the two cases are similar, yet the practical outcomes differ greatly.

It could be argued that the difference is not legal but political. In 1991 the international community, represented primarily by western European states, was loath to upset Russia, which still maintained significant political and military power. In addition, in the euphoria of the demise of Soviet rule, it may have seemed unjustifiable to castigate individuals for the misdeeds of a dead empire. Therefore, it was deemed acceptable that Russophone settlers would remain in place. In contrast, with respect to the Cyprus conflict, the international community, again represented primarily by western European states, more readily aligns with the prospective post-conflict regime. The Republic of Cyprus is already a member of the EU. It is also probable that Turkey's Islamism attracts less sympathy in western Europe.

Another, less cynical, explanation for the difference is that although the Baltic states claimed they were reverting to independence rather than becoming independent for the first time, there was little expectation that the clock would be turned back fifty years. To start with, during the fifty-year annexation of the Baltic states, reversion to independence was not seriously envisaged, except perhaps in the late 1980s. The international community had been more or less resigned to the annexation. In contrast, the unlawfulness of the TRNC has been dealt with by legal means from the first moment. Such a position was upheld by the ECtHR, an international judicial institution, the decisions of which are binding on all parties to the conflict.[59] Under these circumstances, pursuing the logical conclusions does not appear in conflict with reasonable expectations.

Beyond the general political and legal policies, the two situations also differ in the application of law to the specific circumstances. The formula

---

[59] *Loizidou v. Turkey (Merits)*, Judgment of 18 December 1996, Reports of Judgments & Decisions 1996–VI 2216; *Cyprus v. Turkey (The Fourth Interstate Case)*, Judgment of 10 May 2001, Reports of Judgments & Decisions 2001–IV 1.

is identical: the post-conflict regime may expel settlers unless this violates their human rights, most likely the right to private or family life, and unless such expulsion is discriminatory. But the balancing of these elements works differently in each case.

One difference may be the extent to which an alternative arrangement, one that is less injurious to the right to private life, is available. Maintaining the identity of the local population does not necessarily require that the settler population be expelled. Theoretically, protection of the national identity against 'dilution' may be achieved through less severe measures. In Estonia and Latvia, for example, the strategy first attempted was denial of nationality combined with permission to remain. However, it was vehemently opposed by the European institutions, which exerted heavy pressure on both states to enable the settler minority to naturalize, as well as to minimize the differences between nationals and permanent residents with regard to political and other rights. The alternative proposed by the European community was that of integration. The High Commissioner for National Minorities (HCNM) advocated a strategy that diffuses the danger. He encouraged Estonia and Latvia to provide the Russophone population with a genuine opportunity to integrate within the state, formally by acquiring citizenship and substantively through cultural and educational means, so as to enhance the chances that the Russophone minority would embrace Estonian or Latvian identity rather than act to modify it or prevent its consolidation.[60] Programmes have subsequently been undertaken to adapt non-titular citizens into the pre-set titular-dominant state and society (Pettai and Hallik 2002).

The strategy proposed by the HCNM, if it is successful, reduces the threat emanating from the presence of a specific minority community to the national identity by disintegrating the minority's threatening collective character. The HCNM's strategy confronts the threat by a less intrusive measure than expulsion, indeed by one that does not necessarily interfere with any right. As such, it is clearly an alternative which makes expulsion or exclusion from citizenship an excessive and therefore prohibited measure. Integration might also be the answer to the fear of a

---

[60] Letter of the HCNM to the Minister of Foreign Affairs of Latvia, No. 238/93/L (6 April 1993); CSCE Secretariat, CSCE Communication No. 124 (23 April 1993); Letter of the HCNM to the Minister of Foreign Affairs of Estonia, No. 206/93/L (6 April 1993); see also Recommendations by the CSCE High Commissioner on National Minorities about the Latvian Draft Citizenship Law, CSCE Communication No. 8 (Vienna, 31 January 1994), www.osce.org/documents/html/pdftohtml/2729_en.pdf.html p. 3.

'fifth column'. By distancing the settlers from their state of origin, both formally (through acquisition of the post-transition regime's nationality) and substantively (through personal identification with the post-transition regime), integration weakens the capacity of the state of origin, namely the withdrawn illegal regime, to intervene.

However, while theoretically useful, the viability of this strategy in Cyprus can be questioned on a number of grounds. First, alongside the right of the post-conflict regime to protect its identity there is the right of the minority to preserve its character. In other words, while the post-transition regime may encourage the integration of the settler community in the state's national society, it may not demand that the settler community abandon its own identity. Yet it is precisely that identity, with its particular history and weight, which threatens the identity of the state. The tension between creating a nation state while maintaining distinct communities, hardly unique to post-transition regimes, was voiced in Latvian and Estonian politics during the debates on regulating citizenship and residence (Spruds 2001).

Second, integration goes only a limited way towards breaking the attachment of the minority to its state of origin. This is particularly pertinent when the state of origin maintains a formal role with respect to the post-conflict regime. For example, the ethnic link between Turkey and Turkish Cypriots was recognized when Cyprus became independent and was given concrete expression in the 1960 treaties of Guarantee, Establishment and Alliance. The Annan Plan retains the Treaties through Additional Protocols that apply them *mutatis mutandis* to the new state of affairs in Cyprus.[61] It may be overly ambitious to expect a settler population to integrate in the post-conflict regime's society while sanctioning a formal role for the state of origin with regard to the post-conflict regime.

A third element that affects the balancing of rights so that the formal solution adopted by the Baltic states differs from that contemplated for Cyprus is the requirement of proportionality, namely that the detriment caused to the individual must not be disproportionate to the benefit envisaged from the measure restricting his or her rights. The perceived threat presented by mainland Turks to the character of Cyprus may

---

[61] Annexes II, III, and IV to the Annan Plan (see note 8), Part C: Treaty on Matters related to the New State of Affairs in Cyprus. See also the 'special relations and strong ties' between Turkey and Turkish Cypriots are also recognized in the Draft Act of Adaptation of the Terms of Accession of the United Cyprus Republic to the European Union, para. 14.

appear greater than that presented by Russophones in the Baltic states, since mainland Turks already comprise, according to estimates, the majority of the population in the TRNC. The perceived military threat might also be greater than that which was perceived with respect to Russia. Turkey's military involvement in Cyprus was much more recent than the Soviet Union's in Estonia. Importantly, the claims of the two illegal regimes are not on a par. The Russian Federation has renounced any claims over the Baltic states, not only in practice but even formally, by declaring the Molotov–Ribbentrop Pact null and void.[62] In contrast, Turkey remains a guarantor of Cyprus's security. This makes prospects of integration more remote.

Fourth, differences exist also with regard to the hardship which expulsion is likely to cause to mainland Turks compared with Russophone settlers. The mainland Turkish community was only thirty years old (or twenty, counting from 1983) when the Annan Plan was formulated, while the Russophone population in the Baltic states goes back fifty years. There is an entire generation's difference between the two; there are therefore likely to be many third-generation settlers in the Baltic states, but few in the TRNC. The hardship in relocating to the state of origin becomes greater with the passage of time. Third-generation immigrants are generally less familiar with the culture of the state of origin than second-generation ones, and their integration there is likely to be more difficult. Needless to say, in neither case was language an obstacle to integration in the state of origin.

A fifth pertinent difference is the fact that following the breakdown of the Soviet Union, many Russophone settlers found themselves stateless.[63] They may be protected from expulsion either under the Convention relating to the Status of Stateless Persons[64] or under ICCPR Article 12(4). Moreover, had it been decided to expel them, it would have been technically difficult. Statelessness is less of a problem in the case of Turkish settlers.

Sixth, the proportionality of expulsion is measured, *inter alia*, against the behaviour of the individual. A person acting in good faith is entitled

---

[62] Congress of People's Deputies Resolution on a Political and Legal Appraisal of the Soviet–German Non-Aggression Treaty of 1939 (1989).
[63] In 2005, 11 per cent of the residents of Estonia were stateless. Over half of them had been born in Estonia: 'European Commission against Racism and Intolerance', Third Report on Estonia (adopted 24 June 2005, published 21 February 2006).
[64] Adopted on 28 September 1954, entered into force 6 June 1960, Art. 30(1).

to greater consideration than one who has deliberately acted in bad faith.[65] Mainland Turks were never formally forced to relocate to the TRNC. In contrast, Russophones had little choice when they were relocated to the Baltic states. On this ground, too, they and their descendants might have won more sympathy.

Finally, the period of time that has passed since the wrongful act (settlement) may play a role, analogous to the length of time from the commitment of an offence in the case of expulsion on grounds of criminal activity.[66]

In short, the circumstances of the Russophone community and the mainland Turkish community differ in that expulsion was deemed a disproportionate—and therefore unlawful—measure with respect to Russophones in the Baltic states, while not a disproportionate measure with respect to mainland Turks in the TRNC. It is interesting to compare the regulation of nationality and residence with that of property. With respect to the latter, the Annan Plan included a letter from the leaders of Cyprus to the Secretary-General of the Council of Europe, requesting that the ECtHR strike out any proceedings currently before it concerning affected property in Cyprus, in order to allow the domestic mechanism established to solve these cases to proceed.[67] This indicates the understanding of the drafters of the Plan that the provisions on property were not compatible with ECtHR jurisprudence. There is no similar letter with respect to nationality and residence. This suggests that indeed they regarded the provisions as compatible with the obligations of the prospective UCR under the ECHR.[68] The overall picture, then, is that on a comparative basis, in the case of Cyprus, the grounds for expulsion outweigh the right of the settlers to private life.

---

[65] Compare *Shevanova v. Latvia* (see note 49), para. 75 and *Shevanova v. Latvia*, Application No. 58822/00, Judgment of 7 December 2007, para. 49, as well as *Sisojeva and Others v. Latvia*, Application No. 60654/00, Judgment of 16 June 2005, para. 95, with *Kaftailova v. Lithuania* (see note 49), para. 68.

[66] Compare *Boultif v. Switzerland*, No. 54273/00, ECHR 2001–IX.

[67] Foundation Agreement, Annex IX, Attachment 3: Letter to the Secretary-General of the Council of Europe.

[68] The Plan would have been endorsed by the Security Council as Part E: Matters to be Submitted to the United Nations Security Council for Decision. Such endorsement might have precluded any further review by the ECtHR. Compare *Behrami and Behrami v. France*, Application No. 71412/01, and *Saramati v. France, Germany and Norway*, Application No. 78166/01, Grand Chamber Decision (Admissibility) of 2 May 2007. The scope of judicial review of the Plan requires further study, and is outside the scope of the present enquiry.

CONCLUSION

In a post-conflict situation where the settler population is perceived as a threat to the native population there are calls for its repatriation. Even when the calls reflect justifiable concerns, repatriation may be limited by the right of the settlers to remain in their home and social environment.

The difficulty is to balance between these two opposite pulls. In the case of Turkish settlers in Northern Cyprus, national and security concerns have had, at least formally, the upper hand. The resolution of the conflict may result in the repatriation of individuals to a home in which they have never set foot before.

REFERENCES

Anastasakis, O., Bertrand, G., and Nicolaïdis, K. (2004), 'Getting to Yes: Suggestions for Embellishment of the Annan Plan for Cyprus', South East European Studies Programme (SEESP), European Studies Centre, St Anthony's College, University of Oxford.

Crawford, J. (1998), 'State Practice and International Law in Relation to Succession', British Yearbook of International Law, 69: 85–117.

Cuco A. (1992), 'Report of the Committee on Migration, Refugees and Demography', PACE Doc. 6589.

Dodd, C. H. (1998), The Cyprus Imbroglio (Huntingdon, Eothen).

Doob, L. W. (1986), 'Cypriot Patriotism and Nationalism', Journal of Conflict Resolution, 30, 2: 282–96.

Dugard, J. (1987), Recognition and the United Nations (Cambridge, Grotius).

Hatay, M. (2005), Beyond Numbers: An Inquiry into the Political Integration of the Turkish 'Settlers' in Northern Cyprus (Nicosia, PRIO).

—— (2007), Is the Turkish Cypriot Population Shrinking? (Nicosia, PRIO).

Laakso, J. (2003), 'Colonisation by Turkish Settlers of the Occupied Part of Cyprus', Report of the Committee on Migration, Refugees and Demography, PACE Doc. 9799.

Loucaides, L. G. (1995), Essays on the Developing Law of Human Rights (Leiden, Martinus Nijhoff).

Mälksoo, L. (2003), Illegal Annexation and State Continuity: The Case of the Incorporation of the Baltic States by the USSR (Leiden, Martinus Nijhoff).

Necatigil, Z. M. (1993), The Cyprus Question and the Turkish Position in International Law, 2nd edn (Oxford, Oxford University Press).

Nedjatigil, Z. M. (1982), The Cyprus Conflict: A Lawyer's View, 2nd edn (Lefkoşa, A–Z Publications).

Palley, C. (2005), An International Relations Debacle: The UN Secretary-General's Mission of Good Offices in Cyprus 1999–2004 (Oxford, Hart).

Pettai, V. and Hallik, K. (2002), 'Understanding Processes of Ethnic Control: Segmentation, Dependency and Co-optation in Post-communist Estonia', *Nations and Nationalism*, 8: 505–29.

Richmond O. P. (1998), *Mediating in Cyprus, the Cypriot Communities and the United Nations* (London, Frank Cass).

Spruds, A. (2001), 'Minority Issues in the Baltic States in the Context of the NATO Enlargement', NATO Individual Research Fellowship Final Report.

Tiryakioğlu, B. (2006), 'Multiple Citizenship and Its Consequences in Turkish Law', *Ankara Law Review*, 3, 1: 1–16.

Ziemele, I. (2005), *State Continuity and Nationality: The Baltic States and Russia* (Leiden, Brill).

Part II
Repatriation

5.
From *Mohajer* to *Hamwatan*: The Reintegration Experiences of Second-generation Afghans Returning from Pakistan and Iran
Mamiko Saito and Paula Kantor

INTRODUCTION

In contrast to more dominant psychiatric approaches to studying refugee youth in terms of trauma and post-traumatic stress disorder, some recent studies have begun to adopt more of an anthropological perspective towards the impact of prolonged displacement among young refugees, especially in terms of their perception of self, homeland, and future outlook (Chatty et al. 2005; Chatty 2007; Boyden and De Berry 2004). Nonetheless, limited literature exists on the reintegration paths of young refugees returning to their homeland after prolonged forced migration; this applies not only to initial settlement after arrival in the native country but also to the subsequent complex reintegration process and the transformation that occurs in the mid to long term (Cornish et al. 1999).

Questions of homeland for young refugees, many of whom have little or no actual experience of living in this at times idealized place, play a pivotal role in decisions to return and in reintegration experiences. Returning to one's homeland involves significant amounts of psychological stress and does not necessarily represent a return in the conventional sense because many returnees also have a profound attachment to the host country in which they grew up—the place they know the best (Ghanem 2003). However, such issues are often limited to debate within the context of academia, and are neither widely recognized nor prioritized by actors in the process of making and implementing policy to manage and protect forced migrant populations.

This essay is based on the findings of a research project by the Afghanistan Research and Evaluation Unit (AREU) entitled 'Second-generation Afghans in Neighbouring Countries' (Saito and Hunte 2007; Saito 2007; Abbasi-Shavazi et al. 2008; Saito 2009). Initiated in 2006, the project was administered through the United Nations High Commissioner for Refugees (UNHCR) and funded by the European Commission. The primary aim of this study was to promote grounded policy and programme development among the governments of Afghanistan, Pakistan, and Iran along with donors, international organizations, and concerned stakeholders through the generation of a knowledge base for policy making. It sought to delve beneath the surface of Yes/No responses to questions about return and reintegration to illuminate the profound difficulties that Afghan youths and young adults face when deciding about their futures.

The essay aims to address gaps in the understanding of the less visible social and emotional trajectories experienced by young Afghan refugees in the process of return to and reintegration in their 'homeland' and the crucial need for *balance* between these issues and material assistance. The study examines the personal journeys resulting from the respondents' experiences in Pakistan and Iran, their return to Afghanistan, their resettlement, and, for some, onward remigration. It interviewed 199 purposively selected Afghan refugee and returnee respondents in two prominent host countries for Afghan refugees and in Afghanistan. In doing so, the study highlights the meaning of and expectations regarding homeland from the comparative perspectives of both young Afghan refugees and returnees.

The following section gives an overview of the rationale and uniqueness of this research project, followed by a brief description of the approach to selecting the target group. The next section discusses the contradictory characteristics of young Afghans who grew up as refugees among Pakistanis and Iranians, and looks at their perceptions and expectations in regard to Afghanistan. Then, descriptions of barriers to successful reintegration faced by these young people upon return to Afghanistan are provided, and their renegotiation of the meaning of homeland compared to their previous expectations is outlined based on comparative data analysis. The final section concludes the discussion and highlights some key issues to address beyond material assistance to support young Afghans on a journey 'home'.

BACKGROUND TO THE STUDY

After decades of protracted conflict beginning in the late 1970s, Afghanistan was the world's largest source of refugees from a single country under UNHCR's mandate at the end of 2007. While the country's population was dispersed among seventy-two different countries, 96 per cent of displaced Afghans resided in Pakistan and Iran (UNHCR 2008a). See Figure 5.1. The majority of those who remain in these neighbouring countries have lived in exile for more than twenty years; it is estimated that half of all displaced Afghans in Pakistan and Iran were born outside Afghanistan in a second or even a third generation of displacement (UNHCR 2007).

In order to formulate and implement a comprehensive policy solution for the protracted Afghan refugee situation within the context of UNHCR's efforts, AREU undertook research on transnational networks in 2004–5. It stimulated debate to look into the multidimensional Afghan migratory strategy in terms of livelihoods beyond UNHCR's refugee perspectives, thereby addressing the need to better manage continuous cross-border population movements, which should benefit both the migrants and the sending and receiving countries (Monsutti 2006).

This earlier research highlighted a gap in information on the experiences and intentions of the significant numbers of Afghan youths and young adults living in Pakistan and Iran, many of whom were neither born nor grew up in Afghanistan. In 2008 approximately 2.8 million Afghan refugees were living in these two neighbouring countries (UNHCR 2008b). Data from a 2007 report reveal that around 74 per cent of Afghan refugees in Pakistan were under 28 years old (Government of Pakistan and UNHCR 2007); while data from a 2005 report show that 71 per cent living in Iran were aged 29 or younger (Abbasi-Shavazi et al. 2008). In both countries, this sizeable group of young Afghans has grown up in an environment that differs significantly from that of both their parents and their own generation who remained in Afghanistan during the period of conflict. They have had significantly greater access to urban facilities than those who stayed, as well as different opportunities and experiences as refugees living among Pakistanis and Iranians.

Understanding this group's key characteristics and ties to Pakistan, Iran, and Afghanistan in relation to homeland and return holds critical importance for policy making, in that such understanding can be used to potentially shift the fluctuating factors informing their decisions to return voluntarily. Similarly, comprehensive recognition that refugees' past

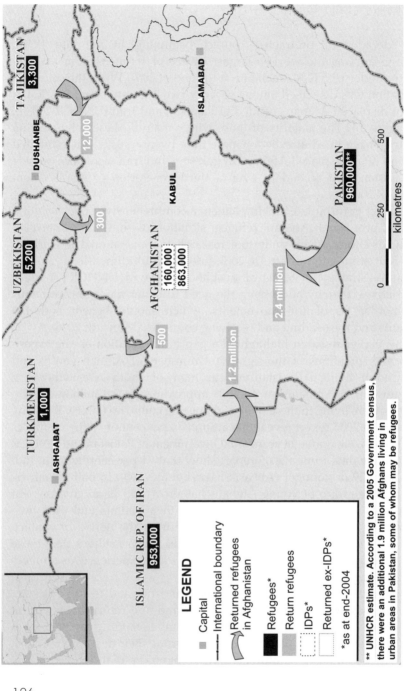

Figure 5.1. Flow of Afghan returnees, 2002–4.

Source: www.unhcr.org/publ/PUBL/3ae6baf34.pdf (reproduced with permission of UNHCR).

experiences directly affect their present situation is essential to the full exploration of their ideas and experiences related to repatriation and their future prospects for long-term settlement in Afghanistan.

The study's strength lies in its use of narrative interviews which allow detailed analysis of the lives and identity formation processes of Afghan youths growing up as second-generation Afghans in Pakistan and Iran, how these experiences influence ideas regarding homeland and return, and how they affect actual experiences of return. During the in-depth interviews, individual respondents often made contradictory statements illustrating ambivalent feelings towards Afghanistan and the places where they grew up, and the struggles of both males and females in deciding where they belong. The collected data reflect particular aspects of these respondents' lives, specifically at the time of interview. However, their perceptions and thoughts are always subject to change due to their position at the intersection of a broad range of political, economic, and socio-cultural factors.

Another aspect of this study is its inclusion of voices from less visible members of the population who reside far from places that are accessible to outsiders, such as rural residents and less mobile females. Special focus was placed on incorporating Afghans with diverse backgrounds. The experiences of the study's diverse respondents clearly show that the situation for Afghans who sought refuge in Pakistan and Iran cannot be over generalized, as the details differed markedly depending on the place of residence, changes experienced over time, and the personal situation of the refugees themselves. Afghan youths and young adults who grew up in neighbouring countries do not form a single homogeneous group; rather, they are individually distinct in terms of the languages they speak, their degree of religiosity, family attitudes, location of origin, level of education, and many other factors. Therefore, decision-making processes about return and experiences of return and reintegration for those deciding or pushed to do so also differ markedly. This makes policy making to support the return and reintegration of young Afghans challenging.

METHODOLOGY

Fieldwork for this qualitative study was conducted in three countries over different periods during a twelve-month period starting in April 2006. The research period included hiring and training Afghan male and female interviewers, conducting meetings with local government institutions and related organizations, identifying respondents and gaining their informed consent, as well as conducting the intensive interviews with respondents and transcribing the data collected. Table 5.1 illustrates the distribution of respondents across study sites.

The main criteria for selecting second-generation Afghan refugee and returnee respondents (both male and female) were as follows:

- candidates were 15–30 years old and had spent more than half of their lives in Pakistan or Iran;
- (for returnees only) they had returned to Afghanistan after the Afghan Interim Authority was established in late 2001, and had lived in Afghanistan for at least six months.

It was crucial to include respondents with various demographic characteristics to ensure that a broad range of opportunities, experiences, and future perceptions would be reflected in this qualitative study. The following key issues were taken into account in the quota sampling process, based on the assumption that these variables would have been likely to affect the personal experiences and return intentions or experiences of young Afghans:

- marital status;
- education level and occupation (of the respondent);
- economic status (of the household);[1]
- ethnicity; and
- location of refuge and/or return (Pakistan/Iran, urban/rural/ camp, main local language spoken in the area).

In addition, more detailed criteria were used where possible to further diversify the sample, including degree of religiosity; positive/negative attitude to Pakistanis/Iranians; and mobility of women (for example, women working outside the home versus those not even allowed to visit relatives). The inclusion of a female-headed household (one where the key income was earned by females) was also set as a selection criterion for each research site. With this range of considerations in place, identifying 'the ideal respondent' was not a simple task.

---

[1] During the initial identification of respondents, their relative economic status (low, middle, upper) was estimated through observation where possible (dress, belongings, housing) and informal conversation about their families. This information was later used during data analysis to further categorize respondents.

Table 5.1. Second-generation Afghan refugee and returnee respondents.

Country	Research site	Female		Male		TOTAL
		Single	Married	Single	Married	
Pakistan 71	Peshawar	10	10	8	10	38
	Quetta	4	3	3	4	14
	Karachi	7	3	5	4	19
Iran 80	Tehran	9	7	9	7	32
	Mashhad	9	7	7	9	32
	Isfahan	4	4	6	2	16
Afghanistan 48	Kabul	4	4	4	4	16
	Herat	3	5	4	4	16
	Baghlan	5	3	4	4	16
TOTAL		55	46	50	48	199
		101		98		

During the fieldwork in Pakistan and Iran, significant fear and suspicion were directed towards the research team because of the refugees' ambiguous legal status. This presented a major obstacle in gaining access to potential respondents, a not uncommon problem in this type of research (Malkki 1992; Kibreab 1999). Some were reluctant to talk, as they believed that revealing their refugee status could lead to their being reported to the police, sent to jail, or deported. This was often the case among both low-income groups (such as garbage collectors) and the wealthier (such as business people). During the fieldwork in Afghanistan, perceptions of outsiders—those working for overseas organizations or NGOs—as people who bring material assistance became a challenge in persuading people to take part in interviews without offering immediate visible benefits; this was particularly true among the urban poor, who tend to work on a hand-to-mouth basis. The research teams made efforts to develop a rapport with local residents when exploring potential respondents prior to the formal interviews.

UNDERSTANDING YOUNG AFGHAN REFUGEES

Complex identities

In the anthropological definition of identity, there are two levels of classification. One refers to the uniqueness of individuals, which differentiates them from others. The other is associated with the sense of sameness, 'in that persons associate themselves, or be associated by others, with groups or categories on the basis of some salient common feature' (Byron 2002). The latter social-level identity, which is closely correlated with the development of individual characteristics, emphasizes links with individuals and individual social and cultural environments. In this research project, focus was placed on self-consciousness as a collective sense of how second-generation Afghans positioned themselves in relation to those around them as they grew up in foreign countries among Pakistanis/ Iranians.

The fluid nature of identity is influenced to a great degree by one's different environments. This is particularly relevant in the context of refugees and migrants as minority groups in society: the 'other' is not only a member of one's own family, kin, or ethnic group, but also a 'national other'. Relating or associating oneself to a particular group or groups becomes crucial for a sense of belonging in the presence of 'others' who are markedly different. In particular, young refugees often possess contradictory, multiple, and conflicting identities, as seen in the common experiences among young Palestinian, Afghan, and Sahrawi refugees drawn from a recent comparative study (Chatty 2007).

Attitudes towards homeland and return

Making decisions about whether or not to return was not easy, especially for the young Afghans who often experienced internal tension over their identities in relation to Afghanistan, a 'homeland' that they knew less about compared to Pakistan or Iran, where they grew up. The balance of these feelings was fragile and constantly in flux because of their experiences as refugees during childhood and adolescence, key periods of identity formation (Mooney 2000). Based on multiple sources of information, many respondents had developed conflicting perceptions of Afghanistan, holding both positive thoughts and negative concerns about life there. The meaning that individuals gave to Afghanistan constantly shifted, informed by life experiences including personal interactions with various Afghans and host populations, along with broader regional political and social dynamics. The delicate, evolving balance of interconnected, and often contradictory, facets of their identity influenced their frequently changing views of homeland and host society.

Data from refugee respondents living in Pakistan and Iran showed that many viewed their lives in exile as non-permanent and accepted the inevitability of eventual return; however, they had yet to make a final decision about whether or not to return to Afghanistan in the short or medium term—an issue open to further influence by the constantly evolving political and economic environment. The correct timing for an individual to return may differ even within the same household, as seen among some respondents whose major concern about return was the fear that their education would be discontinued. Motivated by curiosity, some shared a great interest in going back at least once to see and experience Afghanistan, but they were open to remigrating if this attempt was not successful. The optimistic attitude towards returning and the anticipated potential for movement are the key points to note. This is because these perspectives exist alongside deep links and emotional ties to the locations in which they grew up, making personal decision making about return a highly contradictory and complex process.

Growing up in the mirror of the 'others': expectations of one's homeland

For second-generation Afghans, growing up as refugees in a country that does not consider them its own exacerbates the complexity of establishing 'who they are'; this is due to their participation in two contexts at the same time—the Afghan family sphere and the Pakistani or Iranian social sphere. Regardless of the extent to which respondents integrated into the host society, these dual influences were often seen to result in a degree of intrapersonal conflict since young Afghans tried to balance contradictory values while also navigating the challenges of adolescence. Fundamentally, their values were more or less shaped by Afghan norms, but their behaviour, especially within the Afghan domain, was defined by family expectations which could vary significantly.

In various contexts and spaces outside the family individuals commonly faced situations in which they felt the need to assimilate and adjust to their environment in order to 'belong' either superficially or more profoundly. Such shifts of behaviour were often accompanied by internal conflicts quite simply because second-generation Afghan refugees cannot legally belong to the same category as their Pakistani and Iranian friends and acquaintances. This inability to belong and enjoy rights as a citizen of the host country was another way in which refugees came to learn about themselves and Afghanistan; such experiences at times created feelings of social exclusion that contrasted with their levels of physical comfort in refuge, mainly because they grew up there and were familiar with the environment.

The term *mohajer* originally referred to refugees who had fled their homes to avoid religious oppression or persecution (Centlivres and

Centlivres-Demont 1988) but does not retain this meaning in the eyes of second-generation Afghan refugees. Respondents perceived it as derogatory when used by some of the host country population, for example, in the taunts that many respondents experienced. These were stressful experiences, particularly for children and youth who were already facing the difficult situation of growing up among 'others' and were seeking a base to which they could anchor their values and ideas (Phinney et al. 2001).

It is argued that a certain degree of Afghan national consciousness initially emerged in response to the country's fragmentation due to the war and the intervention of foreign powers. In particular, Afghans in exile started to perceive the territorial border with a sense of nostalgia from the outside, although this was hardly rooted in common traditions or experiences (Schetter 2005). Similarly, prior to the Soviet invasion, the idea of Afghan national unity—in the context of the country's diverse range of ethnic backgrounds—barely existed except as a minor political movement at central government level that was mostly tied to Pashtun nationalism. However, it took on a process of transformation in the face of invasion by 'others' as well as through refugees' experiences in exile among non-Afghan 'others' (Centlivres and Centlivres-Demont 2000; Dupree 2002).[2] For second-generation Afghan refugees, the sense of national awareness of being Afghans in exile was often reinforced against the backdrop of Pakistani/Iranian life, rather than by the sentiments and nostalgia for bygone days that first-generation Afghans felt.

The emergence of identity in relation to sub-groups among Afghans (Pashtuns, Tajiks, Hazaras, etc.) in exile followed a path similar to that of their identity as refugees. Both identities were formed through exposure to differing values over time. It was a common feature of respondents' own childhoods that they played with many different children without taking into consideration ethnicity or nationality. Second-generation Afghans would have certain inherited memories of these divisions from their parents, and some experienced conflict over ethnicity or politics that related to their place of origin in Afghanistan during their time in Pakistan or Iran. However, this was more likely to be an issue for first-

---

[2] Centlivres and Centlivres-Demont add that if Afghan refugees in exile were asked about their identity by foreigners, most would answer that they were of Afghan origin, rather than stating their province or ethnic group. Non-Afghan 'others' (Pakistanis, Iranians, etc.) also tend to regard Afghan refugees as a homogeneous group, rather than distinguishing between ethnicities.

generation Afghan refugees (although it was sometimes transmitted to second-generation individuals). Therefore, for refugees born or brought up in Pakistan and Iran, the more dominant feeling of 'difference' was the sense of being residents with a status inferior to that of citizens native to the country.

For groups of young refugees, intentions to return were less motivated by recovering an idealized past, kept alive through stories from relatives and other refugees, than by the ideas of rights, access to property, and citizenship—which they had not necessarily been able to fully acquire while growing up in refuge (Zetter 1999; Farwell 2001). It is important to note that many second-generation Afghan refugees embraced these expectations of their country as part of their return. If these high expectations were not met, disappointment for some was sharp and led to thoughts of onward movement—remigrating to the host country or moving elsewhere.

THE CHALLENGES OF RESETTLING IN AFGHANISTAN

Those second-generation Afghans who had returned to Afghanistan experience the complexities of both making decisions about returning while in exile, and reintegrating after return to their homeland. These can be seen as part of the same process since the complexities and internal conflicts experienced in refuge did not disappear upon return.

Refugees who had returned to Afghanistan were usually considered economically less vulnerable than those who stayed during the years of conflict because of the education and skills they acquired as well as the savings some accrued. However, from the point of view of many of the study's returnee respondents, repatriation was often accompanied by a complex mix of stresses. Returning for some meant that personal experiences of being a non-citizen in refuge were simply repeated upon returning to their homeland. The extent of this experience depended on the gap between experiences upon return and expectations and hopes.

After arrival, many reported finding differences in their new environment and in people compared to life in refuge. But some found Afghanistan more or less what they had been used to; these were often males, especially those who had maintained close contact with family in Afghanistan while in exile or who had moved to returnee-concentrated areas. However, what native compatriots deemed as 'common sense' was not necessarily naturally understood, particularly by those who had few or no opportunities to see Afghanistan until their arrival. Returning refugees would usually notice: first, changes in material aspects of their new environment; second, differences in social interactions; and, then, less visible differences in values discovered through extended interaction with the society.

Currently in Afghanistan the initial material and security conditions for successful voluntary repatriation and reintegration are not in place. This factor combined with varying degrees of emotional stress related to issues of identity and what being home entails, increasing the risk of unsuccessful resettlement; this prompted some returnees to move else-where or to negatively influence the decisions of others about returning. Those in poorer socio-economic categories were particularly vulnerable to the influence of all of these experiences as they are less able to overcome initial material disadvantages.

Meeting material needs

Meeting material needs is one of the major challenges during the reinte-gration process for many returnees. Finding employment is particularly difficult—for both returnees and those who remained. Among returnees, this study found that skills were not sufficient to gain access to work. Even skilled returnees were not necessarily able to find employment upon return because the skills acquired in Pakistan and Iran were not always useful in Afghanistan. Rather, access to work depends on the needs of the market; the right timing; the location of return; the possibility of acquiring materials and equipment; the availability of initial investment funds; and connections to existing groups or power holders. Despite some having acquired work experience while in exile, a lack of connections and un-familiarity with the local market were formidable obstacles. Notably, some respondents who were relatively wealthy and had strong extended family networks did not mention serious concerns related to employment.

In trying to adjust to life in Afghanistan, labour migration is often used as a livelihood strategy (Monsutti 2006), whereby one or more household members remain in or return to the neighbouring countries for work. This was particularly the case among the average and below-average income respondents in this study. Many faced unemployment in Afghanistan and had no other means to secure livelihoods except sending male household members away again to work. This was a proactive, though illegal and often dangerous, way of adjusting to a new life that allowed most of a household's members to remain in Afghanistan and have their material needs fulfilled. Those who migrated for work, however, had to have at least enough external support (e.g. credit, someone taking care of the remaining family members, networks and information to find employment) as well as money to cover travel expenses. If these were not available and all coping strategies had been exhausted, this study showed that vulnerable returnees reached a tipping point at which they decided to remigrate as a family to the host country where they had achieved a higher standard of living.

Social rejection of returnees

For some second-generation returnees, social rejection by fellow Afghans who had remained during the years of conflict was another difficult experience since the motivation to return was because of experiences of 'non-belonging' in Pakistan and Iran. The degree of social acceptance exhibited by the Afghans who remained in Afghanistan and by the society more generally considerably affected reintegration processes and their outcomes, as did how returnees personally responded to those who remained.

By and large, some of those who remained in Afghanistan appeared to hold negative views of some returnees, especially those whose experiences in Pakistan or Iran led them to have better education, skills, and economic security. One factor involves the fear of competition for resources: those who remained may see the large-scale return of refugees as a threat to their 'territory' in education, work, property ownership, and social status, particularly if the return occurs rapidly in an area with limited absorptive capacity.

Such negative perceptions within the general society may often be directed at particular returnees who are visibly different—physically or culturally—and are easy targets for harassment by their peers. In particular, some respondents who had been highly integrated into a Pakistani or Iranian way of life could not or did not know what is 'normal' for Afghans. Some were subject to contempt, labelled as 'spoiled', 'loafers', or 'not Afghan'. In addition, returnee women are relatively easily identified by what they wear, and their appearance and behaviour can be at odds with local cultural expectations and social codes leading to rejection by others. For example, in areas where symbols and items associated with Iran are viewed negatively Afghans who had remained in Afghanistan used the label *Iranigak* ('little Iran'), for returnees from Iran, showing their lack of welcome. Even for refugees who were fiercely patriotic about

Afghanistan or harboured very negative feelings towards their host country, returning to Afghanistan sometimes meant facing discrimination based on their 'non-Afghan-ness' and a continual sense of 'non-belonging' —even in their homeland.

Unequal treatment in the Afghan context

Facing exclusion because of one's returnee status was only one of the discouraging experiences for respondents. Encountering discrimination based on one's background (such as ethnicity, religion, political ideology, class, and gender) was another stressful experience for second-generation refugees in their native land. They experienced this kind of judgement even more intensely than first-generation refugees or Afghans who remained in Afghanistan and were more aware of these tensions in the country. This was because in refuge the dominant feeling of being 'different' was related to being a refugee compared to a citizen of the host country; this tended to overshadow other ethnic and religious affiliations.

Before returning, many second-generation respondents expected that their feelings of being different would be eased in Afghanistan. Based on their experiences after return, however, they raised the issue of feeling marginalized because access to certain education and work opportunities was heavily influenced by bribery and *wasita* (relations to powerful people). Respondents who had received education in secondary school or higher reported corruption related to achieving success in school and university entrance exams as well as accessing scholarships after return; they said that only those who had power and money could access more favourable opportunities. This experience created frustration and distrust towards the government and, in the end, their homeland. Concerns about being unable to rely upon authorities, including the police, for security and other matters were also commonly voiced, leaving socially and economically less privileged respondents feeling particularly neglected in their own country.

On the other hand, some (more often male) respondents said that they experienced more immediate social acceptance and a welcoming attitude from the receiving population at a relatively early stage of reintegration. They felt this was due to pre-existing social relationships, strong ties that had been maintained with relatives during exile, and other markers of status. If a returnee was considered a socially respectable person in the community (for example, in a position of influence, religiously devout, or able to bring benefit to others), he or she was less likely to face harassment.

Questioning self-identity and belonging

Regardless of their education, gender, level of social acceptance, or emotional contentment, and extent of material difficulties faced, nearly all respondents expressed generally negative, stereotypical images of fellow Afghans who had grown up in Afghanistan during the war years. Many returnee respondents—both educated and uneducated—saw themselves as more open-minded, having experienced new people and cultures in Pakistan or Iran. In particular, educated returnees (more common among those from Iran) criticized the 'inferior' material culture of Afghans who had remained. Based on values formed while growing up in Pakistan or Iran, returnees often felt they saw the situation in Afghanistan through the lens of an 'outsider' and compared this life to the one they experienced in refuge.

In all three countries, some respondents raised serious concerns about the direction in which they perceived Afghanistan to be going in the context of Islamic values. Generally, some second-generation Afghans who grew up in Pakistan criticized Afghanistan's 'less Islamic' environment, which was described as having been contaminated by the influence of foreigners. Those who grew up in Iran, however, tended to perceive Islam in Afghanistan as more fundamentalist and backward. These contradictions sometimes entered into individual and household decisions about an appropriate place to lead their own lives and those of the next generation.

The extent to which returnees eventually feel a shared identity with others in their communities and be socially and emotionally comfortable in that place tends to be closely associated with their process of adaptation. To address or combat feelings of difference, many returnees adjusted their behaviour and actions to fit in with their new environment. For some this process occurred naturally over time, while for others it was an intentional adjustment of their public image in response to social norms. This is a critical point to note: second-generation refugees may have returned to Afghanistan for the moment, but they may neither feel that they fit in nor feel content in the place they are expected to stay in the long term. In combination with material hardships, the social exclusion of some returnees tended to be accelerated by the inability to feel a sense of belonging in Afghanistan, the experience of isolation (in such contexts as family, society, school, and workplace), and related emotional depression.

The impact of the transition on women

After relocating to Afghanistan, women in particular were significantly affected by the changes in physical surroundings. Limited public infrastructure and inadequate availability of material goods resulted in increased domestic work. Compared to their lives in Pakistan or Iran, young women—particularly in rural areas—also had less access to healthcare services due to the lack of nearby health facilities and to movement restrictions resulting from inadequate roads and means of transportation acceptable for women.

Compared to life in refuge, returnee women in Afghanistan tended to experience an unfavourable environment with decreased mobility because of security issues (for example, harassment and kidnapping), more restrictive social norms, and unavailability of facilities (for example, lack of secure public transportation). For economically vulnerable female returnees whose households had no other income earners, few acceptable work options existed. The 'shame' that is at times associated with working women was likely to motivate them to move to Afghanistan's urban areas, or to go back to Iran or Pakistan, where they could earn some income with fewer restrictions.

In relation to physical security, a few female respondents reported experiencing brutal domestic violence from either or both their family and husbands. This led them to perceive deficiencies in the Afghan legal system compared to the system in Pakistan or Iran where they felt 'safer'. For these women, the crucial factor in deciding whether or not to return to Afghanistan, or subsequently to remigrate, was the protection that had been available at the potential destination.

While in refuge many women respondents had become used to behaving in ways that were commonly perceived by those remaining in Afghanistan as too 'free' for women in Afghanistan. The reputation of the family in Afghanistan largely depends on the perception of its women as being 'honourable' and 'Afghan'. Appearance and attitudes that may be perceived as 'foreign' are often cited as evidence of women having abandoned their 'Afghan-ness'; this is particularly significant in a society in transition where women are expected to transfer knowledge of their culture to the next generation (Rayaprol 2005). Thus, second-generation Afghan women who grew up in Pakistan and Iran tended to face greater emotional struggles in relation to return and in the subsequent reintegration process than men.

FROM *MOHAJER* TO *HAMWATAN*: ONGOING NEGOTIATION AND AMBIGUOUS FUTURE

Balancing material, social, and internal fulfilment needs

No simple generalizations can be made about different reintegration paths and their outcomes. This is in part because reintegration is an ongoing process; many respondents did not have fixed ideas about future intentions. Even in the duration of an interview, some of their opinions and ideas appeared to be contradictory—revealing their internal struggles related to the future. It is, therefore, difficult to classify respondents in terms of their future intentions; however, nearly half intended at the time of the interview to remain in their current place of residence in Afghanistan. Some also expressed a preference to settle in urban areas of Afghanistan to enhance their access to facilities, education beyond the primary level (for themselves or their children), and employment. Others, however, expressed thoughts of moving back to the neighbouring countries or elsewhere.

Reintegration outcomes were seen as different points along a continuum reflecting varying degrees of success, ranging from desire to settle permanently in Afghanistan to wish to leave again temporarily or for the long term. Each respondent's complex reintegration experience was influenced by a wide range of factors including personality, background, experiences prior to becoming a refugee, the particular circumstances of displacement, experiences in exile, social networks, conditions of return, and his or her own interpretations of 'home' and 'belonging'.

There was no doubt that the basic material needs for survival must first be secured, but the degree of social acceptance of returnees exhibited by those Afghans who remained, and by Afghan society more generally, significantly affected the situations of returnees. Furthermore, if the process was to lead to long-term settlement, there had to be an adequate sense of internal fulfilment through which returnees felt at ease and that they fitted in. These factors were all interlinked, and a *balance*—with no one area extremely lacking—was crucial for successful reintegration in the long term. In particular, how individual respondents made sense of *watan* (the homeland) in relation to their own identity was found to be a key factor in the overall return and reintegration process.

Watan: a key pull factor

The notion of *watan* for Afghans primarily relates to a limited geographical area in which individuals are well known to each other; it is something treasured and vulnerable—something to be defended—like the females in a man's family. However, in the diaspora context, it takes on a wider meaning: anybody from Afghanistan is regarded as belonging to the same *watan* (Glatzer 2001).

One of the key motivations in the decisions of many refugees to go back to their *watan* was the mental and emotional satisfaction they expected to feel there—despite often hearing about the material hardships. This was often accompanied by the hope of elevating their social status from subordinate *mohajerin* to respected Afghans in a society made up of other *hamwatan* (compatriots) and where they could work with their own people to achieve a stable, prosperous future. The ways in which they found personal meaning from living in their own country, and the sense of comfort derived from this identity, were therefore crucial to successful resettlement.

Living in their own *watan* was also an important 'pull factor' keeping respondents in Afghanistan; it eased the pain of material and emotional hardships. It could raise their inner strength to confront the difficulties of resettling (at least to the extent—different for each individual—at which they felt they could no longer cope). Positive feelings about living in their own *watan* gave the majority of returnee respondents a sense of freedom and often helped them face both the challenges of material needs that went unmet and personal frustrations.

Many returnees expected their *watan* to be a place where their rights to equal treatment and opportunities were ensured because they were respected citizens. These expectations continuously evolved as unanticipated difficulties arose after they returned. (See Table 5.2.) The experience of being 'outsiders' again in *watan*, echoing the experience of their refugee status, hindered psychosocial reintegration for some, and in some cases where that process failed, second-generation returnees were likely to experience a strong desire to go back to the country where they grew up. This was similar to parts of the earlier process of deciding whether or not to repatriate. If they then remigrated because of overwhelming disappointment with (and, for a few, hatred of) their *watan*, even stronger pull factors would be required to bring them back to Afghanistan again.

It must also be recognized that these young returnees often maintained strong ties to the place where they grew up and, in terms of their

Table 5.2. Second-generation refugees' expectations of life in *watan* and its status change.

	Mohajer in Pakistan/Iran	Expected life in *watan*	Actual life in *watan*
Legal rights and official status	Lack of rights, unequal access to services, lack of legal status and opportunities	Property ownership, improved access to services	Freedom, internal peace, comfort of living in *watan* **but**
Social position and definition	Inferior, subordinate, outcast, insulted **but** all Afghans have the same refugee status	A member of a nation where all are Afghans, honour associated with being an Afghan	continued discrimination on the grounds of ethnicity, religion, politics, gender, economic status, or lack of *wasita*
Emotional state	Weak, afraid, tired, worried, uprooted, constant need to defend honour	End of fear and worries, safety, own territory, ancestral home, freedom	Realization of differences in 'others' (other Afghan values)

emotional attachment, did not make much of a distinction between the two countries. This attachment, the degree of which depends on the individual, existed simultaneously among multiple spaces. Regardless of whether or not resettlement was intended to be permanent, many wished or planned to visit Pakistan or Iran in the near future. This was primarily to see relatives and friends (who may be Afghan, Pakistani, or Iranian), to revisit places from their memories, to deal with work-related issues, or to relieve the boredom of life in Afghanistan.

Reintegration processes involved renegotiating core values related to society and people, comparing different lifestyles and ideas in Afghanistan to those experienced in Pakistan and Iran. Coupled with more general challenges related to adolescence or early adulthood, young returnees developed new understandings of home and their future within it as they spent more time there.

This study shows that re-entry difficulties can potentially be relieved by more effectively tapping into external facilitation aimed at meeting both material and emotional needs through such means as land allocation by the government; relief assistance from government and non-governmental organizations; financial support and moral encouragement from relatives; generosity and care provided to youth by elders and parents; having teachers motivate students to serve their own country; and facilitating opportunities for youth participation in community group activities.

These difficulties may also be mitigated by encouraging self-resilience and development of coping mechanisms, promoting the ability and willingness of young returnees to tackle hardships and challenges in order to reintegrate in the *watan*. Improving their emotional security and the ways in which they identify with their homeland could increase the number of young returnees resettling for the long term and, in turn, play a key role in the social and political stability of Afghanistan.

CONCLUSIONS

The process of returning home for many second-generation Afghan refugees was often accompanied by great social and emotional stress, significantly threatening successful long-term resettlement. The meaning of *watan* in relation to self-identity was constantly reconstructed through interaction with different people and their environments, and affected by individual background and context. Second-generation Afghan refugees' values and ideals, shaped by the challenging situations they faced as refugees without a strong connection to their home country, were in many cases markedly different to those of their parents and peers who remained in Afghanistan, as they may have found greater satisfaction in living in Pakistan and Iran and from the ways of life there (despite interpersonal contradictions at times).

Learning about Afghanistan while living outside the country was not a straightforward process: many respondents had developed conflicting perceptions of their own country, holding both positive thoughts and negative concerns about how life might be there. The sense of 'non-belonging' in Pakistani and Iranian society affected their attitudes towards an idealized national homeland, and this was accentuated when they felt that they had been deprived of rights or socially excluded through their unfavourable status as *mohajerin*.

For such refugees, the experience of feeling foreign did not necessarily end as expected in their *watan*, and the related stress combined with a range of interplaying factors to present serious challenges to successful reintegration—materially, socially, and emotionally. This study found that the notion of being in one's own *watan* or homeland was a key pull factor in encouraging Afghan refugees to return from Pakistan and Iran, as it provided expectations that their rights to equal treatment and opportunities as respected citizens of the country would be ensured, and that they would have freedom of movement and residence as well as access to resources, livelihoods, and property. However, these expectations were not always fulfilled.

Despite the profound complexities and challenges involved, the large-scale repatriation of Afghan refugees from neighbouring countries should be seen as a great source of human assets and as a crucial strategy for the reconstruction of Afghan society following decades of conflict. Through gradual interaction with those already in Afghanistan, returnees bringing various skills and values can have a positive impact on Afghan society. The possible benefits include new technical skills, a better understanding of health and hygiene, and the ability to communicate with and accept people who have dissimilar ideas and modes of behaviour.

Material necessity and sustainable livelihoods were first considerations for returnees. However, it was unclear to these young Afghans whether they could achieve successful settlement in Afghanistan, particularly in terms of more long-term permanent reintegration. Returnees, especially those with limited networking resources in the place of repatriation, were often at risk of being socially dislocated and isolated, with wide-ranging social and economic consequences.

Translating aspirations into action was more difficult for those who had less independent decision-making ability in the household. It must be recognized, however, that women—even those less educated and with less freedom of movement—had the potential to pass on their own negative perceptions of their homeland to the next generation and to other relatives still in exile, as data from this study showed. Some who continued to live in Afghanistan sometimes advised their relatives still in refuge never to come back since life in Afghanistan had fallen short of their expectations. The personal fulfilment and social integration of second-generation returnees could not be neglected; it played a role in the broader picture of refugees' decision-making about returning and expectations related to reintegration. More importantly, the research showed that if returnees remigrated after having failed to reintegrate successfully, they were likely to be even more critical of the possibility of returning in the future.

One potential area in which to provide less common but equally necessary non-material assistance to refugees and returnees is collaboration between the governments of Pakistan, Iran, and Afghanistan to support international agencies in the development of information campaigns that utilize media outlets to advocate social acceptance and non-discriminatory treatment of all Afghans (including returnees), particularly in public institutions such as schools, and to show the importance of providing young returnees with understanding and encouragement as they adjust to different values and adapt to being home. Community youth groups which provide spaces for young people to share experiences can also promote acceptance and successful integration. Improving the transparency of procedures for access to higher education and employment could also play a key role in promoting a sense of solidarity and hope among Afghans. It is important to create an atmosphere promoting voluntary return rather than pressuring refugees to return or resorting to deportation, as the latter two are unlikely to result in sustained return or resettlement.

REFERENCES

Abbasi-Shavazi, M. J., Glazebrook, D., Jamshidiha G., Mahmoudian, H., and Sadeghi, R. (2008), *Second-generation Afghans in Iran: Integration, Identity and Return* (Kabul, AREU).

Boyden, J. and De Berry, J. (eds) (2004), *Children and Youth on the Front Line: Ethnography, Armed Conflict and Displacement* (Oxford, Berghahn Books).

Byron, R. (2002), 'Identity', in A. Barnard and J. Spencer (eds), *Encyclopaedia of Social and Cultural Anthropology* (London, Routledge), p. 292.

Centlivres, P. and Centlivres-Demont, M. (1988), 'The Afghan Refugee in Pakistan: An Ambiguous Identity', *Journal of Refugee Studies*, 1, 2: 141–52.

—— and —— (2000), 'State, National Awareness and Levels of Identity in Afghanistan from Monarchy to Islamic State', *Central Asian Survey*, 19, 3/4: 419–28.

Chatty, D. (2007), 'Researching Refugee Youth in the Middle East: Reflections on the Importance of Comparative Research', *Journal of Refugee Studies*, 20, 2: 265–80.

——, Crivello, G., and Lewando Hundt, G. (2005), 'Theoretical and Methodological Challenges of Studying Refugee Children in the Middle East and North Africa: Young Palestinian, Afghan and Sahrawi Refugees', *Journal of Refugee Studies*, 18, 4: 387–409.

Cornish, F., Peltzer, K., and Maclachlan, M. (1999), 'Returning Strangers: The Children of Malawian Refugees Come "Home"?', *Journal of Refugee Studies*, 12, 3: 264–83.

Dupree, N. H. (2002), 'Cultural Heritage and National Identity in Afghanistan', *Third World Quarterly*, 23, 5: 977–89.

Farwell, N. (2001), '"Onward through Strength": Coping and Psychological Support among Refugee Youth Returning to Eritrea from Sudan', *Journal of Refugee Studies*, 14, 1: 43–69.

Ghanem, T. (2003), 'When Forced Migrants Return "Home": The Psychosocial Difficulties Returnees Encounter in the Reintegration Process', RSC Working Paper 16 (Oxford, University of Oxford).

Glatzer, B. (2001), 'War and Boundaries in Afghanistan: Significance and Relativity of Local and Social Boundaries', *Weld des Islams*, 41, 3: 379–99.

Government of Pakistan and UNHCR (2007), *Registration of Afghans in Pakistan 2007* (Islamabad, Government of Pakistan and UNHCR).

Kibreab, G. (1999), 'Revisiting the Debate on People, Place, Identity and Displacement', *Journal of Refugee Studies*, 12, 4: 384–410.

Malkki, L. (1992), 'National Geographic: The Rooting of Peoples and the Territorialisation of National Identity among Scholars and Refugees', *Cultural Anthropology*, 7, 1: 24–44.

Mooney, C. G. (2000), *Theories of Childhood: An Introduction to Dewey, Montessori, Erikson, Piaget, and Vygotsky* (St Paul, MN, Readleaf Press).

Monsutti, A. (2006), *Afghan Transnational Networks: Looking Beyond Repatriation* (Kabul, AREU).

Phinney, J. S., Horenczyk, G., Liebkind, K., and Vedder, P. (2001), 'Ethnic Identity, Immigration, and Well-being: An International Perspective', *Journal of Social Issues*, 57: 493–510.

Rayaprol, A. (2005), 'Being American, Learning to be Indian: Gender and Generation in the Context of Transnational Migration', in M. Thapan (ed.), *Women and Migration in Asia, Vol. 1* (New Delhi, Sage).

Saito, M. (2007), *Second-generation Afghans in Neighbouring Countries: From Mohajer to Hamwatan: Afghans Return Home* (Kabul, AREU).

—— (2009), *Searching for My Homeland: Dilemmas Between Borders: Experiences of Young Afghans Returning 'Home' from Pakistan and Iran* (Kabul, AREU).

—— and Hunte, P. (2007), *To Return or to Remain: The Dilemma of Second-generation Afghans in Pakistan* (Kabul, AREU).

Schetter, C. (2005), 'Ethnoscapes, National Territorialisation, and the Afghan War', *Geopolitics*, 10: 50–75.

UNHCR (2007), *UNHCR Global Appeal 2008–2009* (Geneva, UNHCR).

UNHCR (2008a), *2007 Global Trends: Refugees, Asylum-seekers, Returnees, Internally Displaced and Stateless Persons* (Geneva, UNHCR).

UNHCR (2008b), *Operational Information Monthly Summary Report: March 2008* (Kabul, UNHCR).

Zetter, R. (1999), 'Reconceptualising the Myth of Return: Continuity and Transition amongst the Greek-Cypriot Refugees of 1974', *Journal of Refugee Studies*, 12, 1: 1–22.

6.
Repatriation and Reconstruction: Afghan Youth as a 'Burnt Generation' in Post-conflict Return

Sarah Kamal

The implications of movement in Afghan life are the subject of some debate. In this volume, Monsutti presents transnationalism as an everyday aspect of Afghan nomadism, while Olszewska emphasizes distressing experiences of liminality in refugee experience. My contribution focuses on movement 'back'—specifically on voluntary repatriation, which has been framed as the optimal, durable solution in international political and legal frameworks since the early 1980s.

While still generally put into practice as the solution of choice, repatriation is no longer seen as an unproblematic end to the refugee cycle (Black and Koser 1999; Cornish et al. 1999). Indeed, support for repatriation programmes has waned with growing awareness of their less than exemplary methods, with the coercive nature of some state-sponsored 'voluntary' repatriation programmes and unstable post-conflict conditions awaiting returnees prompting ambivalence on the ethics of assisted return (Bakewell 2000; Blitz et al. 2005; Bradley 2006; Chimni 2002; Stein 1997; Stigter 2006).

However, there is as yet insufficient understanding of the long-term prospects for returnees in their home country (Bradley 2006; Eisenbruch 1997; Chimni 2002; Zetter 1994) to address comprehensively the policy and theory implicated in repatriation studies. In particular, the repatriation perspectives of refugee youth with little or no experience of their family's country of origin (Cornish et al. 1999; Saito and Kantor in this volume) have not been fully explored in existing research. This essay presents a limited account addressing these latter concerns, tracing the stories of four Afghan youths as embedded in their peer and family contexts at three points over a five-year period: in 2003, as they faced the prospect of 'voluntary' repatriation at the hands of the Iranian government; in 2006, as they situated themselves vis-à-vis Afghanistan in the early flush of 'return'[1] to their home country; and in 2007, as they described their hopes and aspirations in view of their growing understanding of their new context.

In general, Afghan refugee youth, often under-investigated in large-scale surveys of male or female heads of refugee households, warrant particularized attention—thick description—to investigate how adolescents influence and are affected by the repatriation choices of their families. The stories I present below offer a longitudinal examination of repatriation from the perspective of long-term forced migrant youth, drawing out themes of concern as embedded in their particular context. While not representative in any scientific sense, their experiences present a small window into the lives of young Afghan men and women repatriating from Iran.

REFUGEE YOUTH AND REPATRIATION

Forty-four per cent of the world's 21 million refugee population are comprised of youth aged 18 years or younger (UNHCR 2005). Youth in exile have been characterized as conflicted and burdened: enduring a loss of cultural pride (Vargas 1999; Blitz et al. 2005), feeling marginalized in the host community (Vargas 1999; Zetter 1999, 1994), and facing constant uncertainty over their futures (Anderson 2001). Bash and Zezlina-Phillips (2006: 126) argue that the 'neither here nor there' psychological limbo of refugee identity along with transition into adulthood can make the emotional instability of refugee adolescence fraught with turmoil. They suggest that within such uncertainty refugee youth do demonstrate resilience in that they can 'act as managers of their own, many sided, frequently fluid, identities in their search for cultural anchors'. Such resilience is not without cost, however: in maintaining and proclaiming the multiple identities required by their context, refugee youth risk undermining the personal cohesion for which they strive.

Refugee youth are often differentiated from the older generation by both their ability to cross cultural boundaries more fluidly and their looser affinity to their country of origin. Refugee youth, in more easily absorbing host country modes of being, can represent a demarcation in refugee families between before and after relative to their parents

---

[1] Return is a problematic term that I use with caution since half of the youth in my study were born in exile.

(Rousseau et al. 2001). Seen within their family networks, refugee youth have been described as a vehicle for the retention of their parents' culture and memory (Dhruvarajan 1993) or a conduit for interpretation of and connection with the host community (Anderson 2001).

For refugee youth, the prospect of return to a land in which they have never been or barely remember can invoke multiple anxieties. Refugee youth can face rekindled uprootedness (Eisenbruch 1997), loss of prosperity, and mismatched skill sets when engaging with their new, often rural, environments (Bradley 2006), and risk becoming reverse refugees in their country of origin (Zetter 1999). Given their limited experience of the family's country of origin, youth at times distance themselves from the older generation's nostalgic longing to return (Kakoli 2000; Zetter 1994; Rousseau et al. 2001) even as they can be influenced by those discourses into visualizing an idealized home (Cornish et al. 1999). Refugee youth's reasons for wanting to return are often different and more politicized than the sentimental discourses of their parents, reflecting claims to rights and property (Zetter 1999, 1994; Rousseau et al. 2001) or more idealistic desires to rebuild their country (Blitz et al. 2005).

The model of re-acculturation developed by Dona and Berry (1999, in Cornish et al. 1999) posits that long-term forced migrants' difficulties upon return are similar to their struggles adapting to life in their host country. Cornish et al. (1999: 281) use the re-acculturation model to study the experiences of Malawian refugee youth upon repatriation. They found that young Malawian refugees experienced 'acculturative stress and ambiguity regarding self and national identity' after repatriating from Zambia. Their study investigates a sample of youth refugees born in exile and brought up in the knowledge of their difference without having experienced transition from their families' original context. They found that for many of the youth, feelings of being outsiders did not abate upon return, but in some cases were actually exacerbated. Some of the youth became unsure of their nationality, and some of them seemed to identify themselves with a 'returnee' identity.

AFGHAN REFUGEE YOUTH IN IRAN

Unlike Pakistan, which has received significant support for its refugee population, Iran has hosted Afghans as one of the largest refugee populations in the world for over twenty years with very little international support. Most Afghan refugees in Iran are integrated with the local population, with only a small percentage living in refugee camps. With the fall of the Taliban, Iran renewed efforts it had made since the 1990s to discourage refugee inflows and promote repatriation. In 2003 the Iranian government signed a tripartite agreement with the government of Afghanistan and the United Nations High Commissioner for Refugees (UNHCR) to facilitate the voluntary repatriation of Afghans. Iran also passed eleven articles entitled 'Regulations on Accelerating Repatriation of Afghan Nationals' which outlawed employment, administrative services, banking, participation in civil society, and accommodation for Afghans without valid residence permits (Abbasi-Shavasi et al. 2005). In the same year, the government implemented mandatory registration of all Afghans in Iran. While the state had conducted repeated campaigns to repatriate Afghans since the 1990s, the more stringent enforcement of its 2003 initiatives instilled anxiety in the Afghan population.[2]

Education had formed a large part of the justification for many Afghan families to migrate to Iran. With the gradual withdrawal of Iranian educational services from the Afghan refugee population over the years, informal Afghan-run schools were organized by the Afghan community, often operating out of people's homes before shifting to larger venues.[3] Many of the Afghan youth who were forced out of Iranian institutions felt the downshift in quality of teaching and resources in Afghan-run schooling keenly. Using second-hand Iranian textbooks, Afghan-run schools had neither the facilities nor staff to provide the level of education of mainstream Iranian schools. 2003 was a pivotal period for the youth, as the Iranian government made clear its intention of, and gradually implemented, the forced closure of many informal Afghan-run schools. For many youth, Afghan schools represented their final link with educational prospects in the country. The closure of most if not all informal Afghan schools (although some reopened after a few months' closure) along with highly curtailed economic viability became a juncture for decision making regarding return for many families after years of socially invisible discrimination in Iranian society.[4]

---

[2] Olszewska presents in this volume an excellent summary of the context in which Afghans in Iran live that I do not duplicate here.

[3] See Hoodfar (2010) for a detailed historical account of Afghan refugee education in Iran.

[4] The relationship between Afghans and Iranians is much more complex than the treatment I am able to offer here. The older refugee generation remembers accommodation and generosity (ration cards, jobs, free schooling) based on historical cultural ties and ideologically based succour offered to Afghans fleeing the Soviet invasion in 1979 by post-

FACING 'VOLUNTARY' REPATRIATION IN 2003

I met the four Afghan youths who are the subjects of this study in 2003 at an informal Afghan school in Tehran. I grew to know them quite well through nine months of intensive collaborative work developing a youth club at their school and organizing the collection of in-depth interviews of them and their peers.[5] Nasir (17-year-old male), Amin (18-year-old male), Maryam (14-year-old female), and Zekya (17-year-old female)[6] were highly active both in their studies and in their peer groups, with only Zekya having some pre-forced-migration memories of Afghanistan. The other three had either been infants or were not born when their family first crossed into Iran. All were the most educated members in their families. The interviewees were not, nor were they meant to be, a representative sample of Afghan refugee youth in Iran. Instead, commonality of refugee context and relatively uniform age and education allowed for a somewhat less complicated analysis of the influence of return on their lives.

The circumstances in which they were living at the time were not conducive to a bright outlook for a future in Iran. Their school, Afghan-run and Afghan-funded, was located in a small, fairly poor southern Tehran suburb sometimes called 'little Kabul' due to its high Afghan population. Life for most Afghans in the Tehran suburb was highly transitory, with many families moving once or twice every year due to steep rent increases by landlords against whom they had no legal protection. Afghan schools were even more vulnerable as recognizable centres of Afghan activity. The school's lack of money, fear of vandalism, its more or less yearly displacement, and legally unrecognized status led it to maintain an anonymous

---

revolutionary Iran. The 1990s saw a shift to impatience, easy disdain, and petty and large injustices from the government and society at large, justified by, among others, the high profile of a number of violent crimes attributed to Afghans and stretched social services and high unemployment in the aftermath of the Iran–Iraq war of the 1980s. From the standpoint of many Afghan refugee youth, however, the dismissive or aggressive attitudes of Iranians and the state loomed large, eclipsing the occasional kindnesses of the few Iranians willing to bend rules or offer sympathy and friendship.

[5] The data I collected in 2003 was part of the 'Children and Adolescents in Sahrawi and Afghani Refugee Households: Living with the Effects of Prolonged Armed Conflict and Forced Migration' (SARC) research project (principle investigator: Dawn Chatty). The project studied coping strategies and issues of identity among long-term Afghan and Sahrawi refugee youth. I helped conduct participatory research for the SARC project in Iran, collecting data on Afghan youth in neighbourhoods settled by Afghan refugees in Mashad and Tehran. In Tehran, more than 100 Afghan youth became involved in SARC participatory research.

[6] The names of the youth have been changed to protect identities.

exterior and low profile. Indeed, students were instructed not to cluster in obvious groups when entering the dank, dark, noisy, and overheated basement housing the school's five classrooms.

The Afghan youth felt the insecurity of their schooling and living quarters keenly, and negative encounters with Iranians also added stress to their lives. As a researcher and participant observer I occasionally experienced[7] the routine discrimination facing Afghans travelling around Tehran, including calls of 'Afghani Afghani!' in the streets, rudeness and dismissive behaviour in markets, and muttered propositions by men walking beside or behind me. Four months into my fieldwork, I had become conditioned to so much negative attention from strangers that if people treated me poorly, I often assumed it was because they thought I was Afghan. Amin and Nasir, meanwhile, reported that male Afghans faced possible harassment and beatings by bands of Iranian youth.

At the start of our collaboration, the four youths and their peers in the school knew very little about Afghanistan: their curricula and media environment were immersed in the Iranian perspective. Footage of ruins and devastation on the television vied with their parents' nostalgic memories of stunning natural beauty and fertile land. The possibility of remaining in familiar but unfriendly Iran evoked ambivalence, with the youth saying they would enjoy a greater standard of living and benefit from a 'higher' culture at the expense of continued discrimination and feelings of not belonging or being second-class citizens. Often present in their discourse was a strong justification for not repatriating in the near future: 'we would go, but . . . our lives would be at risk because the country is insecure/my family would not survive economically/my studies would be disrupted'.

As time progressed and the youths grew more comfortable navigating and vocalizing their often contradictory feelings, pride, defiance, and concern over Iranian discrimination emerged more frequently in their discourse. Nasir and Zekya became heavily involved in the establishment of a student-run school newsletter. The youths decided to include pictures and investigative articles on the Iranian government's 2003 mandatory registration for all Afghan refugees, including 'person on the street' interviews with newly registered Afghans highlighting the injustices and mistreatment of the process.

---

[7] My features are sometimes mistaken as being Hazara (one of the ethnicities in Afghanistan) due to my mixed Chinese–Iranian background.

In another activity, a photography competition, some of their peers at the school chose to highlight the menial, poorly paid jobs that were often the only employment opportunities available to Afghans in Iran. The youths' feelings about their status relative to Iranians were often tinged with battered self-esteem mixed with defiant pride. Most working Afghans were relegated to the low-income, informal economy as labourers or unskilled workers—difficult, low-paying jobs that few Iranians would accept. Their hard-earned self-sufficiency, however, as well as the contribution they believed they made to the Iranian economy, were sources of dignity. Likewise, while often ashamed of their poverty and the poor conditions of their school, the youths circulated stories of Afghan students scoring higher than Iranians in Iranian schools and competitions and being denied their rightful place. In general, the youths seemed vulnerable and defensive about their refugee status and the backwardness of their country, but also characterized themselves as more morally upright, resourceful, academically gifted, and hardworking than the 'soft' Iranians accustomed to the many privileges Afghans lacked.

Nasir and Zekya in particular, given their strong inclinations towards journalistic writing and social justice, often felt overwhelmed by the way their existence seemed to be submerged—their voices muted (Olszewska, this volume)—in mainstream Iranian discourse. Nasir recounted how a youth journalism club in Tehran which had opened its doors to him later unceremoniously rejected him after discovering he was Afghan. He described his feelings of humiliation and bitterness, fearing that he would be forced to remain a faceless manual labourer regardless of his intellectual and creative abilities.

The seemingly inescapable pressure being put on Afghan families—both through curtailment of economic activity and forced closure of Afghan schools by the Iranian state—fed anger over what they felt were unfair violations of their Islamic right to education. Amin was one of numerous students at his school who were convinced that remaining in Iran would be futile. His father had begun careful preparations for travelling to Afghanistan fairly soon. Maryam and Zekya meanwhile reacted to the rejection from Iran by declaring that they preferred to be in Afghanistan anyway, where they could contribute to the reconstruction of their society. When their school was reopened after two months of closure, their school newsletter was revitalized with a change in name from 'The Voice of Today's Generation' to 'The Heart of Asia', to reflect both an emotional response towards Afghanistan and claim to its value and importance regionally. Meanwhile, a quieter stream of opinion within

153

the upsurge in nationalism in the school admitted (privately, often requesting anonymity) that they wished they could move to a third country.

While often aware of what the more 'correct' patriotic responses were to direct questions regarding repatriation, anxiety and uncertainty often dominated the everyday conversations at the school, particularly given the likely difficulty of re-entering Iran after crossing the border into Afghanistan. Where Zetter (1999: 4) suggests that Greek-Cypriot refugees had 'retained the conviction—to varying degrees and despite all the objective evidence—that their exile is temporary and that they will eventually return home', a significant number of Afghan refugee youth appeared more reluctant to admit any eventuality to repatriation, with some declaring definitively that they would not return despite some peer pressure to show preference for repatriation. Peer pressure was such that Nasir refused to comment on his preferences—his friends explained that he did not want to move to Afghanistan despite his vocal criticisms of the Islamic Republic of Iran.

The youths' anxieties over repatriation included concern over Afghanistan's 'lower' culture, lack of infrastructure, Westernization/ degraded Islam, and insecurity, as well as their own job prospect fears, perceived mismatched skill set for daily life in the country, and distress that they would lose their friends. Girls especially feared that the more traditional, conservative culture in Afghanistan would make life unbearable, prohibiting them from engaging in the cultural activities, work, study, and physical mobility they enjoyed in Iran. Having grown up with Islamic codes prevalent in Iran, Maryam was concerned that she would have to wear Afghanistan-style Islamic coverings, which she believed would be less morally correct than the Iranian *magna'eh* (headdress similar in style to a nun's habit). Zekya, on the other hand, felt that she would feel more free in a majority Sunni Afghanistan given the bruising encounters she had had with the predominantly Shi'a Afghan (and Iranian) population in Iran.

In general, positive aspects of life in Afghanistan were less diverse and often expressed more poetically. The youth cited lack of discrimination, feeling empowered, having the opportunity to help rebuild the country, and, quite simply, being in one's own country as advantages of repatriation. Some youth suggested that in Afghanistan they would not be able to reach their potential, whereas others felt they had to repatriate in order to be able to achieve. Educational quality was viewed as higher in Iran, but more freely accessible—where facilities existed—in Afghanistan. The majority believed they would repatriate, some more out of a seeming sense of fatalism ('we have to go back at some point'—Amin) than choice, with several pointing out that they would need to spend several years adjusting to the conditions in Afghanistan. The general understanding was that the Iranian government's policies would make re-entry into Iran difficult if not impossible, and thus the perceived permanence of repatriation was a significant source of anxiety.

PERSPECTIVES ON REPATRIATION IN 2006

The school of Amin, Nasir, Maryam, and Zekya reported that 80 per cent of its students had repatriated by 2005. I remained in contact with Nasir and Amin, who both moved to Afghanistan in late 2004. We worked together on research projects for six months in Kabul in 2005. Nasir subsequently migrated back to Tehran, Iran, while Amin chose to remain in Afghanistan. In late 2006, I contacted them both again with an in-depth questionnaire that focused on significant life events, national affiliation, migration, home, and aspirations for the future. Amin contacted Maryam and Zekya in Kabul, and all four gave me lengthy accounts of their lives since leaving (and, in Nasir's case, leaving and re-entering) Iran.

Life in Afghanistan was difficult in 2006. Given the resurgence of Taliban activity, a weak economy, and the devastated infrastructure in Afghanistan relative to Iran, I expected to hear dissatisfaction from the youth who had chosen to repatriate. I presumed Nasir would be thankful that he had returned to the relative stability of Iran, where informal Afghan schools were still maintaining a precarious but steady existence despite official government prohibitions. In fact the reverse was true: the repatriated youth expressed happiness over their decision to move and were certain they did not want to return to Iran, while Nasir continued to be frustrated and concerned that he had very limited future prospects in Iran.

Amin, Maryam, and Zekya

One of the first questions in my interview asked for stories about 'travel with family', which the youths took to mean the moment of crossing the Iran–Afghanistan border and travelling through different provinces of Afghanistan towards Kabul. The interviews with Amin, Maryam, and Zekya at that point took on the air of an often repeated story—a lodestone of returnee experience—and were remarkably uniform. For all

155

three, the passage across the border was a pivotal and highly emotional moment, where the disparity between Iran's more developed infrastructure and Afghanistan's devastation caused the youth distress, pain, and anxiety, and caused them to think they had made a terrible mistake. In the words of Maryam:

> We were very shocked, it was unbelievable that Afghanistan was so . . . [interrupts herself] Nobody wanted to come to Afghanistan except me. Day and night I would say: let's go to Afghanistan let's go to Afghanistan, we've got to build Afghanistan, and I'd had all these plans for what I would do and all of those dissolved at once. I didn't know what to do, to laugh or to cry. I was like that an entire week, neither crying nor laughing.

The adjustment process was difficult and involved much economic hardship for all the youth and their families. In particular, the two females struggled. Zekya described how she fought on her first day in Afghanistan with a stranger who informed her she was not allowed, as a woman, to approach a heritage site. Maryam recounted how she almost fell into a well because she did not know how to pump water—domestic chores were much more physically taxing in Afghanistan. The youths also had to adjust their behaviour and clothing to integrate with Afghan society. Shifting out of the Iranian accent[8] was particularly important, as was evident in the (in two cases, rather unsuccessful) ways in which the youths tried to adopt Dari phrases and a Kabul accent in their 2006 interviews. Maryam described a painful episode in her integration process as follows:

> When I first came here it was very difficult for me, my accent was very bad, I couldn't speak Dari at all. People would all call me *Iranigak* (little Iranian), and in the streets, or in schools they called me *Iranigak*. In school the teachers seemed to have a particular grudge against us. I went to grade 12 and my algebra teacher—and I'll never forget this, this is the worst memory of my life—I was new at the school and I was wearing a black *magna'eh* and suddenly he pulled it, and he pulled it so hard that it ripped a bit, and he said 'this isn't Iran that you're wearing this, a black headscarf, you've made yourself like a crow, this is Afghanistan.' I took my bag and went home and I felt really bad, and the next day my dad went with me to school and said 'what is going on here that you treat my daughter so badly'—just think, there I was a grade 12 student, taking my dad to school! —and so the teacher did apologize, but it was the worst experience of my life.

---

[8] The Farsi spoken in Iran and Dari spoken in Afghanistan are very similar, differing in some points of grammar, vocabulary, and accent.

After their initial shock and the period of adjustment, their lives improved and, more acclimatized, the youth began to feel that they had made the right choice in repatriating. In general, they reported that their families were also reasonably content. Zekya and Maryam recounted how they believed their families had moved to Afghanistan on their insistence, and how both had struggled with depression and guilt during the re-acculturation period, but how also, in time, they came to see that everyone appreciated having moved. According to Zekya, increased opportunities and access to schooling (even if the educational system in Afghanistan was not as strong) had made her family happy and thankful about the move. In Maryam's family, her older brother who was studying at Kabul University was particularly happy about having moved. The rest of her family was less enthusiastic, with her parents maintaining they were only in Afghanistan for their children's education. Despite their complaints, however, she said that, reading between the lines, one could see that they preferred repatriation as their plans for the future were always about Afghanistan. Amin, meanwhile, said that his family had moved on his father's instigation. Apart from Amin's mother and sister, who had not wanted to move originally and continued to be unhappy with repatriation, his family had passed through the sharp downturn of the adjustment period to a sense of preference for life in Afghanistan over life in Iran.

By 2006, Amin was studying his preferred subject in university; Maryam was working for an international organization, and hoped to be accepted on a midwifery programme in university; and Zekya was a host for Radio Arman, the most popular radio station in Kabul, and planned to apply for university in the coming year. In general, the three demon-strated an acceptance of their situations: although their lives were not perfect, they had clear goals that they believed could be achieved. The youths admitted freely their difficulties in adjusting to life in Afghanistan and earlier unhappiness ('I cursed the fact that I am Afghan'—Maryam), but believed the adjustment was something that they—and, indeed, all Afghans in Iran—would have had to pass through sooner or later. They expressed contentment with their decision to return and were hopeful about and had concrete plans for the future.

Nasir

Having returned to Tehran in 2006, Nasir interpreted 'travel with family' to mean movement and displacement within Iran. He offered in his interview a detailed history of his family's migration from Esfahan, a city in the south of Iran, to Tehran in the north, and subsequent displacement from suburb to suburb in greater Tehran. He identified this movement as the source of much of his later suffering: he was expelled from an Iranian school he loved in the 1990s due to a new government policy regarding Afghan education which required that Afghans only study in the city in which they had been registered—Esfahan, in his case. He was too young to move from Tehran to Esfahan on his own to continue studying in an Iranian school, and thus was forced to enrol in a resource-poor informal Afghan school. While he had travelled across the Iranian border to Afghanistan in 2004, he did not offer a 'border crossing' story, but instead said briefly that he had felt good in Afghanistan since, as a man, he was not vulnerable to the kinds of harassment and beatings Afghan men can face in Iran.

By favouring an 'internal displacement' interpretation of 'travel with family' over others, Nasir seemed to be attempting to highlight his own and others' loss and unhappiness through movement, and their lack of stability within Iran. Nasir's interview demonstrated clearly his frustrations with feeling Iranian but not being accepted, and his helplessness in the face of rejection:

> I had never seen Afghanistan, I'd grown up with Iranian culture and I am like a completely Iranian individual, and I can even speak Farsi much better than many Iranians that are in the provinces, but I'd never seen Afghanistan . . . I grew up in Iran, my memories are Iran's, the good, bad, ugly are all Iran's. I'm 20, and only one of those years, last year, belongs to Afghanistan. The rest belong to Iran. But honestly, I don't feel calm or secure in Iran. I feel like I'm in a cage.

Nasir, as the only youth who had repatriated but then decided to return to refugee life in Iran, maintained that his return to Iran was not of his own choice:

> Why did I come back? Because I was forced to, I couldn't not come, because I believe a person who wants to reach some things has to give something up, I fired my final bullet to go to university in Iran, with [Amin] I wandered around a lot and tried to find other countries to go to but since we weren't young we weren't able to. I never wanted to return again to Iran but I was forced to in order to continue my studies.

The remark that he was 'forced' to return to Iran is somewhat disingenuous as Nasir did have the option of remaining in Afghanistan to study in Kabul like his friend Amin. Unfortunately, after re-entering Iran to try to enter a university in Tehran, Nasir found that his application had been blocked and, despite much effort on his part for five months, was eventually rejected. He lost most of his savings in the process and the stress of the period showed itself clearly in his weight loss and shattered demeanour. He became an illegal worker, living and working at a tailor's shop despite not really knowing the trade, with dreams of finding the means to enter a university in India. A few months after our meeting, Nasir returned to Afghanistan to join his family and again work to find good employment or entry to an educational institution.

IMPRESSIONS OF REPATRIATION IN 2007

In 2007 the security situation in Afghanistan deteriorated further, with the intensification of attacks shifting casualties from being predominantly in the military or law enforcement to formerly 'secure' civilian areas. In May, August, and October, I held a series of meetings and interviews with the four youths. The shift in the youths' attitudes towards their situations was quite clear: Amin described feeling 'weird' when crossing through (now frequently targeted) downtown Kabul; and Maryam, meanwhile, asked to borrow my video camera for what I later found out would be footage to convince Afghans still in Iran not to repatriate. Any 'honeymoon period' there may have been in the youths' relationship with Afghanistan seemed to be over.

The crux of the youths' frustration appeared to centre around feelings of alienation. Amin was continuing his studies at Kabul University and had a job teaching computer skills on the side. While reasonably successful, he was also aware that his opportunities for employment continued to be linked with his identity. Whereas acceptance in Iran was often determined by Afghan-ness versus Iranian-ness, with some Afghan ethnicities such as Tajiks better able to pass as Iranian and hence avoid discrimination, in Afghanistan access to opportunity traversed a complex maze based on factors that could include family, ethnicity, political affiliation, languages spoken, tribe/region of origin, and country of refuge (with Pakistani returnees enjoying much better acceptance than those from Iran).

Nasir and Amin had both resisted shifting their clothing, grooming, and accents at first—in their eyes, urban Afghans sounded like Iranian villagers and looked unkempt. But as time passed they became aware of the disdain their 'fancy' ways earned them, marking them as not having suffered like those who had stayed in Afghanistan, de-Afghanizing them for preferring the cultural modes of a powerful neighbour whose interventions many viewed with resentment. By 2007 both had resorted, in writing as well as in their speech, to the Afghan turns of phrase that to Iranian ears sound like poor grammar. Nasir at one point participated in a university riot protesting the unIslamic influence of Westerners, believing he had found a brief solidarity and acceptance in collective Afghan outrage ('they have insulted our religion') which dissipated shortly thereafter when he was refused a TV hosting job due to, ironically, being too Iranian. His main focus for much of the remainder of the year was to enter a university in Malaysia.

By 2007 the restrictions of gender began to feel ever more confining for the women. Zekya, as the oldest child in a family with only one son (who was in primary school), had set aside her dreams for attending university to take on three jobs for the sake of her family. Despite taking on what would generally be construed as a male role, however, she was still bound by societal conventions requiring her to be chaperoned rather than travel on her own. Maryam, meanwhile, who had spoken in Iran of wanting to stay single forever and enter politics, found that in Afghanistan respectability was much more tied to marriage. She became engaged to a young engineer and worked as a beauty technician. Her strong idealistic desire to work for the reconstruction of her country had been doused by the many hardships and injustices of life in Afghanistan—her father had invested their savings from Iran into building a home in Kabul, but his brother, a military commander, subsequently forced her family out into the streets at gunpoint.

IMPLICATIONS OF REPATRIATION FOR AFGHAN YOUTH

The perspectives I have included above indicate that refugee youth are far from a monolithic category, and more research is necessary to understand the experiences of Afghan returnee youth. I do suggest, however, ways in which the long-term refugee youths in my study may have experienced moving to Afghanistan.

Repatriation as self-reconciliation

Bash and Zezlina-Phillips (2006) suggest that transition, for refugee adolescents, is multifaceted. Refugee youth must position themselves psychologically relative to childhood and adulthood as well as national affiliation in a way that would account for their past, present, and future aspirations. They suggest that the transitions of adolescence mixed with the blurred boundaries of exile and hybrid identity constitute a significant but not insurmountable challenge for youth in finding-defining their identities. Muggeridge and Doná (2006: 424), meanwhile, propose that the first visit home for refugees constitutes an important milestone, causing a shift in inner equilibrium and releasing refugees from the limbo of exile, 'closing one chapter and unlocking a process of engagement with subsequent events'. Brought together, these propositions might suggest that for long-term refugee youth, the first visit to the unfamiliar 'home' of their family's origin enables them to shift into a different plane of engagement with life. Having gained insight into what had been the 'otherness' of their origins, returnee youth are better able to reconcile their inner conflict, anchor their sense of self, and proceed with greater confidence and direction out of adolescence.

Zekya offers her thoughts on how repatriation enabled her to achieve greater coherence and self-knowledge about her place in the world:

> In Iran, it could be said that identity was something that was obscure, not only for me but for all Afghan youth who lived there. We lived there like other individuals and youth, but there was always something unknown that we always lacked, and that was our identity, if we said we didn't have Iranian residency and were Afghan our identity was something that was trodden on and wasn't given any value, which happily in Afghanistan this issue doesn't emerge much. I can say that there's one thing I'm proud of, and that is that I am Afghan. Maybe Afghanistan isn't a place that people think much of, but I am proud to be from here.

Not only had repatriation solidified her identity as definitively Afghan, but it also put into perspective her relationship with Iran. She and her peers recognized the positive contributions of their time in Iran (awareness of a larger world, greater gender sensitivity, a strong education) while separating themselves from Iranian society. Nasir, on the other hand, who had achieved his first visit home but declined to stay, remained conflicted over his identity. In his case, his internalization of what Hoodfar (2010) terms the 'cultural chauvinism' of Iran may have factored in his decision to reject educational opportunities in Afghanistan and attempt, in vain, to return to the 'superior' culture and better established educational system of Iran.

Repatriation as mystical–moral destination

While in Iran in 2003, the youths at the informal Afghan school spoke of Afghanistan in poetic terms, as a space of purity and healing. Placing 'the spirit' in Afghanistan appeared to allow them to preserve their sense of worth and dignity in the face of Iranian rebuffs, even when—as in the case of Nasir– they were reluctant to repatriate.[9] It also allowed the youths to take a moral high ground: whatever harassment they may have faced from Iranians, they were adamant that they would not reciprocate in treating Iranians poorly in Afghanistan. Through morality discourse the youths were able to claim one important area in which Afghanistan was more developed relative to Iran, and challenge or break the hold of the Iranian nationalism in which they had been immersed most of their lives.

Given their lack of political and economic clout, the youths made Islamic obligation and morality a central platform in their analysis of Iran's coercive repatriation programme. They appropriated human-rights discourse and notions of 'borderless Islam' to assert their right to access refugee education in Iran (Hoodfar 2010). Their analysis sat uneasily, however, alongside their sense of obligation towards their country, for whose soil they ostensibly held great esteem. As dutiful and devoted Afghans, how could they justify overstaying their welcome in Iran now that the conflict in Afghanistan was officially over and the collective task of reconstruction had begun?

Thus, contrary to my expectations, the youths had a strong voice in the repatriation decision-making processes in their family, in some cases reportedly convincing their reluctant family members to repatriate against their economic best interests. Their hope for access to education in Afghanistan held great weight in the decision-making process of the family, but their idealism and less trammelled sense of possibility were also highly potent forces. Repatriation was a moral imperative for the youths, at a personal rather than political level, as well as an idealized solution to their discomfort in Iran.

---

[9] For all his later unwillingness to relocate to Afghanistan, in 2003, Nasir asked me to bring back a small box of Afghan soil from one of my trips to Afghanistan. He welled up with emotion when I presented it to him on my return, kissing it before putting it away reverently.

Repatriation as rite of passage

Monsutti (2007) suggests that economic migration by young Afghan men is a masculine rite of passage—young males migrating to Iran reached adulthood in proving their ability to be economic providers for their families in Afghanistan. Perhaps for Afghan refugee youth born in exile, enduring the suffering of return is a rite of passage as well, initiating the youth into Afghan society. Their initiation includes economic distress, facing derision at being *Iranigak*, and adjusting to the customs and lack of infrastructure of Afghanistan. For all the youths in this study, crossing the border into Afghanistan was a painful and pivotal event even as its repeated story was a well worn badge of honour. Nasir, as the one reluctant returnee in the study, declined to share his own border-crossing story, perhaps demonstrating his rejection of the symbolism and transformative power of the border crossing.

Acculturation stress was a commonality among the returnees and a marker differentiating their coming of age from those still in exile: 'When I was in Iran, I thought Afghanistan was a place where all my dreams would come true . . . When I came here, I put all those dreams aside, they seemed really plastic to me. This place needs dreams that are somehow stony' (Maryam). Asked what they thought of the youth who had remained in Tehran, the returnees said that they were unsure what their former classmates were trying to gain—were they cowards?—by remaining in Iran, as quite simply it was hard to live in a country that wasn't your own. Surviving the pain of repatriation gave the youths a basis for reclaiming the stoicism of Afghan identity, expressing solidarity with those who had remained in the country, and earning the right to join the larger community in Afghanistan as insiders.

Repatriation as loss of a generation

While the youths may have felt they deserved to be accepted as fully Afghan after repatriating, however, that designation was not always accorded them by their external world. Their painful tension and limbo between Iranian-ness and Afghan-ness continued, as manifested in discrimination by Afghans towards 'Iranianized' Afghans. Such lack of community acceptance and the curtailed economic and social opportunities it portends led Maryam to characterize herself and her peers as a 'burnt generation': just as her parents had relinquished their life goals in the narrowed choices of forced migration, so would she have to set aside her hopes for greater achievements in the face of battles over land claims, livelihoods, educational placement, and the right to belong in her purported home country.

CONCLUSIONS: CONSTRUCTIONS AND RECONSTRUCTIONS

This study presents the stories of four Afghan youths who had lived in a very specific refugee context in Tehran. By the very nature of the participatory research style, which emphasized self-expression and dialogue among the youths and a fair amount of contact with me, the sample I have studied is 'contaminated' and unlikely to represent most Afghan refugee youth in Iran. I would suggest, however, based on long-term research I have conducted with dozens of youth and their families in a number of neighbourhoods in Tehran and Mashad, that the youths' reactions and concerns during the crises of repatriation decision making and acculturation evoke the experiences of many Afghan youth.

Their stories raise a number of questions. First, the differing positions presented by Olszewska and Monsutti in this volume over the 'naturalness'—whether rupture or nomadism—of migration offer a possible mirror to the naturalness of repatriation. It may indeed be helpful to think of repatriation in light of the nature of the original movement. Is the original movement predicated on trauma, does it include significant ties back to the origin (via remaining family, protected assets, regular remittances, return visits), what perceived or real degree of choice was there in the migration and its destination, and so on? In turn, how natural might be the perception and experience of the repatriation?

Second, it is also possible to look at the 'naturalness' dichotomy from the standpoint of the construction of the self, as reflected in international policies. There is a strong critique of the concept of a 'natural' identity being anchored in an 'original' place or community (Gupta and Ferguson 1997; Malkki 1997; Black 2002). By this argument, the (wrongful) assumption that identity is 'rooted' in place designates dislocation as unnatural, and as a consequence (wrongfully) promotes repatriation as optimal relative to any other outcome in a refugee crisis. In contrast, it is argued, on decoupling identity and place and presuming that physical origin allows for a 'construction, rather than merely a discovery, of difference' (Gupta and Ferguson 1997: 13), displacement would indicate mobility rather than rupture. Emphasis on the right of return could well be set aside in favour of the right to stay and belong, regardless of original identity.

Finally, 'naturalness' reflects both the individual and their external world. For the youths in this study, one of the most painful aspects of their exile was its continuation in the promised land, post-repatriation. The optimal durable solution of repatriation assumes a natural fit for refugees in their country of origin, offering (often limited) support for returnees, but rarely investing adequately in preparing the society to which they return. Such investments would need to include infrastructural support for the influx, as well as address attitudes and identity constructions of the society towards the returnees.

These concerns are important for dehomogenizing any 'durable solution' to particularized contexts and populations. They are also important for addressing, at the local level, the ruptures and tensions that occur in repatriation. Repatriation is presumed to fit based on the construction of a 'natural' self, when in fact in many cases it may cause the *destruction* of an imagined self as the frameworks of international agencies and policies, those of their families' land of origin, and those within refugees themselves collide painfully. And when, as was the case for long-term forced migrant Afghan youth in Iran, the 'liberation' of the 'homeland' presents opportunity/obligation/coercion to return, repatriation can engender a highly conflicted outlook and many suboptimal solutions.

Note. This essay draws on material I have presented in Kamal (2010). My thanks to the Social Sciences and Humanities Research Council and the Trudeau Foundation for providing funding for my ongoing doctoral research in Afghanistan.

REFERENCES

Abbasi-Shavasi, M. J. et al. (2005), *Return to Afghanistan? A Study of Afghans Living in Iran* (Kabul, Afghanistan Research and Evaluation Unit).

Anderson, P. (2001), '"You Don't Belong Here in Germany": On the Social Situation of Refugee Children in Germany', *Journal of Refugee Studies*, 14, 2.

Bakewell, O. (2000), 'Uncovering Local Perspectives on Humanitarian Assistance and Its Outcomes', *Disasters*, 24, 2.

Bash, L. and Zezlina-Phillips, E. (2006), 'Identity, Boundary and Schooling: Perspectives on the Experiences and Perceptions of Refugee Children', *Intercultural Education*, 17, 1.

Black, R. (2002), 'Conceptions of "Home" and the Political Geography of Refugee Repatriation: Between Assumption and Contested Reality in Bosnia-Herzegovina', *Applied Geography*, 22.

—— and Koser, K. (1999), *The End of the Refugee Cycle?: Refugee Repatriation and Reconstruction* (New York, Berghahn Books).

Blitz, B. K. et al. (2005), 'Non-voluntary Return? The Politics of Return to Afghanistan', *Political Studies*, 53.

Bradley, M. (2006), 'Return of Forced Migrants', Forced Migration Online, www.forcedmigration.org/guides/fmo042/.

Chimni, B. S. (2002), 'Refugees and Reconstruction of "Post-conflict" Societies: A Critical Perspective', *International Peacekeeping*, 9, 2.

Cornish, F. et al. (1999), 'Returning Strangers: Children of Malawian Refugees Come "Home"?', *Journal of Refugee Studies*, 12, 3.

Dhruvarajan, V. (1993), 'Ethnic Cultural Retention and Transmission among First Generation Hindu Asian Indians in a Canadian Prairrie City', *Journal of Comparative Family Studies*, 24.

Eisenbruch, M. (1997), 'The Cry for the Lost Placenta: Cultural Bereavement and Cultural Survival among Cambodians who Resettled, were Repatriated, or Stayed at Home', in M. van Tilburg and A. Vingerhoets (eds), *Psychological Aspects of Geographical Moves: Homesickness and Acculturation Stress* (The Netherlands, Tilburg University Press).

Gupta, A. and Ferguson, J. (1997), *Culture, Power, Place: Exploration in Cultural Anthropology* (Durham, NC, Duke University Press).

Hoodfar, H. (2010), 'Refusing the Margins: Afghan Refugee Youth in Iran', in D. Chatty (ed.), *Deterritorialized Youth: Sahrawi and Afghan Refugees at the Margins of the Middle East* (Oxford, Berghahn Books).

Kakoli, R. (2000), 'Repatriation and De-territorialization: Meskhetian Turks' Conception of Home', *Journal of Refugee Studies*, 13, 4.

Kamal, S. (2010), 'Afghan Refugee Youth in Iran and the Morality of Repatriation', in D. Chatty (ed.), *Deterritorialized Youth: Sahrawi and Afghan Refugees at the Margins of the Middle East* (Oxford, Berghahn Books).

Malkki, L. H. (1997), 'National Geographic: The Rooting of Peoples and the Territorialization of National Identity among Scholars and Refugees', in A. Gupta and J. Ferguson (eds), *Culture, Power, Place: Explorations in Critical Anthropology* (Durham, NC, Duke University Press).

Monsutti, A. (2007), 'Migration as a Rite of Passage: Young Afghans Building Masculinity and Adulthood in Iran', *Iranian Studies*, 40, 2.

Muggeridge, H. and Doná, G. (2006), 'Back Home? Refugees' Experiences of their First Visit back to their Country of Origin', *Journal of Refugee Studies*, 19, 4.

Rousseau, C. et al. (2001), 'Going Home: Giving Voice to Memory Strategies of Young Mayan Refugees who Returned to Guatemala as a Community', *Culture, Medicine and Psychiatry*, 25.

Stein, B. (1997), Paper presented at the 'Promoting Democracy, Human Rights, and Re-integration in Post-Conflict Societies Conference' held on 30–1 October, http://pdf.dec.org/pdf_docs/pnacd092.pdf on April 2007.

Stigter, E. (2006), 'Afghan Migratory Strategies', *Refugee Survey Quarterly*, 25, 2.

United Nations High Commissioner for Refuges (UNHCR) (2005), *Measuring Protection by Numbers* (UNHCR).

Vargas, C. M. (1999), 'Cultural Mediation for Refugee Children: A Comparative Derived Model', *Journal of Refugee Studies*, 12, 3.

Zetter, R. (1994), 'The Greek-Cypriot Refugees: Perceptions of Return Under Conditions of Protracted Exile', *International Migration Review*, 28, 2.

—— (1999), 'Reconceptualizing the Myth of Return: Continuity and Transition amongst the Greek-Cypriot Refugees of 1974', *Journal of Refugee Studies*, 12, 1.

Part III
Identity in Exile

7.
When the Self Becomes Other: Representations of Gender, Islam, and the Politics of Survival in the Sahrawi Refugee Camps
Elena Fiddian-Qasmiyeh

INTRODUCTION

As embodied in this volume and the conference upon which it is based, refugees and other forcibly displaced populations are frequently examined and analysed by external observers, be they policy-makers, governments, academics, or non-governmental organizations (NGOs). At the same time, however, observational flows are multidirectional, with refugees and their political representatives identifying and acting in response to the priorities and assumptions of aid providers and analysts alike for a number of reasons.[1] This essay traces the ways in which the protracted Sahrawi refugee context has been represented by its political body, the Polisario Front, to its non-Sahrawi 'audience' in order to secure their continued political and humanitarian support.

This essay builds upon the recognition that the delivery of development aid has often been dependent upon recipients fulfilling a set of non-economic conditionalities, including the creation of democratic political structures, the protection of human rights, and the promotion of gender equality (Kandiyoti, in Hammami 2005: 1352 and Kandiyoti 2007: 509; Moghadam 1997: 36). With reference to refugees more specifically, Harrell-Bond equally stresses that 'refugees [are] expected to *conform* to the values of their sponsors' (1999: 145, emphasis in the original) as a

---

[1] My conceptualization of these multidirectional observations develops Foucault's notion that 'he [*sic*] who is subjected to a field of visibility, and who knows it, assumes responsibility for the constraints of power; he inscribes in himself the power relations in which he simultaneously plays both roles; he becomes the principle of his own subjection' (1979: 203).

means of guaranteeing the continued arrival of humanitarian supplies. However, such conditionalities do not necessarily lead to recipients modifying their socio-political structures as sponsors or aid providers might expect. Rather, analysts are increasingly documenting the ways in which multiple forms of dependence on externally provided aid and support have directly impacted the ways in which recipients represent or 'market' (Bob 2005) themselves to their aid providers. Since NGOs and solidarity networks habitually differentiate between groups which are or are not worthy of support, their continued engagement with a 'cause' often depends on their being convinced as to the cultural 'authenticity' of the recipient (Conklin 1997),[2] or the usage of particular political discourses and methods by recipients (Bob 2005; Jasper 1997; Jean-Klein 1997). In this way, 'broader political contexts' often influence the particular identity which is presented by social and political movements (Jasper 1997: 329–30). Thus, Bob stresses that 'movements must often alter key characteristics to meet the expectation of patrons' (2005: 5) who often act as 'auditors' (Jean-Klein 1997), observing both the implementation of their projects, and what I term the 'justifiability' of their engagement.

In the following pages I therefore argue that the Polisario Front not only observes 'its' refugee population, but has also developed a particular representation of the Sahrawi 'Self' based upon its observations of its own observers, including non-Sahrawi academics, policy-makers, and solidarity movements. In the present case, I argue that the Polisario Front places one particular social group (Sahrawi refugee women) and a specific set of characteristics at the forefront of its representations of the camps.

METHODOLOGY

This essay is informed by over 100 in-depth, semi-structured interviews conducted with Sahrawi refugees as part of my ESRC-funded doctoral research in the Algerian-based Sahrawi refugee camps, Cuba, Syria, and Spain.[3] Sahrawi youth live and study in the last three of these locations, often spending up to (and sometimes over) a decade without contact with

---

[2] MacCannell (1973) also discusses the enactment of 'staged authenticity' in order to attract tourists to certain locations. In this context, I argue that a particular representation has been developed to attract solidarity workers and networks to the Sahrawi refugee camps.

[3] Additional interviews were conducted in South Africa. I draw upon this data-set in Fiddian-Qasmiyeh (2009a).

their families in the camps.[4] All interviews completed in Spain and Cuba, as well as with camp-based Sahrawi youth who have graduated from Cuban universities, took place in Spanish: this is the interviewees' second language and the author's mother tongue. I interviewed Syrian-based students and Sahrawi families in the refugee camps in either Spanish or Hassaniya-Arabic (the language spoken in the camps), without the need of a translator.

A BRIEF HISTORY OF THE WESTERN SAHARAN CONFLICT

From 1884 until the mid-1970s, the phosphate-rich territory currently known as the Western Sahara was a Spanish colony (see Figure 7.1). Despite being placed on the UN Decolonization Committee's agenda in October 1964, and although Spain conducted a census of the colony's population in December 1974 to prepare for an eventual referendum for self-determination, by the end of 1975 Spain had decided to withdraw without holding a referendum. With General Franco (Spain's military dictator) gravely ill, and the Spanish mainland itself experiencing violent threats from political and military groups, Spanish forces rapidly left the colony to 'maintain the peace' in the metropolis. During May 1973 the main anti-colonial movement, the Polisario Front, was born and gained popular support, first resisting Spanish colonialism, and later Moroccan and Mauritanian claims over the territory.

Although the International Court of Justice ruled in October 1975 that neither Morocco nor Mauritania had legal claims to the territory that should impede holding a referendum for self-determination,[5] 350,000 Moroccan civilians faced no resistance from Spanish or international forces as they crossed into the territory in early November 1975 as part of the 'Green March' designed by the Moroccan state to recover its 'Southern Provinces'. Some 20,000 Moroccan soldiers soon joined their civilian compatriots from the north (Chopra 1999), while Mauritanian forces entered from the south, ignoring UN resolutions which deplored the

---

[4] The impact of this long period of separation from the camps is explored in Chatty, Fiddian-Qasmiyeh and Crivello (2010), and Fiddian-Qasmiyeh (forthcoming a).
[5] The ICJ ruling reads as follows, '. . . the Court has not found legal ties of such nature as might affect the application of resolution 1514 (XV) in the decolonization of Western Sahara and, in particular, of the principle of self-determination through the free and genuine expression of the will of the peoples of the Territory': *Western Sahara, Advisory Opinion*, ICJ Reports 1975, p. 12.

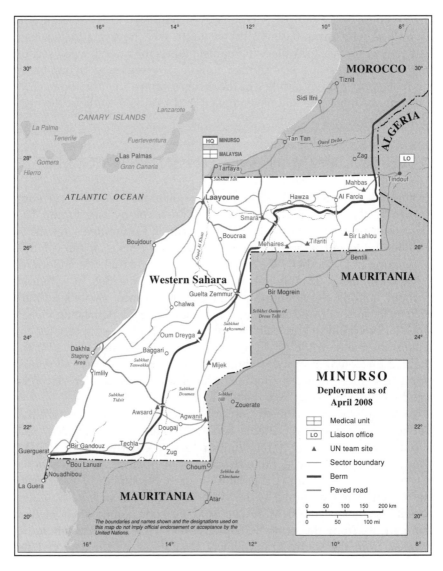

Figure 7.1.   Map of Western Sahara, MINURSO Deployment April 2008, no. 3691, Rev. 57,
April 2008.
Source: www.un.org/Depts/Cartographic/french/htmain.htm   (© UN Cartographic
Section).

March and called for its termination (i.e. Res. 380, 06/11/75). After General Franco died (20 November 1975), the armed conflict between Morocco, Mauritania, and the Polisario Front intensified, with a mass exodus of Sahrawis to other parts of the territory and, later, following the bombard-ment of these first encampments with napalm and phosphate bombs (Lippert 1987; Andrade 2003; Mercer 1979), to the nascent Algerian-based refugee camps near these countries' common border.

On 26 February 1976, Spain officially withdrew from its colony and unilaterally declared that it was no longer the administrating power. A day later, the Polisario Front proclaimed the birth of the Sahrawi Arab Democratic Republic (SADR), which to this date governs and administers the Sahrawi refugee camps and its refugee population as a 'state in exile'. Given the extensive overlap of members of the Polisario Front and the representatives of the SADR (i.e. Mohamed Abdelaziz is both the secretary-general of the Polisario and the president of the SADR) I henceforth refer to 'the Polisario/SADR'.

Political conflicts ensued between states which recognized and lobbied in favour of the Polisario/SADR's struggle for independence and those which did not. Such conflicts were both bilateral (for example, between Algeria and Morocco) and multilateral, playing out in arenas such as the Organization of African Unity. Hence, when this body, which has since been reborn as the African Union, recognized the SADR in 1982, Morocco suspended its membership and officially withdrew from the organization in 1984 (Damis 1983; Lynn Price 1981). From 1976 to the present, the conflict over the Western Sahara has thus been dominated by the main parties (Morocco and Polisario) attempting to convince influential state and non-state actors to support their respective political standpoints, and recognize the legitimacy of their claims over the territory and its inhabitants.

THE SAHRAWI REFUGEE CAMPS

The Sahrawi refugee camps are currently inhabited by between 125,000 and 165,000 refugees from the former Spanish Sahara,[6] and are still

---

[6] Despite contradictory census data, in 1999 a preliminary registration carried out by UNHCR concluded that at least 107,000 camp-based refugees (potential voters and their immediate families) would wish to return to the Western Sahara under the auspices of a UNHCR repatriation programme after/if a referendum for self-determination is conducted (UNHCR 2000: 187; WFP 1999: 4). The total camp population, including 'non-voters' living in the camps, is thus now calculated by UNHCR and WFP as being over 155,000.

managed by the Sahrawi refugees' only political representatives, the Polisario Front, who continue to demand self-determination from Morocco. Upon the camps' creation, the Polisario/SADR developed its own constitution, camp-based police force (and prisons), army, and parallel state and religious legal systems (the latter of which implements a Maliki interpretation of Islam). A number of 'national' institutions, such as the national parliament and national council, national hospital and pharmaceutical laboratory, the national war hospital and the landmine victims' centre, are all located close to Rabouni, the administrative capital of the camps and where the SADR's camp-based ministries are found.

There are currently four major established refugee camps named after main cities/towns in the Western Sahara: Aaiún, Ausserd, Smara, and Dakhla. A fifth, smaller camp has developed around the National Women's School, called 27 February School/Camp: this was the location of the majority of my fieldwork in the camps. The main camps are headed by a *wālī* (governor) who is appointed by the 'head of state' (Shelley 2004: 183), with administrative and managerial functions completed by camp residents employed by the Polisario/SADR. Each of the camps is divided into a number of districts, and each district is subdivided into neighbourhoods. In the case of the 27 February Camp, the camp is managed not by a *wālī* or *wāliya* (fem. sing.) but by the director of the National Women's School. The relatively small population (estimated at 2,000–2,500) is shared between four neighbourhoods: three on one side of a recently paved road running through the camp, and the fourth on the other side, where the women's and primary schools, the National Union of Sahrawi Women (NUSW) headquarters, local hospital, state court building, and national museum are all located.

Sustaining the Sahrawi refugee camps

Camp inhabitants are dependent on a number of international and transnational networks which provide both refugees and the Polisario/SADR with material aid and political support. Humanitarian aid is provided by organizations such as the European Commission's Humanitarian Aid Office (ECHO), the United Nations High Commissioner for Refugees (UNHCR), and the World Food Programme (WFP), by states including Algeria, and by individual refugees and the Polisario Front. Further, however, significant 'solidarity' networks have arisen from Spanish civil society in particular, and play a pivotal role in maintaining the camps and their inhabitants. Indeed, WFP notes in a recent report that '[t]he resources from UNHCR do not cover all needs: they are complemented by inputs from the Government of Algeria, *solidarity groups*, and a number of NGOs' (2008: 9, my emphasis). Solidarity groups in this respect refer to the organized mobilization of members of civil society who define themselves as being 'in solidarity with' or 'friends of' the Sahrawi people and the Sahrawi cause for self-determination. I use the term solidarity as it is employed in popular Spanish (*solidaridad*), to mean the 'humanitarian'[7] act of offering moral, political, and/or material support to individuals and collectivities which are conceptualized as being 'in need' of and deserving such support. Individuals who support and 'care' for others in need are referred to in Spanish as *solidarios* (sing. *solidario*), which is a more precise meaning than that encompassed by the English term 'solidary' (more broadly defined by the Oxford English Dictionary as 'characterized by or having solidarity or coincidence of interests'). While multiple solidarity actors are engaged in working to support the camps and the cause, in this essay I focus on the largest and most active network: the Spanish solidarity movement.

In Spain, the Coordinadora Estatal de Asociaciones Solidarias con el Sahara (CEAS: 'State Coordinator of Associations in Solidarity with the Sahara')[8] organizes the activities of over 200 associations which support the Sahrawi people through humanitarian, development, and political means. CEAS estimates that the groups which it coordinates have a total of over 14,700 active members, and CEAS itself is supported by over 5,000 volunteers, the majority of whom are reportedly women aged 35–50, men aged 40–55, and young people aged 18–30. *Solidarios* include men and women from across Spain's autonomous communities and regions and from all points of the political spectrum. In addition to CEAS, the Federación Estatal de Instituciones Solidarias con el Pueblo Saharaui (FEDISSAH) is a federation of Spanish state institutions which are 'in solidarity' with the Sahrawi people. Reflecting the high level of Spanish institutional support for the Sahrawi 'cause', the second state conference of institutions 'twinned' with the Sahrawi camps and in solidarity with the Sahrawi people was attended by over 140 Spanish state institutions including municipal and city councils. As a further example, it is noteworthy that in the Basque country 71 per cent of all cooperation and development

---

[7] The first meaning of the adjective *solidario* in the *Collins Spanish–English Dictionary* (Butterfield 2003) is '(= *humanitario*) caring'. I question the nature and implications of the Spanish solidarity network upon the camps and their inhabitants in Fiddian-Qasmiyeh (2009a).

[8] The following information was accessed at www.saharaindependiente.org/spip.php?rubrique15.

projects financed and managed by Guipúzcoa's twenty-seven municipal councils were related to the Sahrawi people in 2007–8 (M.O. 2008).

Overall, these solidarity groups lobby the Spanish government to take an active role in resolving the international dispute through the implementation of a referendum for self-determination; regional and local organizations run significant development programmes in the camps, promote awareness-raising and fund-raising campaigns in Spain, and ensure that the protracted refugee situation is kept on the political radar both nationally and internationally. They also help to coordinate the *Vacaciones en Paz* (Holidays in Peace) programme which allows some 10,000 Sahrawi refugee children to spend two months each summer in Spain. Spanish host-families then travel to the camps en masse during the Easter and Christmas holidays, bringing food, money, medicine, clothes, and toys to 'their' Sahrawi family (see Crivello and Fiddian-Qasmiyeh 2010), in addition to having the opportunity to see living conditions in situ. The material significance of such connections should not be understated: WFP identifies 'the very vulnerable households' as those which 'had not built any contacts with the civil societies of Spain and of other countries that provide support to refugee *families*' (WFP 2008: 3, my emphasis).

It is the palpable connection and physical proximity to the *solidarios* who provide Sahrawi refugee families with much needed material and financial assistance, alongside social capital, which leads many Sahrawis to recognize the significance of the solidarity network. This is in direct contrast with the less visible, and more taken-for-granted humanitarian projects which are, according to my research, marginalized in both the popular and the 'national' imagination. Following Betteridge's analysis of formal and personal gift exchange in Iran (1985), I suggest that we can conceptualize this as a perceived distinction between invisible and anonymous 'official aid', and hyper-visible and personally granted 'intimate aid' (Fiddian-Qasmiyeh 2009a).

Hence, although international non-governmental organizations and certain states provide quantitatively substantial amounts of humanitarian aid to the Sahrawi refugee camps, my research indicates that the Polisario Front and refugees themselves appear to prioritize the various forms of support which are provided by Spanish families and Spanish solidarity groups.[9] In a context where individuals, families, camps, and a political project (that created and run by the Polisario/SADR) depend upon the

---

[9] I discuss this dynamic further in Fiddian-Qasmiyeh (2009a).

provision of humanitarian aid and solidarity networks, I argue that ensuring the sympathy of those visiting or observing the camps surpasses meeting 'physical necessities', and rather becomes a matter of physical and political survival.

Representing the Sahrawi refugee camps: sustaining solidarity

Throughout my multi-sited research with Sahrawi refugees I began to identify a range of means through which this sympathy, or 'solidarity', could be ensured by the Polisario/SADR. While there are different components underpinning this 'international public relations' strategy, one key element arising throughout my interviews with Sahrawis and Spaniards alike—as well as in the literature reviewed in English, Spanish, French, and Arabic—is the centrality which is given by the Polisario/SADR to specific social groups and social characteristics of the refugee population (Fiddian-Qasmiyeh 2009b). Hence, I repeatedly and consistently encountered the same terms, concepts, and labels being invoked by the Polisario/SADR to describe life in the refugee camps to Western audiences. In particular, Sahrawi women emerged as being central to official (i.e. Polisario/SADR) representations of camp social structures and of the 'Sahrawi nation in exile'.

Through a range of discursive and representational mechanisms, including 'parades' staged for Western visitors to the camps and official statements made by Polisario/SADR representatives to the Western media, NGOs, and academics, an archive of common knowledge about the camps has been created and maintained by the Polisario/SADR.[10] The central tenets of the Polisario/SADR's representation of the camps have in turn been adopted and reproduced by the camps' Western observers. The following extract from a report written in 1986 following an Oxfam desk-officer's visit to the camps clearly highlights the principal claim which is systematically made by the Polisario/SADR to Western observers:

> Perhaps the most impressive thing about Sahrawi society is that it is the most fundamentally balanced society I have ever come across in terms of the relationships between men and women (Mowles 1986: 9).

Indeed, since the creation of the Sahrawi refugee camps in the mid-1970s, gender equality and women's 'empowerment' have become central and

---

[10] Following Foucault (1989: 25), I consider that this archive has been created through accumulation and repetition, and that it may be viewed as embodying a source of 'knowledge' to be consulted by and transmitted to both Sahrawis and non-Sahrawis.

recurrent features in both Polisario/SADR and Western accounts of life therein.

In part, that women's participation in the camps should have been highlighted is understandable given that women have always been highly visible in the refugee camps, and were even more so when men were as a whole absent from the camps during the war against Morocco. However, Westerners' descriptions of the camps and their socio-political structures are based on their visits to the camps, where visitors are accompanied by Sahrawi 'guides' who explain the situation on the ground in European languages, alongside Polisario/SADR officials who welcome guests and take them on what I call the camps' 'tourist route': a tour around the main SADR buildings (the national hospital, the war museum, the administrative capital of Rabouni, etc.), and a demonstration of the camps' success stories. These include the vegetable plots which have grown in the arid desert; the primary and secondary schools where Sahrawi students are taught by Sahrawi teachers; and the National Union of Sahrawi Women, which allows for women's participation in local decision-making processes, and coordinates courses run by NGOs in the camps (including computing, driving, weaving, and language courses).

Importantly, during these camp tours, visitors tend to be exposed to particular claims regarding life in the camps, the content of which is reflected in the following extracts from Polisario/SADR representatives and officials. Hence, al-Kuttab, the Syrian-based Polisario Front representative to the Middle East, informed me:

> There are many differences between Sahrawi and Syrian societies . . . Sahrawi women have more freedom . . . Unlike in Jordan, where honour killings and sexual abuse prevail, and in Spain, where violence against women is common, women do not suffer from domestic violence in the camps—[a wife] would be able to divorce [her husband] immediately if he did so, and a Sahrawi man would be unable to remarry if he hit his wife or abused her in any way, his reputation would be destroyed . . . Sahrawi women do not accept polygamy, for there is a 'law of never before or after', and the woman can demand a divorce, which is common. So too is a total rejection of violence against women[11] (interview, Damascus, July 2006, my translation).

Elsewhere, Mariem Salek, who was then the SADR minister of culture in the camps (and is now the minister of education), reported to a journalist:

---

[11] Drawing on fieldwork conducted in the camps, I examine the nature and motivations behind these claims in Fiddian-Qasmiyeh (2009a, 2009b, forthcoming b).

I sometimes ask myself . . . if Arab women exist. In the Arab world, the [form of] feminism which has developed up until now lacks depth; there is nothing serious. If they wanted to recognize us, they would have to admit that what we have achieved is a treasure [una joya] (quoted in Petrich 2005, my translation).

Further, Es-Sweiyh, the former Polisario Front representative to France and the UK, and former permanent SADR representative at the UN, wrote:

women are not marginalized . . . There is space for everyone, and especially for women, for whom the values and traditions of the bidhan (maure) society in general and Sahrawi society in particular, give a privileged place, clearly different from the position of their sisters[12] in the rest of the Arab and Muslim world. In contrast with what you find in other Arab and African societies, the Sahrawi woman plays an important role, in both the productive-economic sector and in the political and administrative structures of the SADR (Es-Sweyih 2001: 36, my translation).

In these Polisario/SADR representations of life in the refugee camps, Sahrawi women are presented as liberated and empowered, and habitually as secular and modern. Such representations are closely based upon the creation and solidification of difference between Sahrawi women, on the one hand, and 'the rest of the Arab and Muslim world' on the other. The implicit message is that 'other Arab and Muslim women' as a unified whole embody the opposite of these virtues and successes. In such examples, the terms 'Arab' and 'Muslim' are consistently used interchangeably, as false synonyms which fail to recognize the religious and ethnic heterogeneity of the Arab world, and the marked differences which exist between Muslim women both in and outside of the Middle East.

It is not the aim of this essay to evaluate the claim that Sahrawi women are 'free' and 'empowered'. Rather, I reflect on the reasons why the Polisario/SADR has focused so intently on equating the Sahrawi refugee camps as a space for female empowerment and gender equality. Simultaneously, I ask why it has done so through distancing the Sahrawi refugee community from the Muslim Middle East. In particular, I propose that the creation, representation, and Western acceptance of Sahrawi society as being based on 'gender equality' and even 'the most fundamentally balanced society . . . ever come across', is an indispensable part of the foundation upon which the solidarity network that maintains the camps is based. I consider that this female-centred strategy of 'international public

---

[12] I explore the apparently contradictory invocation of the concept of 'sisterhood' to refer to both Spanish and 'Arab' women in Fiddian-Qasmiyeh (2009a).

relations' reflects the extent to which the Polisario/SADR has identified that a language of women's rights, female participation, and empowerment is able (or even necessary) to capture the attention of external observers, and guarantees the continuation of humanitarian and political support for the camps and the Sahrawi 'cause' for self-determination.

Indeed, my research with and on Spanish solidarity providers reveals the conditional nature of the solidarity network, demonstrating that this particular representation of camp life is directly related to the Polisario/SADR's 'politics of survival'. Hence, the head of one Spanish solidarity group wrote in *El País* (Spain's principal national newspaper):

> those of us who have always defended the legitimacy of the Sahrawi cause in their fight for their legitimate independence . . . [do so] because we have always defended the democratic basis upon which the SADR's constitution is founded and upon the values of equality between all Sahrawi men and women (Vallbé-Bach 2002, my translation).

As this extract indicates, support for 'the Sahrawi cause' is perceived to be both justifiable and necessary when the refugee camps are concurrently conceptualized as a location for democracy, and home to a society characterized by gender equality. Importantly, the international incident which instigated this letter demonstrates that cases which contradict the Polisario/SADR representation of Sahrawi women threaten not only to undermine its veracity, but the entire solidarity framework upon which the camps and the 'national project' are based.

The cases of three adolescent Sahrawi girls fostered in Spain in the early 2000s allow us to better understand the ways in which official claims of gender equality have been developed as part of what I have called the Polisario/SADR's politics of survival.[13] I submit that Spanish responses to these girls' situations explicitly demonstrate the power which interconnected ideas/ideals about gender have to potentially destabilize the solidarity network which is perceived as both keeping Sahrawi refugees physically alive, and the 'cause' on the political agenda in the West. This case study also clearly demonstrates the dangers which may arise when boundaries are strategically brightened (following Alba

---

[13] It is noteworthy that no parallel male-centred high-profile cases have emerged in Spain (despite boys/young men also having been asked to return to the camps), highlighting the extent to which the 'abduction' of girls and young women has attracted the Spanish public's imagination and media coverage. Numerous other female-centred cases have been reported in the Spanish press. For example, see M.P. (2008a and b) regarding 20-year-old Mimouna Bachir Mostar, whose family reportedly 'kidnapped' her in 2008.

2005) and solidified between Sahrawi refugees and their solidary aid providers through reference to gendered and religious difference.

Conditional solidarity and the 'liberation' of Sahrawi women

Aicha, Huria, and Fatimetu lived and studied in Spain for seven, four, and three years respectively before becoming the centre of a chain of Spanish media campaigns between 2001 and 2003. Two of the three girls had arrived in Spain primarily for medical reasons: Huria due to serious dental complications, and Fatimetu because of her condition as a celiac (Fernández 2003). Indeed, hundreds of Saharawi children have moved to Spain for humanitarian and medical reasons, while others, like Aicha, have been invited to live in Spain specifically to allow them to access secondary and tertiary education (see Crivello and Fiddian-Qasmiyeh 2010).

Prior to leaving the refugee camps, the girls' birth and host families signed agreements before a Sahrawi state judge from the SADR Ministry of Justice and Religious Affairs, indicating that the host family would be granted temporary custody and guardianship of the child, that the child would be returned to her birth family at the family's request, and that the host family would be responsible for maintaining the child's family and cultural ties and facilitating regular communication with the child's parents and family (RASD 2000). These contracts reflect Sahrawi families' concerns that their children might lose their cultural identity and linguistic abilities whilst abroad.[14] Simultaneously, they echo an Islam-based understanding that adoption (and much less so fostering) creates neither legal nor relational ties between individuals (sura 33: 4; Mernissi 2003: 57).

Despite these contracts, Aicha returned only once in seven years to visit her family in the refugee camps, while Huria had not seen her biological parents for over two years (Díaz 2003). These experiences reinforced the families' anxieties that they might eventually lose their daughters entirely. Shortly after the girls reached puberty, their parents separately asked them to return to the camps to help care for their mothers.[15] One girl's mother

---

[14] See Chatty, Fiddian-Qasmiyeh, and Crivello (2010) and Crivello and Fiddian-Qasmiyeh (2010).

[15] A female Sahrawi graduate whom I interviewed in Cuba in November 2006 reflected that 'around adolescence, some families started to ask for their daughters to return to the camps. They would contact the [SADR] Embassy who would in turn contact the Cuban Ministry

was enduring a high-risk pregnancy after having contracted hepatitis, another had suffered a miscarriage, while the third had just recently given birth (Castaño-Boullón 2003; Guijarro 2003). All three mothers therefore required assistance in looking after their younger children, and turned to their eldest daughters accordingly. In each case, the girls' Spanish host families eventually acceded to their returning to the camps 'for a short visit'. However, when their birth families told the girls that they had to stay in the camps rather than return to Spain, the Spanish host families claimed that the girls had been 'abducted', and proceeded to vigorously lobby for their 'return home' (i.e. to Spain).

The degree of Spanish public support mobilized cannot be overstated. In Aicha's case, 17,000 Spaniards in the city of León alone signed a petition for her immediate return (Cazón 2004; Peregil 2002).[16] The relevant debates and legal arguments reached not only the Spanish public via the media, but also higher political institutions such as the Spanish congress, foreign ministry, and senate. Many local-level and several high-ranking politicians (including the then-vice president of the Spanish senate) offered Aicha and Huria their backing, and the senate voted in June 2002 in support of Aicha's return to Spain (Cazón 2004: 187).

Alongside general claims that the girls' rights to health and education were being denied in the camps, the Spanish families and the girls themselves mobilized the Spanish press and political institutions through reference to social conditions in the camps, in particular claiming that Sahrawi traditions violently oppress women's rights. Importantly, the extreme representation of the subjugation of Sahrawi refugee women which was repeatedly and purposefully projected by the girls, their host families, and much of the Spanish media was diametrically opposed to the Polisario/SADR discourse vis-à-vis Sahrawi gender relations. At the same time, it was directly in line with the monolithic depictions of subjugated, isolated, and violated 'third world women' which Mohanty (1988) and Spivak (1990) vehemently reject. Before turning to the case study in question, a brief note is necessary to clarify the significance of this last point.

Building upon Fanon's work (in particular, his seminal piece 'Algeria Unveiled' (1965), first published in 1959) and Said's *Orientalism* (1979),

---

asking for their daughters to conclude their studies and leave Cuba. They did this, and girls started returning to the camps (Fiddian-Qasmiyeh 2009b).'

[16] 12,000 signatures were collected in Avilés supporting Huria's 'liberation' (González 2003a).

authors including Yeğenoğlu (1998), Lewis (1995), and Abu-Lughod, (1998, 2001, 2002) have developed gendered post-colonial studies of the Middle East and North Africa (MENA) region which concentrate on various forms of, and motivations for, interconnected representations of the national and gendered Self and Other (also Chatty and Rabo 1997: esp. 14–15).[17] Much of this work explores and critiques 'the metonymic association between the Orient and its women, or more precisely the *representation* of woman as tradition and as the essence of the Orient' (Yeğenoğlu 1998: 99, my emphasis; also Chatty and Rabo 1997: passim).

Yeğenoğlu stresses that within Orientalist constructions 'of Muslim cultures, the harem, the veil and polygamy were highly charged symbols and they all functioned as synonyms of female oppression' (1998: 100). Equally, Almond argues:

> Among Muslim female writers, the most frequently encountered objection against Western feminism is one of ethnocentrism: a number of European and American theorists, it is alleged, simply devote their attention to chadors, polygamy and honour-crimes (2007: 134).

Importantly, the body of work produced by post-colonial feminists has provided insights into the ways in which representations of women are connected to systems of domination and subordination on national and transnational levels (see Hyndman and Walton-Roberts 2000; Abu-Lughod 2002).[18]

Bearing the above framework in mind, I now turn to Spanish responses to these three girls' 'abductions', demonstrating that support was explicitly obtained for the girls' 'liberation' from the refugee camps via continuously pinpointing oppressive veiling and marriage practices, and identifying different forms of violence against women. The images mobilized parallel the Orientalist imagery which is reproduced by the West, and indeed by the Polisario/SADR in the official representations outlined above with regard to the Muslim Middle East.

'Saving' oppressed Sahrawi women

Undoubtedly the most powerful factor prompting thousands of Spaniards to support the girls' return to Spain was the perception that

---

[17] On post-colonial nationalism, see Chatterjee (1986 and 1993).
[18] One such element is highlighted by Nzenza (quoting Alcoff) who stresses that 'the practice of privileged people speaking for or on behalf of less privileged persons has actually "resulted [in many cases] in increasing or reinforcing the oppression of the group spoken for"' (1997: 222).

their rights, as young women, were being denied in the camps.[19] This led to many members of Spanish civil society advocating the girls' 'liberation' from their 'oppressive' birth parents and culture in the refugee camps, thereby directly engaging in 'an Orientalist logic that paternalistically seeks to protect women' (Stabile and Kumar 2005: 775, also 770). Such a 'protection scenario' is dependent on both a 'polarization between "us" and "them," but also [upon] caricatures and stereotypes which bear little resemblance to reality' (Stabile and Kumar 2005: 771; also Abu-Lughod 2002; Ayotte and Husain 2005).

In her letter to the Spanish authorities, Aicha writes:

> Here in the Saharawi Refugee camps [sic] I feel I have been kidnapped, forced to adapt myself to so many traditions that I don't even know where to start . . . If [X] doesn't manage to speak with [the smuggler] I will spend the rest of my life as a prisoner of my own family, and I will be the crazy one who tried to escape because she didn't agree with her clan's rules (Embarek n.d., my translation).

Parallelling claims that Aicha's 'clan' had imprisoned her and forced her to adapt to alien 'traditions', in a letter to the Queen of Spain, Huria denounces the Sahrawi way of life as follows:

> That is the reason why I ask for your help. Do you think this is just? Here the women wear the burqa. Their lives are like Afghan women's lives. So, please, help me to leave this place, I beg you. I don't want to live the life that they lead, I want them to see that it is possible to change all this and to have rights[20] (Hamoudi 2003, my translation and emphasis).

The terms and descriptions offered in these accounts, and especially the explicit references to Afghan women and the burqa[21] are clearly under-

---

[19] The extent to which refugees can be considered, as a whole, to be 'voluntarily' living in refugee camps is of course contestable, since many (if not all) inhabitants would 'prefer' to live elsewhere but are unable to do so for a range of reasons. Or, as one *solidaria* wrote, 'Dear Aicha, whether you like it or not, you're a Sahrawi refugee . . . Whether you like it or not, your family, those who gave you life, live there in regrettable conditions' (Tapias 2003).

[20] Huria's personal (and political) identification rejects the Sahrawi 'way of life', speaking of (and thus othering) her birth-parents and refugee community as *ellos* ('them' and 'they'), whilst aligning herself with Spanish civil society and national institutions (her imagined 'we' and 'us').

[21] It is important to stress that Sahrawi women do not in fact wear the burqa but rather the *milḥafa* (derived from the Arabic verb *laḥafa*, meaning to cover), which is a long piece of fabric worn by women over an existing layer of clothing, and which is loosely wrapped around their bodies and head. It is also pertinent to note that conventional Sahrawi representations of this item of clothing to Westerners purport to distance the *milḥafa* from religious obligations or connotations, even overtly declaring that Sahrawi women 'do not veil' (Kuttab 2002: 63; Harrell-Bond 1999: 156). Rather, Western observers are systematically

stood by these young women as epitomizing the 'worst' possible conditions for Muslim women (also see Ayotte and Husain 2005: esp. 117). These terms have undoubtedly been strategically exploited by the girls to convince Spanish observers that their plight to flee the refugee camps and their birth families was simultaneously understandable, just, and necessary. As such, they seem to have recognized that a key factor which may pressure Western powers to intervene in a crisis, or may at least be provided as a justification for intervention, is a particular representation of a cultural and religious prison which unjustly oppresses and subjugates women. Indeed, as has now been extensively documented, summoning the image of forcibly veiled Afghan women is particularly pertinent given the extent to which 'the plight of Afghan women was invoked as a humanitarian crisis justifying military intervention' (Kandiyoti, interviewed by Hammami 2005: 1352; also Ayotte and Husain 2005; Stabile and Kumar 2005: 766ff.).

These images were parallelled and expanded upon by those members of the Spanish media who supported the teenaged refugees' 'release',[22] basing their reports on the specific details delineated in the young women's letters and the Spanish families' press releases, but concurrently drawing upon their own perceptions and beliefs surrounding Sahrawi gender relations. Hence, one internet journalist who has not visited the refugee camps describes Sahrawi society as:

> a hell of ancestral customs which stamp on women's most elemental rights; . . . where women never come of age to obtain these [rights] and choose their way of life, not even to choose a husband because their own father chooses one for them when they are still girls, or they sell them or trade them for two camels, two goats or two donkeys; where men make laws only for themselves, always leaving their women in the margins (Suarez 2003, my translation).

Other journalists and commentators stated that Aicha had 'won the battle against her parents' ignorance and egoism', parents who expected her to fulfil 'the role that is reserved . . . for all of her nation's first-born

---

informed by Sahrawi men and women that the *milḥafa* is a traditional or national item of clothing, rather than a religiously motivated one (i.e. Martín 1985; Sanz 1997; Velázquez-Gaztelu 2001).

[22] A selection of articles and debates surrounding these cases is posted on www.entendersahara.com/articulo.php?sec=documentos&id=11 and at http://elguanche.net/dosopinionesaicha.htm. The articles often contain elements which are present in the Spanish host-families' own representations of the Sahrawi families in the camps (as discussed in Fiddian 2006).

women: little more than slavery in the *khayma* [tent] in the refugee camps' (Alonso 2003, my translation). Alonso continues by stating: 'Some religions and a certain Bedouin atavism keep women tied to the leg of the bed.'

In all these statements, Sahrawi society is 'constructed as timelessly misogynistic, barbaric and uncivilized', naturalizing both a 'rhetoric of the "clash of civilizations"' and Orientalist constructions of the East upon which such a clash is predicated' (Stabile and Kumar, on representations of Afghanistan, 2005: 774). Indeed, one Spanish *solidario* recognized that 'for [Spanish] trash TV ... what is useful is to ... build upon an anti-Muslim prejudice which is sufficiently widespread to guarantee an audience' (Guijarro 2003, my translation), while another *solidaria* rejected the ways in which the Spanish press (including the popular TV station, Antena 3) and the host family 'should have utilized and exploited the over-used argument of the Muslim woman at home, veiled and with a broken leg' (Tapias 2003, my translation).

In fact, it is important to note that a large proportion of Spanish solidarity groups denounced the ways in which the 'liberation' campaigns had been run, pointing to the xenophobic nature of the comments made,[23] and highlighting that most reporters had not visited the camps and were therefore unfamiliar with the 'real' position of Sahrawi women there. Many high-ranking *solidarios*, including de la Vallina, Medina, and Suárez-Montiel,[24] formally indicated that they shared the Sahrawi parents' concerns about their daughters' prolonged absences from the camps (Díaz 2003; González 2003b), and argued (alongside the Polisario Front) that the Sahrawi families' decisions should be designated 'private' matters to be discussed only by Sahrawis rather than by Spanish individuals and organizations. Such a request for 'privacy' was directly related to the *solidarios'* recognition that '[the Sahrawi] people's right to self-determination is too serious a matter to be frivolized' and:

---

[23] Martín-Corrales (2004: 45), however, argues that 'almost all Spanish society' supports the Sahrawi cause through reinforcing an antagonistic paradigm in which the 'noble, loyal, democratic and brave Sahrawi [is] clearly contrasted with the traitorous, fanatic and despotic Moroccan'. In his view, the Sahrawi solidarity system is revealed as a key proponent of what he terms Maurophobia (the fear and/or hatred of Muslims in general and Moroccans in particular; ibid: 39).

[24] The first two were the president and vice-president of the Friends of the Sahara group at the time of Huria's 'abduction'. Suárez was representing CEAS at the time, and is currently its vice-president (see http://elistas.egrupos.net/lista/afaan/archivo/indice/1685/msg/1726).

> In the end, the least important question is what Aicha will do, whether she will study or not . . .; what matters is that [this case] causes a lot of damage, not only to the Sahrawi people but to its women who have created camps from nothing and direct them as no-one else could (Tapias 2003, my translation).

Such responses to these crises demonstrated *solidarios'* commitment both to the Sahrawi quest for self-determination, and to the central features of the official representation of the camps.[25]

Hence, one *solidario* drew readers' attention to 'an undeniable reality which has been indicated by many people with a minimum level of honesty: that the women of the Sahara have been the authors of this miracle . . . [creating] a survival structure which was first a seed for, and subsequently a real democratic State'. Further, he asked:

> Who are we to criticize those whom have exalted the meaning of the word Woman [*sic*]? . . . It's not for nothing that for 25 years they have been a model to be followed by many women who know about [the situation] . . . by their side, the situation of other women in the West, Spain included, pales in comparison (Guijarro 2003, my translation).

Nonetheless, despite many *solidarios'* commitment to both the Sahrawi cause and the official discourse, the power of the interconnected representations of gender and religion mobilized by the host families and the Spanish media was so great that certain 'solidary' individuals and groups were prepared to threaten disengagement from, and even a rejection of, the Sahrawi 'cause' in order to obtain the girls' 'liberty'. At the same time, this indicates the leverage which granting or withdrawing humanitarian and political support may have over recipient populations.

Politicians, journalists, NGOs, and the Spanish host families all mobilized their public statements to inform both the Spanish audience and the Polisario/SADR of the serious political and humanitarian damage which the Polisario/SADR, and Sahrawi refugees more broadly, could face by losing the Spanish public's support over this matter. Hence, a small number of Spanish solidarity groups, including the Riojan community's 'Friendship' Group, either explicitly or implicitly threatened the Polisario/SADR that, unless each of the girls was allowed to return to 'their Spanish family', they would stop campaigning for the cause:

---

[25] Further, those politicians who supported the girls' return to Spain stressed that their demands for the young women's individual rights to be respected accompanied their unequivocal support for the Sahrawi people to be given the right to self-determination and to return to their territory.

> You must consider, obviously, that these incidents can affect future solidarity relations of a whole Autonomous Community like that of La Rioja with The Sahara. The news about the girls' retention has become a matter of public opinion [sic] . . . And, sadly, such disheartening news spreads quickly and ends up affecting everybody, even their perception of the causes and their desire to collaborate with them (Riojan Community's 'Friendship' Group 2001, my translation).[26]

Such implicit and explicit threats were ultimately highly effective in 'resolving' these cases. Before the extent of Spanish public support for Aicha's 'liberation' had become clear, the Polisario Front's main representative in Spain at the time (Brahim Gali) officially indicated that the Front would not become involved in Aicha's case since it was 'a very personal problem, between families'. He argued that 'if more silent methods had been used, this case could have been resolved', and reiterated *solidarios'* claims that these girls' cases were 'private' rather than 'political' matters (quoted in Peregil 2002).[27] However, having recognized that these Sahrawi families' decisions and acts in reality had the potential to destabilize this highly important support network, the Polisario/SADR ultimately succumbed to the pressure applied by Spanish civil and political organizations and 'negotiated' the girls' 'release' from their biological parents, and their 'return' to Spain (see Fiddian 2006).

Although these are highly complex cases which illustrate the precarious balance and the power play which may exist between aid providers, refugee recipients, and their political representatives, I conclude the current discussion with reference to two main points. First, the public outrage prompted by these crises partly demonstrates the reasons why the Polisario/SADR has consistently distanced the Sahrawi Self from the Muslim Middle East: in a context where many Western observers perceive the Muslim Middle East through, essentially, Orientalist lenses (as demonstrated in a selection of extracts included above), recreating the Sahrawi camps as the antithesis of the Middle Eastern Other becomes a strategic means of protecting public support for the camps. Second,

---

[26] My translation of the Group's letter to the SADR Ministry.

[27] The Sahrawi Delegation to Castilla-León indicated: 'The Saharawi authorities never become implicated between Saharawi families and the host families given that they do not support temporary adoptions. In the case of Aicha . . . the Saharawi authorities are making an effort to convince Aicha's parents, but, they do not guarantee anything given the sensitive nature of the case in Saharawi society, and it is not possible to launch a crusade for the liberation of Saharawi women, using Aicha's name as its motto, without knowing about the history and achievements in relation to Saharawi women's position today' (2002, my translation).

Spanish responses to these girls' cases, and the threat to withdraw multi-faceted and essential support unless the Polisario/SADR guaranteed their 'liberation', appear to substantiate my broader argument that Sahrawi gender relations have become emblematic of the justifiability of 'the cause'. The future of the solidarity network therefore depends upon the careful protection (and projection) of idealized notions of Sahrawi women's position in the camps to ensure the Western audience's support.

CONCLUSION

While refugees and their representatives are habitually under close scrutiny by foreign visitors and funders, and aid is often 'conditional' upon certain socio-political provisos, this case illustrates the extent to which such observations are multidirectional, and to what effect. On one level, the Sahrawi refugee camps and their inhabitants are observed by their 'representatives' (the Polisario/SADR) and by non-Sahrawi NGO members, journalists, academics, and solidarity groups, including those referred to and quoted earlier. At the same time, the Polisario/ SADR is in turn observed by both other Sahrawis (who are, as a whole, limited in their ability to challenge the ways in which they are represented) and by different actors and agencies in the international community. Lastly, in this essay I suggest that the priorities, beliefs, and assumptions of aid providers and political supporters have themselves been identified and noted by the Polisario/SADR, which has accordingly designed a specific international public relations strategy in line with its observations.

Since NGOs and solidarity groups habitually differentiate between groups which are or are not worthy of support, or even attention, their continued engagement with a population often depends on these external observers being convinced that their engagement is 'justifiable' and acceptable. It is within this framework, characterized by the non-economic conditionalities prioritized by the new development agenda, that the Polisario/SADR engages with Spanish civil society and Spanish institutions. Having reproduced the Sahrawi refugee camps as spaces for gender equality and female empowerment, 'conditional solidarity networks' have both accepted and become a part of the perpetuation of this image. Such networks, however, are subsequently at risk whenever cases come to light which contradict that which has been taken for granted and has become 'common knowledge'.

I conclude this essay by proposing that the dangers and ethical issues presented by such a situation are multiple, with a particular risk of the 'audience' (in this case Westerners, and especially Spaniards, who support the Sahrawi 'cause') directing the rhetoric, and therefore reproducing systems of Othering and marginalization both inside and outside the camps. In this case, the homogenized and essentialized representation of Other Arab and Muslim women in accounts of the Sahrawi refugee camps must be highlighted. I therefore propose the particular urgency of both the 'observed' and their 'observers' developing and structuring critical approaches to the multifaceted dimensions of engagement which exist not only between refugees and Western observers, but also between refugees, their representatives, and those who purport to either provide them with humanitarian assistance, or to document and analyse their experiences in their refugee camps and/or hosting countries.

REFERENCES

Abu-Lughod, L. (1998), 'Introduction: Feminist Longings and Postcolonial Conditions', in L. Abu-Lughod (ed.), *Remaking Women: Feminism and Modernity in the Middle East* (Princeton, NJ, Princeton University Press), pp. 3–31.

—— (2001), 'Orientalism and Middle East Feminist Studies', *Feminist Studies*, 27: 101–13.

—— (2002), 'Do Muslim Women Really Need Saving? Anthropological Reflections on Cultural Relativism and Its Others', *American Anthropologist*, 104: 783–90.

Almond, I. (2007), *The New Orientalists: Postmodern Representations of Islam from Foucault to Baudrillard* (London, I. B. Tauris).

Alonso, L. M. (2003), 'Esperanza', *El Faro de Vigo*.

Andrade (2003), *El territorio del silencio: un viaje por el Sáhara Occidental* (Tegueste, Tenerife, Ediciones Baile del Sol).

Ayotte, K. J. and Husain, M. E. (2005), 'Securing Afghan Women: Neocolonialism, Epistemic Violence, and the Rhetoric of the Veil', *National Women's Studies Association Journal*, 17: 112–33.

Betteridge, A. H. (1985), 'Gift Exchange in Iran: The Locus of Self-identity in Social Interaction', *Anthropological Quarterly*, 58: 190–202.

Bob, C. (2005), *The Marketing of Rebellion: Insurgents, Media and International Activism* (Cambridge, Cambridge University Press).

Butterfield, J. (2003), *Collins Spanish Dictionary; Collins diccionario inglés* (Glasgow, HarperCollins).

Castaño-Boullón, M. C. (2003), 'Sr. Director', www.entender-sahara.com/articulo. php?sec=documentos&id=11.

Cazón, P. (2004), *Lágrimas de arena: la historia de Aicha Embarek* (Barcelona, El Aleph).

Chatterjee, P. (1986), *Nationalist Thought and the Colonial World: A Derivative Discourse?* (London, Zed for the United Nations University).

—— (1993), *The Nation and Its Fragments: Colonial and Postcolonial Histories* (Princeton, NJ, Princeton University Press).

Chatty, D. and Rabo, A. (1997), *Organizing Women: Formal and Informal Women's Groups in the Middle East* (Oxford, Berg).

——, Fiddian-Qasmiyeh, E., and Crivello, G. (2010), 'Identity With/out Territory: Sahrawi Refugee Youth in Transnational Space', in D. Chatty (ed.), *Deterritorialized Youth: Sahrawi and Afghan Refugees at the Margins of the Middle East* (Oxford, Berghahn Books).

Chopra, J. (ed.) (1999), *Peace-maintenance: The Evolution of International Political Authority* (London, Routledge).

Conklin, B. (1997), 'Body Paint, Feathers, and VCRs: Aesthetics and Authenticity in Amazonian Activism', *American Ethnologist*, 24: 711–37.

Crivello, G. and Fiddian-Qasmiyeh, E. (2010), 'The Ties that Bind: Sahrawi Children and the Mediation of Aid in Exile', in D. Chatty (ed.), *Deterritorialized Youth: Sahrawi and Afghan Refugees at the Margins of the Middle East* (Oxford, Berghahn Books).

Damis, J. J. (1983), *Conflict in Northwest Africa: The Western Sahara Dispute* (Stanford, CA, Hoover Institution Press).

Delegación Saharaui Castilla Y León (2002), *Memorando*, Valladolid, 2 May 2002, http://es.geocities.com/aichaembarek2/constitucion/carta_ayunta_2.JPG.

Díaz, L. (2003), 'La Asociación Critica a la Familia Asturiana: Amigos del Sáhara rechaza la vuelta de Huria', *La Voz de Asturias*, 16 July.

Embarek, A. (n.d.), 'Para las autoridades españolas', http://es.geocities.com/aichaembarek2/primeracarta/cartaautoridades.

Es-Sweyih, M.-F. (2001), *El Primer Estado del Sahara Occidental*, www.arso.org/1estadosaharaui.pdf.

Fanon, F. (1965), *Studies in a Dying Colonialism* (New York, Monthly Review Press).

Fernández, E. (2003), 'Movilización por la niña mariposa', *El Mundo*, 7 September.

Fiddian, E. (2006), 'Education in Exile: Gendered Dilemmas', Theory and Methodology Seminar Series, Gender Studies Centre, University of Cambridge, 9 February.

Fiddian-Qasmiyeh, E. (2009a), 'Gender, Islam and the Sahrawi Politics of Survival', DPhil thesis, University of Oxford.

—— (2009b), 'Representing Sahrawi Refugees' "Educational Displacement" to Cuba: Self-sufficient Agents and/or Manipulated Victims in Conflict?', *Journal of Refugee Studies*, 22, 3: 323–50.

—— (forthcoming a), 'Internationalist Scholarships: Situating Muslim Middle Eastern and North African Students in Cuba', *Journal of North African Studies*, 14, 3.

—— (forthcoming b), 'Concealing Violence Against Women in the Sahrawi Refugee Camps: The Politicization of Victimhood', in G. Lewando-Hundt and H. Bradby (eds), *Living Through Intended and Unintended Suffering: War, Medicine and Gender* (Aldershot, Ashgate).

193

Foucault, M. (1979), *Discipline and Punish: The Birth of the Prison* (Harmondsworth, Penguin Books).

—— (1989), *Foucault Live: Interviews 1966–84* (New York, Semiotext).

González, J. (2003a), 'Denuncian la "retención" de una joven saharaui por su familia. La pareja con la que vivió una adolescente en Avilés reúne 12.000 firmas de apoyo', *La Voz de Asturias*, 13 July.

—— (2003b), 'Servicios sociales no cree que la niña saharaui vuelva a Avilés', *La Voz de Asturias*, 5 August.

Guijarro, F. (2003), 'La mujer saharaui sigue', www.entender-sahara.com/articulo.php?sec=comentario&id=23.

Hammami, R. (2005), 'Deniz Kandiyoti', *Development and Change*, 37: 1347–54.

Hamoudi, H. (2003), 'Carta a la Reina de España', www.elparchedigital.com/pags/huria/ruedadeprensa_20Dic2003.htm.

Harrell-Bond, B. E. (1999), 'The Experience of Refugees as Recipients of Aid', in A. Ager (ed.), *Refugees: Perspectives on the Experience of Forced Migration* (London, Pinter).

Hyndman, J. and Walton-Roberts, M. (2000), 'Interrogating Borders: A Transnational Approach to Refugee Research in Vancouver', *Canadian Geographer*, 44: 244–58.

International Court of Justice (1975), *Sahara occidental: avis consultatif du 16 octobre 1975. Western Sahara: Advisory Opinion of 16 October 1975* (The Hague).

Jasper, J. M. (1997), *The Art of Moral Protest: Culture, Biography, and Creativity in Social Movements* (Chicago, University of Chicago Press).

Jean-Klein, I. (1997), 'Palestinian Militancy, Martyrdom and Nationalist Communities in the West Bank during the [First] Intifada', in J. Pettigrew (ed.), *Martyrdom and Political Resistance: Essays from Asia and Europe* (Amsterdam, VU University Press).

Kandiyoti, D. (2007), 'Old Dilemmas or New Challenges? The Politics of Gender and Reconstruction in Afghanistan', *Development and Change*, 38: 169–99.

Kuttab, M. (2002), *Riwaya min as-Sahra' al-Gharbiya: autaad al'arḍ (The Pegs of the Land: A Novel from Western Sahara)* (Damascus, Syria, Muasasat al-Tibaa al-Taswiria).

Lewis, R. (1995), *Gendering Orientalism: Race, Femininity, and Representation* (New York, Routledge).

Lippert, A. (1987), 'The Sahrawi Refugees: Origins and Organization, 1975–1985', in T. Lawless and L. Monahan (eds), *War and Refugees: The Western Sahara Conflict* (London, Pinter).

Lynn Price, D. (1981), *The Western Sahara* (London, SAGE Publications).

M.O. (2008), 'Guipúzcoa ve en decadencia los proyectos de hermanamiento', *El País*, 21 May.

M.P. (2008a), 'El juez investiga una denuncia de secuestro de una saharaui', *El País*, 20 August.

—— (2008b), 'El padre de la supuestamente secuestrada dice que está a salvo en Tinduf', *El País*, 21 August.

MacCannell, D. (1973), 'Staged Authenticity: Arrangements of Social Space in Tourist Settings', *American Journal of Sociology*, 79: 589–603.

Martín, C. (1985), 'Guesmula Ebbi', *El País*, 2 July.

Martín-Corrales, E. (2004), 'Representaciones e interculturalidad: Maurofobia/ islamofobia y maurofilia/islamofilia en la España del siglo XXI', *Revista Cidob d'Afers Internacionals*, 66–7: 39–51.

Mercer, J. (1979), *The Sahrawis of Western Sahara* (London, Minority Rights Group).

Mernissi, F. (2003), *Beyond the Veil: Male–Female Dynamics in Modern Muslim Society* (London, Saqi Books).

Moghadam, V. M. (1997), 'Women's NGOs in the Middle East and North Africa: Constraints, Opportunities, and Priorities', in D. Chatty and A. Rabo (eds), *Organizing Women: Formal and Informal Women's Groups in the Middle East* (Oxford, Berg).

Mohanty, C. T. (1988), 'Under Western Eyes: Feminist Scholarship and Colonial Discourses', *Feminist Review*, 30: 61–88.

Mowles, C. (1986), 'Desk Officer's Report on Trip to the Sahrawi Refugee Camps near Tindouf, Southern Algeria, June 16–21, 1986', Oxfam.

Nzenza, S. (1997), 'Women in Post-colonial Africa: Between African Men and Western Feminists', in P. Darby (ed.), *At the Edge of International Relations: Postcolonialism, Gender, and Dependency* (London, Pinter).

Peregil, F. (2002), 'El tormento de Aicha', *El País*, 26 May.

Petrich, B. (2005), 'Los avances de las saharahuíes ejemplo para el mundo árabe', *La Jornada* (n.d.).

RASD (2000), 'Acogimiento provisional', www.elparchedigital.com/pags/huria.

Riojan Community 'Friendship' Group (2001), 'Estimado Sr. Ministro', http://es. geocities.com/aichaembarek2/otroscasos/Maribel_Carta1.gif on 01/11/2005.

Said, E. W. (1979), *Orientalism* (New York, Vintage Books).

Sanz, J. C. (1997), 'Los saharauis seguirán en el desierto si no hay independencia', *El País*, 27 April.

Shelley, T. (2004), *Endgame in the Western Sahara: What Future for Africa's Last Colony* (London and New York, Zed Books in association with War on Want).

Spivak, G. C. (ed.), (1990), *The Post-colonial Critic: Interviews, Strategies, Dialogues* (London, Routledge).

Stabile, C. A. and Kumar, D. (2005), 'Unveiling Imperialism: Media, Gender and the War on Afghanistan', *Media Culture Society*, 27: 765–82.

Suarez, I. (2003), 'Aicha Embarek, la Hurí de ojos negros y piel canela', *El ParcheDigital*, www.elparchedigital.com/pags.huria/ruedaprensa_20Dic2003. htm.

Tapias, A. (2003), 'Querida familia acogedora', www.entender-sahara.com/articulo. php?sec=documentos&id=11.

United Nations High Commissioner for Refugees (UNHCR) (2000), *Global Report 1999* (UNHCR).

Vallbé Bach, F. (2002), 'Cartas al Director: Aicha', *El País*, 29 May.

Velázquez-Gaztelu, J. P. (2001), 'Solos en el desierto', *El País*, 9 March.

World Food Programme (WFP) (1999), *Protracted Relief and Recovery Operation Approved by the Executive Director (1 January–30 June 1999): Algeria 6099.00: Assistance to Western Sahara Refugees* (WFP).

—— (2008), *Protracted Relief and Recovery Operation: Algeria 10172.2: Assistance to the Western Saharan Refugees* (WFP).

Yeğenoğlu, M. (1998), *Colonial Fantasies: Towards a Feminist Reading of Orientalism* (Cambridge, Cambridge University Press).

8.
'Hey, Afghani!' Identity Contentions among Iranians and Afghan Refugees

Zuzanna Olszewska

> The street was empty at noon, and he, full of tumult and din
> Was walking, drowning himself in long [rambling] thoughts
> From the path, he kicked a rotten apple into the gutter
> How useless is this world, buried in its abundance
> He took another puff of his cigarette and closed his eyes:
> The world is bitter, bitter, full of discord and darkness
> Ahead there was a pedestrian bridge, steps leading up, then
> He glanced up, both eyes turned towards the ruins
> How quiet and how cold is the sky, death so out of reach
> Just one stain of a cloud in a corner, busy with [its own] distress
> . . .
> Under his breath, he hummed a song and with him hummed along
> The hundred thousand ghosts imprisoned in his chest
> He leaned against the balustrade, then closed his eyes
> From behind, someone called out: Hey, Afghani![1]

This melancholy poem is by an Afghan refugee in Iran, Seyyed Zia Qassemi, who has a degree in television film-making from Tehran and is a poet and literary activist acclaimed by both Afghans and Iranians. Although in a classical *ghazal* form, it speaks in an entirely contemporary language of an ordinary urban landscape.[2] It also describes something that we might see as a very modern urban malaise—a sense of meaninglessness and alienation. We do not know why this man might be so

---

[1] From '*Afghani*', Qassemi (2007: 16–17). This and all subsequent translations from original Persian texts are by the author.

[2] The *ghazal* is a short metric poem with a monorhyme (i.e. rhyming *aa ba ca)* that has been recorded throughout the thousand-year history of Persian poetry. Although originally widely known as a love lyric, it is extremely versatile and has been used to express a variety of mystical, social, and political feelings and opinions.

depressed until the last line of the poem makes it clear—he is an Afghan, and someone is taunting him for it. For the word 'Afghani' in Iran has unfortunately acquired the overtones of a pejorative epithet.

During my time conducting fieldwork on poetry among young Afghans in Iran, I was intrigued by the despondency and rootlessness that many of them made into their poetic hallmarks, and was curious to investigate the reasons for this. Why should second-generation refugees who spent most of their lives in Iran still write poems about the 'pain of exile'? Other essays in this volume describe young returnees to Afghanistan who suffer from an identity crisis, not knowing if they are Afghan or Iranian (see Kamal; Saito and Kantor). This essay explores some of the reasons for this liminal confusion, offering conclusions which complement and complicate the picture presented by Monsutti (also this volume).

AFGHAN REFUGEES IN IRAN: SOCIAL AND LEGAL CONTEXTS

In August 2007, there were just over 920,000 Afghans living as registered refugees in Iran, as well as a number of undocumented Afghans estimated by the Iranian government at between 1 and 1.5 million. (See Figure 8.1.) Despite Iran's being a signatory to the 1951 Convention relating to the Status of Refugees, their legal status has instead been based on the Act on the Entry and Residence of Foreign Nationals in Iran of 1931 (Ebadi 2008: 12) and policies towards them have been characterized by an inconsistency and arbitrariness that keep most of them in a perpetual state of insecurity. Thus Iran has veered between great generosity to refugees in the 1980s, when they were greeted as fellow Muslims fleeing oppression, and a much more restrictive approach from the early 1990s onwards.[3] The government has permitted the vast majority of Afghans to self-settle in or on around cities, with only 3 per cent living in refugee camps. They have also been entitled to receive government subsidies on basic commodities such as bread, flour, petrol, etc., like Iranian citizens, as well as (until

---

[3] It must be noted that the international community shoulders a good deal of responsibility for this situation. According to Loescher, 'Between 1979 and 1997, the UNHCR spent over one billion US dollars on Afghan refugees in Pakistan but only $150 million on those in Iran because Muslim fundamentalist-ruled Iran was a pariah state to the West after the fall of the Shah' (2001: 216). When the United Nations High Commissioner for Refugees (UNHCR) cut its educational subsidies in 2004, Iran promptly imposed school fees for refugee children.

Figure 8.1. Map of Afghanistan and Iran.
Source: Map produced using digital data (© www.collinsbartholomew.com, reproduced with kind permission of HarperCollins Publishers).

recently) social insurance. The majority, however, are economically and socially marginalized and live in relative poverty. Documented Afghan refugees—even those with professional qualifications obtained in Iran— are legally permitted to work only in a small number of menial professions, such as construction, brick-making, well-digging, etc. (Turton and Marsden 2002: 31; Abbasi-Shavazi et al. 2005b: 17). Whether documented or undocu- mented (in which case they work illegally), their work tends to be insecure and low-waged. In addition, although hundreds of thousands of Afghan children and youth have attended state schools, theological seminaries, and universities, access to these has recently been curtailed and heavy fees and other restrictions imposed. This has led to the flourishing of dozens of informal schools run by Afghans for Afghans, pointing to the extent to which they have embraced the importance of a modern education.[4]

---

[4] For more background on Afghan refugees in Iran, see Olszewska (2008), the contributors to the *Iranian Studies* special issue on Afghans in Iran (April 2007, vol. 40, no. 2), Hoodfar (2004), and Abbasi-Shavazi et al. (2005a, 2005b, 2005c).

In 2007, not for the first time but on an unprecedented scale, Iran's hard-line interior minister Mostafa Pur-Mohammadi launched a deportation campaign against Afghans. In theory, it targeted undocumented 'illegal immigrants', but in practice many vulnerable people, including unaccompanied women and children, and also those who simply didn't have their documents with them, were detained and deported. By June 2008, about 490,000 had been arrested, kept in deportation camps for days, and then expelled from the country. In the process, families were reportedly separated, people were beaten, abused, or told to pack their belongings at an hour's notice, and in some cases women and children were deported without their families. The campaign continued through the worst winter the region had suffered in decades and during which many died of cold. It sparked a humanitarian crisis in Afghanistan and led to the sacking of two ministers, and yet went generally unnoticed in the wider world (IRIN 2007b, 2007c, 2007d, 2007e, 2008).

IRANIAN NATIONALISM AND THE AFGHAN 'OTHER'

Aside from these legal challenges to their everyday lives, there is also the discrimination Afghans face at a more existential level. Afghans in Iran frequently cite the pan-Islamic slogan of Ayatollah Khomeini (not without a hint of irony) that 'Islam has no borders' in order to justify their presence in Iran, but the slogan seems particularly empty in the wake of the exclusionary policies I have described. Although western Afghanistan was part of Iran until the mid-nineteenth century, Iran is now seen as a 'territorially satisfied' state with no irredentist claims (Farhi 2005: 10), despite extensive economic, political, and security interests in its neighbour. It appears that the forces of Iranian nationalism and the rationalizing order of the nation state have won the contest with pan-Islamism and other, older cross-border ties.[5]

In fact, the discourse and sentiment of nationalism have become a prevailing philosophy in the culture and politics of Iran, although their precise content has shifted over time (Kashani-Sabet 2002: 164). Defining the 'authentic Iranian Self' has always involved implicit or explicit comparisons to, or a distancing from, a number of other cultural reference

---

[5] For historical accounts of the emergence of Iranian nationalism and the transformation of the former Qajar empire into a modern nation state, see Tavakoli-Targhi (2001), Kashani-Sabet (1999, 2002), and Boroujerdi (1996).

points. This might be an identification with European culture combined with a distancing from Arab–Islamic culture (cf. Tavakoli-Targhi 2001: 103), or the exact opposite. Mehrzad Boroujerdi has argued that, from the mid-twentieth century onwards, the process of asserting an 'authentic' native Iranian identity by Iranian intellectuals in the face of Western cultural, political, and economic domination was a kind of 'Orientalism in reverse' (1996: 10–14). That is, it revalued the aspects of Iranian culture that may have been portrayed as retrogressive by Western Orientalists, such as mysticism and pre-Islamic statecraft and philosophy. But it did not abolish the idea of an ontological dichotomy, an essential difference between 'East' and 'West'.[6] In conversations with Iranians (and indeed with Afghans), I was often surprised and frustrated by their earnest insistence on the differences between 'us Orientals' and 'you Occidentals' (*mā sharghihā* and *shomā gharbihā*). The 'West', when people are in a mood to generalize, is still spoken of as the abode of rationality ('*aql*) and order (*nazm*), while the East is the home of *ehsās* (emotion), of mysticism, spirituality and religious feeling, and of poetry.[7]

Perhaps curiously, the older admiration for and sense of inadequacy vis-à-vis *Gharb*, the West, persist as an uncomfortable and guilty indulgence of many Iranians even after the Islamic Revolution. I heard them expressed with surprising regularity, and they are a recurring theme in much scholarship on Iran.[8] Many of my Afghan interlocutors, having been educated in Iran, unselfconsciously echoed this belief.

But in a classic case of projections of the Other really being a story about the Self's preoccupations, their ideas about Afghans enable Iranians

---

[6] Boroujerdi writes: '[O]rientalism in reverse uncritically embraces orientalism's assumption of a fundamental ontological difference separating the natures, peoples, and cultures of the Orient and the Occident. Orient and Occident are depicted as essentialistic geographical, historical, and cultural entities asymmetrical to one another. Each is supposed to possess its own distinct and easily identifiable history, imagery, tradition of thought, mode of discourse, ethics, and culture' (1996: 12).

[7] This dichotomy should not be confused with the revolutionary slogan of 'Neither East nor West', which represented Iran's desire to avoid political alignment with either the West (the USA) or the East (Soviet Russia). Today 'East' is more commonly used to refer simply to Asia, although it remains a generalization which is difficult to locate exactly, much like the English 'Orient'.

[8] For example, Jahanbegloo writes: 'This complex sentiment of inferiority mixed with that of the loss of the Iranian self through the global domination of the West has been the foundation for theoretical elaborations on the two concepts of tradition and modernity among four generations of Iranian intellectuals; how to resolve this remains an "agonizing question"' (2004: xii).

to reflect on the distances they have already travelled. In fact, rather than being a simple dichotomy, there exists a triad of points of reference through which the Self is reflected upon, which might be termed West, East, and Further East. Seeing Afghanistan, the Further East, as more 'backward' (*aqab-mānde*, lit. 'remaining-behind') than Iran, is perhaps helpful for Iranians to mark off the 'progress' (*pish-raft*, lit. 'going-forward') they have already made in becoming more modernized, and an admonition not to slip backwards: the temporal–spatial metaphors implied by these common terms are revealing. Afghanistan is thus cast as the lurking, darker side of the Self; particularly so during the time of Taliban rule, seen as the victory of a religious fanaticism that was a little too close to home for comfort. Many Iranian Muslim reformers have identified conservative Islamists of Iran with the Afghan Taliban. One leading Iranian feminist who, polemizing against a proposed law for sex segregation of hospitals in 1998, wrote: 'The path you have taken ends in Afghanistan!' (Tohidi 2002: 219). Similarly, the filmmaker Samira Makhmalbaf, when asked why she had made *Panj-e 'asr* ('Five in the Afternoon'), her film on Afghanistan, replied: '[T]his film is not only about Afghanistan but it could very well have taken place in Iran. *The Taliban are our backwardness*' (Makhmalbaf Film House 2003, emphasis added). And, in a comedy series screened on Iranian public television beginning in the summer of 2007, *Chāhār Khuneh* (starring popular actor Javad Razavian), an 'Afghan' charlatan, complete with a funny name, a quaint (though inaccurately 'Afghan') accent, and 'traditional' dress, insinuates himself into the life of an Iranian family, wreaking much slapstick havoc. Yet the viewer learns in an early episode that he is in fact from a remote desert village in Iran, merely posing as an Afghan to gain sympathy. So, in a subtle way, his deceit, avarice, laziness, and other vices reflect poorly on and satirize Iranians rather than Afghans, and dramatize the fluidity of identity and social status as indexed by external appearances in Iran.

Here it must be noted that Afghans in Iran are not only greeted with taunts and xenophobia. As evidenced by the mother character in *Chāhār Khuneh*, there has also been a great deal of sympathy for their plight— along with fund-raising campaigns, donations, charitable acts, and sincere friendships. Iranians' perception of Afghans is contingent on class, region, level of mutual interaction, and political orientation. For example, Iranian upper-class employers often value Afghans for being honest and efficient workers—but this is probably mostly because they are a cheap source of labour. Lower-class Iranians may actively participate in the same social networks as their Afghan neighbours, and indeed there are thousands of intermarriages (Zahedi 2007). But other lower-class Iranians often feel most threatened by this group which is described by populist politicians as the source of unemployment, a drain on the Islamic welfare state, as criminals and drug smugglers, and as carriers of infectious diseases (Tober 2007).[9] Furthermore, they are a topic of internal political contention among conservatives and those reformists who hope for a more open civil society in Iran—certain Iranian pro-refugee activists had close ties to the Khatami presidency, and two of the few articles to publicly denounce the 2007 deportations were published in the pro-reformist *Hammihan* newspaper just weeks before it was banned for the second time by the conservative government of the time. Sympathetic comments are often made by Iranian readers in the weblogs of young Afghans. However, sympathy notwithstanding, Afghans for the most part remain politically mute and invisible in Iran, except as a problem to be managed.

Their muteness, or perhaps Iranians' unwillingness to hear what they say, is elegantly illustrated by two films generally hailed as 'sympathetic' portrayals of Afghan refugees and Afghanistan. They are Majid Majidi's *Bārān* ('Rain', 2001) and the aforementioned 'Five in the Afternoon' (2003) by Samira Makhmalbaf. In the former, the heroine, a young Afghan girl who dresses as a boy in order to take her father's place on a construction site when he is injured, does not speak a single word in the whole film. When she cries out in pain in one scene, she is not even given the dignity of her voice ringing out—instead, it is muffled by sound effects which make it sound other-worldly. That is perhaps the point—the film is not really *about* Afghans, but, as in most of Majidi's films, the plot is a vehicle for a mystical allegory. The mysterious Afghan girl functions unwittingly as a spiritual guide for the self-realization of an Iranian boy who falls in love with her and gives up everything, including his national identity card, to help her and, in so doing, learns how to be selfless. The heroine of 'Five in the Afternoon' has a voice, but speaks remarkably little for a young girl who dreams of becoming president of Afghanistan and presumably has a lot to say. Instead, the film is filled with languid scenes of her walking up and down the corridors of the ruined Dar al-Aman palace in Kabul, symbolically clicking her no-longer-banned high-heeled

---

[9] During a stint as a volunteer English teacher in an informal Afghan school in a poor area of south Tehran, I once witnessed a distressing scene as small Iranian schoolchildren passed by on the street and shouted through the small window into our bare basement classroom, 'Afghāni kesāfat!' (meaning something like 'filthy Afghanis'). My pupils barely registered this incident, a regular occurrence for them.

shoes beneath a burqa which is now pulled back off her face. But she rehearses her political speeches silently, so we can only guess at their content. The mute image replaces any real dialogue or intersubjective understanding that might have been achieved. The figure of the Afghan in public discourse is thus a mirror turned towards the Iranian subject's own fears and fantasies.[10]

REFUGEE INTELLECTUALS IN IRAN: LITERARY RESPONSES TO MARGINALIZATION

How do Iranian-educated Afghan intellectuals respond to this situation? They are caught in a double bind—they feel excluded in Iran, not simply legally (being deprived of all of the political rights and many of the social rights that their Iranian counterparts enjoy), but also existentially. And yet, being educated people who have been exposed to the state's ideology of 'Islamic modernity', like Iranians, they have internalized the idea that Iran is civilizationally superior to Afghanistan. One friend, studying for a master's degree in French literature at Tehran University, sent me an e-mail about her depression at her potential imminent repatriation to Afghanistan in 2004: 'Can you believe that in the twenty-first century there is a country whose cities resemble poor, small and isolated villages?' It is indeed diffi-cult to believe that these worlds exist contemporaneously; Afghanistan has been left behind. Among the most popular NGO-sponsored courses for young Afghan women in Iran is basic medical and first-aid skills training. When I met a group of women taking such a course, they passionately described to me their reasons for joining—their horror at Afghanistan's lack of modern medical facilities. If Iranians are caught in a limbo between East and West, educated Afghans in Iran are in a more complicated state, somewhere between West, East, and Further East.

The young generation of refugees born or raised mostly in Iran is thus a disenchanted one. They have seen opportunities for education and advancement alternately offered to them and taken away without notice.

---

[10] Few scholars of Iranian society have remarked on the important role played by Afghanistan and Afghans in the Iranian imagination and, clearly, much more work could be done than I have in this short survey. Adelkhah and Olszewska (2007) begin to scratch the surface of this issue by showing that the figure of the Afghan is actually central to questions about Iranian identity and citizenship. Nonetheless, it remains a spectral figure—one used to frighten children in the same way as the Taliban are used to instil fear in adults.

Many have been educated at Iranian universities, but have been denied the opportunity to practise their professions in Iran. They have absorbed many of the values and practices of Iranian working-class modernity such as the pursuit of social advancement through education, and the pursuit of social justice through political and cultural engagement: this is one reason why so many of them were idealistic enough to want to return and rebuild Afghanistan after 2001. The two youngest candidates in the Afghan parliamentary elections in 2005—both 25 at the time, one male and one female—were returnees from Iran. However, they are also keenly aware of the failures and paradoxes of the Islamic Revolution, as a group that might have benefited most from its stated commitment to the welfare of the *mostaz'afin* (or 'dispossessed'), but which has been increasingly excluded from its purview due simply to its nationality. They have found themselves written out of (in some cases literally expelled from) the Islamic Republic in a manner analogous to what Wali Ahmadi (2004) has called the 'exclusionary poetics' of Iranian discourse about literary history, from which non-'Iranian' poets writing in Persian have been written out altogether, while poets born in what is today Afghanistan, such as Rumi or Jami, have been appropriated as belonging to Iran alone.[11]

The large number of Afghan refugees who have received a secular or religious education in Iran has led to the rise of a group of Shi'a Afghan intellectuals influenced by the intellectual currents present in the Islamic Republic (cf. Olszewska 2007: 210–14). They call themselves *roshanfekr* (or 'enlightened thinkers') and, like their predecessors in both Iran and Afghanistan from the late nineteenth century onwards, for them cultural activity has largely become synonymous with taking a political stance, even if that means opposing a particular ideology without proposing one in exchange.[12] Writers and poets, writes Dabashi (1985), formed a subset (the 'literati') of the intelligentsia, for whose political and cultural beliefs

[11] Mowlana Jalal al-Din Mohammad 'Rumi' (1207–73), who was born in Balkh in what is today Afghanistan and died in Konya in modern-day Turkey, is considered one of the greatest classical Persian poets, a master of mystic and philosophical verse. Nur al-Din Abd al-Rahman 'Jami' (1414–92), who was born in Jam in what is today Afghanistan's Ghor Province and died in Herat, was a Sufi and considered by many to be the last great poet of the golden age of classical Persian poetry that ended in the sixteenth century.
[12] For discussions of the genesis and different definitions of the term *roshanfekr*, as well as intellectual developments and engagements with modernity and imperialism in Iran, see Boroujerdi (1996), Gheissari (1997), Mirsepassi (2000), and Jahanbegloo (2004). On twentieth-century intellectuals in Afghanistan, see Ahmadi (2008).

their works were the mouthpiece. For example, from the 1940s to the time of the Revolution, the proponents of a major literary current known as 'Committed Literature' (*adabiyyāt-e mota'ahed*) largely espoused leftist and Marxist ideas and opposed the monarchy, while much of the literature officially published in the 1980s was deeply ideological, praising the Revolution and the war with Iraq and forming the first literature that was both religious and modern to appear in the Persian language (Talatoff 2000).

Many Iran-educated Afghans have embraced the role of the 'committed intellectual', using their writing to bring about social, political, and cultural change.[13] During the 1980s, much of their literary work, whether polemical essays or poetry, was devoted to supporting various Shi'a armed factions fighting against the Soviets inside Afghanistan (and later against each other). This was published in magazines they produced on their own but with support from various Iranian government bodies.[14] From the mid-1990s onwards, however, their work has become less obviously ideological, frequently deals with individual, subjective feelings and experiences, and also increasingly addresses Iranian audiences or other Afghans specifically within the Iranian context. Their marginal position in Iranian society and their ongoing 'exile' is one preoccupation of their work. Many writers and poets are now self-publishing their work in weblogs, allowing for a greater degree of freedom and outspoken criticism than was possible in printed work, which is subject to government censorship.[15]

The well known poet, critic, and literary historian Mohammad Kazem Kazemi, born in Herat in Afghanistan but educated in Iran and a resident of Mashhad for thirty years, has devoted much of his career to promoting

[13] For a historical overview of Afghan refugee political, cultural, and literary organizations in Iran, and their changes according to the political context, see Olszewska (2007).

[14] Notably, the Howze-ye Honari-ye Sazman-e Tablighat-e Eslami, or Arts Centre of the Organization for Islamic Propaganda. This, a public body not subject to the oversight of the Ministry of Culture and Islamic Guidance, but directly responsible to the supreme leader, became the most important Iranian state patron of Afghan refugees' literary activities. Its membership consisted of religious supporters of the Revolution who were interested in promoting Afghan refugee literature because their ideology had a pan-Islamic rather than a nationalist basis.

[15] One example of critical writing on the internet is an entry by Afghan poet Mohammad Sarvar Rajai in the weblog of the House of Afghan Literature, a Tehran-based Afghan literary association (Rajai 2008), in which he criticizes the distortions and stereotypes of the *Chāhār Khuneh* television series about the 'Afghan' charlatan, described above. It was later published in an Iranian newspaper, *Sarmāyeh.*

the cultural activities of his compatriots. He also seeks to remind Iranians of their shared literary, linguistic, and cultural heritage with Persian-speaking Afghans, rather than of their differences. In a book called *Hamzabāni va bizabāni* ('On Sharing a Tongue and Being without a Tongue', 2003), he cites a survey he conducted among educated people in Mashhad in which most did not know that people in Iran, Tajikistan, and Afghanistan speak the same language, and most could name few or no contemporary Persian writers from outside Iran. The book arose from his indignation at this state of affairs, but it is telling that he has to adopt an apologetic tone and emphasize that he does not mean to offend anyone:

> I am aware that raising such debates is like walking on the blade of a sword. Expressing certain realities may lead the speaker to be accused of Afghan nationalism by Iranian friends, while raising other matters may make him appear to be a sell-out and identity-less in the eyes of Persian speakers from Afghanistan; and I have kept both these probabilities in mind (Kazemi 2003: 8).

This book was published by a small Afghan publisher in Tehran and it is not clear how many Iranians it reached. But Kazemi is more famous for *Bāzgasht* ('Return'), a long poem in a classical form which he published in an Iranian newspaper in the early 1990s, of which many Iranians still remember the opening lines. It is ironically addressed to 'The Muslim nation of Iran'. In it, he variously accuses Iranians of indifference and of scapegoating Afghans and blaming them for all social ills. Yet he reminds them that in the 1980s they suffered together, each nation fighting a war of invasion, each suffering heavy losses. Ultimately, he defiantly says that he will return to Afghanistan, because he is organically connected to his homeland, to its mosques, the tombs of its martyrs, its struggle for freedom. It is the place where the exile is made whole again:[16]

> At sunset, in the hot breath of the road I will go
> On foot just as I once arrived, on foot I will go
> My talisman of exile shall be torn apart tonight
> The tablecloth that I could never fill, be folded up
> And in the air on eves of happy feast days, neighbour!
> No longer shall you hear the sound of weeping, neighbour!
> The stranger with no penny to his name shall be gone
> The child that had no doll or cradle, too, shall be gone.

---

[16] Of course, there was more rhetoric than substance to this claim, given that seventeen years after publishing this poem, Kazemi is still living in Iran and has little intention of going back to Afghanistan. For a discussion of the poem and the interest and responses it aroused among both Iranians and Afghans, see Olszewska (2007: 211–12).

How could I not return? when my battle trench is there
How? Oh, the memory of my brother's grave is there
How could I not return? when the mosque and the *mihrab*,
The sword which waits to kiss my head, all of these are there?
A time to build, a time to pray, were all that I had here
My fight for freedom and my cries of 'God is great!' are there
My wings are broken here, perhaps, but not my fortitude
The skies through which I long to fly with joyful ease are there
Do not find fault that I have only one leg and one crutch
Do not find fault: my other leg is firmly planted there.[17]

In this poem, like many critical intellectuals in the past, Kazemi was able to say in elegant and memorable verse what few others had been given the right to say in a public forum, and to engage in a critical dialogue with his Iranian counterparts and Iranian society in general.

It is important to note that not only self-described intellectuals attempt to combat Iranian nationalist exclusion of Afghans, both physical and metaphysical. The following poem, a cry of outrage apparently composed by an anonymous Afghan worker deported from Iran in 2007, was sent to me by an Afghan friend. Its rhetoric is simple and direct, and appeals clearly to the ideals of Islamic unity and equality rather than nationalism:

Your hospitality, what strange hospitality it is, O Republic of Islam
I, an Afghan guest, became a prisoner in my home; I'm neither a traitor
    nor a murderer, what description of Islam is this?
I have been driven out for the crime of being an Afghan.
Islamic kindness has been sacrificed to a national feeling
Neither Islamic behaviour, nor humane treatment: one is snatched from the
    street, another is snatched from the well, one is snatched without
    warning;
I have no place to hide; I have neither a civilized country, nor am I comfort-
    able here, free
To whom might I cry out an appeal from this suffering and distress?
Have you not read the verses of the Koran? The earth is the dominion of
    God
Why are you silent, Mr. Sheikh and Mr. Mullah? To a Muslim, Muslim
    treatment.
One should not say 'foreigner', according to the command of Islam,
    according to the word of the Koran, whether you are a scholar or a
    wise man, whether you are a Sayyed or a lord.

---

[17] Fragments; reprinted in Kazemi (2005: 40). This translation is literary rather than literal, aiming to preserve the formal structure of the original by using a familiar English metre and maintaining the 'over-rhyme', the phrase that is repeated at the end of certain lines. All of the images, however, have been preserved as faithfully as possible.

It is not clear, however, whether or not this poem ever reached Iranian ears, and what effect it had on them, though it was reportedly republished in a number of weblogs.

In the meantime, the poetry of the younger generation is becoming a repository of the indignities suffered by them as refugees. In one poem, written in modern blank verse, Elyas Alavi mentions some of the phantom horrors that haunt the Afghan–Iranian borderlands: the kidnapping or selling of Afghan girls in the border region near Zabol, and Tall-e Siah, a notorious desert deportation camp for Afghans allegedly surrounded by the mass graves of those who tried to escape or resist:

> Your legs carry the smell of landmines
> Your mouth of hunger
> Your shoulders of wander wander
> > wandering.
> Wipe away your sweat
> The men of Zabol are buying gold to take away your daughter
> In the well-shafts of Tall-e Siah your son's thirst has been quenched
> > for eternity[18]

The vast majority of Iranians would not recognize the name Tall-e Siah, so much so that Alavi included a footnote explaining it, still rather obliquely, as 'a camp for refugees'.

Alavi frequently plays up his 'victimhood' in poems which he enters into Iranian poetry competitions, and he has won a growing number of awards and accolades for them in recent years. This tactic has invited criticism from some of his compatriots for exoticizing Afghanistan and flaunting its misery for personal gain. However, it seems that simple appeals to the early revolutionary ideals of solidarity with the weakest members of society—ideals which are felt to have been betrayed by harsh political and economic realities—fall on receptive ears among contemporary Iranian audiences. Indeed, Alavi was honoured by Iranian revolutionary poet Ali Moallem at one award ceremony for his *bidāri-ye vahshatnāki* ('terrible wakefulness') with respect to the suffering of people in the region. Unfortunately, such educated, literary audiences do not seem to have any say in creating policy towards refugees.[19]

Another poet, Qanbar Ali Tabesh, a student of the religious seminary in Qom who was born in a small village in the Hazarajat region of

---

[18] Fragment of 'Āvāz-e gharib' ('A Desolate Voice'), in Alavi (2008: 24–5).
[19] See Olszewska (2007: 221–2) for a more thorough discussion of this poem.

Afghanistan, tackles the state of exile itself, saying with a hint of irony that it is simply the 'destiny' of migrants and refugees to be 'trampled underfoot', rather than free, like birds, to make their home anywhere they please (Tabesh 2006: 77):

> A man is not a bird
> That he might make his homeland on any shore he flies to
> A man has the destiny of a leaf
> A leaf, when it separates from the heights of its branch,
> Is trampled underfoot by passers-by in the streets.

Meanwhile, Afghanistan itself, when it appears in post-2001 refugee writing, is represented in very ambivalent terms. The following poem is by Mahbubeh Ebrahimi, a prize-winning female poet with a degree in public health, born in Kandahar but raised and educated in Iran. Written after her first visit to Afghanistan since her childhood on a journey to visit her parents who had returned to their native city, it is titled 'Solh' ('Peace') and describes the longing, pity, and horror she feels for her homeland, personified as a man—a father perhaps—both loved and feared.

> A rifle on your shoulder
> You come out to greet me
> Unkempt, dressed in rags
> This
> Is not you
> You were supposed to be
> A rider on a red horse. . .
> Upon my hair you place
> A crown of opium poppy blossoms
> Roses?
> You smile
> And half-dead butterflies
> Fall to the dust.
> Release me!
> I'm afraid of you
> You've hidden minefields in your pockets
> They've killed men
> And thrown them into the wells of your heart
> Your kisses say—
> But your voice
> Tired and hoarse reaches me
> —Come, let's go home
> If you kiss me
> The mines will be disarmed
> The guns

The poppies
Your kiss
Is a white dove
With a delicate flower in its beak.[20]

CONCLUSION

The poems discussed above illustrate the distressing ambivalence experienced by second-generation Afghan refugees in Iran, a confusion which they themselves describe as an 'identity crisis'. Perhaps such ambivalence may be extrapolated to many other groups in long-term situations of displacement, in which there appears to be no possibility of a return to full citizenship, whether in their country of origin or their new home. Of course, such confusion is only a problem when citizenship—for our purposes, the sense of belonging to and living in a particular state which is considered to be a guarantor of one's social and political rights and, indeed, one's identity—becomes a desirable thing to hold. This was not always the case in this region, which was once a vast area criss-crossed by trade routes and by shifting and permeable boundaries of empires, but linked together by a common language (Persian) and religion (Islam), and the literary and scholarly traditions of both. Monsutti (this volume) points out that even today movement is a normal feature of Afghan social life and people maintain multiple ties in multiple societies, and that transnational mobility, adaptation, and 'flexible citizenship' carry many benefits.[21]

However, as the first part of this essay showed, movement may have consequences not entirely intended or predicted by the migrant. Whether in the schools of the host country, through its media, or in its deportation camps, migrants and refugees encounter the normative power of the modern concepts of nation state and nationalism. In today's Iran, this nationalism overrules the pan-Islamic aspirations of the Islamic Republic and excludes even fellow believers with a long

[20] Ebrahimi 2007: 42.

[21] The alert reader may notice a discrepancy between the two chapters in this volume on the difficulties of Afghan returnees from Iran in fully embracing their Afghan 'identity' and feeling cheated and unfulfilled by life (Kamal; Saito and Kantor) and Monsutti's chapter describing a much more enthusiastic embracing of migration and adaptability as livelihood strategies. To some extent, this may be a result of studying distinct groups within the same broader population and, to some extent, of their different methodologies. If, like Monsutti, one's research consists of following those who have been successfully mobile, one selects against those who have not been mobile or those who would prefer not to be mobile.

common history. Long-staying refugees in Iran, particularly those who have been educated there, have inevitably been shaped by the ideologies of the state as well as by the discontents of Iranian society. Territorial nationalism, social consciousness, participation in the public sphere (especially for women), and social justice within the framework of political Islam are among the values they have absorbed. Denied outlets for implementing these values in Iran, many young people hoped they would find them in Afghanistan, to which they attached almost mystical value, even if they had never seen it. Many of those who returned, however, were thwarted there too, as other authors in this volume explain (e.g. Kamal).

Such disillusionment can be creatively channelled by literary activity, which provides rhetorical tools with which social and legal marginalization may be protested and discussed. But a culture of despondency itself, or a feeling of liminality and being neither-here-nor-there, are not merely rhetorical stances—they are real subjective experiences which must be taken seriously by social scientists. Monsutti's bottom-up, migrant action-focused study draws much needed attention to the blurred lines between forced and economic migration in practice, and the insufficiency of these categories as analytical tools. It is my hope that my work will complement his picture by focusing on the important roles of the state and its discourses, the normative power of ideology and ideas, and the ways in which these affect subjectivity and creative expression.

Note.   Parts of this essay draw on my DPhil dissertation entitled 'Poetry and Its Social Contexts among Afghan Refugees in Iran' (University of Oxford, 2009). It is based on twelve months of ethnographic fieldwork in Mashhad and Tehran, Iran, between 2004 and 2007. I am grateful to the Scatcherd European Scholarship, the British Institute of Persian Studies, and the Institute of Social and Cultural Anthropology at the University of Oxford for funding, and to the Department of Literature, Ferdowsi University of Mashhad, for an affiliation that made this research possible. I would also like to thank the participants of the 'Dispossession and Displacement' conference for their helpful comments.

REFERENCES

Abbasi-Shavazi, M. J., Glazebrook, D., Jamshidiha, G., Mahmoudian, H., and Sadeghi, R. (2005a), *Return to Afghanistan? A Study of Afghans Living in Tehran, Islamic Republic of Iran* (Kabul, Afghanistan Research and Evaluation Unit).
—— (2005b), *Return to Afghanistan? A Study of Afghans Living in Mashhad, Islamic Republic of Iran* (Kabul, Afghanistan Research and Evaluation Unit).

—— (2005c), *Return to Afghanistan? A Study of Afghans Living in Zahedan, Islamic Republic of Iran* (Kabul, Afghanistan Research and Evaluation Unit).

Adelkhah, F. and Olszewska, Z. (2007), 'The Iranian Afghans', *Iranian Studies*, 40, 2: 137–65.

Ahmadi, W. (2004), 'Exclusionary Poetics: Approaches to the Afghan "Other" in Contemporary Iranian Literary Discourse', *Iranian Studies*, 37, 3: 407–29.

—— (2008), *Modern Persian Literature in Afghanistan: Anomalous Visions of History and Form* (London and New York, Routledge).

Alavi, E. (2008), *Man gorg-e khiālbāfi hastam: Majmu'eh-ye she'r* (*I am a Daydreamer Wolf: A Poetry Collection*) (Tehran, Ahang-e Digar).

Boroujerdi, M. (1996), *Iranian Intellectuals and the West: The Tormented Triumph of Nativism* (Syracuse, NY, Syracuse University Press).

Dabashi, H. (1985), 'The Poetics of Politics: Commitment in Modern Persian Literature', *Iranian Studies*, 18, 2: 147–88.

Ebadi, S. (2008), *Refugee Rights in Iran* (London, Beirut, San Francisco, UNHCR/Saqi).

Ebrahimi, M. (2007), *Bādhā khāharān-e man and* (*The Winds Are My Sisters*) (Tehran, Sureh-ye Mehr).

Farhi, F. (2005), 'Crafting a National Identity amidst Contentious Politics in Contemporary Iran', *Iranian Studies*, 38, 1: 7–22.

Gheissari, A. (1997), *Iranian Intellectuals in the Twentieth Century* (Austin, University of Texas Press).

Hoodfar, H. (2004), 'Families on the Move: The Changing Role of Afghan Refugee Women in Iran', *Hawwa*, 2, 2: 141–71.

Integrated Regional Information Network (IRIN) (2007a), 'Afghanistan–Iran: Afghan Refugees Given Repatriation Extension', UNOCHA, www.irinnews.org/report.aspx?ReportId=70450, 28 February 2007.

—— (2007b), 'Afghanistan–Iran: Iran Deports Thousands of Illegal Afghan Workers', UNOCHA, www.irinnews.org/Report.aspx?ReportId=71865.

—— (2007c), 'Zahraa, "I Was Told to Leave My Home for Good within One Hour"', UNOCHA, www.irinnews.org/HOVReport.aspx?ReportId=72149.

—— (2007d), 'Afghanistan–Iran: UN, Afghan Government Call for Humane Deportations from Iran', UNOCHA, www.irinnews.org/Report.aspx?ReportId=72127.

—— (2007e), 'Afghanistan–Iran: Afghan Deportees Complain of Lack of Aid', UNOCHA, www.irinnews.org/Report.aspx?ReportId=73721.

—— (2008), 'Afghanistan: Stream of Deportees from Iran Continues', UNOCHA, www.irinnews.org/report.aspx?ReportId=78881.

Jahanbegloo, R. (2004), 'Introduction', in R. Jahanbegloo (ed.), *Iran: Between Tradition and Modernity* (Lanham, MD, Lexington Books), pp. ix–xxiii.

Kamrava, M. (2008), *Iran's Intellectual Revolution* (Cambridge and New York, Cambridge University Press).

Kashani-Sabet, F. (1999), *Frontier Fictions: Shaping the Iranian Nation, 1804–1946* (London and New York, I. B. Tauris).

—— (2002), 'Cultures of Iranianness: The Evolving Polemic of Iranian Nationalism', in N. R. Keddie and R. Mathee (eds), *Iran and the Surrounding World: Interactions in Culture and Cultural Politics* (Seattle and London, University of Washington Press), pp. 162–81.

Kazemi, M. K. (2003), *Hamzabāni va bizabāni* (*On Sharing a Tongue and Being without a Tongue*) (Tehran, Entesharat-e Erfan).

—— (2005), *Qesse-ye sang va khesht: Gozineh-ye she'r* (*A Tale of Stone and Brick: A Selection of Poems*) (Tehran, Ketab-e Neyestan).

Loescher, G. (2001), *The UNHCR and World Politics: A Perilous Path* (Oxford, Oxford University Press).

Makhmalbaf Film House (2003), 'An Interview with Samira Makhmalbaf for the Movie "5 in the Afternoon" in the Cannes Film Festival 2003', www.makhmalbaf.com/articles.php?a=379.

Mirsepassi, A. (2000), *Intellectual Discourse and the Politics of Modernization: Negotiating Modernity in Iran* (Cambridge, Cambridge University Press).

Olszewska, Z. (2007), '"A Desolate Voice": Poetry and Identity among Young Afghan Refugees in Iran', *Iranian Studies*, 40, 2: 203–24.

—— (2008), 'Afghan Refugees in Iran', *Encyclopedia Iranica Online*, www.iranica.com/newsite/index.isc?Article=http://www.iranica.com/newsite/articles/unicode/ot_grp14/ot_afghanrefugees_20081215.html.

Qassemi, S. Z. (2007), *Bāghhā-ye mo'allaq-e angur* (*Suspended Vineyards*) (Tehran, Sureh-ye Mehr).

Rajai, M. S. (2008), 'Adabiāt-e ajib dar tanz-e Chāhār Khuneh' (Strange Manners in the Comedy *Four Houses*), House of Afghan Literature, www.farkhar.blogfa.com, 11 dey 1386/1 January 2008.

Tabesh, Q. A. (2006), *Ādami parandeh nist* (*A Man is Not a Bird*) (Tehran, Entesharat-e Erfan).

Talatoff, K. (2000), *The Politics of Writing in Iran: A History of Modern Persian Literature* (Syracuse, NY, Syracuse University Press).

Tavakoli-Targhi, M. (2001), *Refashioning Iran: Orientalism, Occidentalism and Historiography* (Hampshire and New York, Palgrave Macmillan).

Tober, D. (2007), '"My Body is Broken Like My Country": Identity, Nation, and Repatriation among Afghan Refugees in Iran', *Iranian Studies*, 40, 2: 263–85.

Tohidi, N. (2002), 'International Connections of the Iranian Women's Movement', in N. R. Keddie and R. Mathee (eds), *Iran and the Surrounding World: Interactions in Culture and Cultural Politics* (Seattle and London, University of Washington Press), pp. 205–31.

Turton, D. and Marsden, P. (2002), *Taking Refugees for a Ride? The Politics of Refugee Return to Afghanistan* (Kabul, Afghanistan Research and Evaluation Unit).

Zahedi, A. (2007), 'Transnational Marriages, Gendered Citizenship, and the Dilemma of Iranian Women Married to Afghan Men', *Iranian Studies*, 40, 2: 225–39.

9.
Narrative as Identity: Perspectives from an Iraqi Women Refugees' Oral History Project

Laura Hamblin and Hala Al-Sarraf

INTRODUCTION

Our research consists of collecting oral histories of Iraqi women refugees who are now living in Amman, Jordan. To date we have collected seventy interviews, and are creating transcripts of the interviews to be archived as historical documents, thus giving ear to the women refugees' issues, concerns, and hopes. From the narratives, we analyse different aspects of the refugees' experience and identity, including current legal options, class, and socioeconomic status, religious identification, and changes in gender roles. In this essay we look at the identity of the Iraqi women refugees as revealed through their personal narratives. As we began working on the essay, we immediately recognized that we (as an American scholar and as an Iraqi scholar and public health policy maker) have rather different ideas about what identity is and how identity is created.

From an Iraqi perspective, a new Iraqi identity is currently struggling to emerge in light of the changes following the American invasion of 2003. The thirty-five years of Ba'athist rule enhanced and reinforced the Iraqi identity as an Arab identity. In alignment with this policy, Iraqis watched Arabs of other nationalities enjoying privileges of free education, work opportunities, housing, etc. while they lived in Iraq. Most Iraqis accepted such sharing of Iraqi benefits with other Arabs as part of their 'Arab nationalism responsibility'. With the fall of regime, the interim government emphasized Iraqi identity as being separated from other Arab nations by introducing the concepts of a system based on sectarian and ethnic power sharing. Iraqis found themselves grouping under different umbrellas of Shi'ite, Sunni, Arab, Kurd, Assyrian, Sabean, Christian, etc. When conflict pushed Iraqis from their homes and country, their new struggle for identity became even more complicated among their host country's perceptions of old and new Iraqis. Iraqi women refugees are Arabs who cannot now enjoy the same privileges the Arabs of other nationalities had in Ba'athist Iraq, and they still do not accept their sectarian differences as the main criteria by which they identify themselves. From an Iraqi perspective, the current Iraqi identity is yet to emerge based on outcomes of the conflict.

From a Western, postmodern perspective, identity is understood as a factor of one's cultural, social, familial, and individual sense of self. According to identity and social identity theory, one's social identity is based on a person's knowledge that she belongs to a social category or group that holds a common social identification; individuals place themselves (or are placed) in a society structured in relationship to other contrasting categories (Stets and Burke 2000). When different roles are imposed or negotiated, disruptive effects can and do occur. When a woman lives as a refugee, the understanding and significance of her individual and social identity shifts. All of the women we have interviewed expressed the sense that their identity is challenged as their life circumstances demand of them that they somehow accommodate the dramatic changes they experience. The war itself has highlighted both the similarities *and* the differences of their identity and experiences, and although there are shared aspects of the women's identities, each woman's oral history exemplifies how each woman's identity is unique. From this perspective, identity emphasizes the uniqueness of each individual's experiences and the way in which narrative is actually a process by which identity is created.

CURRENT LEGAL OPTIONS FOR IRAQI REFUGES

Jordan did not sign the 1947 United Nations compact, so the people who flee to Jordan are not recognized as 'refugees' and hence are not afforded the rights and privileges accorded to refugees (IRC 2007). Instead, Iraqis arriving in Jordan are received as 'temporary visitors' or 'guests' and may stay for three months, after which they are expected to leave or become a resident of Jordan (Frangieh 2007). However, one may become a resident only by depositing 50,000 Jordanian dinars (JDs) in a frozen Jordanian bank account, or by investing 75,000 JDs in a Jordanian company. Of course, for the majority of the refugees, such sums of money are impossible to acquire; hence, the majority of Iraqis lose their legal status after the allotted three months guest stay. Of the women we interviewed, only four were actually legal residents. Once one has lost legal residence, she is charged a fee of 1.5 JD per day of illegal stay. In order to become a legal resident again, such fines have to be paid. Those who are illegal residents live with the continual anxiety of being confronted by the Jordanian immigration police with the possibility of being deported, or of an Iraqi official visiting Jordan and putting additional pressure on the Jordanian government to ensure their return to Iraq.

Recently, the Jordanian government issued a resolution that allows Iraqis who have stayed beyond the legal permissible period to leave the country without paying penalties (Hindi and Hazaimeh 2008). Once an Iraqi refugee has left Jordan, she must submit a visa request to reenter. As for those who do not wish to return to Iraq, they are allowed to pay 50 per cent of their penalty to correct their legal status in Jordan and give them an additional three months' legal residency in Jordan. With these criteria in place, we calculate the following:

$$
\begin{array}{rl}
540 \text{ days} & \text{average duration of illegal stay in Jordan} \\
\times \quad 1.5 \text{ JD} & \text{penalty/day} \\
\hline
810 \text{ JD} & \text{penalty/person}
\end{array}
$$

$$
\begin{array}{rl}
810 \text{ JD} & \text{penalty/person} \\
- \quad 405 \text{ JD} & \text{payment of 50\% of penalty to correct person's status} \\
\hline
405 \text{ JD} & \text{amount of penalty still owed after correcting illegal status}
\end{array}
$$

In other words, a family of four members would have to pay 1,620 JD to gain three months' secured legal status. This correction of legal status covers only an additional three months' stay, after which the daily 1.5 JD fee begins to accrue again. To most of the refugees, this option is untenable—they are likely to see the offering as illogically allowing them to pay 405 JD to wave what would otherwise be a 135 JD fee. Additionally, the majority of the women have the dream of resettling in a third country, and on acceptance to a third country all the fines are waived. So, for most of the refugees, maintaining an illegal status is the only viable financial option they can see for themselves. However, without legal status, many refugees live in fear of and are vulnerable to exploitation (NGO Statement 2007).

We begin with this information on the women's legal status to highlight the legal pressures that overlay all their experiences. For this essay, we focus on four aspects of identity that the women we have interviewed have expressed as being challenged and changing: (1) class and socioeconomic status, (2) religious identification, (3) gender roles, and (4) child rearing. Of course, these four categories are not separate categories—rather, they overlap one another.

CLASS AND SOCIOECONOMIC STATUS

To have legal status as a refugee in Jordan, one must register with the United Nations High Commissioner for Refugees (UNHCR). As refugees, Iraqis cannot find legal employment with an illegal status. For a very few refugees with political connections, the Jordanian government has granted special resident permits.

About half of the women we interviewed worked outside the home while they were living in Iraq, employed in various positions and fields including as a school principal, seamstress, pre-school teacher, medical doctor, veterinary doctor, industrial engineer, special education teacher, chemist, textile engineer, university professor of religion, attorney, and Caritas worker. Only one of the women was working in her professional discipline while in Amman (Sahar, anchorwoman at Babelyia TV station). Of the thirty-five women who were employed in Jordan, one, who had been an employee in the Ministry of Education while in Iraq, was selling cigarettes on the sidewalk; another, who was an engineer in Iraq, was selling homemade food; and a third, a maths teacher, was selling cosmetics in a cosmetics shop in East Amman.

When we asked how the women supported themselves, the answers varied from selling gold and possessions, to having family members from abroad give a little, to receiving charity, to selling handiwork, to peddling cigarettes on the streets, to working illegally, to having their children work. None of the women spoke directly of working as prostitutes. Erika Feller of the UNHCR reports a rising problem of 'weekend marriages' where 'families make available young girls for a "traditional marriage ceremony" for the weekend to those who are prepared to pay and the divorce takes place on Sunday in accordance to traditional practices' (Aziakou 2007). Two of the women stated that they frequently received sexual proposals and that they sometimes considered accepting and did not know how long they could keep refusing. One woman had a child after she arrived as a widow in Amman. Her neighbours stated that they suspected she had an affair which resulted in her last child. Because sexual relations outside of marriage are taboo, it is likely that women who might actually support themselves through prostitution would not speak of it (Associated Press 2007). Consequently, when some women spoke of the possibility of prostitution as a means of supporting themselves and their family (using the subjunctive mood), it caused us to wonder if in fact they were describing their actual circumstances in an oblique fashion.

RELIGIOUS IDENTIFICATION

By using snowball sampling,[1] we managed to contact and interview women from a variety of religious backgrounds. Some of the connections were unexpected: we contacted Christians though Sunni Muslim referrals, Sabeans through Sunni, and Sunni through Shi'ite. Apparently, unlike Iraqis in contemporary Iraq, sectarian differences were not the main criteria by which the women refugees formed relationships and community. On the contrary, the women often expressed a denial of there being sectarian conflict; they particularly seemed to want the West to know that the sectarian conflict originated with the Anglo-American Coalition's occupation of Iraq and is not natural for Iraqis.

During Ashura (the tenth day of Mohrram, a sacred holiday for Shi'ites, commemorating the death of their Imam Hussein) we witnessed the fact that both Shi'ite and Sunni Iraqi women refugees cooked and distributed food to those around them, whether Sunnis, Shi'ites, Christians, Jordanians, or Americans. We interpreted this as a real attempt (neither a perfect attempt nor one without its awkwardness, but a real attempt) to interact with one another as Iraqis and not as Sunnis, Shi'ites, or Christians.

In spite of their insistence on solidarity, we did see manifestations of old prejudices. For example, two women (Iptisam, a Sunni, and Nida, a Shi'ite) told us that we should not distribute heaters to the Sabeans as they claimed that the Sabeans were rich and hoarded money and had more access to international support—none of which we observed. Several specific concerns were expressed to us. Some of the Christians felt that George Bush's rhetoric of the war being a 'crusade' encouraged Muslims to magnify the Sabeans' identity as Christians. The Christians spoke of others seeing them in close alliance with Bush and as benefiting from the Coalition, so they saw themselves as being targeted with negative stigma.

---

[1] Snowball sampling is quite common in situations where the population being studied is vulnerable and wary of contact with outsiders. In snowball sampling, one contact recommends another, the other then recommends a further contact, and so on.

Sabeans are thought by many Iraqis to have close ties with Christians, so many Iraqis assumed that Sabeans were also in close alliance with the West. Because of their specific persecution, Sabeans have expressed a need for more assistance from the Coalition. In Jordan, Sabeans are not recognized as a religious group at all. On a Jordanian birth certificate, there are only two boxes in which to mark the family's religion—Muslim or Christian. The Sabeans' religious leader resettled in Sweden, so the Sabeans in Jordan have no one in Amman to marry or bury them. Additionally, the Sabeans require naturally flowing water to perform their religious rituals and thus cannot practise even the basic rituals of their faith while in Jordan.

The identity of the Shi'ite Muslims in Jordan is also altered. Many of the Shi'ites do not openly claim to be Shi'ite because Jordan is a Sunni country, and as Shi'ite they are perceived (or they have the perception of being perceived) as having close affiliation with Shi'ite Iran. (We noticed this is not the case: almost everyone expressed uniform resentment against the Iranians.)

CHANGES IN GENDER ROLES

One of the challenges we heard the women express over and over again is that of assuming the traditionally masculine role of being the head of the family. In cases where the father is not present, the children often look to the women exclusively, seeing strong female role models in the house. In one instance, when we entered a large family's apartment, the father began telling us his story. I stopped him, saying, 'Right now I'm just taking the women's stories.' He responded, 'Well, I *am* a woman—I cannot work, I stay at home all day. They have turned me into a woman—so why don't you interview me!' His comment, met with nervous laughter by everyone, underlined the anxiety many of the refugees feel about the reversals in gender roles with which they are faced.

Many of the women interviewed were responsible for the main income of the family. Most Iraqis in Jordan, because of their illegal status, are not allowed to work legally; thus if an individual works, it is by taking illegal employment (which is typically at a significantly lower pay rate than a legal worker, with little recourse if the employer makes unrealistic or illegal demands). We saw women taking illegal employment more than men because the perception (and it may be a correct perception) is that women are less likely to be deported by police if they are caught working.

The shifts in gender roles cause a number of problems to arise. Most couples expressed frustration on both sides which often resulted in an increase in domestic violence and family disturbances (Women's Commission 2007). We saw a greater sense of independence on the part of the women who were working, further exacerbating the situation as they became less dependent on their husbands. Some of the women seemed to be enjoying their newfound independence; in the future, these women may not return to the home and comfortably assume their previous domestic roles.

We also speculate that if women are working at ages as young as 12 or 13 (with the negative image that this creates), and if men cannot work, the traditional forms of marriage proposal and the possibilities of traditional marriages will of necessity alter. Of the women we interviewed, not one family member was engaged or preparing for marriage.

CHILD REARING

Of the various challenges of child rearing that the women we interviewed faced, perhaps the most pressing was ensuring their children's education. The enrolment of Iraqi children in public schools has fluctuated according to the Jordanian government's discretion with policies changing from open to closed enrolment. Initially, the government of Jordan was hopeful that the duration of Iraqi refugees' stay would be minimal, thus not requiring that the schools open up enrolment to Iraqi children. Additionally, the schools could not accommodate the anticipated increase in students. In autumn 2007, the public schools changed their policy and allowed Iraqi children to attend. At the beginning of the school year only 7,000 new students had registered. This number is out of an estimated 50,000 children or more who were of school age (Seeley 2007). Indeed, only 3 per cent of the Iraqi refugees held residency permits which are necessary for their children to attend school (Women's Commission 2007). In 2007 some international NGOs allowed Iraqi children to be admitted to private schools including Christian schools. Although their programmes cover books and tuition, they do not cover transportation costs.

Through our direct contact with families, we found a number of reasons why children were not attending schools in greater numbers. The parents who might be in Jordan illegally were afraid that the act of registering their children for school would result in the parents being identified and deported. The family might have had difficulty accessing the necessary official papers needed to register the children in school as many left Iraq in a hurry without gathering the family's governmental papers. Many families cannot afford the 20–30 JDs fee for primary or secondary education. (Although UNICEF made an agreement with the Ministry of Education to cover the costs, some families were not aware of this offer and so did not take advantage of it.) Some children were not attending school because they were actually working and the family could not support itself without their income (Washington and Ejeilat 2007). Of the children who worked, one woman's (Nidal's) daughters (aged 8 and 12) worked in a shoe factory, and another's (Majid's) daughters (aged 12 and 13) worked as waitresses for a catering company at wedding parties. The waitresses often worked late into the night and then walked home alone with men sexually taunting them along the way.

A third woman's son (Sahar's son, Omar) was working at a bakery. He had dropped out of school two years before when in ninth grade. In Jordan, any child who has missed three years of school is not allowed to go back. Statistics show that once a child has missed three years of schooling, he or she rarely returns for more education (Seeley 2007). The children who are not attending feel socially alienated, teased, and bored, resulting in feelings of helplessness and hopelessness.

Education is not the only challenge of child rearing the Iraqi women refugees we interviewed faced. We saw a number of teenagers, particularly young men, who embraced Western fashion and activities (to varying degrees), often to the distress of their mothers. The mothers, while wanting their sons to be traditional, conservative Iraqi teenagers, had little or no control over the boys' attitudes and dress. For some of these women, their worst fears for their children were manifested within two years of leaving Iraq. Additionally, the children of the Iraqi women refugees had spent a good part of their childhood in a war-torn country; the emotional and psychological effects of such an upbringing are difficult to calculate.

CONCLUSIONS

Our findings and conclusions are based on the answers the women gave from the uniform questions we asked them. We see the women's identities as continuing to shift until their status as refugees is resolved. When we asked the women, 'Where do you see yourself in five years', only two out of the seventy women saw themselves as being able to return to Iraq. However, the Iraq they envisioned returning to is and will be very different from the Iraq they left. Seventy per cent of the women we interviewed had applied for resettlement to a third country, but their cases were pending. Some cases had been pending for more than three years. During the time we conducted interviews, only one unmarried woman was resettled in the United States; she worked as an interpreter for the military, but it took four years for her application to be processed.

In reality, we see the two options of either returning or resettling as being unrealistic because so few of the refugees are actually accepted into third countries and because conditions in Iraq have not improved to the point where return is possible. We predict that the majority of the women will remain in Jordan in their current dire situations as in a state of limbo. The recording and presenting of oral histories should continue. The information gathered from Iraqi women refugees can be an invaluable part of understanding who the refugees are so that the West, other Arab nations, and Iraq itself can better understand and assist with the needs of the Iraqi women refugees.

REFERENCES

Associated Press (2007), 'Among Desperate Iraqi Refugees, Prostitution a Growing Problem', *International Herald Tribune*, 23 October.

Aziakou, G. (2007), 'UN Spotlights "Survival Sex" among Iraqi Women Refugees', United Nations (Middle East Online), 15 November, www.iraqupdates.com.

Frangieh, G. (2007), 'Who Is a Refugee?', email to Liz Heaney, 4 November.

Hindi, L. and Hazaimeh. H. (2008), 'Iraqis Exempted from Fines', *Jordan Times*, 14 February, http://admin.jordantimes.com.

International Rescue Committee (IRC) (2007), *Uprooted Iraqis: An Urgent Crisis* (IRC).

NGO Statement on Regional Consequences of the Humanitarian Crisis in Iraq (2007), International conference on addressing the humanitarian needs of refugees and internally displaced persons inside Iraq and neighbouring countries, Geneva, Switzerland, 17–18 April 2007.

Seeley, N. (2007), 'Breaking into School', *JO Magazine*, September: 48–51.

Stets, J. E. and Burke, P. J. (2000), 'Identity Theory and Social Identity Theory', *Social Psychology Quarterly*, 63, 3: 224–37.

Washington, K. and L. Ejeilat (2007), 'When Is It OK to Make Kids Work?', *JO Magazine*: 48–52.

Women's Commission for Refugees and Children (2007), 'Iraqi Refugees in Jordan: Desperate and Alone', www.womenscommission.org.

Part IV
Policy

10.
The Refugee Factor in Two Protracted Conflicts: Cyprus and Palestine Compared

Peter Loizos and Tobias Kelly

In the early years of the twenty-first century two peace processes at the eastern end of the Mediterranean, that had once widely been seen as very promising, came to a halt. In Cyprus, the Annan Plan was rejected by the majority of Greek-Cypriots. In Israel/Palestine, the Oslo Peace Process collapsed into the second *intifada*. Despite their obvious differences, not least in the levels of political violence, the fate of the refugees caused by both conflicts has played a major role not only in how the relative paths of the conflicts in Cyprus and Israel/Palestine developed, but also in the eventual collapse of the respective peace processes. This essay is a comparative exploration of the roles that refugees—as individuals, as groups, and as political issues—have played in the eventual failure of both peace processes. Although there have been Turkish-Cypriot refugees from the southern part of the island, and Jewish refugees from the Arab states, this essay focuses on Greek-Cypriot refugees and Palestinian refugees respectively, as it is the ways in which the rights of these two groups have been treated that has been the most controversial issue in both peace processes.

In comparative sections, we explore the historical conditions, legal statuses, access to political representation, and geopolitical factors that have influenced the ways in which the wider conflict and the refugees have been dealt with. The following section explores the failures of the Annan Plan in Cyprus and the Oslo Process in Israel/Palestine, and the role of the refugee issue in these failures. We conclude with some wider suggestions about the implications of refugee issues for attempts to settle long-term political conflicts.

THE DEVELOPMENT OF THE REFUGEE PROBLEMS

The Palestinian refugee crisis was created by a struggle between an indigenous Arab nationalism shaped by the British colonial project in the Middle East, and a Jewish settler nationalism rooted in European anti-Semitism. Following the creation of the British Mandate for Palestine at the close of the Ottoman Empire, the Balfour Declaration committed the British to the promotion of a 'Jewish national home' in Palestine. In the mid-1940s militant Zionists turned their guns on the British with the aim of establishing a Jewish state and, following the Holocaust, Jewish immigration to Palestine increased greatly. By 1947 the British Mandate could no longer control either the Jewish or Arab communities. In response, the United Nations passed Resolution 181, which supported the partition of Palestine into two states: one Jewish, one Arab. The British left it to the two groups to fight it out. The Zionist forces accepted the partition, whilst the Palestinian leadership—divided or in exile—rejected partition on the basis that Palestine was not a legitimate British possession that it could grant to the Zionist movement. Throughout 1947 and 1948, Zionist and Palestinian Arab forces fought across Mandate Palestine. The better trained, organized, and equipped Zionist *Haganah* were largely victorious against the ad hoc Palestinian Arab forces. Shortly after the leadership of the Jewish community declared Israeli independence in mid-May 1948, the surrounding states of Egypt, Jordan, Syria, Lebanon, and Iraq sent in their troops. However, the efforts of the Arab states were limited by their often contradictory agendas. By the end of October, Israeli forces controlled over 78 per cent of Mandate Palestine, a space considerably larger than that which had been allotted to it under the UN partition plan.

After its declaration of independence in 1948, the new state of Israel was quickly recognized by the international community. The Arab state envisaged in the UN partition plan was never established, and the areas of Mandate Palestine not under Israeli control were either annexed to the Hashemite Kingdom of Jordan, or placed under Egyptian military rule. The majority of Palestinians became stateless persons. By the time the armistice agreements were signed in January 1949 only 150,000 of the original 950,000 Palestinian Arab residents remained in the area now under Israeli control (see Figure 10.1). The refugees had fled, fearing forced removals or worse from the rapidly advancing Zionist forces. By 2003 the UN estimated that these people and their descendants numbered

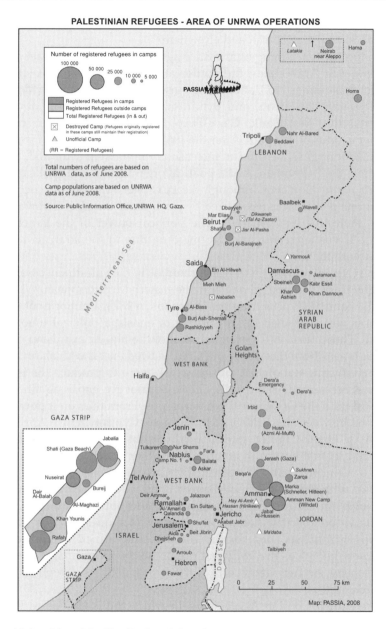

Figure 10.1. Map of the West Bank and Gaza Strip, 2000.
Source: www.passia.org/palestine_facts/MAPS/Refugees-UNWRA-2001.html (© Palestinian
Academic Society for the Study of International Affairs).

229

more than 4 million people, spread across Jordan, Syria, Lebanon, the West Bank and Gaza Strip, and elsewhere.[1]

Following the signing of armistice agreements between Israel and its neighbouring Arab states, the border areas remained sites of sporadic conflict. In summer 1967, after rising tension, the Israeli military defeated the Egyptian, Jordanian, and Syrian armies in a matter of days and occupied the West Bank, Gaza Strip, and Sinai peninsular, causing another exodus of refugees. After the 1967 defeat the Palestine Liberation Organization (PLO) became an increasingly influential actor and, for the first time, the Palestinians had a political organization that spoke directly in their name. However, although the PLO was a diplomatic success, in that at one point it was recognized by more states than Israel, it was militarily ineffective (Sayigh 1997). The political power of the Israeli state became unchallengeable, in large measure due to the strategic alliance forged with the USA.

The Cypriot refugee crisis was formed, as in the Palestinian case, in the twilight of British imperial power in the eastern Mediterranean. When the British acquired Cyprus from the Ottomans in 1878, a minority of Greek-Cypriots were attracted to the concept of enosis, a political union with Greece. Those Turkish-Cypriots mindful of the bloody expulsion of their co-religionists from the Morea and Crete viewed enosis with alarm. It was these conflicting nationalist visions which were to produce the island's refugees between 1955 and 1974. Greek-Cypriot pro-enosis agitation was peaceful until the October 1931 disturbances. From then on it dominated relations between the British and the Greek-Cypriots. On 1 April 1955, EOKA, a Greek-Cypriot guerrilla movement for national liberation, exploded its first bombs in an effort to further the enosis project. These actions were politically supported by Greece, whose leaders had lost patience with Britain's Prime Minister Eden who refused to show flexibility over the future of the island and would not contemplate Cyprus ceasing to be a British colony, as Greece had requested. The Turkish-Cypriot nationalists soon formed a clandestine armed organization of their own, known as the TMT, and promoted the idea of partitioning the island between the Greek and Turkish populations (Stephens 1966; Bahcheli 1990).

The Zurich–London Agreements, in which the NATO allies Britain, Turkey, and Greece had decisive voices, resulted in an independent

---

[1] Available at www.un.org/unrwa/english.html.

Cypriot state with a complex power-sharing constitution, which excluded *both* enosis and partition. However, this compromise failed to satisfy the more extreme nationalists in each community, and after three troubled years the fragile state was riven by fresh intercommunal fighting. In 1964, Turkey threatened to make a full-scale military incursion, and only decisive intervention by the USA, UK, and UN prevented this. A further flare-up in 1967 led to a second invasion threat by Turkey, which again the USA spent more political capital in order to prevent. Subsequently, the Greek-Cypriots sought to pursue enosis through diplomacy. However, in 1967 an anti-communist military dictatorship had taken power in Greece, and in 1972 it started to fund a new insurrectionary movement among the Greek-Cypriots aimed at achieving enosis by destroying democratically elected President Makarios. This movement began a coup on 20 July 1974 and, having crushed pro-Makarios democrats, faced invasion by Turkey, which then occupied 38 per cent of the island. The resulting violence meant that within a few months, there was an almost total separation of the two major ethnic groups behind two opposed armies, with a UN peacekeeping force in between (see this volume, Figure 4.1). Technically, the situation in Cyprus remains a ceasefire. The south of the island, which the Greek-Cypriots control, has international recognition as the Republic of Cyprus. The north of the island, occupied by Turkey, has declared itself as the 'Turkish Republic of Northern Cyprus' (TRNC), but is recognized by Turkey only, while Turkey refuses to recognize the Greek-controlled Republic of Cyprus.

The Palestinian and Cypriot refugee crises were the result of clashes between an indigenous nationalism and a settler colonial movement on the one hand, and a clash between two indigenous ethno-national movements on the other. Both conflicts developed in the wake of the Ottoman Empire, as the British Empire weakened and contracted. Although sizeable proportions of both populations were displaced, the ultimate result was a Greek-Cypriot state, but no state for the Palestinians. As the Greek-Cypriot internally displaced persons (IDPs) retain full citizenship in the Republic of Cyprus, an internationally recognized state, and as the Palestinian refugees lack either a state of their own or first-class citizenship anywhere, major differences in the statuses of these two groups persist. At the same time, although Cyprus remains tense and deadlocked, there are only rare casualties; in contrast Palestine–Israel is regularly caught up in cycles of lethal violence.

A COMPARISON OF THE LEGAL STATUS OF THE REFUGEES

Since 1948 the Palestinians refugees have existed in a legal limbo. The Israeli state refused to allow the 1948 refugees to return to their homes, arguing that they represented a security threat which would endanger the Jewish majority in Israel; and the refugees' property was confiscated, without compensation. In 1950 the UN established the United Nations Relief and Works Agency for Palestine Refugees in the Near East (UNWRA) in order to deal with the immediate humanitarian aspects of the refugee crisis. Although most of the Palestinians who fled had not crossed an international frontier, the UN decided to designate them as 'refugees' on a needs basis. Refugee status was also passed down to the descendants of those initially displaced, meaning that the number of official refugees has now more than quadrupled. In this context, Palestinian refugees were granted limited legal rights by the various states in which they found themselves. In general this meant that most Arab states treated the refugees as a temporary presence and gave them some residency rights but no permanent legal footing. The notable exception was Jordan, where after 1948 all Palestinians resident in Jordan were claimed as Jordanian citizens. However, although, or even because of the fact that over 70 per cent of the population of Jordan was of Palestinian origin, the Jordanian government has attempted to stress their status as Jordanians rather than Palestinians refugees. The vast majority of 1948 refugees have remained stateless persons, and have relied on refugee documents issued by the states in which they are resident. The Casablanca Protocol issued by the League of Arab States in 1965 was supposed to stabilize rights of movement, residency, and work, but has been honoured more in the breach. In practice, Palestinian refugees have largely only contingent rights to residency, movement, and work—making them subject to discrimination in virtually every Middle Eastern state (Shiblak 1996).

The legal status of the Greek-Cypriots displaced in 1974 is relatively more straightforward. In contrast to most Palestinians, who became stateless, the Greek-Cypriot refugees remained citizens of the Republic of Cyprus. In international refugee law, they are 'internally displaced persons' (IDPs), rather than refugees. However, some of those who left the island after 1974 have claimed refugee status in the countries to which they migrated—chiefly the UK, Canada, the USA, and Australia. Like Palestinian refugees, the Greek-Cypriot refugees lost access to their former properties, which were now in Turkish-occupied Cyprus and were inhabited either by Turkish-Cypriots or settlers from Turkey. However, in addition to their retention of citizenship rights in a modern democratic state, Greek-Cypriot refugees received special entitlements granted by that state to ease their transition to a semblance of normal life. Unlike the Palestinian refugees, the Greek-Cypriot IDPs were granted social and economic rights to compensate for their displacement.

The major distinction between Palestinian and Greek-Cypriot refugees is that of citizenship and statehood. Greek-Cypriots enjoy full citizenship rights. With the notable exception of Jordan, most Palestinians are stateless, and have only temporary residence rights. Although both populations lost property and livelihoods, most Palestinians were also denied residence, social, and civil rights.

A COMPARISON OF THE ECONOMIC CONDITIONS OF THE REFUGEES

The precarious legal status of most Palestinian refugees has been translated into their economic conditions. Whereas middle-class and upper-class refugees were often able to make use of the contacts and relatives they had developed in Beirut or Damascus, the majority of refugees were small-scale peasant farmers who, by losing their land, also lost their only means of livelihood. Without property and largely unskilled, the refugees have faced the same difficult economic conditions as the citizens of the countries in which they reside. Syria, Jordan, and Egypt have long-term stagnating economies, whereas Lebanon has faced the instability of years of civil war. Ironically those refugees in Gaza and the West Bank have, until recently, fared best economically, because, like the other residents of the area, they have often found employment in the Israeli economy.

As well as facing the economic conditions of the countries in which they live, many refugees have had additional problems arising from their legal status—such as severe restrictions placed on their employment, particularly in Lebanon. Even where they have not been subject to legal discrimination, they have often faced socio-economic prejudices on the basis of their refugee status. In Jordan, for example, despite making up the majority of the population and formally having full rights of citizenship, Palestinians constitute only 10 per cent of all government employees. Many refugees work in the underground economy or fill the lowest paid jobs in agriculture, construction, and manufacturing. The PLO, formed in the mid-1960s, became a major employer of camp residents. As a result of this economic marginalization, Palestinian refugee camps have been centres of deprivation and poverty. In the Gaza Strip in 2002 over 40 per cent of refugees were unemployed; in Jordan, 31 per cent of all camp households fall below the poverty line (Shiblak 1996: 43). A 1993 UNICEF survey found that in Lebanese refugee camps only 37 per cent of men aged between 15 and 49 were employed (Shiblak 1996: 43). Refugees receive few, if any, social services from the states that they are resident in. In Lebanon, for example, they are entitled to no state services, despite the fact that they pay social insurance contributions on their wages.

In stark contrast, although the Greek-Cypriots faced relatively major economic losses in 1974, they managed to turn a potential economic and political disaster into what has been termed an 'economic miracle'. Mass unemployment lasted less than eighteen months, and major reconstruction projects, both state-led and private-sector, redeployed refugees as a development resource—a labour force keen to work on almost any reasonable terms (Zetter 1992; Strong 1999; Christodoulou 1992). Furthermore, after 1974 trade unions agreed to suspend confrontations with employers, a concordat lasting into the late 1980s. The Greek-Cypriot economy grew rapidly from the late 1970s and throughout the 1980s due to the purchasing power of the OPEC countries, the growth of mass tourism from northern Europe, the backwash effects of the Lebanese civil war, and the development of the Cyprus merchant fleet, one of the world's largest. The consequence for those displaced in 1974 was that there were many opportunities for remaking livelihoods, and these were energetically grasped by the refugees. Few of them were forced to remain in refugee camps for more than the first year of displacement. Whilst rehousing the poorer refugees typically took three to four years, by 1980 virtually everyone displaced in 1974 had a weatherproof home and a stake in the economy, however small.

Although both the Greek-Cypriot and Palestinian refugees largely originated in rural and relatively poor areas of their home countries, the Greek-Cypriot refugees have fared a great deal better economically than their Palestinian counterparts. In large measure this is due to three factors. First, the Greek-Cypriots had a recognized state which allowed them international credit and trade. Second, the secure legal status of the Greek-Cypriot refugees meant that they could plan for the future, and also receive considerable economic support from the state. In contrast, Palestinian refugees have always faced an uncertain future, have received little in the way of welfare and social support from their host states, and have often had their economic opportunities restricted. Third, when it mattered most, in 1976–85, Cyprus boomed—unlike war-torn Lebanon, stagnant Jordan, and sluggish Egypt.

A COMPARISON OF THE POLITICAL REPRESENTATION OF THE REFUGEES

Although the 'right of return' has been a central feature of the wider Arab and Palestinian national agenda, refugees themselves have largely remained politically marginalized. There was, for example, no refugee representation at the armistice talks between the Arab states and Israel in February 1949. As stateless persons they have little influence on the decisions—that directly affect them—of the states in which they dwell. Although Jordan and Lebanon both set up branches of government with direct responsibility for Palestinian refugees, these mainly took on a regulatory rather than a representative function, being closely linked to the security forces. The dispersal of refugees across Lebanon, Syria, Jordan, the West Bank, the Gaza Strip, and further afield, all with very different economic, political, and legal experiences, has also meant a dilution of influence, such that a unified 'refugee' position has been hard to produce.

However, a common experience of discrimination, combined with the 1967 defeat of the Arab states by the Israeli military, prompted a sense that only through an independent Palestinian infrastructure could refugees improve their individual positions and national aspirations. It was this realization that led to support for the creation of the Palestine Liberation Organization (PLO) in the mid-1960s. Although, in the early years at least, the expressed goal of the PLO was the return of refugees, and refugees held senior positions in the original leadership, they have played a limited role in its decision-making. The majority of senior PLO positions have gone to people from the West Bank and Gaza Strip (Sayigh 1997: 671). Furthermore, there has been even less representation of Palestinian refugees *as refugees* within the PLO. Although the PLO has had a Department of Refugee Affairs, this has been a largely administrative body, rather than a forum through which refugees could voice their concerns. This situation reflects the wider process of PLO state building, which has tended to favour the reproduction of top-down resource allocation rather than grass-roots mobilization (Robinson 1997). Since the start of the second *intifada* in September 2000 refugee camps have arguably played a central role in popular militancy, but it is difficult to tell to what extent they are doing so as refugees, or merely as part of a wider group of the politically and economically marginalized.

In large part, the relatively marginal role of refugees as political actors has been due to the very centrality of the refugee issue to the Palestinian national movement. No one political faction could be said to be more refugee-orientated than any other. Fatah, Hamas, and the Popular Front for the Liberation of Palestine (PFLP) have all placed the refugee issue high on their agendas. Originally, refugee expulsion was not seen as a tragedy for individual refugees only but as a national catastrophe that thwarted attempts at national self-determination (Khalidi 1992: 30). Until 1968 the 'right of return' was usually subsumed within the wider struggle for the liberation of all of historical Palestine. It was implicitly assumed that once Palestine had been liberated the refugees would return. However, following the 1967 war, the occupation of the West Bank and Gaza Strip, and the increasing dominance of the two-state solution, the 'liberation of Palestine' and the 'right of return' became distinct issues. This has left a crucial ambiguity over the meanings of 'return'. In particular, there is a dispute over whether return should be seen as an issue of individual rights to return to former homes, or as an issue of national self-determination, and therefore potentially fulfilled through the creation of a Palestinian state, wherever that maybe (Khalidi 1992: 19).

In contrast to the Palestinians, displaced Greek-Cypriots remained citizens of the Republic of Cyprus, and as a result their right to political representation was never in doubt. They could vote in elections and make their preferences known. For much of the last thirty years the president of the day has consulted an all-party National Council and, throughout the years, national unity has been a dominant theme. As a result, it can be argued that the refugees as an interest group have never felt forgotten or been left out in the cold. They have their own national association which speaks directly for them collectively, and they also have regional political associations, with more or less symbolic functions most of the time, but which may find their voices whenever a political solution is under national discussion.

The Greek-Cypriot refugees were sufficiently numerous that had they acted in a concerted manner, they might have acted as a radical force to demand a major restructuring of the polity (Loizos 1981: 135–8). Their discontent was potentially explosive. However, no important radical pro-refugee movement arose, nor did any radical challenge to the pre-1974 modes of politics arise. Although the names of the refugees have been inscribed on the electoral register by reference to their pre-1974 communities of residence, this appears to be a matter of more symbolic than substantive significance. The refugees have voted for the four major pre-war political parties, and have distributed their votes across the party spectrum in such a way that their impact as a collective pressure group has tended to be diffused, preventing the radical challenge which they could have made had they all voted for a single pro-refugee party. In an important sense, the way non-displaced Greek-Cypriots responded to those who were displaced meant that a politics of radical challenge was neither necessary nor particularly appropriate. One senior member of the key planning bureau, which authored the three emergency plans which were to take Cyprus from the threatened economic collapse of 1974 to healthy development said: 'My mother was from Kythrea. She was a refugee. We did not have to be told to think about the refugees—they were our parents and grandparents!'[2]

In both the Palestinian and Greek-Cypriot cases the refugees have been seen as a concern of wider nationalist politics and not just about the refugees themselves. However, the Greek-Cypriots had greater levels of electoral leverage, largely because they were incorporated into an already functioning democracy. The stateless Palestinians faced the task of building their own representative structures through the PLO, which developed largely as a top-down organization. Although refugees were a central part of the nationalist agenda and numerically dominant, refugees themselves were relatively marginalized and had little access to mechanisms of accountability.

A COMPARISON OF THE GEOPOLITICAL ISSUES

The Israeli–Palestinian conflict and the Palestinian refugee issue are heavily internationalized and subject to wider geopolitical pressures. Not only are refugees subject to the foreign-policy considerations of their host countries, but also US support for Israel has been increasingly influential. At a military level, US support has made the position of Israel unassailable. As a result, through the late 1970s and the 1980s, the pragmatic wing of the PLO sought to play down the armed struggle in favour of a more diplomatic approach, and in 1988 the PLO implicitly recognized the two-state solution. Such a diplomatic approach, which recognizes Israel, has increasingly found favour among the Arab states. Egypt signed a peace

---

[2] Interview with Iakovos Arestides, Nicosia, 2001.

agreement with Israel in the late 1970s, and Jordan eventually followed suit in the 1990s. Even Saudi Arabia and Syria have indicated their willingness for a two-state solution. However, at the diplomatic level, Israel has had considerable support from the USA, and in particular the USA has vetoed critical resolutions on Israel at the UN. After 11 September 2001 support for Israel seemed to become increasingly entrenched, with the administration of George Bush becoming allied with right-wing governments in Israel. Within this general approach, the USA has largely favoured the integration of Palestinian refugees into their current host countries, rather than their return to Israel. In this context, pressure on the Israeli state to accept the return of Palestinian refugees is unlikely to come from the USA. In practical terms EU influence in the area is limited, partly because of Israeli mistrust of alleged European pro-Palestinian sympathies, and partly because of an unwillingness to force the issue.

The Greek-Cypriot refugee problem has also been internationalized, albeit largely at a regional, rather than a global level. As the very essence of the conflict has concerned the nature of links to Greece and Turkey, it has never been a simple matter of whether the two local communities 'get on with' each other. The very way each saw the other was, for many years, ever more intensely affected by how they saw their 'mother countries', and how their left-wing movements saw the UK, the USA, and the USSR. This is best understood as a 'double-minority problem': the Greek-Cypriots were a majority on the island but a minority in an Ottoman-dominated province, and later in an eastern Aegean dominated by Turkey. Turkish-Cypriots were a minority vis-à-vis Greek-Cypriots and feared they would be even more powerless if Cyprus were to have become a province of Greece (Loizos 1976).

When, in 1952, Greece and Turkey entered the North Atlantic Treaty Organization (NATO), the relations between the alliance and the island became complicated by the anti-communism of NATO, as the communist movement was strong among the Cypriot workers of both communities. The USA decided in the mid-1950s that the British were mismanaging the EOKA rebellion, and briefly favoured a pro-enosis solution for some years (Nicolet 2001). The 1959 Zurich–London Agreements were an attempt by the British to keep both Greece and Turkey sweet after a period (1955–8) of serious estrangement, particularly between London and Athens, and Athens and Ankara. In 1962, President Kennedy was concerned about Cyprus as a Mediterranean Cuba, and the Greek-Cypriot Communist Party's fraternal solidarity with Moscow aggravated those anxieties, as did reports of Greek-Cypriots receiving light-missiles training from Russian instructors in Egypt (Stephens 1966). The period from 1960 until 2003 can be characterized as a time when the UK and USA attempted further damage limitation as the conflict on Cyprus threatened to disrupt the eastern flank of NATO, while the USSR attempted to exploit the situation by overtures to Turkey and arms sales to the Makarios regime. Since 1964 the UN and more recently the European Union have sought a negotiated settlement to the island's divisions.

Both the Cypriot and Israeli–Palestinian conflicts have been heavily influenced by wider geopolitical concerns. At a regional level both Greece and Turkey have played major roles in Cyprus; and the neighbouring Arab states are an integral part of the Israeli–Palestinian conflict. It is at the wider international level that the contrast is most marked. Although the USA, the UK, and NATO have been involved in Cyprus, it has mainly been in order to maintain stability between NATO allies Greece and Turkey in the eastern Mediterranean. Engagement has therefore been tactical, rather than reflecting a deep-seated ideological commitment to either side. In contrast, US, and to some extent European, support for Israel has been based on what is seen as a strong moral commitment to the existence of the Israeli state (Allin and Simon 2003). As a result, the USA and the EU have been unwilling to push solutions to the Palestinian refugee crisis that they have considered would be unacceptable to majority opinion in Israel.

THE FAILURES OF THE OSLO PROCESS AND THE ANNAN PLAN

By the late 1980s the unofficial consensus, albeit a highly contested one, had been reached among many Israelis and Palestinians, as well as the international community, that any eventual solution to the Israeli–Palestinian conflict, if there was to be one, would have to be based on a two-state model. Important questions remained however about the exact nature of these states and the place of the refugees within them. In the early 1990s, Israel and the PLO, under the supervision of the USA, UN, and Russia, signed up to the Oslo Peace Process. For the PLO, the Oslo initiative came at a key juncture as it had been marginalized by its support for Iraq in the First Gulf War. For the Israelis, it offered the opportunity of handing over day-to-day responsibility for Palestinians, after the violence of the first *intifada* in the late 1980s demonstrated that it was difficult to simultaneously maintain claims to be a liberal democracy and control occupied populations. Crucially, Oslo was not a final peace agreement but a process, that was signed to lead eventually to final-status negotiations. Central issues, such as refugees and borders, were left unexamined and delayed until these negotiations would take place. In the interim period, Israel retained ultimate security control over the West Bank and Gaza Strip but passed limited administrative powers to the newly created Palestinian National Authority (PNA). Final-status negotiations were scheduled for 1999 but were delayed several times and have not been completed.

There was a general perception among Palestinians that the Oslo Process had at best left the refugee issue on the back burner and at worst threatened to abandon refugees altogether. In the 1990s the main focus of the PLO became the West Bank and Gaza, rather than the refugee camps of the diaspora. When PNA President Arafat and the PLO sided with Iraq in the First Gulf War, the Arab states cut off funds and the PLO could no longer fund the refugee camps. The PNA, restricted to the West Bank and Gaza Strip, became the main centre of focus and source of power for the Palestinian national leadership.[3] The result was a further marginalization of the refugee populations outside the West Bank and Gaza Strip. There was also a wide sense that the replacement of the PLO by the PNA as the main centre of gravity in Palestinian politics had created further incentives for the Palestinian leadership to compromise on refugee issues in favour of issues such as settlements that were of significance mainly to the West Bank and Gaza Strip. However, despite the marginalization of the refugee issue, opposition to the Oslo Process did not primarily come from refugees *as refugees*, but from nationalist organizations such as Hamas and the PFLP, as well as younger elements within the Fatah movement. Furthermore, in general refugees did not see the Oslo Process solely through the refugee lens and assessed its likely impacts in terms of other factors, such as the continued building of settlements across the West Bank and Gaza. However, there is no doubt that refugees did feel increasingly marginalized by the Oslo Process. The constant deferral of final-status negotiations where refugee issues (and the status of Jerusalem) were to be addressed, and the lack of precise communications from the PLO, led to a sense of confusion and dislocation.

Grievances around the issues of refugees have to be understood at two interacting levels. The first level is the individual political and civil rights

---

[3] The PNA is formally a subsidiary of the PLO, but in practice the PLO has been starved of funds and has become largely moribund.

of the people displaced, dispossessed, and denied return in 1948. It is hard (although not impossible) to see how those displaced in 1948 or their descendants can ever return to their original homes and property. Many of those homes have been destroyed, or are now occupied by Israeli citizens. The issue of return therefore represents a claim to political and economic resources for a marginalized population, as much as a desire for a physical return. The second level concerns Palestinians as a collective. Here the issue of return has a much broader political significance than individual displacement and dispossession. The events of 1948 were a humiliating disaster for Palestinians at a collective and national level. The 'return' of refugees would signify that the Palestinians were wronged in 1948. The legacy of the past fifty years has meant that very few are willing to forgive Israel or forget the *nakba* (disaster).

When the final-status negotiation collapsed in the summer and autumn of 2000, the issue of refugees was a decisive, if not the only important, factor. Although the events are much disputed, according to several commentators considerable agreement was made on the issues of the borders of the Palestinian state, the nature of its sovereignty, and the future of Israeli settlements (Pressman 2003). However, refugees (and the status of Jerusalem) remained the most sizeable gap between the two negotiating positions: Ehud Barak, at that time prime minister of Israel, claimed that through the implementation of the 'right of return', the PLO was seeking the destruction of the state of Israel as a Jewish state via the back door. Before the final-status negotiations he had publicly stated that the resolution of the refugee issue would have to be found in the countries in which they currently resided, and not in Israel (Tamari 1999: 86). The PLO negotiating position is hotly disputed, but it seems that the PLO was trying to separate the issue of the right of return from its practical implementation (Pressman 2003). While the PLO argued that Israel had to recognize the absolute right of return for Palestinians refugees, it was willing to negotiate various mechanisms through which this could be realized, and argued that the vast majority of refugees would not seek to return to Israel. However, the Israeli negotiators would not accept moral responsibility for the refugee issue, would not trust Palestinian promises that most Palestinians refugees would not return to Israel, and feared that their return was a euphemism for the 'destruction of Israel'. The Palestinian negotiators would not compromise on the 'right of return' in the abstract sense, even if they could come to agreements on its practical implementation. The talks eventually collapsed with no agreement on the refugee issue, and have since been sidelined by the reciprocal violence of the second *intifada*.

It is hard to tell whether both sides were right in arguing that they could not have sold the other side's proposals to their own populations. Polls suggest that 76 per cent of Jewish-Israelis would refuse any deal that saw anything more than a token number of Palestinian refugees settled in Israel (*Haaretz*, 7 August 2000). It is even more difficult to tell exactly what Palestinian refugees felt about the various options that were put forward. This is partly due to the lack of political mechanisms through which they could express their views. It is also due to the politically sensitive nature of the refugee issue, which goes far beyond the concerns of individual refugees. In large measure refugee opinions were not distinguishable from those of the wider Palestinian public. According to another report more than 95 per cent of Palestinians saw the 'right of return' as a 'sacred right that can never be given up' (PSR 2003). However, the same poll also showed that only 10 per cent of Palestinian refugees would seek to exercise the right of return if it meant living under Israeli security. Since the collapse of the Oslo Peace Process, there have been several 'unofficial' draft peace agreements, most notably the Geneva accords. The most controversial aspects of these agreements, among Palestinians at least, have been the way they have dealt with the refugee issue. Whilst the Palestinian participants were keen to stress that they had not formally renounced the 'right of return', they were widely criticized for treating the refugee issue merely in terms of immigration and not as a national issue.

The most likely 'shape' of any agreed constitutional settlement between Greek- and Turkish-Cypriots has been implicitly clear to the political leadership of both sides. Since the Makarios–Denktash high-level agreements of 1977, a settlement has implied a state with two ethnically homogenous and largely self-governing components. Greek-Cypriots have sought a state with stronger central powers; Turkish-Cypriots have sought equality in all governmental institutions. It has also been supposed that the Turkish-Cypriot-controlled component would amount to at least 25 per cent of the island. However, as in Israel–Palestine, the issues over which there has been most speculation involve the refugees' right of return, their right to property reinstatement, and matters of compensation for those who would not or could not return.

Crucially, as with 1948 and the Palestinians, 1974 did not affect the Greek-Cypriot refugees alone. All Greek-Cypriots were affected in two ways. First, in the practical, materialistic sense they could not visit the occupied lands, nor invest in them. Thus, even if they were not themselves IDPs they were affected by the shrinking of opportunities in their already small state. Second, most Greek-Cypriots felt spiritually impoverished and politically less secure from the humiliation of 1974. As in Palestine, the creation of the refugee crisis was a major blow to national pride. Prior to 1974, Greek-Cypriots had made economic progress, seen their children increasingly better educated, fought a successful campaign to remove the vastly more powerful colonial state, and worsted the Turkish-Cypriots in several intercommunal conflicts. Just as 1922 was 'the Catastrophe' for mainland Greeks, and 1948 was *an-nakba* (the catastrophe) to the Palestinians, so 1974 was the catastrophe for Greek-Cypriots. The article of faith they had learned in primary school, a catechism of confident and resurgent Hellenism, was 'Cyprus is a Greek island!' After 1974, that sentence had to continue 'but a portion of it is under occupation'.

However, unlike in Israel–Palestine, the political leadership of both sides in Cyprus came close to agreeing to what the UN and the EU hoped would be a final peace agreement. The 2003 UN-sponsored Annan Plan would have seen the establishment of the United States of Cyprus (Palley 2005). In essence this would have been a federal umbrella state, with two 'constituent states', territorial in character, and with implicitly ethnic criteria for residence. To achieve the new state, Turkey was required to release 9 per cent of the island's territory under its occupation, which would have reduced the zone reserved for Turkish-Cypriots (and Turkish settlers) to 25 per cent. Graduated Turkish troop withdrawals were envisaged. The Greek-administered zone would thus have increased to 75 per cent, as the Buffer Zone (the 2 per cent under UN control) would have been reabsorbed by the two constituent states. The property issue was to be dealt with in rather complex ways. The Greek-Cypriots in that part to be returned by Turkey as a Greek-administered zone would get all their property back, but would not be able to return until fresh provision had been made for the Turkish occupants. For the remainder of formerly Greek-Cypriot land, there was a formula that would allow the current occupant to retain the property if he or she had spent more on it since acquisition than it had originally been worth in 1974. If this was not the case, the Greek-Cypriot owner had a theoretical right to reinstatement or compensation. There were to be restrictions on the number of Greek-Cypriots who could return to the Turkish-Cypriot constituent state as residents, and the formula would allow the oldest back first, and accept the next age groups, downwards, until that ceiling was reached. For those not able to reside in their properties, there was to be compensation. For Turkish-Cypriots the basic provisions of rights to reinstatement and to compensation if they did not seek reinstatement would have been the same as those of the Greek-Cypriots, but the Greek-Cypriots did not fear any demographic 'swamping' by returning Turkish-Cypriots, because the numbers of Turkish-Cypriots in the Greek-Cypriot constituent state would have been too few to change the majority–minority relationship. As the settlers from Turkey owned no property in the Greek-Cypriot constituent state, there was no question of their 'returning'.

In the event, and despite the formal preparatory participation of the two leaderships, the Annan Plan was rejected at a referendum. While two-thirds of the Turkish-Cypriots voted in favour of the Plan, following a strong rejection speech from Greek President Tassos Papadopoulos, three-quarters of the Greek-Cypriots voted against it. For Turkish-Cypriots it offered an end to their marginal status as persons in a non-state living in limbo under administration from Turkey, and it also offered immediate and much desired entry into the EU. The Greek-Cypriots had been guaranteed entry into the EU on 1 May 2003 as the Republic of Cyprus, and to them the 'leap in the dark' meant too much economic and political uncertainty, fear of possible instability, a continuing Turkish military presence in the island, but no defence force of their own. This added up to a perception of more risks than guaranteed benefits. It was seen as 'too little' and many voters insisted that 'a better Plan was possible' and would be forthcoming.

How far has the existence of the refugee issue been the main obstacle, or one of the core obstacles, to a settlement in Cyprus? There is no doubt that all Greek-Cypriot negotiators have had a careful eye on the demographics of proposed settlement packages. (How many refugees could have returned to their properties? How many would have been permanently excluded?) The Turkish-Cypriots and Turkey's minimum demands— 25–30 per cent of the island under their near exclusive control—would always have made a negotiated settlement 'risky' for any Greek-Cypriot leader who might have been tempted to 'sign away' Kyrenia and Karpassia. By voting against the Annan Plan, Greek-Cypriots stressed their claims to the north of the island, but more of them might have forgone this gesture had they not also felt that great uncertainties might follow a major new change in their lives had they agreed to the Plan. The 'return' of the refugees, in and of itself, was not the major reason for rejecting the Plan. The most recent analysis (Trimikliniotis 2006) suggests that 35 per cent of the refugees voted 'yes' to Annan, against 25 per cent of the non-refugees. This is a notable difference, but hardly an overwhelming one. If it had been a much greater difference, we might have had measurable indicators of the strength of the refugees' desire to return.

However, the fact is those refugees who cared most because they put most of their lives into the pre-1974 homes and properties are now dead or elderly. Many who were young in 1974 are now rooted in the south and see their children's and grandchildren's futures as keeping them there.

CONCLUSIONS: REFUGEES AND PEACE PROCESSES

What lessons do the collapse of the Annan Plan and the Oslo Peace Process have for the way in which refugee issues are dealt with in attempts at settling long-term political conflicts? Talk of 'solutions' to such protracted and complex disputes is of course overly simple. There are no magic formulas, but only complicated and painful compromises that must build up trust and address the grievances of all involved in a meaningful manner. However, at least four important points can be taken from a comparison of the different place that refugees have in both conflicts, and the very different ways in which both peace processes collapsed.

The first and perhaps most important point is that refugees became a national issue and not just a sectional issue for the refugees and their descendants. In this sense, it is difficult to separate refugees from non-refugees in their opinions and demands over refugee issues. This means that not only do non-refugees have strong opinions over how refugees should be treated, but also that refugees do not look exclusively through the lens of 'refugeeness' when assessing the implications of peace processes. As a result, agreements made over the fate of refugees do not have to be sold only to refugees, but also to the wider population.

The second related point is that refugees are an issue of morality and memory, as well as of rights, citizenship, and property. While the restitution/recognition of rights is undoubtedly an important issue for both Palestinians and Greek-Cypriots, the creation of the refugee problem is above all perceived as a national humiliation. This means that in addition to dealing with individual claims, any serious attempt to deal with refugees needs to find ways of coming to terms with this sense of damaged national pride. Crucially, this is not possible without some form of restitution, but it also requires those responsible for the creation of the crisis to admit moral agency.

The third point is that access to political and economic resources matters. While Greek-Cypriots feel better off than the people who now occupy their former homes, Palestinians are not only worse off than the

Israelis who inhabit their former villages, but they are also worse off than those Palestinians who remained in what is now Israel. Many Greek-Cypriot refugees would find 'return' to northern Cyprus economically difficult and disruptive, and would need major economic resettlement packages which are not on offer; meanwhile they are politically and economically adjusted to life in the south. In sharp contrast, the widespread economic and political marginalization of the Palestinian refugees means that the political and civil rights that are attached to their claims to 'return' are very much a live issue. While they may not necessarily want to return to their former homes (and it is unclear whether they do), a claim to 'return' is a way of making a claim to wider rights which they presently lack.

The fourth and most tentative point relates to the very different ways in which the Annan Plan and the Oslo Peace Process collapsed. An unsolved refugee issue is not enough, on its own, to lead to violence. For Greek-Cypriots, while the refugee issue can be seen as a perceptual or psychological obstacle, the heat seems to have gone out of it as the primary refugees have grown old or died. For Palestinians, although the rights of those displaced in 1948 are as hot a political issue as they were sixty years ago, it would be problematic to reduce explanations for the violence of the second *intifada* to the refugee issue. While the impasse over refugee issues did play a key part in the collapse of the Oslo Peace Process, any comprehensive analysis of why the second *intifada* broke out would have to include the wider economic and political disenfranchisement of West Bank and Gaza Strip Palestinians, the resort to disproportionate violence by the Israeli military, and the tactical decisions made by a disjointed Palestinian leadership. However, in seeking to understand why the Annan Plan and the Oslo Peace Process collapsed in such different styles, the crucial difference between both cases is that the Greek-Cypriots have a politically and economically stable state, with attendant rights and resources, whereas Palestinians are stateless. Armed struggle has never quite made sense in the same ways for Greek-Cypriots as it did for Palestinians, because they had far more economic and political options.

Note. This essay was published at greater length in a collection of essays edited by Thomas Diez and Nathalie Tocci, entitled *Cyprus: A Conflict at the Crossroads* (2009) and grateful acknowledgement is made to Manchester University Press for permission to reproduce it.

REFERENCES

Allin, D. and Simon, S. (2003), 'The Moral Psychology of US Support for Israel', *Survival*, 45, 3: 123–44.

Bahcheli, T. (1990), *Greek–Turkish Relations since 1955* (Boulder, CO, and London, Westview Press).

Christodoulou, D. (1992), 'Inside the Cyprus Miracle', *Modern Greek Studies Yearbook*, Supplement 2 (November) (Minneapolis, MN, University of Minnesota).

Khalidi, R. (1992), 'Observations on the Right of Return', *Journal of Palestine Studies*, 21, 2: 29–40.

Loizos, P. (1976), 'Cyprus: An Alternative Analysis', *Minority Rights Group Report* no. 30, part 2 (London, Minority Rights Group).

—— (1981), *The Heart Grown Bitter: A Chronicle of Cypriot War Refugees* (Cambridge, Cambridge University Press).

Nicolet, C. (2001), *United States Policy Towards Cyprus 1954–1974: Removing the Greek–Turkish Bone of Contention* (Mohnesee, Bibliopolis/Peleus).

Palestinian Center for Policy and Survey Research (PSR) (2003), 'Results of PSR Refugees' Polls in the West Bank/Gaza Strip, Jordan and Lebanon on Refugees' Preferences and Behavior in a Palestinian–Israeli Permanent Refugee Agreement, January–June 2003', www.pcpsr.org/survey/index.html.

Palley, C. (2005), *An International Relations Debacle: The UN Secretary General's Mission of Good Offices in Cyprus 1999–2004* (Oxford, Hart).

Pressman, J. (2003), 'Visions in Collisions: What Happened at Camp David and Taba?', *International Security*, 28, 2: 5–43.

Robinson, G. (1997), *Building a Palestinian State: The Incomplete Revolution* (Bloomington, Indiana University Press).

Sayigh, Y. (1997), *Armed Struggle and the Search for State: The Palestinian National Movement, 1949–1993* (Oxford, Oxford University Press).

Shiblak, A. (1996), 'Residency Status and Civil Rights of Palestinian Refugees in Arab Countries', *Journal of Palestine Studies*, 25, 3: 36–45.

Stephens, R. (1966), *Cyprus: A Place of Arms* (London, Pall Mall Press).

Strong, P. (1999), 'The Economic Consequences of Ethno-national Conflict in Cyprus: The Development of Two Siege Economies after 1963 and 1974', PhD thesis, London School of Economics and Political Science.

Tamari, S. (1999), 'Palestinian Refugees and the Palestinian–Israeli Negotiations', *Journal of Palestine Studies*, 29, 1: 81–9.

Trimikliniotis, N. (2006), 'A Communist's Post-modern Power Dilemma: One Step Back, Two Steps Forward, "Soft No" and Hard Choices', *Cyprus Review*, 18, 1: 37–86.

Zetter, R. (1992), 'Refugees and Forced Migration as Development Resources', *Cyprus Review*, 4, 1: 7–39.

11.
There Go the Neighbourhoods: Policy Effects vis-à-vis Iraqi Forced Migration
Nabil Al-Tikriti

Commentators frequently affirm that sectarian violence in Iraq springs from age-old ethnic tensions which long pre-date American involvement in the region. While the relevant sectarian *identities* do date back several centuries, sectarian *violence* has not persisted as a social constant throughout the millennia of regional history. Rather, outbreaks of sectarian violence have erupted on highly specific occasions, most of which can be explained through careful analysis of the particular social stresses at the time. As in other societies, when long-term shifts such as dwindling natural resources, mass migration, or changes in social identity are inflamed by deliberate and short-term policy choices, violence can break out.

In accordance with this presumption and projection of age-old ethnic tensions is the perception of Iraqi society as little more than an unnatural British creation of the early twentieth century, held together solely by brute force. Those who see Iraq this way envision three distinct ethno-sectarian regions: a Shi'i Arab southern Iraq, Sunni Arab central Iraq, and Sunni Kurdish northern Iraq. Particularly uninformed observers tend to view these Iraqi geographic divisions according to the tripartite 'no-fly zone' borders of 1991–2003. While this simplified portrayal does bear some general resemblance to ethno-sectarian reality, it provides insufficient contextual information to competently engage with Iraqi society.

In the wake of the 2003 Anglo-American invasion, occupation authorities instituted policies which in their effect—if perhaps not in their intent—encouraged a gradual, progressive, and incessant increase of social chaos and sectarianism that eventually culminated in the violent geographic consolidation of Iraq's ethno-sectarian mapping. Ironically, this remapping has all but created the Iraq that American policy makers imagined already existed in 2003.

IRAQ'S SOCIAL AND POLITICAL ORDER

The ethno-sectarian geography of Iraq which has recently undergone a violent remapping has its modern origins in—and often before—the era of Ottoman rule. The relevant groups do not neatly correlate with solely religious, ethnic, tribal, or national categories, since every unit is described in a way that is unique to it. For example, while Chaldo-Assyrians are defined by religion, Kurds are defined primarily by linguistic and tribal identity.

Most such groups emerged in the wake of what is widely described as the Ottoman 'millet system'. Under the nineteenth-century version of this regional social order, millets were defined on an exclusively extra-Muslim religious basis, with such groups including the ancestors of today's Greek Orthodox, Armenians, Chaldo-Assyrians, Jews, Egyptian Copts, Maronites, and several others.[1] Such groups largely governed their own communal affairs under the protection of an umbrella imperial system limiting itself to sovereignty fields such as defence, foreign policy, taxation, and domestic security. Throughout the Ottoman era, the millets lived in various rural and urban locales, largely apart and usually in peace. Meanwhile, Muslims were lumped together as majoritarian loyal subjects of the Ottoman ruler, the protection of whom justified the empire's existence. Muslim opponents of Ottoman rule—Anatolian Kızılbaş, Safavids, Wahhabis, and others—were occasionally classified as 'heretics' and faced intense persecution.

Following the brutal intercommunal violence and population displacement which accompanied the empire's destruction, a more secular, urbanized, and nationalistic twentieth century emerged. Throughout this more recent era in Iraq, members of these groups increasingly came to intermarry, or at least live next to each other in progressively more heterogeneous and diverse urban neighbourhoods.[2] At the same time, such groups experienced several redefinitions of identity, most prominently adding intra-Muslim layers of previously unrecognized communal categ-

---

[1] This Ottoman system of ethno-sectarian classification dates only to the nineteenth-century era of *tanzimat* reforms. Prior to that, Ottoman usage of the term 'millet' was far less systematic, applying equally to Ottoman Muslim populations, foreign Christian communities, and certain ad-hoc instances of Ottoman Jewish populations. For further discussion of the evolution of Ottoman conceptions of 'millet', see Braude (1982).

[2] This is less true of rural spaces, where communities appear to have maintained a geographically 'mosaic' structure. Under this structure, in evidence on the Ninevah plains, the region is quite heterogeneous but each village usually contains just one group.

ories such as Kurdish, Turcoman, and Arab while grappling with attempts at creating national identities. Although violent eruptions did occur on occasion under both the Ottomans and various twentieth-century rulers, and the identity of such groups has never been completely stable, this more recent social system had reached a recognizable modicum of relatively mixed stability towards the end of the century. Intense cases of violence and forced migration which broke out in the 1980s and 1990s can be equally characterized as the result of violence between state and anti-state actors as between inter-communal actors.[3]

If we attempt to divide Iraq according to ethno-sectarian identity, then there are far more than the three major ethno-sectarian groupings frequently mentioned. Sizeable groups include Chaldo-Assyrian, Turcoman, Yazidi, Sabaean-Mandaean, Shabak, Jewish, and Roman. In addition to these indigenous groupings, several third-country national (TCN) groups, including Palestinians, Mujahidin-i Khalq (MEK) Iranians, Iranian Kurds, and guest workers, have settled in Iraq over the past several decades, and have found their situations deteriorating following the collapse of the former Government of Iraq. Finally, even the three largest ethno-sectarian groups do not often act in an internally consistent fashion (Al-Tikriti 2003b).[4]

Sunni Islam, as its full name *ahl al-sunna wa al-jama'a* ('the people of custom and consensus') implies, is the umbrella grouping within Islamic identity, comprising approximately 80 per cent of the Arab world and worldwide Islam. As an umbrella construct, however, 'Sunni' is often not a very useful term for describing beliefs. Various ideological strands—Wahhabi, Naqshbandi, Deobandi, Nurcu, Ahmadi, secularist—within this umbrella constellation often say far more about individual religious identity than the reductionist term 'Sunni'.

The Iraqi Sunni Arab community, although constituting only about 15 per cent of the Iraqi population, has provided most of the ruling elite since the fifteenth century—which pre-dates the modern sense of the ethno-sectarian term 'Sunni'. The political elite status of this community thus pre-dates even the Ottoman era. Perhaps due to their ruling status—or perhaps due to the self-image of Sunni Islam as being the 'party of

---

[3] This violence can persuasively be classified as intercommunal in nature only if one accepts the proposition of complete Sunni Arab domination of all levers of state. While some do perceive the violence this way, it is by no means a consensus view.

[4] Much of the information for this section was previously posted by the author in a web forum which is no longer maintained.

consensus'— Sunni Arabs did not often see themselves as a group per se, and clan groupings or ideological strands have often carried more weight than this ethno-sectarian umbrella identity. Today, Sunni Arabs can be said to play a social role within Iraq somewhat resonant with 'whites' in the USA, whereby they no more think of themselves as 'Sunni' than most American whites see themselves as particularly 'white'.

The Iraqi Sunni Arab community has historically been quite supportive of pan-Arab ideologies. Since unification of Iraq with other Arab states would adjust demographic proportions in favour of Sunni Arabs, many Iraqi Shi'is and most Kurds remain deeply suspicious of this ideology. Just as Shi'i groups historically oscillated between Iraqi nationalist and pan-Shi'i ideological orientations, Sunni factions have tended to oscillate between Iraqi nationalist and pan-Arab orientations. When Iraqi nationalist opinions are in the ascendant, these two communities are perfectly capable of political cooperation against foreign elements. This was the case during the 1920 rebellion against the British occupation, and may yet be the case again.

Shi'i Islam is the second largest branch of Islam, originating from a seventh-century political movement. The most significant holy sites of Shi'i Islam are found in Najaf and Karbala, with other significant sites in Kadhimayn (Baghdad) and Samarra. These sites provide the religious focus for Shi'i Muslims worldwide and Iraqi Shi'is in particular. Although the origins of Shi'i Islam date back to the seventh century, it has been claimed that the Iraqi Shi'i community itself has been the majority communal grouping only since the nineteenth-century mass conversion of most southern Iraqi tribal units to Shi'ism (Nakash 1994).

One difference between Sunni and Shi'i communities worldwide is the relatively high level of political participation of Shi'i clerics. The clerics, or 'ulama, have long dominated communal leadership within the Shi'i community and were well on their way to setting up semi-independent state structures in Iraq prior to the First World War. Throughout the twentieth century, this clerical class was undermined by state efforts to control, co-opt, and subvert it. However, immediately after the 2003 evisceration of the Iraqi state, several 'ulama figures came to play the primary political role within southern Iraq despite over eighty years of state opposition. Certain clerical families exert great influence on Iraqi politics, and their influence has grown rapidly since. Following the 2003 invasion, a power struggle emerged within the major Shi'i political factions. Although many Shi'is refuse to follow a political line defined by clerics, it is evident that the vacuum caused by the fall of the Iraqi state created a situation conducive to a sudden and impressive resurgence of clerical power.

While Shi'i Arabs are the majority of Iraq's population, they have not historically acted as a single bloc due to the great variety of opinions and interests evident in that population. In the 1940s–70s the most popular following among Shi'is was the Iraqi Communist Party (ICP). After this party was broken in the 1970s, many Shi'is turned to the religious Da'wa Party. It is mistaken to believe (as many commentators do) that Iraqi Shi'is are beholden to Iranian interests. One proof of their lack of attachment to Iran is that the vast majority of Iraqi troops fighting against Iran in the 1980–8 Iran–Iraq War were Shi'i. At the same time, each religiously defined Shi'i faction appears to maintain connections of some sort with counterparts in Iran.

As the Shi'is consider themselves to have been systematically oppressed throughout the past century (and beyond), they are unlikely to accept anything less than a predominant role in Iraq's new political order. The political language used by Shi'i communitarian groups has revolved around the creation of an Islamic Republic in Iraq following the protocols of the *hawzas* (committees of leading clerics). Donald Rumsfeld's statement on 27 April 2003 that an Islamic government in Iraq was 'unacceptable' might have caused conflict between the clerics and US occupation forces, if US officials had not backed down.

The Kurdish population is predominant in northern Iraq, with additional population centres in south-eastern Turkey, north-western Iran, north-eastern Syria, Armenia, and Azerbaijan. Although most Kurds are Sunni, their ethnic identity carries far more weight than their religious affiliation—even while their common membership with Sunni Arabs in certain groups like the Naqshbandi Sufi order is indicative of cross-affiliations which were once more important than ethnicity. Since the fall of the Ottoman Empire, Kurds in the four states with the largest Kurdish populations (Iran, Iraq, Syria, and Turkey) have consistently sided with foreign interests against those of their host nation states. This legacy, combined with widespread linguistic differences between the three major Kurdish dialects, has rendered the Kurdish polity extremely fractured throughout the twentieth century.

The Kurds in Iraq have enjoyed de facto independence since 1991, following an extremely difficult period fighting the Iraqi state in the 1970s and 1980s. Kurdish northern Iraq weathered the 1990s far better than the rest of the country due to the relatively greater attention they received from non-governmental organizations (NGOs), their international financial support, and their ability to act as a trading intersection—and free trade zone—between Iraq, Turkey, Iran, and Syria.

Iraqi Kurds are politically divided between two party confederations, led by Mas'ud Barzani (who inherited the role from his father) and Jalal Talabani. Both of these leaders have struggled for over forty years to gain control of the Iraqi Kurds, and both have failed. They have each worked variously with the Iraqi state, the USA, Israel, Turkey, Iran, and any other actor that has suited their short-term plans. The two groups together have proven able to maintain Kurdish self-rule in northern Iraq since 1991. No regional actor is willing to grant them independence, so they invariably remain locked in a delicate and tricky position of semi-sovereignty. Throughout the 1990s, Barzani's faction controlled the transit fees between Turkey and Iraq, while Talabani controlled more of the land and population of northern Iraq. This changed somewhat in 1996, when Barzani (with Iraqi state backing) temporarily pushed Talabani's supporters across the Iranian border until they returned several months later with Iranian backing and US mediation. If the reconstituted Iraqi state should ever violently attack northern Iraq (as occurred in 1991 and 1996), Barzani's supporters might again be expected to head for Turkey, and Talabani's supporters for Iran.

In the course of the 1990s, a nascent 'Kurdistan Regional Government' (KRG) was established, led primarily by Barham Salih. However, the KRG remained weaker than both of Iraqi Kurdistan's main factions until recent years. Although these two factions dominate Iraqi Kurdish politics, they neither encompass all of Kurdish politics nor do the views of their followers remain constant over time.

Ethno-sectarian categories are not the only ways to classify actors within Iraqi society. Tribal interests frequently count for more than religious or ethnic identity, and do not always intersect neatly—especially considering the high level of intermarriage. According to one source, there are some seventy-four tribal groupings in Iraq. While this source unrealistically treats tribal groupings as distinct geographic entities that can be mapped as such, at the very least it demonstrates that there are alternative ways to map Iraq than as a tripartite ethno-sectarian entity.[5] Several of the most important players in Iraqi politics are descendants of prominent families from several different groups who have dominated

[5] www.humanitarianinfo.org/iraq/maps/284%20A4%20Tribes%20in%20Iraq.pdf. This map, issued by the Humanitarian Information Centre for Iraq (HIC) in 2003, does not list its own source.

the old social classes of the country since at least the Ottoman era.[6] Other important figures in recent Iraqi history are 'new' in the sense that their immediate ancestors were largely or completely insignificant in yester-year's political scene.[7] Although the significance of such familial lineages should never be underestimated in the Iraqi context, the importance of such affiliations is not constant over time.

Finally, in Iraq as elsewhere, political ideology has often counted for more than any other factor in terms of individual loyalty and identity. This was true for several potent political forces in modern Iraqi history, such as communism, Iraqi nationalism, Ba'athism, Nasserism, and certain others.

PRIOR POPULATION DISPLACEMENTS

Although the scale of Iraqi forced migration experienced in recent years is unprecedented, there are earlier cases in modern Iraqi history. The first major case of forced migration in modern Iraq was that of the Chaldo-Assyrian Christian community following widespread massacres in 1932. This was actually the second displacement of Chaldo-Assyrians in the century, the earlier case being before the establishment of Iraq during the last years of Ottoman rule, when great numbers fled traditional home-lands in south-eastern Anatolia and north-western Iran for what is today northern Iraq following state-sanctioned violence during the First World War. Upon their arrival, they were recruited into the Assyrian Levies— military police units organized by the British to guard airports and attack their opponents within Iraq. Not surprisingly, once the British turned over full sovereignty to Iraq in 1932, many in the country turned against this group. Within a year, the newly independent Iraqi army massacred several thousand Chaldo-Assyrian villagers while the ailing King Faysal was in Switzerland seeking treatment.[8] Following these massacres, thousands fled Iraq. Most ended up in diaspora communities spread throughout Europe and the USA, particularly in Chicago.

---

[6] Prominent public figures such as Messrs Barzani, Chaderchi, Chalabi, Jabr, Khoei, Pachachi, and Sadr descend from families who exercised power and influence throughout the twentieth century.

[7] Public figures such as Saddam Hussein and the Tikriti clans, Jalal Talabani, and others exercised no power prior to their own rise.

[8] These massacres remain a highly contentious issue among historians. For an account placing most of the blame on the Chaldo-Assyrians, see Husri (1974).

The next major population displacement was suffered by Iraqi Jews, who numbered more than 100,000 prior to their departure in the early 1950s. Why did the Iraqi Jews leave in such great numbers, and so quickly? There were certain outbreaks of communal violence, such as the 1941 *Farhud* riots and several celebrated bombings of Jewish congregations—some of which were later alleged to have been committed by Mossad provocateurs.[9] While Iraqi Jews did suffer these violent outbreaks prior to their exodus, this migration was largely an organized movement resulting from secret intergovernmental agreements between the newly established state of Israel and Iraq. Wealthier Iraqi Jews tended to migrate to Europe and the USA (including families whence sprung the corporate giants of Sassoon and Saatchi), while poorer families were mostly settled in a suburb of Tel Aviv. As demonstrated in Hanna Batatu's magisterial *The Old Social Classes and Revolutionary Movements in Iraq* (1978), and portrayed through several interviews in the 2002 UK television documentary 'Forget Baghdad', many of these Iraqi Jews were cadres and leaders of the Iraqi Communist Party, and many resented being essentially 'sold' by Iraqi Prime Minister Nuri al-Said to Israeli Prime Minister David Ben-Gurion.

Following the 1958 overthrow of the Hashemite monarchy, thousands of monarchy supporters fled the country. This migration, while not so large in absolute terms, was significant due to the elite nature of and the wealth held by the population involved. Many prominent politicians and merchant families felt obliged to leave in the course of the revolutionary chaos, and most such families did not return—one notable exception being Ahmad Chalabi. These migrants largely moved without difficulty to the UK, Jordan, and other locations.

The next major population displacement was the first initiated by former Iraqi President Saddam Hussein, and involved expelling Iraqis considered by the state to be 'Persians'. The origins of this distinction between 'Persian' Iraqis and all others dates back to the nineteenth century, when the Ottoman government provided a military draft exception to all those who claimed to be Persian subjects of the Qajar empire rather than Ottoman subjects. Not surprisingly, many individuals hoping to avoid military service claimed at that point to be Qajar subjects. When the modern state of Iraq was created in the 1920s, the descendants of these nineteenth-century Ottoman draft dodgers continued to be classified as

---

[9] For a summary of the *Farhud*, see Cohen (1966).

'Persian'. By the 1970s, when Shi'i communalism was on the political rise, and the 1980s, when Iraq was at war with Iran, the Iraqi state expelled over 200,000 such 'Persians' as a fifth-column security threat in a time of war—even though a great many of these people were not 'Persian' in any meaningful sense of the word. Following the failed 1991 uprising against the central government, another estimated 200,000 Iraqis fled from southern Iraq to Iran. As a result of the earlier mass expulsion and the 1991 mass flight from violence, some 200,000 registered Iraqi refugees resided in Iran just prior to the Anglo-American invasion of 2003. Since then, some three-quarters of these refugees were said to have returned to Iraq, although an estimated 10,000–50,000 of these subsequently returned to Iran (*Boston Globe* 2007).

The most renowned population displacement in recent Iraqi history is commonly referred to as the 'Arabization of Kirkuk'. Kirkuk, historically a cosmopolitan urban centre with sizeable Turcoman, Kurdish, Arab, Christian, and Jewish populations (in that order of magnitude), had long been a focus of politically resonant demographic competition since its development as an oil-drilling centre in the 1920s. Following the 1988 *Anfal* Campaign, which led to the deaths of tens of thousands of Kurds, the Iraqi government forced the collectivization and urbanization of the Kurdish countryside as a whole, and the displacement of the Kurdish population from what are today considered the 'Disputed Territories'. Combined with resettlement incentives offered primarily to Shi'i peasants from southern Iraq, the goal of this policy was to increase the Arab proportion in sensitive areas straddling the historical border regions between Arab and Kurdish rural populations.[10]

By attempting to Arabize the population in the 1980s and 1990s, the Iraqi state under Saddam Hussein laid the seeds for an aggressive counter-policy following the 2003 invasion. As if on cue, since the 2003 fall of the Iraqi state, Kurdish militias have moved into Kirkuk and Mosul, setting off increased sectarian tension and occasional bouts of ethnic cleansing and violence. In an effort to reverse thirty years of 'Arabization', KRG officials encouraged what can best be described as the 'Kurdification of Kirkuk' in the months and years after the invasion. In the course of this initiative, Kurdish militias reportedly ejected Arab families from farmland around Kirkuk, causing the deaths of dozens of people. Similar dynamics led to reports of summary executions of Turcoman individuals

---

[10] One Arab informant reported using government-subsidized loans to build a new house in Kirkuk town in the 1990s—which he subsequently rented to Kurds.

at Kurdish checkpoints (and vice versa) since 2003. One highly contested point about this reversal of the Arabization policy since 2003 is the proportion of 'original' Kurdish Kirkukis now settling in Kirkuk.

The final example of population movement prior to 2003 is what might be called the 'Sunnification' of a ring south of Baghdad. This ring, including the towns of Mahmudiyya, Iskandariyya, and Musayib, was settled with Sunni Arab residents throughout the 1990s. Not much is known about this migration, although the probable goal of the policy was to fortify the Sunni population of Baghdad in case of sectarian conflict. Resembling Israeli settlement policies in the ring around East Jerusalem, one of the legacies of this policy was a great outbreak of violence after the invasion, which led to US soldiers nicknaming the region as the 'triangle of death'.

All of these prior population displacements were in their own way as socially influential—and often as individually traumatic—as the more recent displacement. However, while the intent was similar in each case—the consolidation and homogenization of various Iraqi regions through the expulsion of unwanted populations—the scale was far more modest than today's displacement, at least in absolute terms.

SOCIAL CAPITAL DESTRUCTION SINCE 2003

Under Iraq's *ancien régime*, national space was dominated by a self-defined and self-consciously secularist approach, whereby communi-tarian or ethnic nationalist actors were violently suppressed by the state on behalf of those actors allied with the state. Within this paradigm, social divisions primarily reflected level of urbanization, class attainment, political power, tribal membership, or national identity.

Before 2003, one might usefully classify Iraqi society as being divided between Baghdad and the rest of the country, Ba'ath Party members and the rest of society, Kurdish nationalists and their opponents, communi-tarian activists and secularists, exiles and residents, tribal confederations, various class actors, and several other categories which no longer carry the same relevance today. Rather than recognizing the relevance of such clas-sifications, American policy makers tended to force Iraq into a tripartite box allowing for only Shi'i, Sunni, and Kurdish divisions.

Through a process punctuated by assassinations, executions, bomb-ings, intimidation, and other tactics forcing ethno-sectarian consolidation, the communal variety previously evident has been transformed yet again.

As a result, Washington's tripartite trap has taken on a life of its own and become something of a self-fulfilling paradigm, largely creating the Iraq that this policy community imagined. Forced migration and population displacement cemented the new communal make-up, and served to form geographic realities in line with the imagined vision of American policy makers. In effect, Iraq's 'imagined community' was imagined in Washington, DC—and continues to be so imagined.[11]

Invasion enthusiasts were quite clear that the Iraq encountered upon arrival would no longer be allowed to exist. Consistent with Condoleezza Rice's doctrine of 'creative chaos', early policies effected the complete elimination of the Iraqi state and symbols of common national identity. The first such decision was as much a passive non-decision as an active decision. In the wake of the initial entry of US forces into Baghdad, widespread looting broke out throughout the capital. Occupation forces—apparently in line with specific Pentagon orders—chose to protect sites deemed of financial and strategic importance to US interests while allowing facilities critical to either Iraqi state functionality or national cohesion to be looted down to the office furniture.[12] As a result, looters bred generalized anarchy, destroyed the administrative organs of state, and eviscerated institutions of common national identity such as the National Archives, (Saddam) Museum of Modern Art, Iraqi National Museum, Ministry of Religious Endowments Library, and several other prominent symbols of national culture.[13] Some of the most egregious looting appears to have been carried out by mysterious provocateurs more focused on symbolically significant destruction than self-enrichment.

This first passive decision of the occupation set the tone for much of what followed, with Coalition authorities consistently neglecting institutions supportive of Iraqi national cohesion. The destruction of the nuts and bolts of state machinery and dismantling of national assets rapidly

---

[11] Benedict Anderson (1983) describes the process whereby national identity is socially constructed by elites. According to Anderson, no such identity exists without this creative process, and the existence of various nationalist communities depends on the imagination of the people involved.

[12] US forces proved fully capable of protecting sites considered worthy of protection, such as the Baghdad (formerly Saddam) International Airport; what would become the 'Green Zone', including the Republican Palace, the Rashid Hotel, and the Convention Centre; the Ministry of Oil; the Palestine Meridien, Ishtar Sheraton, Rashid hotels; and several other strategic locations.

[13] For an early situation report of the effects of looting on libraries and archives, see Al-Tikriti (2003a).

led to the breakdown of social capital, defined as the extent to which 'people in a community feel responsible for each other'. As Shankar Vedantam has argued, such social capital cannot be reconstructed from above, and once it has diminished it is exceedingly difficult to recover (Vedantam 2007). Easily destroyed, not so easily repaired. In the wake of this breakdown of social capital, sectarian-minded actors stepped into the vacuum while occupation forces continued to passively observe the unravelling of the national.

Soon after arrival, Coalition Provisional Authority (CPA) adminis- trator Paul Bremer issued his infamous de-Ba'athification order in May 2003, justified as leading the construction of a new social order entirely free from the taint of the former regime's crimes. With this order Bremer effectively dismissed the entire Iraqi management strata—more than 120,000 people—from state service, while at the same time forcing under- ground the single most visible remaining group of nationalist actors within Iraqi society. What was forgotten at the time, and remains unknown by many, is that so many members of the urban middle class had been Ba'ath Party members that this order effectively alienated most of those who had held Iraqi society together for the previous forty years. Usually portrayed as anti-Sunni Arab in effect, in light of which groups the Ba'athist government had favoured, this order could equally be seen as damaging to secularists, Christians, smaller minorities, and feminists. However, by reductively tarring Sunni Arabs with the brush of Ba'athism, American policy makers encouraged revenge actions expressed in a sectarian fashion. At the same time, in light of the high correlation between the former cadres of government technocrats and Ba'athist membership, this order allowed exile groups—largely sectarian in nature—to fill nearly all governmental posts being opened up by occupation authorities at the time. This last outcome exacerbated tensions between exiles and locals who had never left the country.

In the same week, Ambassador Bremer announced the dissolution of the entire Iraqi military, an estimated 500,000 men under arms. Bremer's argument that the Iraqi military had demobilized itself in the course of the invasion ignored the financial reality of military patronage and the pyschological perception of American imperiousness on the local popula- tion. While CPA officials generally perceived the Iraqi military as 'Saddam's Army', most non-Kurdish Iraqis saw this same institution as a professional, secular, and national institution capable of keeping the country unified in a time of crisis. While certain units, such as the Special Republican Guards, were widely perceived as tribal protectors of the former regime, the vast majority of the military was seen as largely outside of politics—and therefore clean and capable. The security vacuum caused by the final dissolution of this national institution was quickly filled by sectarian militias returning from exile in the summer of 2003.

Once Bush administration officials conceded that functioning Iraqi security forces were a necessity amid a growing insurgency, they began stating that US forces would 'stand down' when Iraqi forces would 'stand up'. Concurrent with this rhetorical statement, US officials strove to quickly re-form the Iraqi military in order to enable it to share security duties with Coalition forces. However, rather than integrating militia members into Iraqi security forces while disarming militia units, advisers usually incorporated into security and police forces entire units of party militias, leaving such units intact, legitimized, and better armed. At the same time, former Iraqi military officers were largely frozen out of the new institution, consistent with the earlier policies. As a result, civilians who did not share either the sectarian make-up or the political perspectives of the respective units quickly came to fear and oppose these new units.

One prominent example of this phenomenon was the second Falluja siege in November 2004, whereby Iraqi commando units comprised of former Kurdish militiamen and Badr Corps members supported the American attack on the city. Overall, this attempt to make up for Bremer's dissolution of the Iraqi military ended up encouraging sectarian tensions through its implementation. In an effort to reverse the damage, immediately following the January 2009 provincial council elections Prime Minister Nouri al-Maliki invited several senior pre-invasion military officers to rejoin the Iraqi army—belatedly demonstrating their legitimacy and value.

Contending that thirteen years of sanctions and the invasion had rendered Iraq's economic structures obsolete, Bremer ordered the complete and immediate dismantling of Iraq's massive state sector.[14] Including dairy plants, cigarette factories, battery production lines, cement factories, and several others, this sector had long employed the

---

[14] Order 39 allowed for 'the privatization of Iraq's 200 state-owned enterprises, 100 per cent foreign ownership of Iraqi businesses, national treatment of foreign firms, unrestricted, tax-free remittance of all profits and other funds, and 40-year ownership licenses'. For further detail, see Douglas et al. (2007: 28).

largest bloc of the country's workforce. Arguments in support of this policy largely parallelled those used to support the dissolution of the Iraqi military, characterized by a search for a new start to replace a hopeless past. According to Naomi Klein, Bremer's 'shock doctrine' approach to Iraq's economic restructuring was intended to establish a model and utopian free trade regime—an approach applied equally in Iraq after the 2003 invasion and in New Orleans in the wake of Hurricane Katrina.[15] In Iraq's case, the dissolution of hundreds of thousands of stable jobs further degraded social capital and led individuals to seek financial shelter through employment in sectarian militias.

Parallel with efforts to instantly privatize Iraq's state sector was a comprehensive $US18 billion reconstruction programme announced with some fanfare by the Bush administration shortly after the completion of the invasion. As 'no-bid' contracts were almost exclusively channelled to US corporate entities, Iraqi institutions were effectively frozen out of any stake in their own reconstruction programme. While Iraqi returnees frequently subcontracted several tasks on these contracts, locals often found that the only option open for them in this process was as manual labour. Not surprisingly, this programme orientation tended to alienate the Iraqi domestic elite, while its failure to share out reconstruction patronage resources added to the general economic collapse unfolding in the wake of the invasion.

On 13 July 2003, Ambassador Bremer appointed—according to an explicitly sectarian population formula—a 25-person Interim Governing Council (IGC) to act as an advisory body to the CPA. A preponderance of diaspora returnees was chosen for this council at the expense of locals who had never left Iraq throughout the previous regime's rule—which increased tensions between these two categories of actors. Most notably, the nationally minded Muqtada al-Sadr was kept out of the IGC, even though his followers included a great deal of the urban poor of Baghdad and the rural poor of several southern provinces. Reacting to his exclusion from power, a month later Sadr announced the formation of his 'Mahdi Army', which quickly flourished into one of the major sectarian militias in Iraqi politics. Although Sadr's movement reflects something of a sectarian agenda, his ideology has always remained nationalist in orien-

---

[15] Naomi Klein (2007: 49–74) characterizes the 'shock doctrine' approach to post-conflict economic restructuring as the intentional use of widespread societal trauma—natural or caused by humans—as a cover for establishing free trade regimes in place of whatever had been present before.

tation, as opposed to several parties who found seats on the IGC. Such parties, notably al-Da'wa, SCIRI, PUK, and the KDP, advanced agendas incompatible with Iraqi nationalist goals. Notably, once al-Da'wa under Nouri al-Maliki adopted a more Iraqi nationalist viewpoint in 2007, it grew more popular at the ballot box—which appears to demonstrate the preference of the Iraqi public. Overall, the privileging of diaspora returnees over locals, combined with the population formulas used to structure the nascent government, forced a newly sectarian political reality from which Iraq has yet to recover.

In January 2004, Ambassador Bremer issued an order intended to facilitate the return of Iraqi refugees from outside the country, a policy goal that has only grown in urgency since that time. In a strong—some would say unrealistic—defence of property rights, Bremer's order stipu-lated that properties must be returned to their original, formerly expelled, 'Persian' Iraqi owners. While compensation was included in the order, it reportedly amounted to only about one-third of a home's original value. Occupants, in many cases consisting of large, extended families who had resided in the homes for more than twenty years, were given sixty days to leave the properties.[16] Although the defence of property rights was a posi-tive goal of the order, its harsh terms encouraged Badr Corps militia members to expel Sunni families from homes without due process once they became part of the new Iraqi government in July 2005—which led to a new round of population displacement. While CPA officials established a property adjudication commission to decide cases concerning pre-2003 property disputes, its writ does not extend to more recent disputes, and there remains no similar entity to adjudicate post-2003 property disputes.

In June 2004, John Negroponte was appointed the first US ambassador to the new (re-)sovereign state of Iraq, and immediately became the senior US civilian official in the country. Due to his earlier career profile in Central America in the 1980s, several observers speculated about the policy reasoning behind his appointment, and by January 2005 the cele-brated 'Salvador Option' came to be discussed openly as an option for counter-insurgency operations in Iraq. According to this doctrine, one party can end public opposition to its policies by eliminating those who publicly oppose those policies. Nicknamed after unproven counter-insurgency doctrines applied in El Salvador in the 1980s, this doctrine is characterized by the use of death squads targeting prominent individuals.

---

[16] Juan Cole's posting (2005b) included a pdf file of a petition in Arabic requesting that the order be rescinded.

During this same period in 2004–5, the kidnapping, assassinations, and disappearances of prominent professors, doctors, engineers, and lawyers rose dramatically.[17] The same military officer who advised Salvadoran police squads in the 1980s, Colonel James Steele, advised Iraq's Interior Ministry's 'Special Police Commandos' in 2005. It later emerged that Ministry of Interior officials were running their own prisons, dominated by former members of the Badr Corps.

Although much of this aspect of US policy in Iraq remains unproven due to the classified nature of the policies, fear of such a policy led to a mass migration of middle-class professionals by the middle of 2005. The mass migration, set off by a combination of dozens of prominent assassinations and individual death threats, further depleted the managerial cadre of Iraqi society and left behind a population dominated by sectarian militias with their young, poor, male, unemployed followings fighting over whatever was left behind.

Coalition counter-insurgency operations appear in some cases to have promoted sectarianism while aiding ethnic cleansing. In 'Operation Restoring Rights' in autumn 2005, the US military introduced its 'clear, hold, and build' strategy of counter-insurgency operations in Tal Afar (Poole 2005). Returning war veteran Scott Ewing described how US forces aided the ethnic cleansing of Tal Afar during that operation in the interest of promoting social stability. After evacuating the population of the Saray neighbourhood to nearby camps, US forces bombed the neighbourhood, regular US Army units aggressively searched all homes in the area, and US special forces assisted Kurdish Pesh Merga units in rounding up all military-age men remaining in the area for the final clearing of that neighbourhood (Ewing 2008). Months after President Bush cited this Tal Afar operation as a successful example of counter-insurgency operations, in March 2006 a massive truck bombing attributed to al-Qa'ida in Iraq (AQI) killed 152 people in a primarily Shi'i neighbourhood market, demonstrating the sectarian repercussions of such operations (Al-Khairalla 2007).

As the security situation continued to deteriorate throughout 2004, voters began seeking safety in parties who promised to protect them in their neighbourhoods, villages, and towns throughout the country—a phenomenon especially aggravated by the sectarian nature of bombings

---

[17] According to the US Army's counter-insurgency manual, non-combatant supporters of insurgents are never less important than combatants, and are often more important. This may be seen as indicative of military policy vis-à-vis the population as a whole.

that had taken place up until that point. As a result, transitional parliamentary elections of January 2005 resulted in a landslide for sectarian grounded parties. In summer 2005, US diplomats shepherded a new constitution through a series of intense and heated negotiations among these elected parties and certain unelected political groups. As in previous processes enacted since the invasion, this negotiation was designed to progress along sectarian and regional lines rather than either tribal lines or along strict governorate borders—and the process was driven primarily by parties defined by specific ethno-sectarian agendas. Since there were many obstacles to such a constitution being passed, a deadlock arose in August 2005, which was broken only when a fait accompli draft constitution was agreed upon by such officials—with American blessing—in September 2005. As if to institutionalize the newly sectarian face of Iraqi politics, the constitution included provisions allowing for three or more governorates to band together as federal regions with certain prerogatives of sovereignty—creating the potentiality of de facto regional partition. At the same time, clauses ensuring the funnelling of oil revenues through such provincial structures, combined with ambiguous statutes concerning the freedom of such regional institutions to negotiate international contracts, encouraged fiscal fracturization of the national whole. Finally, the Kirkuk referendum guaranteed by the constitution ensured a sectarian poison pill for the future.

The next milestone—the one which consensus opinion holds started the ethnic cleansing—was the February 2006 bombing of the Ja'far al-'Askari shrine in Samarra. This major event, which set off an eighteen-month orgy of sectarian Sunni–Shi'i killing throughout the country, was blamed on AQI, yet there was no complete investigation of the event itself. While an AQI strike makes a certain amount of sense strategically, in that it would increase sectarian violence and potentially help AQI come to power, many Iraqis remain unconvinced that AQI actually committed the crime. The bombing was somewhat unusual according to al-Qa'ida's normal modus operandi in that the perpetrators were disguised by black balaclavas and did not kill anyone in the course of the bombing. Whoever perpetrated the act, this wholly symbolic event did more than any other to feed the mass migration of individuals within, throughout, and beyond Iraq.

In December 2006, following a lengthy trial which many criticized for being improperly executed, US officals handed former Iraqi President Saddam Hussein to the Government of Iraq. Within hours of the handover, the Iraqi government carried out his highly contentious execution. As it turned out, the execution fully pleased only certain factions within the Iraqi body politic, and proved to be yet another divisive policy choice. The timing of the execution, held on the morning of a religious holiday exclusive to Sunni Muslims, sent an intentionally sectarian signal to Sunni factions. Mr Hussein was executed for the lesser crime of ordering the attack and summary execution of over 143 Shi'i men and boys in the village of Dujail following an assassination attempt. Meanwhile, he was never legally charged for invading Iran or Kuwait, or for the execution of several thousand Kurdish Barzani tribespeople in the early 1980s, or for ordering Operation Anfal—which caused the massacre and displacement of tens of thousands of Kurdish civilians in the late 1980s. That such crimes were not even addressed during the trial upset not only Kurds, but also those who wanted to pursue information about Mr Hussein's connections with various Western governments in the 1980s (Cole 2005a). As it turns out, many of the facts about such connections appear to have died with the former president, whose dignity in the face of death has cast him posthumously as a saintly martyr to those inclined to support him. Finally, following internet broadcasts of the execution, rumours spread that Muqtada al-Sadr personally carried out the hanging of Saddam Hussein. Such rumours were based on the Sadr family history, whereby Mr Hussein personally ordered—and may have carried out—the 1980 execution of Muqtada al-Sadr's uncle Muhammad Baqir al-Sadr and aunt Bint al-Huda. The rumours were also based on the actions of the crowd at the execution, chanting 'Muqtada, Muqtada, Muqtada', as well as on similarities—possibly 'photoshopped' similarities—between the executioner's beard and ring and Muqtada al-Sadr's. Whether or not Muqtada al-Sadr personally carried out the execution is not as important as the impression gained by many of an execution carried out as a form of personal and sectarian revenge rather than provision of justice.

Since February 2007 a policy regime which has generally received positive reviews in US government circles appears to have encouraged population displacement—the completion of which contributed to the great reduction in violence. In the course of the 'Surge strategy', credited to General David Petraeus, Iraq suffered the peak of sectarian violence and population displacement, and Baghdad's neighbourhoods experienced the greatest amount of sectarian consolidation, whereby formerly mixed areas became either more fully Sunni or Shi'i. Some have referred to this process as the 'Shi'itization' of Baghdad, as those sectarian factions appear to have gained the most in the past year. Others have suggested that this process occurred due to nightly violence carried out under the passive gaze of US soldiers who concentrated on attacking Sunni militias seen as their primary enemy during the day. As if to formalize this process, General Petraeus ordered the erection of several walls to divide and separate opposing neighbourhoods. While this tactic has been praised for reducing violence, neighbourhood residents themselves protested against these walls which appear to have been modelled on walls erected by the Israeli military on the West Bank.

Another policy carried out as part of the Surge strategy has been the financing and arming of Sunni Sahwa 'Awakening Councils' to attack al-Qa'ida elements within their midst, especially in the al-Anbar governorate. While the tactic has been credited with reducing violence against the US military, it has effectively empowered yet another sectarian group, which may contribute to the further break-up and consolidation of this formerly mixed society.

POST-2003 DISPLACEMENT

In 2009 there were estimated to be as many as 4.8 million forcibly displaced Iraqis out of a total population of approximately 27 million, or roughly 15 per cent of the whole. Although these estimates must be handled with extreme care, the general magnitude of the displacement is not in doubt. For perspective, the displacement of 15 per cent of the US population would equal some 45 million people, roughly the population of the entire east or west coast.

The total of 4.8 million displaced includes roughly 2.8 million international refugees seeking official status and 2 million domestic internally displaced persons (IDPs). An approximate estimate of the distribution of this forced migration includes the following: Iraq (northern Iraq—750,000, central and southern Iraq—1.25 million), Syria (1.4 million), Jordan (450,000), Egypt (100,000), Lebanon (50,000), Turkey (10,000), Iran (100,000), Sweden (27,000), and the USA (15,000).

The forced migration resulting in the above figures did not occur in a single wave, and there has been some disagreement concerning the characteristics of this migration (Chatelard 2008). While the numbers of the displaced and the origins of the forced migration are highly contentious, one can outline several waves of migration since 2003.[18] The first wave consisted largely of former regime elites who either anticipated or quickly

---

[18] For discussions of pre-2003 displacement, see Romano (2005) and Chatelard (2005).

realized the difficulties to come of remaining in Iraq after the invasion. These migrants tended to be sufficiently wealthy, highly educated, and well connected to move without great difficulty to comfortable destinations within the region. The second wave consisted of middle-class technocrats, professionals, and intelligentsia who were targeted as a class following the breakdown of social capital in 2003–5. Concurrent with the second wave began the movement of Iraq's 'micro-minorities', smaller groups who found themselves particularly vulnerable as order collapsed and society descended into widespread sectarian violence. While each of these groups—including Chaldo-Assyrians, Sabaean-Mandaeans, Yazidis, Shabaks, and others—experienced their own types of danger and obstacles, they all shared the common imperative to move. Many of these micro-minorities ended up taking refuge in northern Iraq, with others leaving the country for Syria or Jordan. The final, and largest, wave followed the Samarra bombing of February 2006. This movement involved all ethno-sectarian groups throughout the country, depending on where they found themselves in a locally vulnerable minority status. It is this final wave which brought about the consolidation and homogenization of Iraq's ethno-sectarian mapping.[19]

DISPLACEMENT POLICIES

Since Iraq's social breakdown accelerated in the wake of the 2006 Samarra bombing, certain policy choices appear to have been taken with the aim of solidifying the new reality rather than attempting a return to the *status quo ante*. In Baghdad, US officials have overseen the construction of partition walls between certain neighbourhoods considered mutually hostile. While these walls are credited with reducing violence, they have not proven popular with residents of those neighbourhoods—in fact, their announcement led to immediate protests in at least Adhamiyya (Iraq Updates 2007). The primary intention behind these walls may well be to augment security through restricting militants' access between such opposing, hostile, and relatively homogenous neighbourhoods. At the same time, however, such walls prevent interaction between non-militant residents, solidify the homogenizing nature of each neighbourhood

---

[19] The most detailed indications of this phenomenon are provided in International Organization of Migration (IOM) reports which have been posted since 2005.

behind the walls, trap whatever minority populations remain walled in and expose them to further violence by majority militias without a reduced possibility of external intervention, and tend to confirm ethno-sectarian boundaries due to their sheer physicality. In a nutshell, such walls may save lives in the short run, but they contribute to more permanent communal demarcations in the longer term.

Concurrent with the policy of walling off certain neighbourhoods within Baghdad, several provinces have initiated restrictions on civilian freedom of movement in an effort to limit the influx of an IDP population. Through such limitations, provincial officials are hoping to both reduce the risk of security transgressions from outsiders and reduce the human-itarian burden such population influxes might put on their social service networks. One prominent example of such limitation is the policy in the KRG stipulating that no one can enter the territory without first securing a Kurdish sponsor. While those who have reached KRG have generally been well protected, and while the KRG has emerged as something of a refuge for non-Muslim minority populations, this limitation is both legally problematic and another example of a policy regime which encourages sectarianization of Iraqi society.

Certain policy choices by NGOs and intergovernment organizations appear designed to encourage *in situ* settlement of IDPs rather than even-tual return. One prominent example is the Iraqi Red Crescent Society's 2007 multimillion dollar appeal for IDP housing, structured in terms of model villages. This decision is usually defended as the more realistic approach, which it may very well be. At the same time, however, when coupled with the lack of emphasis on post-2003 property rights until this time, such a policy will likely encourage the solidification of the legacy of ethnic cleansing which has taken place in the past five years.

The Government of Iraq announced a major initiative in July 2008 to assist in the reversal of the ethno-sectarian remapping described in this essay. This initiative promised incentive packages to return to place of origin, an increased emphasis on property rights and protection of returnees, and other elements that might promote the reversal of post-2003 forced migration. Unfortunately, policy details have remained some-what opaque and implementation uneven since this initiative's initial announcement. Up to April 2009 the return of Iraqi populations to their pre-2003 place of origin remained minimal.

CONCLUSIONS

The effects of the ethno-sectarian remapping described here are wide-spread, potentially permanent, and highly problematic for the cohesion of the future Iraqi state and society. Communal consolidation has progressed to such an extent that Iraq has already evolved somewhat from a mosaic patchwork of geographically mixed sectarian clusters into the rough outline of three large regions coinciding with an idealized conception of the majoritarian ethno-sectarian identities of Shi'i Arab, Sunni Arab, and Kurdish. Those who either refuse or are not allowed to fit within these majoritarian identities have mostly been forced out, causing the nearly complete erasure of certain micro-minority communities such as the Sabaean-Mandaeans and Shabak; the external migration of roughly half of Iraq's Chaldo-Assyrian Christian populations; the entrapment and/or external migration of prominent third-country nationals such as the Palestinians, certain Iranian Kurds, and the Mujahidin-i Khalq Iranians; and the expulsion of minority clusters of majoritarian ethno-sectarian groups caught outside their region of dominance.

After allowing mass looting, destroying all remnants of Iraq's state structure, abolishing the military, alienating the country's secular and nationally minded professional class, and institutionalizing sectarian interests, US officials proceeded to blame 'age-old ethnic conflicts' when sectarian violence exploded throughout the country after the February 2006 Samarra shrine bombing. Some prominent commentators and policy makers even argued for tripartite state partition as a solution to this violence.[20] While a noticeable shift in US policy in 2007 eventually contributed to a calming of the violence, the remapping of Iraq's ethno-sectarian geography has not yet been—and may never be—reversed.

Note. I would like to thank the US Institute of Peace for supporting the research behind this essay. I would also like to thank Zaid al-Ali, Joe Balmos, Elizabeth Campbell, Géraldine Chatelard, Chantal De Jonge Oudraat, Elizabeth Ferris, Paul Hughes, Amanda Johnson, Dana Graber Ladek, L. Rashad Mahmood, Phebe Marr, Scott Portman, Daniel Serwer, Zainab Shakir, Kimberly Stoltz, Samira Trad, Kristele Younis, and several other figures who may wish to remain unnamed.

---

[20] Prominent advocates for partition, whether 'soft' or otherwise, have included Sen. Joe Biden, Peter Galbraith, Leslie Gelb, Michael O'Hanlon, and Kenneth Pollack.

REFERENCES

Anderson, B. (1983), *Imagined Communities* (London and New York, Verso).

Batatu, H. (1978), *The Old Social Classes and Revolutionary Movements in Iraq* (Princeton, NJ, Princeton University Press).

Boston Globe (2007), 'Iraqi Refugees in Iran', http://boston.com/news/world/middleeast/articles/2007/05/13/iraqi_refugees_in_iran/.

Braude, B. (1982), 'Foundation Myths of the *Millet* System', in B. Braude and B. Lewis (eds), *Christians and Jews in the Ottoman Empire: The Functioning of a Plural Society* (New York and London, Holmes & Meier), vol. 1, pp. 69–88.

Chatelard, G. (2005), 'Iraqi Asylum Migrants in Jordan: Conditions, Religious Networks and the Smuggling Process', in G. Borjas and J. Crisp (eds), *Poverty, International Migration and Asylum*, Studies in Development Economics and Policy (Basingstoke, Palgrave Macmillan), pp. 341–70.

—— (2008), 'Constructing and Deconstructing the Iraq Refugee Crisis', International Association of Contemporary Iraqi Studies Conference, London.

Cohen, H. (1966), 'Anti-Jewish "Farhūd" in Baghdad, 1941', *Middle Eastern Studies*, 3, 1: 2–17.

Cole, J. (2005a), 'At Hussein's Hearings, U.S. May Be on Trial', *Znet*, www.zmag.org/content/showarticle.cfm?SectionID=15&ItemID=9229.

—— (2005b), 'Iranian-Iraqis Returning, Expelling New Owners', *Informed Comment*, www.juancole.com/2005/07/iranian-iraqis-returning-expelling-new.html.

Douglas, I., Al-Bayaty A., and Al-Bayaty, N. (2007), 'U.S. Genocide in Iraq', *Brussels Tribunal*, www.brusselstribunal.org/pdf/NotesOnGenocideInIraq.pdf.

Ewing, S. (2008), 'Racism and War: The Dehumanization of the Enemy: Part 1', *Winter Soldier: Iraq and Afghanistan. Eyewitness Accounts of the Occupations*, Iraq Veterans Against the War (IVAW), www.ivaw.org/wintersoldier/testimony/racism-and-war-dehumanization-enemy/scott-ewing/video.

Humanitarian Information Centre for Iraq (2003), www.humanitarianinfo.org/iraq/maps/284%20A4%20Tribes%20in%20Iraq.pdf.

Husri, K. (1974), 'The Assyrian Affair of 1933', *International Journal of Middle East Studies*, 5: 161–76, 344–60.

Iraq Updates (2007), 'Baghdad Merchants Wonder if Blast Walls Are Really Worthy It', www.iraqupdates.com/p_articles.php/article/18070.

Al-Khairalla, M. (2007), 'Deadliest Bomb in Iraq War Kills 152', *Reuters UK*, http://uk.reuters.com/article/topNews/idUKPAR34073020070401.

Klein, N. (2007), *The Shock Doctrine: The Rise in Disaster Capitalism* (London, Metropolitan).

Nakash, Y. (1994), *The Shi'is of Iraq* (Princeton, NJ, Princeton University Press).

Poole, O. (2005), 'Iraqis in Former Rebel Stronghold Now Cheer American Soldiers', *The Daily Telegraph*, www.telegraph.co.uk/news/main.jhtml?xml=/news/2005/12/19/wirq19.xml.

Romano, D. (2005), 'Whose House Is This Anyway? IDP and Refugee Returns in Post-Saddam Iraq', *Journal of Refugee Studies*, 18, 4: 430–53.

Al-Tikriti, N. (2003a), 'Iraq Manuscript Collections, Archives, and Libraries Situation Report', *Iraq Crisis List*, www-oi.uchicago.edu/OI/IRAQ/docs/nat.html.

—— (2003b), 'Social and Political Forces in Contemporary Iraq: An NGO Primer', Joint NGO Emergency Preparedness Initiative (JNEPI).

Vedantam, S. (2007), 'One Thing We Can't Build Alone in Iraq', *Washington Post*, www.washingtonpost.com/wp-dyn/content/article/2007/10/28/AR2007102801477.html.

Epilogue
Dispossession and Forced Migration in the Twenty-first-century Middle East and North Africa: The Way Forward

Dawn Chatty

THE PAST IS PROLOGUE

When we think of refugees in the Middle East, the 750,000 thousand who fled Palestine in 1948 generally come to mind. Palestinians are certainly not the first case of large-scale dispossession and forced migration in the Middle East, but they are perhaps the best known because of the length of their liminal status as refugees; neither citizens of any country nor a people with a clearly demarcated state to return to. They now enter their seventh decade in exile. They have been studied for years, but the studies make little impact. They are a people to whom the term 'warehousing' largely applies (US Commission on Refugees and Immigrants 2008). Many Palestinian refugees have been herded into refugee camps from which there is little chance of escape. Why has this happened and is it likely to be repeated with other refugee populations?

Every refugee situation is *sui generis*. The Palestinian refugee crisis was a League of Nations and then United Nations 'problem'. It was initially compartmentalized by the UN when responsibility for providing relief to the dispossessed Palestinians was given to a specially created agency, the United Nations Relief and Works Agency (UNRWA). The search for a durable political solution was given to another specially created agency, the United Nations Conciliation Commission for Palestine (UNCCP). Created as part of the United Nations General Assembly Resolution 194 (III) in December 1948 its membership was made up of representatives from the USA, France, and Turkey. By the early 1950s the UNCCP became largely inactive, recognizing that there was no political will,

Figure 12.1. Palestinians fleeing in 1948.
Source: 2001–2009 IMEMC NEWS (reproduced with permission).

certainly not in the new state of Israel, to see a return of refugees to the former British Mandate territory of Palestine. Sixty years on, these refugees and their offspring still maintain the wish to return to their homes; the political will to effect a solution to this crisis, however, is not held by all parties to the conflict. Seemingly intractable situations are sometimes overcome when empirical research offers up constructive and lateral analysis, or reveals misunderstandings and unsubstantiated fears to be at the base of political positioning. In such situations, understanding the past is a step in solving the crises of the present.

The Middle East has been witness to largely forgotten waves of Muslim and Jewish groups dispossessed and forced into the region at the end of three empires—Ottoman, Russian, and Austro-Hungarian. From the middle of the nineteenth century mass migration, largely from territory newly conquered by Russia, entered into the Middle East. Between 1850 and 1870, 1.5 million Tatars from the Crimea settled in Ottoman Rumeli, Anatolia, and Syria. Between 1880 and 1930 more than 2 million largely Circassian but also Chechnyan, Abhazi, Kosovar, and Albanian people found refuge in the Ottoman Empire and its successor states in the

Middle East. From 1861, when the Ottoman Refugee Commission was created (based on the Refugee Code of 1857), refugee individuals and families arriving in the Ottoman Empire were granted plots of state land to farm. They were exempted from taxes and conscription for six years, if they settled in Rumeli (the European Ottoman Empire), or twelve years, if they settled in Anatolia or in the Syrian provinces. They were to cultivate the land and not sell it or leave it for twenty years; they automatically become subjects of the Ottoman sultan and were expected to accept his laws and justice. They had freedom of religion, whatever their faith, and were allowed to build churches if not already available to them. They were not herded into refugee camps, denied legal protection, or warehoused as is commonly the case at the beginning of the twenty-first century.

In the closing years of the Ottoman Empire, the world witnessed the dispossession and death marches of the Armenians and other Christian groups. Between 1 and 1.5 million people died. This was followed by the international denial of Kurdish nationalism at the Treaty of Lausanne and the flight of many Kurds as their homeland was carved into four new nation states (Turkey, Iran, Iraq, and Syria). As many as 150,000 to 200,000 Kurds are stateless in Syria alone. Though many live in territory which is part of their Kurdish homeland, they have few legal rights and are identified as 'muted' (*maqtumeen*) rather then as citizens of a state. Nearly 750,000 Palestinians were dispossessed in 1948 in the former British Mandate Palestine shortly after the end of the Second World War. These refugees now number more than 4 million, and are largely warehoused in refugee camps in Lebanon, Syria, Jordan, the West Bank, and the Gaza Strip (see Table 12.1). They are perhaps one of the most studied refugee groups with the issues of right of return, self-determination, statelessness, and coping and resilience into the third and even fourth generation commonly examined. They are a people with a specialized UN agency to provide relief, but no UN agency to provide international protection, which the rest of the world's refugees have with the creation of the United Nations High Commission for Refugees (UNHCR) in 1951. Other long-term refugee groups include the Sahrawi refugees from Western Sahara, who are provided with shelter in a border area near the Algerian town of Tindouf, courtesy of the Algerian government. The Sahrawi number about 165,000 and have lived in UNHCR-provided tents in Algeria since the late 1970s. All food and water is provided by a combination of UN agencies and the Algerian government. Sudanese refugees have sought refuge in Egypt as well since the 1970s. Afghan refugees began fleeing their country with the overthrow of their king in the late 1970s in a

Table 12.1.   Total numbers of registered Palestinian refugees in 2009.

Host	
Jordan	1,930,703
Lebanon	416,608
Syria	456,983
West Bank	754,263
Gaza Strip	1,059,584
TOTAL	4,618,141

Source: UNHCR Global Trends.

communist-inspired coup. At one time as many as 4 million Afghan refugees could be found in Pakistan and Iran. Today that number is closer to 3.5 million or 27 per cent of the entire Afghan population. And most recently we have seen, as a result of the Anglo-American invasion of Iraq in 2003 and the uncontrolled rise in sectarian violence, a further 2 to 2.5 million Iraqis in exile. Understanding these dispossessions and forced migration is surely the key to finding solutions to current, largely protracted crises. Supporting research which goes beyond immediate needs assessment and, rather, steps back to understand the original and present predicaments, the perceptions of all parties, and the aspirations of the dispossessed is one step in the direction of finding durable answers. Supporting such research, as the British Academy affiliated organizations have begun to do, is to be applauded.

North Africa has two significant sets of prolonged refugee situations: Sahrawi refugees in Algeria and Sudanese refugees in Egypt. The Middle East, however, shows a very different picture. This region has seen large-scale dispossession, limited successful return (unlike Africa), and serious problems of statelessness (both for the Palestinians and the Kurds). There is little research into or understanding of the predicaments, perceptions, and aspirations of these peoples. Hence encouraging such research is a priority for future funding.

UNHCR figures show that the Middle East and North Africa (MENA) hold 25 per cent of the world's refugees. These figures include estimates of the number of refugees from Iraq. They exclude, however, UNRWA figures of 4 million Palestinian refugees. If the UNWRA figures of 4 million are added to the existing UNHCR figures of 12 million, there is a world total of nearly 16 million refugees; the total in the MENA region would be over 6 million—more than one third of the world's total refugees. Such enormous figures warrant a concerted effort from academic funders, researchers, policy makers, and practitioners to undertake research into forced migration in the Middle East and North Africa to help the search for durable solutions to these humanitarian crises.

Four out of the ten major refugee hosting countries of the world are in the Middle East (see Table 12.2). Pakistan has the single largest number of refugees (Afghans), followed by Syria (Iraqis), then Iran (Afghans), Germany (mainly Kurds from Turkey and Iraq), and Jordan (Iraqis). If the figure of 4 million Palestinian refugees spread out between Lebanon, Syria, Jordan, the West Bank, and the Gaza Strip is added to these numbers, then the top four refugee hosting countries in the world become Pakistan, Syria, Jordan, and Iran.

Clearly the Middle East is a major refugee-producing region of the world; it also hosts more than a third of all the world's forced migrants. Such realities demand greater understanding which can be accomplished only through research that addresses the issues of prolonged force migration among the Sahrawi, Palestinians, Sudanese, and Afghan refugees, as well as internally displaced Kurds (in Iraq, Iran, and Syria), and Palestinians (in Israel, the West Bank, and the Gaza Strip). Furthermore, those who remain open up a new area of research to understand the individual and group decision-making processes regarding whether to stay or flee.

The essays in this volume have opened up areas of research which are important to pursue further. They have looked at displacement and the impact of generation and gender as well as the physical and mental stress of refugee situations. They have explored the phenomenon of repatriation, including the voluntary and sometimes not so voluntary return to

Table 12.2.   The major refugee hosting countries.

Host	Refugee numbers
Pakistan	2,003,100
Syria	1,503,800 + 456,983 Palestinians
Iran	963,500
Germany	578,900
Jordan	500,000 + 1,059,584 Palestinians
Tanzania	435,600
China	301,100
UK	299,700
Chad	294,000
USA	281,200

Source: UNHCR Global Trends.

places such as Afghanistan and northern Iraq. They have considered the Palestinian 'right of return' both in its legal manifestations as well as emotional and cultural expression. Identity in exile has been addressed in order to understand the processes of integration, assimilation, and alienation. Policies towards refugees have also been considered in order to understand both the international refugee regime as well as national and regional interpretations.

The very recent crisis of Iraq's exiles has been addressed in this volume, highlighting its special features which warrant a concerted effort to better understand this complex tragedy. We know that more than 4 million Iraqis have fled their country since 2003. By 2008 nearly one seventh of Iraq's population had been displaced in a regular outflow rather than a sudden flood of people. Jordan and Syria have received over 2 million of these forced migrants who have largely 'self-settled' into urban, largely middle-class neighbourhoods, mainly in Damascus and Amman. These exiles have an unusual profile in the contemporary world of refugees. They are largely middle-class professionals. They have settled in urban centres and become 'invisible'—many are unwilling to register their families with aid agencies for fear of being discovered and sent back. The lack of trust with officialdom is as likely a reflection of the collapse of their own government, armed services, civil service, and private sector in Iraq as a result of decisions taken by the Anglo-American occupying forces. Their situation is unique, and without detailed study of their predicaments, perceptions, and aspirations it is unlikely that either the academic world or practitioners in the humanitarian aid regime will be able to effectively assist such vulnerable people.

Most UN agencies and other humanitarian aid organizations have commissioned needs surveys and other basic data collection efforts. Yet little social science academic or applied research has been carried out with Iraq's exiles. Most research has considered these refugees as 'objects' rather than agents. The existing research has been piecemeal and generally lacks coherence. There is an urgency to address this situation, not only because of its scale but also because of its unusual character—largely urban and middle class. Previous refugee movements have been mainly rural, agrarian, and largely uneducated. The humanitarian aid regime traditionally responded to these situations by establishing rural camps. However, urban, middle-class refugees represent a new, difficult-to-reach phenomenon. The difficulties which host states have in providing refuge to their fellow Arab brothers is also of pressing concern. International agencies must find appropriate solutions based on accurate information about the situation of Iraqi exiles to anticipate future needs and acceptable conditions for return or possible third-country resettlement. At present we are playing a guessing game. We do not know what conditions Iraq's refugees will accept to remain where they are, when they might consider a return to Iraq, or under what conditions they would consider seeking third-country resettlement. We need to understand their current livelihood predicaments, their perceptions of their conditions, and their aspirations for their future. Once these issues have begun to be addressed by researchers, they will provide much needed information and conceptual understanding for policy makers and practitioners alike. This volume is a small step in that direction.

REFERENCE

United States Commission on Refugees and Immigrants (2008), 'End Warehousing', March, Washington, DC.

Abstracts

Géraldine Chatelard
What Visibility Conceals: Re-embedding Refugee Migration from Iraq

This essay connects the mass refugee migration from Iraq that has followed the fall of the regime of Saddam Hussein April–May 2003 with previous and concomitant social and spatial migratory trends from Iraq. Focusing on the case of refugee migration from Iraq to Jordan between 1990 and 2008, it is argued that the international humanitarian engagement with the post-2003 Iraq refugee crisis conceals previous dynamics of forced migration from Iraq that have long taken a regional and global scope, the embeddedness of current refugee migration in other types of migration movements from and to Iraq, regional dynamics that span Iraq and the neighbouring countries that have played hosts to the majority of refugees from Iraq pre- and post-2003, and the variegated experiences, self-perceptions, and expectations of the refugees themselves.

Keywords: Iraqi migration to Jordan, forced-migration continuum, mobility and security, refugeeness and Arabism, urban refugees, social networks, regional migration

Alessandro Monsutti
The Transnational Turn in Migration Studies and the Afghan Social Networks

This essay examines how the study of migration and transnationalism contributes to scholarly anthropological debate. Migration is not seen here as mere passage from one location to another, but instead as a complex phenomenon characterized by recurrent and multidirectional movements during which a variety of links are woven. Moreover, sociocultural groups are not considered as discrete territorially defined entities. The dispersal of family groups can be the result of a strategy aimed at diversifying resources and minimizing risks; it does not always lead to a weakening of social ties.

The essay illustrates the broad potential of the transnational approach by analysing one particular group, Afghan refugees and migrants, particularly the Hazaras who originate in the mountainous centre of Afghanistan. The argument draws upon a multi-sited ethnography conducted between Afghanistan, Pakistan, Iran, Australia, and the USA. Afghans have been able to adapt to each context. In their case, escape from violence is not necessarily incompatible with a real migratory strategy— the geographical dispersion and the resulting economic diversification can become an asset.

Keywords: transnationalism, migrants and refugees, multi-sited ethnography, social networks, Afghanistan, Hazaras

Maher Anawati Bitar
Internal Displacement in the Occupied Palestinian Territories: Politics and the Loss of Livelihood

Internal displacement in the West Bank and East Jerusalem can be traced back to a combination of military and land expropriation policies that have continued unabated since Israel's military occupation of the occupied Palestinian territories in 1967. The Israeli government's construction of a wall mostly within the West Bank has served to simultaneously accelerate and localize the displacement. This essay analyses the diverse, albeit reinforcing, triggers of displacement—both direct and indirect—that have and continue to alter the demographic and territorial realities in the occupied Palestinian territories. These triggers include settlement construction and expansion, home demolitions, forced expulsion, military incursions, the revocation of residency rights, directed violence by Israeli settlers, as well as the consolidation of the wall and its associated permit and closure regime.

Building on preliminary data, this essay highlights the manner in which internal displacement of Palestinians has and continues to be spatially concentrated and highly targeted, in a manner that significantly correlates with the larger political, territorial, and demographic aims of the government of Israel in East Jerusalem and the West Bank. In doing so, the essay seeks to demonstrate that research on displacement cannot be conducted without a critical assessment of larger territorial and political consequences arising from, if not predicated on, displacement. Nevertheless, significant further research is needed to ascertain the extent of the present predicament of internal displacement, to determine the location and needs of internally displaced persons, and to identify communities and individuals at risk of displacement.

Keywords: Palestinians, Israel, occupied Palestinian territories, internally displaced person

Yaël Ronen

Displacement by Repatriation: The Future of Turkish Settlers in Northern Cyprus

This essay concerns prospects for the future of Turkish immigrants to Northern Cyprus, in the framework of a peaceful settlement of the Cyprus conflict. In the early 2000s, the UN Secretary-General attempted to broker a settlement of the Cyprus conflict. The framework for settlement, commonly known as the Annan Plan, was rejected by the Greek Cypriots in 2004 but, at the time of writing, it once again serves as the basis for resumed negotiations. Under this framework, Turkish immigrants are to be repatriated to mainland Turkey. In many cases the repatriated individuals would arrive at a country in which they have never set foot before. The notion of forced post-conflict repatriation of foreign settler communities is hardly new; yet it has not taken place under international approval since the end of the Second World War. Since then the legal standards governing such action have developed, suggesting that the repatriation of Turkish settlers may not be as straightforward as it may appear. The essay examines the international human rights standards that govern potential removal of Turkish settlers. It also compares the proposed arrangements against those adopted in the Baltic states in the early 1990s, where similar legal problems led to a different political solution.

Keywords: displacement, repatriation, immigrants, Northern Cyprus, Cyprus conflict, Annan Plan, settlers, human rights, international law

Mamiko Saito and Paula Kantor

From *Mohajer* to *Hamwatan*: The Reintegration Experiences of Second-generation Afghans Returning from Pakistan and Iran

This essay addresses the knowledge gap in the complex reintegration process that occurs over time upon returning to one's 'homeland'. It does so from the viewpoint of Afghan youth and young adults who have grown up in Pakistan and Iran, away from their home country. It is based on qualitative research involving 199 respondents aged 15–30 living in Pakistan, Iran, and Afghanistan.

Currently in Afghanistan the conditions for successful voluntary repatriation and reintegration are poor, meaning that material difficulties may combine with emotional stress to increase the risk of unsuccessful resettlement. The essay investigates the complex struggles of young returnees, some of whom fail to reintegrate into Afghan society because of the significant distress associated with issues of identity and the meaning of 'homeland'—as well as material and financial hardship—leading to the desire to remigrate.

Keywords: refugee youth, second-generation, identity and homeland, return and reintegration

Sarah Kamal
Repatriation and Reconstruction: Afghan Youth as a 'Burnt Generation' in Post-conflict Return

Coercive repatriation programmes often create circumstances in which families return under less than optimal conditions to the land they had fled. The long-term fortunes of young refugees who return, as a result, to unstable post-conflict societies are difficult to determine. In this essay, I follow the movements and perspectives of four long-term Afghan refugee youth across a five-year period. I draw on in-depth interviews and participant observation in 2003, 2006, and 2007 to contrast the youths' pre-repatriation perspectives in Iran against their post-repatriation experiences in Afghanistan. I demonstrate that where their parents often characterized themselves as the 'burnt generation' of the exile period, the youth feel that they themselves are bereft of opportunity post-'return' as building blocks for future generations in the country. Such perspectives are tempered and change with time as they work through ambivalence over their relationship with Iran and changing circumstances in Afghanistan.

Keywords: repatriation, Afghan refugees, youth, Iran

Elena Fiddian-Qasmiyeh
When the Self Becomes Other: Representations of Gender, Islam, and the Politics of Survival in the Sahrawi Refugee Camps

This essay traces the ways in which the longstanding Sahrawi refugee camps have been represented by the Sahrawi political body, the Polisario Front, to their Western 'audience'. With particular reference to Spanish solidarity networks which provide essential humanitarian aid and political support to the Sahrawi camps and their inhabitants, I argue that ensuring the sympathy of those observing the camps has become a matter of both physical and political survival. In this context, the Polisario Front has strategically placed one particular social group (Sahrawi refugee women) and a specific set of characteristics at the forefront of its representations of the camps to secure the continuation of this support. Focusing on the Polisario Front's claims pertaining to gender and Islam, I examine the 'conditional' dimension of Spanish public support for 'the Sahrawi cause'. A case study of Spanish civil society's responses to the ostensible 'abduction' of three young Sahrawi women by their families in the refugee camps highlights the reasons why the Front is so determined, in its interactions with Western audiences, to separate the Sahrawi self from the Muslim Arab world.

Keywords: conditional solidarity, gender, Islam, Polisario Front, politics of survival, Sahrawi refugees

Zuzanna Olszewska
'Hey, Afghani!' Identity Contentions among Iranians and Afghan Refugees

In this essay, based on research among Shi'a, Persian-speaking Afghan refugees in Iran, I describe the rather negative representations and stereotypes of Afghans current in Iranian society, including its state-run media, and argue that these are connected to debates on the essence of Iranian identity itself. I explore the efforts made by refugee intellectuals educated in Iran to counter these negative representations in their own work—through poetry festivals and journals, newspapers, and, increasingly, weblogs—by appealing to the common faith, language, or literary heritage that they share with Iranians. The young generation, however, sees itself as going through an identity crisis, feeling neither fully Iranian nor Afghan. I argue that contentious identity discourses and feelings of uprootedness should be considered alongside other studies which depict transnational mobility as an unproblematic and intrinsic aspect of Afghan life. Similarly, the role that state institutions play in the formation of refugee subjectivity should be examined.

Keywords: Iran, Afghanistan, second-generation refugees, poetry

Laura Hamblin and Hala Al-Sarraf
Narrative as Identity: Perspectives from an Iraqi Women Refugees' Oral History Project

The humanitarian crisis of over 4 million Iraqi refugees has been highlighted only recently in the Western media. Sixty per cent of all Iraqis are women, yet women have had little or no say concerning the Iraq War. We have been gathering oral histories specifically of Iraqi women refugees, recording the interviews on HDV (to be compiled in a documentary), and creating transcripts of the interviews to be archived as historical documents, thus giving ear to the women refugees' issues, concerns, and hopes. In our essay, we look at how narrative is a means of the construction of identity for Iraqi women refugees. The challenges the women face are affected by their lived experiences in Iraq and Jordan, which are then overlaid with the identity of self as a refugee. We highlight four aspects of identity that the women we have interviewed have found challenged and changed: (1) class and socioeconomic status, (2) religious identification, (3) gender roles, and (4) child rearing. We believe that the oral histories of Iraqi women refugees are an important part of understanding who these refugees are so that the West can better understand their situation and assume appropriate responsibility.

Keywords: socioeconomic status, religious identification, gender roles, child rearing, Iraqi women refugees, oral histories

Peter Loizos and Tobias Kelly
The Refugee Factor in Two Protracted Conflicts: Cyprus and Palestine Compared

This essay compares Cyprus with Israel/Palestine, to assess how far the existence of refugees and IDPs has contributed to the failures to reach negotiated solutions. The two territories were once Ottoman provinces, later British colonies, which experienced violent challenges to British rule. The essay considers the presence or absence of legal citizenship rights for the displaced, the influence of economic factors such as livelihood opportunities and the overall economic environment, issues of political representation, and the international factors which have affected the outcomes. The essay concludes with the thought that in neither case do the displaced seem to be the primary reason for failure to reach a 'solution', because in neither case have the displaced been prominent among key decision makers. In both cases the political implications of national humiliation rather than displacement in and of itself are seen as the chief obstacle to resolution.

Keywords: refugees, political conflicts, peace, legal status

Nabil Al-Tikriti
There Go the Neighbourhoods: Policy Effects vis-à-vis Iraqi Forced Migration

Commentators frequently affirm that sectarian violence in Iraq springs from age-old ethnic tensions which long pre-date American involvement in the region. While the relevant sectarian *identities* do date back several centuries, sectarian *violence* has not persisted as a social constant throughout the millennia of regional history. Rather, outbreaks of sectarian violence have erupted on highly specific occasions, most of which can be explained through careful analysis of the particular social stresses at the time. In accordance with this presumption and projection of age-old ethnic tensions is the perception of Iraqi society as little more than an unnatural British creation of the early twentieth century, held together solely by brute force. In the wake of the 2003 Anglo-American invasion, officials holding like views instituted policies which encouraged a gradual increase of social chaos and sectarianism that eventually culminated in the violent geographic consolidation of Iraq's ethno-sectarian mapping. This remapping has effectively created the Iraq that American policy makers imagined already existed in 2003.

Keywords: forced migration, Iraq, population displacement, sectarianism

Index

The letter *n* refers to a footnote; numbers in italics indicate illustrations; numbers in bold indicate tables.

Afghan refugees in Iran 9, 125, 128–9, **128**, 149–50
  estimated numbers 198
  intellectuals' responses to marginalization 204–11
  Iranian response to 200–4
  social and legal contexts 198–200
Afghan youth (second-generation refugees) 7–8, 125, 127–33, 147–65, 204–5
  attitudes to homeland and return 123, 124, 130–1, 149, 154–5
  challenges of resettling in Afghanistan 133–44, 155–60, 204
  complex identities 129–30, 137, 160–1
  economic status 128*n*
  employment for returnees 134–5
  expectations of life in *watan* 140–2, **141**
  migration as rite of passage 56 *and n*, 163, 164
  moral imperative of repatriation 162, 164
  and national identity 132–3, 137, 153–4, 161, 164
  repatriation as self-reconciliation 160–1
  research interviews 127–9, **129**
  status in host countries 131–2, 133, 148, 154
  'voluntary repatriation' from Iran 147, 151–5
'Afghani', as pejorative (in Iran) 152, 198
Afghanistan 55, *199*
  Communist coup (1978) 55
  discrimination against returnees 136, 159–60, 163–4, 165
  flow of refugees *126*
  Hazaras 57–63
  Iranian view as backward 202, 204
  migration strategies 47–8
  outcomes for returnees 139, 155–60
  policies towards returnees 143–4
  problems for women returnees 138, 143, 154, 160
  return to 47–8, 56
  role for returnees 143–4
  seasonal migration 47, 57
  shared identity of returnees 137, 159
  social rejection of returnees 135–6
  and transnational networks 55–6
  US intervention (2001) 55
Afghans,
  identity of sub-groups 132
  notion of *watan* 140–2
  refugees 275–6
  second-generation returnees 6–7, 123–44
  social networks 3–4, 53
  transnational marriage networks 62 *and n*
Alavi, Elyas, Afghan poet 209
Algeria, Sahrawi refugee camps 172–91
Amman, Jordan,
  hotel bombings 17, 30
  Iraqi women in 215–23
  role as Iraqi meeting point 32–3
Annan Plan, Cyprus 5–6, 99–100, 105–7, 112, 113, 116, 118
  rejection 227, 243–5, 246
anthropology,
  and fieldwork 49
  transnationalism 45–8, 50–1
Appadurai, Arjun 49–50
Arab Gulf States, Iraqi migration to 28, 32
Armenians 1, 48, 250, 275
Assyrians, Anatolia 1, 255
Australia,
  Afghan migrants 58–60, 62
  Iraqi migrants 20, 29
  Pacific Solution 59
  refugee scheme 27, 59
Austro-Hungarian Empire 274

Ba'ath Party, US purge of 260
Badr Corps militia, Iraq 261, 263, 264

289

Baghdad, partition walls 268–9
Balfour Declaration 228
Baltic states,
    compared with Annan Plan for TRNC
        113–18
    statelessness of Russophones 117
Barak, Ehud, Israeli prime minister 241
Barnes, John A. 53
Barzani, Mas'ud, Kurdish leader 254
Batatu, Hann, *The Old Social Classes . . . in
    Iraq* 256
Ben-Gurion, David, Israeli prime minister
    256
Bremer, Paul, US Coalition Provisional
    Authority (CPA) administrator 260,
    261–3
British Army, 106th Hazara Pioneers 57
Bush, George, US president, administration
    238, 261, 264
business, Jordanian–Iraqi links 32–3

California, Iraqi migrants 29
Canada 27
    Afghan migrants 60
    Iraqi migrants 29
Casablanca Protocol 232
Chad, refugees in **277**
Chalabi, Ahmad 256
Chaldo-Assyrian Christians 11, 250, 255,
    270
China, refugees in **277**
Chrisafios, president of Cyprus 106
Christians,
    Chaldo-Assyrian 11, 250, 255, 270
    Iraqi and Jordanian 25
    Iraqi migrants in Jordan 22, 31, 219
Circassian Muslims 1
class 278–9
    Afghan intellectuals in Iran 204–11
    and Afghan migrants 58, 60
    Iraqi women in Jordan 218–19
    and solidarity networks, Iraq 24–5
    and transnational marriage 60–1
Clifford, James 49
Clifford, James, and Marcus, G., *Writing
    Culture* 45
communications, mobile phones and
    internet 35
corruption, Afghanistan 55

Council of Europe,
    and Cyprus 99*n*
    and TRNC population 101–2
CSCE High Commissioner for National
    Minorities 115
Cuco Report (1992), on Turkish settlers 112
culture,
    Iraqi national 259
    as journey 49
Cyprus 5–6, *98*
    compared with Palestine 10–11, 227–46
    comparison with Baltic states on
        repatriation of settlers 113–18
    dispossession of Greek Cypriots 103–4
    economy 234–5
    enosis movement 230–1
    geopolitical issues 237–9
    Greek-Cypriot coup 98, 231
    history of conflict 97–100
    human rights constraints on repatriation
        of Turkish settlers 107–13
    independence 98
    legal status of Greek-Cypriot refugees
        232–3
    Makarios–Denktash agreements (1977)
        242
    origins of refugee problem 230–1
    political representation of Greek Cypriots
        236–7
    problems of property 113, 118, 243–4
    provision for citizenship of United
        Cyprus Republic 105–6
    reunification dilemma 103–5, 116
    treaties of Guarantee, Establishment and
        Alliance (1960) 116
    Turkish invasion (1974) 98, 231, 242–3
    Zurich–London Agreements (1959)
        230–1, 238
    see also Annan Plan; TRNC
Cyprus v. Turkey 109

Da'wa party,
    Iraqi migrants 29
    and Iraqi nationalism 263
    Shi'i faction 253
decolonization 49, 173
diaspora,
    definition of concept 48–9

and deterritorialization 4
links between 52
redefinitions 49
diaspora, Cypriot 104
diaspora, Iraqi, and Amman (Jordan) 32
displacement 3–6
  see also forced migration; internal
    displacement
Dugard, UN Special Rapporteur 85

Ebrahimi, Mahbubeh, Afghan poet 210–11
Eden, Anthony, UK prime minister 230
education,
  informal Afghan schools in Iran 150,
    151–2, 153–4, 199
  in Iran 198*n*, 205
  in Jordan 24, 221–2
Edwards, D.B. 54–5
Egypt 32, 275
emigration, cost of 22
enosis (Cypriot union with Greece) 230–1
EOKA (Greek-Cypriot guerrilla movement)
  230, 238
Es-Sweiyh, Polisario representative 181
Estonia, Russophone settlers in 115, 117
ethnography, multi-sited 52–5
European Commission,
  Humanitarian Aid Office (ECHO) 176
  see also Council of Europe
European Convention of Human Rights
    and Fundamental Freedoms (ECHR),
    and Annan Plan 107, 118
  Article 8 (right to private life) 108–9
European Court of Human Rights (ECtHR),
    and Cyprus 109, 118
European Union, and Cyprus 239
Europeanism 20
expulsion, proportionality 111, 116–18

FAFO (Norwegian research institute) 18*n*
Falluja, siege (2004) 261
Fanon, F. 184
Fatah 236, 240
Faysal, King 255
fieldwork,
  multi-sited 54
  nature of 49

films, Afghani 202, 203–4
forced migration,
  Iraq 19–20, 40, 256–7
  and transnational networks 46
Foucault, Michel 171*n*
Franco, General 173, 175

gender 12–13
  Iraqi women's roles 220–1
  and Orientalist imagery 185–6, 188, 190
generation 12–13
  see also Afghan youth
Germany,
  Iraqi migrants 20
  Kurdish migrants 29
  refugees in **277**
Global Commission on International
    Migration 46*n*
'global Ecumene' 52 *and n*
globalization, and transnational networks
  50–1
Greece, and Cyprus 238–9
Greeks, as diaspora 48

Haganah militia 228
Hamas 236, 240
Hannerz, U. 52, 53–4
Hazarajat society, Afghanistan 56
Hazaras, Afghanistan 4, 47, 56, 57–62
  migrants to Australia 58–60
  migrants to Iran 57–8
  migrants to Pakistan 57
  migratory networks 60, 61–3
'homeland', for young Afghan refugees
  123, 124, 130–1, 149, 154–5
Howard, John, Australian prime minister
  59*n*
human rights,
  and Palestinian Wall 86 *and n*
  possible limitations right to private life
    110–13
  and right to private life (ECHR Art. 8)
    108–9
humanitarian aid,
  institutional actors 35–7
  in Sahwari camps 176, 179
Hussein, King of Jordan 24

identity formation,
  Iranian 200–1 *and n*, 204*n*
  Iraqi 215–16
  and place or community 164–5, 212
  second-generation Afghan refugees 127,
    129–30, 132–3, 137, 148, 211
  and social identity 216
India, Hazaras in British Raj 57
Indonesia, Afghan boat people from 59
information flows, Iraq–Jordan 35
internal displacement,
  definition and identification 72–5
  direct causes 74, 77–82
  indirect causes 75, 82–3
  Iraq 17, 263–5, 266–9
  Palestine 69, 70, 72–5, 89–90, 91–2
'internally stuck persons' (ISPs), Gaza Strip
    69, 89–90
international aid 13, 278–9
  conditionalities 171–2
  and Iraqi refugees 18
International Convention on Civil and
    Political Rights 86 *and n*
International Court of Justice,
  Advisory Opinion (AO) 85, 86 *and n*, 87
  and Western Sahara 173 *and n*
International Displacement Monitoring
    Centre 70, 89
  definitions 73
international law,
  on repatriation of settlers 107–13, 114–18
  see also ECHR; United Nations
Iran *199*
  Afghan refugees in 9, 125, 128–9, **129**,
    149–50
  Afghani films 203–4
  employment 58, 150, 199, 205
  Hazaras in 57–8, 62
  informal Afghan schools 150, 151–2,
    153–4, 199
  Iranian view of Afghan refugees 152,
    200–4
  Iraqi forced migrants 19–20, 40, 256–7
  nationalism 200–4, 211–12
  provision for Afghan refugees 150–1 *and
    n*, 198–9
  refugees in 277, **277**
  view of West 201 *and n*
  'voluntary repatriation' from 150, 151–5,
    200, 204

Iranian Revolution,
  Arts Centre of the Organization for
    Islamic Propaganda 206*n*
  'Committed Literature' 206
Iraq 3, 256–7
  American policy 258–9, 260–5, 266–7, 270
  Anfal campaign against Kurds 257–8
  Anglo-American invasion (2003) 17, 249,
    257
  conditions leading to migration 25–6, 27,
    249
  counterinsurgency operations 263, 264–5
  de-Ba'athification order (2003) 260
  destruction of social capital (from 2003)
    258–67
  displacement policies 268–9
  economic privatization policy 261–2
    and n
  expulsion of Jews and Christians 11–12,
    255–8
  Interim Governing Council (IGC) 262
  internal displacement 17, 263–5, 266–9
  long-term migration trends 18–19, 223
  migrant links with Jordan 24, 28–9, 32–4
  national identity 215–16, 259
  'Operation Restoring Rights' 264
  overthrow of monarchy 256
  Palestinian support in First Gulf War
    239–40
  provision for return of refugees 263
  refugee migration from 17–42
  refugees' view of 223
  regionalism 265
  sectarianism 11–12, 219, 249, 250–5,
    258–9, 264–7
  secularism in 258
  security forces 260–1, 264
  'Surge strategy' 266–7
  tribal groupings 254–5
  war with Iran 257
Iraqi Communist Party (ICP) 253
Iraqis 1, 276, 278, 279
  as asylum-seekers in Jordan 36
  as asylum-seekers in West 28
  diaspora formation 30, 41–2
  middle-class migrants, to Jordan 22, 30–1,
    33, 41, 278
  migration to Jordan (1990–2003) 22–9
  post-2003 migration to Jordan 30–9
  'refugeeness' 37–9
  women as refugees 9–10, 215–23

Islam,
  gendered Orientalist imagery 185–6, 188, 190
  and non-Muslim communities 39
  pan-Islamism 20, 200
  see also Shi'i Islam; Sunni Islam
Israel,
  1949 Armistice Line 89, 90, 228, 230
  1967 war 230, 235
  assault on Gaza (2008–2009) 69
  'closure regime' 82–3
  demographic policies 91
  employment of Palestinians in 233
  forcible expulsions 79–80
  geopolitical issues 237–9
  home demolitions 78–9
  independence (1948) 228
  and Iraqi Jews 11, 256
  land policies in oPt 76–7, 85
  military incursions 80
  and Oslo Peace Process 239–42
  partition 228, *229*
  revocation of residency rights 81, 88
  settlement expansion 77–8
  settler violence against Palestinians 81–2
  the Wall and associated regime 84–7

'Jami' (Nur al-Din Abd al-Rahman), Afghan poet 205 *and n*
Jerusalem,
  family reunification ban 88–9
  revocation of Palestinian residency rights 81, 88
  as seam zone 87–9
  Wall around 87, 88
Jewish diaspora, Roman Empire 48
Jewish groups,
  expulsion from Iraq 250, 255
  expulsions from Eurasia 1
Jewish state, commitment to 228
Jordan 26, 277, 277
  asylum regime 23, 36, 216–18
  employment 37, 218, 220–1, 233, 234
  further migration from 25, 26–7, 28–9, 32–5
  institutional humanitarian actors 35–7
  Iraqi migration (1990–2003) 22–9, 279
  Iraqi women refugees in 9–10
  Iraqis in 1, 17, 22–9

legal status of Palestinians as citizens 232
migrant links with Iraq 24, 28–9, 32–4
migrant smuggler organizations 27
Palestinians in 23, 41–2
post-2003 Iraqi migration 30–9
residence conditions 216–17
security of migrants in 26
Shi'ite Muslims in 25, 219, 220
spatial distribution of Iraqis 31
status of Iraqi migrants 23–4, 34–5
Sunni religious identity 38, 219
UNHCR in 23, 27, 31, 36
visa restrictions 17, 28, 30, 35–6, 217
Jordanians,
  expelled from Kuwait 23
  view of Iraqi migrants 26, 31–2

Kazemi, Mohammad Kazem,
  Afghan poet 206–8*nn*
  Bāzgasht 207–8
Kennedy, John F., US president 238
Khirbet Qassa, West Bank, forcible relocation 80
Kirkuk,
  'Kurdification of' 257–8
  referendum 265
Kızılbaş, under Ottomans 250
'Kurdistan Regional Government' (KRG) 254, 269
Kurds 1, 275
  Anfal campaign against 257–8, 266
  in Germany 29
  in Iraq 253–4
  and US policy in Iraq 258, 264
al-Kuttab, Polisario representative 180

Latvia, Russophone settlers in 115, 117
Lausanne, Treaty of 275
League of Arab States, Casablanca Protocol 232
Lebanon, Palestinians in 233–4
legal rights 10–11, 13, 59
  constraints on repatriation 107–13
  in Jordan 23, 35–6, 216–18
  and 'voluntary repatriation' 150, 151–5, 198–200, 204
  see also human rights

legal status 36, 41, 117
  Australia 59
  Iraqis in Jordan 23–4, 34–5
  Palestinians compared with Cypriots
    232–3
Libya, Iraqi migration to 28, 29

Majidi, Majid, film-maker 203
Makarios, President 231, 242
Makhmalbaf, Samira, film-maker 202
al-Maliki, Nouri, Iraqi prime minister 261,
  263
Malkki, Liisa 51
Manus island, Australian detention camp
  59
Marcus, George 52
marriage, transnational 60–1, 62 *and n*
Mauritania, and Western Sahara 173, 175
metaphor, for migrations 51
Middle East,
  definition 2
  prospects for 273–9
migrants,
  self-perceptions 21, 37–9
  and territory 45
migration,
  and networks 46, 54
  as rite of passage 56 *and n*, 163, 164
  see also forced migration
migration strategies 46–7
  Afghanistan 47–8
  complexity 40–1
  and economic diversification 61–2
  and relational identities 39
migration studies 45–8
Moallem, Ali, Iranian poet 209
mobility, in modern world 49, 50, 52*n*
mohajer,
  expectations in Pakistan/Iran **141**
  use of term (refugee) 131–2
money transfers *see* remittances
Morocco, and Western Sahara 173, 175
Mughayir Al Dir, West Bank, forcible
  relocation 80

Naqshbandi Sufi order 253
nation states, and transnational migration 51
National Union of Sahwari Women 176

NATO (North Atlantic Treaty
    Organization), and Cyprus 230,
    238–9
Nauru, Australian detention camp 59
Negroponte, John, US ambassador to Iraq
  263
Nestorian Chaldeans 1
network analysis 52
networks 53, 54
  Afghan social 3–4, 53
  Hazaras 60, 61–3
  Iraqi class 24–5
  transnational 46, 50, 55–6
NGOs (non-governmental organizations),
  delivery of development aid 171, 172
  and internal displacement in Iraq 269
  in Iran 204
  and 'justifiable' engagement 191
  and Kurds 253–4
  and middle-class refugees 278–9
  and schools for Iraqis in Jordan 221
nomads, Afghanistan 47

Occupied Territories *see* Palestine
Olmert, Ehud, Israeli prime minister 85
Orientalism,
  gendered imagery 185–6, 188, 190
  Iran 201 *and n*
Oslo Peace Process 227, 239–42, 246
Other,
  Afghans in Iran as 200–2
  Muslim Middle East as 185–6, 190
  and Self 9
Ottoman Empire 274
  end of 11, 228, 250–1, 274–5
  millet system 250 *and n*
Oxfam, and Polisario/SADR 179

Pakistan,
  Afghan refugees in 125, 128–9, **129**
  Hazara migrants 57, 62
  refugees in 277, **277**
Palestine, British Mandate for 228
Palestine Liberation Organization (PLO)
    230, 235, 237, 240
  and right of return 241
Palestine, Occupied Territories (oPt) 4–5, *71*
  access to services 90

administrative cantonization 76–7
'closure regime' 82–3
compared with Cyprus 227–46
East Jerusalem 70, 76, 79, 87–9
Gaza Strip 69–70, 80, 234, 275
geopolitical issues 237–9
home demolitions 78–9
internal displacement 70, 72–5, 241
Israeli assault on Gaza (2008–2009) 69
land expropriation 85
military incursions 80
movement of Israelis within 91–2
Oslo Peace Process 227, 239–42
permit regime 89–90
popular militancy in refugee camps
    235–6
'seam zones' 84, 87, 89–90
settlement building 77–8
settler violence 81–2
the Wall 5, 70, 83–7, 88, 89, 91–2
West Bank 70, 76, 79, 89–90, 275
Palestinian National Authority (PNA)
    240
Palestinians 1, 273, **276**
economic conditions 233–4
forced expulsion 79–80, 241, *274*, 275
in Jordan 23, 41–2, 232
origins of refugee problem 228–31
political representation 235–6
refugees 228, *229*, 230, 277, **277**
restriction of movement 86
revocation of residency rights 81, 88
and right of return 241–2
statelessness 228, 230, 231, 232
pan-Arabism 20, 38
pan-Islamism 20, 200
Papadopoulos, Tassos, Greek president
    244
passports, forged Pakistani (for Afghans)
    58, 60, 62
Petraeus, General David 266–7
poetry,
    ghazal form 197–8
    as response to marginalization 204–11
policy 10–12
    US in Iraq 258–9, 260–5, 266–7, 270
Polisario Front 8–9
    and administration of Sahwari camps 176
    and development aid 171, 172
    and empowerment of women 179–82

and Muslim Middle East 190
    origins 173, 175
    public relations strategy 190–1
    and Spanish solidarity groups 178–9
    see also Sahrawi refugee camps
political conflicts,
    and access to resources 245–6
    and peace processes 245–6
    see also Annan Plan; Cyprus; Oslo Peace
        Accords; Palestine
Popular Front for the Liberation of
    Palestine (PFLP) 236, 240
prostitution 218–19

al-Qa'ida in Iraq (AQI) 264, 265
Qalqiliya, Palestine 90*n*
Qassemi, Seyyed Zia 197–8
Quetta, Pakistan, Hazaras in 57

Rajai, Mohammad Sarvar, Afghan poet
    206*n*
re-acculturation, of repatriating youth 149,
    163
Refugee Code (1857) 275
refugee identity 13, 129–30, 137, 148
    in exile 8–10, 132–3
    see also 'refugeeness'
'refugeeness', Iraqis in Jordan 37–9
refugees 273–9
    major hosting countries **277**
    and national conflicts 245–6
    visibility of 40
    see also Afghans; Iraqis; legal rights;
        Palestinians; Sahrawi
regionalism 38, 265
    and migration trends 21
remittances,
    Afghanistan 56
    Iraq–Jordan 24, 35
repatriation 6–8, 277–8
    and international law 107–13, 114–18
    'voluntary' 150, 151–5, 198–200, 204
Rice, Condoleezza 259
Roman Empire, Jewish diaspora 48
roshanfekr ('enlightened thinkers') 205
Rumeli (European Ottoman Empire) 275
'Rumi' (Mowlana Jalal al-Din Mohammad),
    Afghan poet 205 *and n*

Rumsfeld, Donald 253
Russia,
    Empire 274
    relations with Baltic states 116, 117

Sabeans (Iraqis), in Jordan 22 *and n*, 25, 31,
    219, 220
Saddam Hussein,
    campaign against Kurds 257–8, 266
    execution 265–6
    expulsion of 'Persian' Iraqis 11, 256–7
al-Sadr, Muqtada, 'Mahdi Army' (Iraq)
    262–3, 266
Safavids, under Ottomans 250
Safran, William, concept of diaspora 48
Sahrawi refugee camps 8, 172–3, 175–91,
    275
    interviews 172–3
    return of girls fostered in Spain 183–91
    solidarity groups 177–9
    see also Polisario Front; Spain
Sahrawi refugees 175, 276
Sahwari Arab Democratic Republic (SADR)
    175
Said, Edward, *Orientalism* 184–5
al-Said, Nuri, Iraqi prime minister 256
Salek, Mariem, SADR minister of culture
    180–1
Salih, Barham, Kurdish leader 254
'Salvador Option', counterinsurgency
    policy 263–4
Samarra, Iraq, Ja'far al-'Askari shrine
    bombing 265, 270
schools, Jordan 24, 221–2
secondary migration, Jordan 25, 26–7, 28–9,
    32–5
sectarian affiliation,
    identification of 31
    Iraq 11–12, 219, 249, 250–5, 258–9, 264–7
sedentarity 51
September 11, 2001 attacks 238
settlers,
    human rights constraints on repatriation
        107–13, 114–18
    integration of 115–16
    Russian, in Baltic states 113, 115, 117–18
    Turkish in TNRC 100–3, 104, 108–13
Shi'i Islam,
    in Iraq 252–3, 266

role of clerics 252–3
Shi'ites, Iraqi migrants 25, 29, 31, 39, 219,
    220
social identity 216
solidarity (*solidaridad*), use of term 177
    and n
Somali refugees 1
Soviet Union,
    in Afghanistan 55
    collapse of 113–14
    and Cyprus 238–9
Spain,
    and reaction to return of fostered
        Sahwari girls 183–90
    Sahwari Delegation 190*n*
    and solidarity groups in Sahwari camps
        177–8, 182, 187–90, 188*n*
    and Western Sahara 173, 175
sponsorship,
    for Afghan migrants to Canada 60
    for migrants to Jordan 27, 30, 33–4
statelessness 41, 117
    see also Kurds; Palestinians
Steele, Colonel James 264
Sudanese 1, 275
Sunni Islam,
    ideological strands 251
    in Iraq 251–2, 258, 266–7
Sunni Muslims,
    'Awakening Councils' (Iraq) 267
    and Iraqi Ba'ath party 260
    and Jordanian identity 38
    Kurds 253–4
Sweden, Iraqi migrants 20, 29
Syria,
    Iraqis in 1, 17, 29, 30, 278
    refugees in 277, **277**
    UNHCR in 36

Tabesh, Qanbar Ali, Afghan poet 209–10
Tal Afar operation, Iraq (2005) 264
Talabani, Jalal, Kurdish leader 254
Taliban, in Afghanistan 55, 150, 202
Tanzania, refugees in **277**
territory,
    and deterritorialization 4
    links with sociocultural groups 45
TMT (Turkish-Cypriot guerrilla
    organization) 230

transnationalism 45–8
  networks 46, 50, 55–6
  theories of 50–1
TRNC (Turkish Republic of Northern
    Cyprus) 98–9, 231
  citizenship 102–3
  displaced Turkish Cypriots 100
  ethnic links with Turkey 116
  and human rights of Turkish settlers
    108–13
  nationalization 102–3 *and n*
  settlers 100–3
  Turkish mainland settlers 100–1, 104, 117
  see also Cyprus
Turkey,
  and Annan Plan 243
  and Cyprus 238–9
  Iraqi forced migrants 20
  possible political intervention in Cyprus
    111–12
  and TRNC 102–3 *and nn*, 117

UN Convention relating to the Status of
    Stateless Persons (1954) 117
UNCCP (UN Conciliation Commission for
    Palestine) 273–4
UNCHR (UN Commission on Human
    Rights), and East Jerusalem 87–8
UNFPA (UN Fund for Population
    Activities) 56
UNHCR (UN High Commission for
    Refugees) 275, 276
  offices in Jordan 23, 27, 31, 36
  and refugee status 36
  and Sahwari camps 176
  statistics on Afghan refugees 47, 56, 198*n*
  statistics on Iraqi refugees 18 *and n*, 22
  statistics on Sahrawi refugees 175*n*
  study of second-generation Afghans 124,
    125, 127
  in Syria 36
United Kingdom,
  and Cyprus 230
  refugees in 20, 29, **277**
United Nations,
  61st session (2006) 46*n*
  Committee against Torture 78
  and Cyprus 231

Decolonization Committee 173
General Assembly Resolution 194 (III)
    273
Guiding Principles on Internal
    Displacement 73–4
Office for the Coordination of
    Humanitarian Affairs 70*n*, 76, 89
Resolution 181 (1947) 228
and Turkish Cyprus 98–9
United States of America 60, **277**
  Afghan migrants in 60–1, 62
  and Cyprus 238–9
  invasion of Iraq (2003) 17, 249, 257
  Iraq reconstruction contracts 262
  Iraqi migrants in 20, 255
  and Israeli-Palestinian conflict 237–8
  policy in Iraq 258–9, 260–5, 266–7, 270
  and state of Israel 230
UNWRA (UN Works and Relief Agency)
    23*n*, 72–3, *229*, 232, 273

Vertovec, Steven 46

Wahhabis, under Ottomans 250
watan, notion of (community) 140–2
  expectations of **141**
  as key pull factor 140, 142–3
Western Sahara,
  history of conflict 173, *174*, 175
  see also Polisario Front; Sahrawi refugee
    camps
women,
  child rearing in Jordan 221–2
  class identity 218–19
  constraints on in Sahwari camps 186–8
    and nn
  empowerment in Sahwari camps 176,
    179–83
  gender roles in Jordan 220–1
  Iraqi migrants in Jordan 31, 36
  Iraqi oral histories 9–10
  Iraqi refugees in Jordan 215–23
  religious identity 219–20
  returning to Afghanistan 138, 143, 154,
    160
  Sahwari girls fostered in Spain 182,
    183–91

women (*cont.*)
    social identity 216
Woomera, Australia, detention camp 59*n*
World Food Programme, and Sahwari
    camps 176–7, 178

Yemen, Iraqi migration to 28, 29, 32

Zionism 228
Zolberg, Aristide 19